Britain and the World

Edited by The British Scholar Society

Editors:
James Onley, University of Exeter, UK
A. G. Hopkins, University of Cambridge, UK
Gregory Barton, The Australian National University, Australia
Bryan Glass, Texas State University, USA

Titles in the *Britain and the World* series include:

Benjamin Grob-Fitzgibbon
IMPERIAL ENDGAME
Britain's Dirty Wars and the End of Empire

Brett Bennett and Joseph M. Hodge (*editors*)
SCIENCE AND EMPIRE
Knowledge and Networks of Science in the British Empire,
1850–1970

John Fisher
BRITISH DIPLOMACY AND THE DESCENT INTO CHAOS
The Career of Jack Garnett, 1902–1919

Spencer Mawby
ORDERING INDEPENDENCE
The End of Empire in the Anglophone Caribbean 1947–1967

Richard Scully
BRITISH IMAGES OF GERMANY
Admiration, Antagonism and Ambivalence, 1860–1914

Joe Eaton
THE ANGLO-AMERICAN PAPER WAR
Debates about the New Republic, 1800–1825

Helene von Bismarck
BRITISH POLICY IN THE PERSIAN GULF, 1961–1968
Conceptions of Informal Empire

James Burns
CINEMA AND SOCIETY IN THE BRITISH EMPIRE, 1895–1940

Martin Farr and Xavier Guégan (*editors*)
THE BRITISH ABROAD SINCE THE EIGHTEENTH CENTURY
Vol. 1: Travellers and Tourists
Vol. 2: Experiencing Imperialism

Forthcoming titles include:

Barry Gough
THE PAX BRITANNICA
Navy and Empire

John Griffiths
IMPERIAL CULTURE IN ANTIPODEAN CITIES, 1880–1939

Britain and the World
Series Standing Order ISBN 978–0–230–24650–8 hardcover
Series Standing Order ISBN 978–0–230–24651–5s paperback
(*outside North America only*)

You can receive future titles in this series as they are published by placing a standing order. Please contact your bookseller, or write to us at the address below with your name and address, the title of the series and one of the ISBNs quoted above.

Customer Services Department, Macmillan Distribution Ltd, Houndmills, Basingstoke, Hampshire RG21 6XS, England

The British Abroad Since the Eighteenth Century, Volume 2

Experiencing Imperialism

Edited by

Martin Farr
School of History, Classics and Archaeology, Newcastle University, UK

and

Xavier Guégan
Department of History, University of Winchester, UK

First published 2013 by
PALGRAVE MACMILLAN

Palgrave Macmillan in the UK is an imprint of Macmillan Publishers Limited, registered in England, company number 785998, of Houndmills, Basingstoke, Hampshire RG21 6XS.

Palgrave Macmillan in the US is a division of St Martin's Press LLC, 175 Fifth Avenue, New York, NY 10010.

Palgrave Macmillan is the global academic imprint of the above companies and has companies and representatives throughout the world.

Palgrave® and Macmillan® are registered trademarks in the United States, the United Kingdom, Europe and other countries.

ISBN 978–1–137–30417–9

This book is printed on paper suitable for recycling and made from fully managed and sustained forest sources. Logging, pulping and manufacturing processes are expected to conform to the environmental regulations of the country of origin.

A catalogue record for this book is available from the British Library.

A catalog record for this book is available from the Library of Congress.

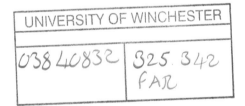

To our colleagues, friends and lovers in Newcastle

Contents

Figures

Series Preface

Experiencing Imperialism is the second part of a two-volume project called *The British Abroad since the Eighteenth Century* (the companion volume being *Travellers and Tourists*). It is published as the eleventh volume in The British Scholar Society's *Britain and the World* series from Palgrave Macmillan. From the sixteenth century onward, Britain's influence on the world became progressively more profound and far reaching, in time touching every continent and subject, from Europe to Australasia and archaeology to zoology. Although the histories of Britain and the world became increasingly intertwined, mainstream British history still neglects the world's influence upon domestic developments and Britain's overseas history remains largely confined to the study of the British Empire. This series takes a broader approach to British history, seeking to investigate the full extent of the world's influence on Britain and Britain's influence on the world.

Rather than considering imperialism in conventional terms, Martin Farr and Xavier Guégan's collection of innovative international and interdisciplinary contributions from both new and established scholars seeks to contribute to our understanding of the subject by emphasising the actual experiences of those who travelled abroad during the colonial era and subsequently. Establishing empire took intellectual and physical form, as the first section discusses. The individuals' experiences of imperialism on the part of different social groups both produced and challenged stereotypes, and none more than that of gender. Moving from the internal to the external, contributors then consider other empires, and how the British perceived them. The passing of Empire brought with it new and proliferating ways of remembering, and of being remembered. Throughout these chapters, a wide variety of motivations – diplomatic, military, religious, commemorative, political, artistic – are used to illustrate how the British experienced imperialism in its widest senses, and the impact the resulting relationships had on the perceptions of the colonialists, the colonised, and the metropolitan British themselves. Such considerations are of course far from being unproblematic, but are essential to our understanding of imperial identities and their implications within the colonial and post-colonial worlds, and for Britain and Britishness.

Editors, *Britain and the World*:

James Onley, University of Exeter, UK
A. G. Hopkins, University of Cambridge, UK
Gregory Barton, The Australian National University, Australia
Bryan S. Glass, Texas State University, USA

Preface and Acknowledgements

As we hope is not too apparent to even the casual reader, this volume, and its companion, *The British Abroad Since the Eighteenth Century, Volume 1: Travellers and Tourists*, were derived from a conference, which in their wisdom, and heathen ignorance, the organisers scheduled for Holy Thursday and Good Friday. Not all of the proposed papers for the conference were accepted, and not all of the papers that were accepted led to an invitation to publish. Nevertheless, the majority of the contributors in each book were those who decided to come to Newcastle and share their research so congenially. The element of serendipity in such an undertaking should not be understated, nor apologised for. Serendipity does mean that no collection of essays is likely even to attempt to present itself as a comprehensive view of its subject, and neither of our volumes does. There are omissions and absences, though they are stronger for our having invited some contributors who were not at the conference to write articles which complement those of our original colleagues, and fill some of the larger gaps, though by no means all.

The range of imperial experiences is so vast that a collection of essays such as this can hope to do no more than offer some fresh insights, and this one, with its companion volume, does so as part of a broader shift in historiographical perspectives, and it shares the outlook and purposes of the Society of whose book series they are part. *Britain and the World* is the book series of the British Scholar Society which originated at the University of Texas at Austin in 2008, and its five-member board are based in the United Kingdom, the United States, Australia and New Zealand. There is an annual conference (alternating between the US and the UK), a journal (*Britain and the World*), public lectures and seminars, and a website (www. britishscholar.com). Each in its way examines Britain's relations with the wider world, and is pioneering the future of the international study of British history, in that its future seems likely to be 'Britain the world' history: the ways in which Britain has interacted with other cultures and societies since the seventeenth century. The present volume is very much a part of this process, and through the experiences contained within we hope to offer some sense of how the British experienced the wider world, and why it was important.

The British Abroad has been a collective endeavour, and we would like to thank each contributor for their efforts and co-operation. The editing of 12 chapters – and with the companion volume, another 12 – was expected to be the academic equivalent of herding feral cats. Though not without moments when events appeared to be beyond our, or indeed any, control, the experience has been a pleasurable as well as a fulfilling one. Ultimately.

We would like to thank Professor Tim Kirk, Head of School at the School of History, Classics and Archaeology, Newcastle University, for stepping in to keep the original conference afloat when 'institutional support' proved something of an oxymoron, and also for demonstrating that the words 'Yorkshireman' and 'munificence' can exist in the same sentence. Dr Joan Allen and Dr Richard Allen characteristically and selflessly girded their loins in the collective interest, and we were blessed with the assistance of Ms (soon to be Dr) Melinda Sutton during those two days in April 2010 (the morning of the second being a particular trial for the editors). Mention should be made of our friends and colleagues at Newcastle University for helping to create an environment so sociable as to make it a challenge to get anything done, and in this last particular special recognition goes to the ancient wisdom of Professor Tony Spawforth, the late Professor James Wilberding (late in that he took his leave and went to Düsseldorf, rather than departed to the next world), Dr Diana Paton, Dr Matt Perry and Dr Meiko O'Halloran. It also goes to Dr Alejandro Quiroga, Dr Felix Schulz, Dr Carolyn Pedwell, Dr Claudia Baldoli, Dr Samiksha Sehrewat, Dr Ben Houston and Dr Neelam Srivastava, who in their respective Spanish, German, Canadian, Italian, Indian, American and Italian-Indian-American persons demonstrate the transformative benefits of migration. If only the League of Nations had been anything like as harmonious.

Thanks are also due to Dr Bryan Glass, Dr James Onley, Dr Greg Barton, Dr S. Karly Kehoe, Dr Michelle Brock and Dr Helene von Bismarck at the British Scholar Society, and to Jen McCall, Holly Tyler, Sumitha Nithyanandan and Kate Boothby at Palgrave Macmillan.

Falling very much into their own categories, we would also like to convey our gratitude to Kate Barnes and Paul Taylor.

The Anglo-French editors took the spirit of the project so seriously that the editing process on occasion required them to substitute Tyne and Wear for Languedoc Roussillon, the Italian lakes, Sardinia, Ostwestfalen-Lippe and the Côte d'Azur. They hope that the resulting volumes demonstrate further the fruits of venturing beyond one's own shores.

Martin Farr and Xavier Guégan
Newcastle, October 2013

Contributors

Marc Alexander is Lecturer in English Language at the University of Glasgow, UK. His work primarily focuses on cognitive and corpus stylistics, digital humanities and the semantic development of the English language. His current research projects centre on digital humanities, and in particular the computational analysis of meaning in legal, political and scientific contexts. He is Director of the STELLA Digital Humanities lab in Glasgow, Associate Director of the Historical Thesaurus of English, former researcher on the JISC Parliamentary Discourse corpus project and co-investigator on the AHRC-funded Mapping Metaphor with the Historical Thesaurus project.

Anna Bocking-Welch is Lecturer in History at the University of Liverpool, UK. She has recently completed her PhD on British civil society at the end of the British Empire and has also published on the Freedom from Hunger Campaign and the changing nature of humanitarianism in the 1960s. She is a member of the Voluntary Action History Society New Researchers committee.

James Canton teaches in the Department of Literature, Film and Theatre Studies, University of Essex, UK. His book *From Cairo to Baghdad: British Travellers in Arabia* (2011) explores the shifting patterns of British travel writing on the Middle East from Britain's occupation of Egypt in 1882 until 2003 when British forces returned to invade Iraq. His *Out of Essex: Re-Imagining a Literary Landscape* (2013) is a collection of writing inspired by rural wanderings in the county.

Matthew Day is Head of English at Newman University College, Birmingham, UK. He has research interests in print culture, having published work on running titles in *Renaissance Paratexts* (eds. Smith and Wilson, 2012), and he recently co-edited *From Compositors to Collectors* (2012). He also works on the production and reception of texts and has published on both the censorship and the reception of travel writing in the early modern period. He is currently working on a reception history of Richard Hakluyt's *Principal Navigations* and is co-editor of Volume IX of the Oxford University Press edition of that work.

Martin Farr is Senior Lecturer in the School of History, Classics and Archaeology, Newcastle University, UK. He has published on subjects concerning British politics throughout the twentieth century and is currently working on a book entitled *Margaret Thatcher's World*.

John Fisher is Senior Lecturer in International History at the University of the West of England, UK. He has written extensively about British interests in the Middle East and North Africa, c. 1870 to 1930. His latest book is *British Diplomacy and the Descent into Chaos: The Career of Jack Garnett, 1902–19* (2012).

Xavier Guégan is Senior Lecturer in colonial and post-colonial history in the Department of History at the University of Winchester, UK. He specialises in the history of British and French imperial and post-colonial history, and in particular the cultural implications in South Asia, the Maghreb and the Ottoman Empire. His most recent publications include *The Imperial Aesthetic: Photography, Samuel Bourne and the Indian Peoples in the Post-Mutiny Era* (2014) and 'Transmissible Sites' in *Sites of Imperial Memory: Commemorating Dominion in the 19th and 20th Centuries* (eds. Müller and Geppert, 2013).

Henrika Kuklick is Professor in the Department of History and Sociology of Science at the University of Pennsylvania, US. She obtained her PhD at Yale University. Previous publications include contributions to British colonial history, and to the overlapping histories of the human sciences and the field sciences. Her publications with special relevance to her contribution to this volume include *The Savage Within. The Social History of British Anthropology* (1991) and 'Contested Monuments: The Politics of Archaeology in Southern Africa' in *Colonial Situations* (ed. Stocking, 1991).

John M. MacKenzie is an honorary professorial fellow at Edinburgh University and a Fellow of the Royal Society of Edinburgh, UK. He is the author and editor of many books on the cultural history of the British Empire. Recent publications include *Museums and Empire: Natural History, Human Cultures and Colonial Identities* (2009) and (as editor) *European Empires and the People* (2011) and *Scotland and the British Empire* (2011). He has long been interested in the subject of travel and tourism, together with their related publications, in the British Empire.

Jane McDermid is Reader in Women's and Gender History at the University of Southampton, UK, with research interests in British and Russian women's history in the nineteenth and early twentieth centuries. She was an advisor and contributor to the *Biographical Dictionary of Scottish Women* (2006), and was on the Steering Committee of the UK's Women's History Network, 2004–9. She is a member of the editorial board of the journal *History of Education*.

David Rock has been Professor of History at the University of California, Santa Barbara, US, since 1977. He was born in Lancashire and educated at St. John's College Cambridge. His books include *Politics in Argentina, 1890–1930* (1975), *Argentina 1516–1987* (1987), *Authoritarian Argentina* (1992), *Latin America in the 1940s* (1993) and *Political Movements in Argentina, 1860–1916* (2002).

Kerry Sinanan is Lecturer in English at the University of the West of England, UK. She specialises in the writings of slaves and slave masters, abolitionist poetry and prose, the black Atlantic and identity, travel writing and the construction of 'race' and gender in the period. Her publications include *Slave Masters and the Language of Self: 1750–1833* (2011) and *Romanticism, Sincerity and Authenticity* (co-edited with Milnes, 2010).

Andrew Struan is a political historian at the University of Glasgow, UK, and is an associate of the STELLA Digital Humanities Lab. He was previously the Gilder-Lehrman Research Fellow at the International Center for Jefferson Studies at Monticello, Virginia, where he worked on Jeffersonian ideas and their impact in the British political world. His research investigates shifting conceptions of empire in the eighteenth-century Anglophone world, and British political reactions to colonial expansion and discovery. In particular, he is interested in the ways in which networks of knowledge influenced imperial and colonial policy, and the political authority/capital that such knowledge gave individual politicians. He has conducted research using various digital humanities approaches, notably through the Historical Thesaurus of English based at the University of Glasgow.

Michael Talbot studied history at Jesus College, Cambridge, following which he pursued a master's in Middle Eastern History at the School of Oriental and African Studies (SOAS), University of London, UK. He recently received his doctorate from SOAS for a thesis that examined British-Ottoman relations in the long eighteenth century from a financial and cultural perspective. His research focuses on the Ottoman Empire from the seventeenth to the mid-nineteenth century, with a broader interest in financial and commercial history, as well as Ottoman interactions with the states of Christian Europe.

Introduction

Martin Farr and Xavier Guégan

The British have a long history of travelling beyond their Isles. From the eighteenth century they developed a taste for discovery and self-discovery through the exploration – and exploitation – of other lands and peoples, and through their encounters with other societies and civilisations. The development of imperialism and travel and tourism – indeed, the development from one to the other – challenged the perceptions that the British had of the world – and the world of the British. These journeys also impacted on the representation and formation of 'Britishness', the exploration of national identity by defining a non-British world or a world becoming 'British'. By encountering the 'other' in an era of new relationships between power and knowledge (through experience), the British participated in the representation and politics of a world that moved from traditional to modern, from colonial to post-colonial. This collection of essays is concerned with that imperial experience.

This book has a companion: *Travellers and Tourists*. Each volume examines the roles that different actors played in creating and disseminating ideas and values about Britain and the world – actors who included travellers, artists, writers, politicians, diplomats, service personnel, tourists and consumers. Each volume is interested in understanding how different values and practices – be they social, economic, cultural, military, medical, artistic or political – have influenced international exchanges, and how the evolution from elite travel to mass tourism, and the varied experiences of empire, transformed perceptions and representations of Britons' view of the world. They bring interdisciplinary and transnational perspectives to bear on British travel experiences and their impact on their interactions with the world, from the eighteenth to the twenty-first century.

The volumes have been designed to analyse the main aspects apparent when one considers the two principal reasons for the British to have travelled outside their Isles and experienced other cultures: tourism and imperialism. The chapters develop the subjects and approaches that defined the relationships between Britain and the world. Those subjects highlight the definition of Britishness at home and abroad; the exportation of ideas as well as individuals; modern forms of impression and expression; gender, faith and class perspectives. These approaches are distinct yet highly complementary, which is why they have been conceived of in this dual form. They help to explain the experiences of the British abroad. Each volume has significant geographical and chronological breadth. With the creation of popular destinations in Europe, *Travellers and Tourists* explores both the closest overseas and the most remote – such as escapism in Tibet, Japan and Australia. *Experiencing Imperialism* focuses on colonised lands and peoples, from the British Empire and those of other Western powers, from territories ruled by the West to those that gained independence. Together they hope to offer fresh perspectives on the exploration, over 300 years characterised by the dominance of new means of transport and communication, of a world defined by those travellers, explorers, tourists and colonialists.

One of the underlying arguments of the *British Abroad* volumes is that the enormous global impact of exploration and travel since the eighteenth century is dependent on the process of defining travel as a cultural and political experience, generating images, dreams and promises of alternatives to a life at home. The representation of the world through the long process of constructing a historical cultural baggage is what has turned the practice and discourse of travelling in its different forms into a means of perception and self-perception. This book thus explores crucial dimensions in modern British history through the prism of the development of travelling modes – exploration and imperialism – through the case study of British travellers. Modernisation, globalisation and personal experiences are here connected to the analysis of different dimensions of social, economic and technological change in a period when industrialisation pushed travelling to new heights. Also they explore cross-references to issues of identity and space, definitions of self and others, processes of economic and cultural globalisation, as well as memory and performance. The chapters also show different dimensions of the evolution of British society, political systems, social classes, gender perspectives, migration, urbanisation and its implications, means of travelling, capitalism and the middle class, art, exhibition and traditions versus modernism.

Themes and context

Experiencing Imperialism seeks explicitly to avoid suggesting a certain 'greatness' of Britain and that it made the modern world. Rather, it aims to understand, in the context of British imperialism, how the British 'diaspora' experienced that world and what it made of it.[1] Crucially, it is about how those experiences influenced the building of a national identity, something that came to be known as 'Britishness'.[2] It is also concerned with how these men and women affected those people and places they travelled to and colonised – or witnessed others colonising. Although the following chapters focus on the British experiences, many also explore the connections to the local populations. Britishness, nationhood and the feeling of belonging – or not – to the Empire assume a layered identity for the travellers to think of themselves as simultaneously British and also Scottish, English, Welsh and being part of a broader sense of community within the British Empire and outside its borders. In this volume we also ask whether this Britishness could truly be defined as a homogenous identity.

Since Edward Said's *Orientalism*, the representation of a traveller during the height of colonisation – and particularly a traveller who writes, paints or composes music – is as an agent of imperialism. Through the traveller's artistic, political or economic production, the perception 'at home' of the world – or at least the colonised world – seems racially formed and thus a justification for a concept of supremacy leading to the validity and legitimacy to rule over other peoples and territories. If Said's seminal work has indeed implied putting at the centre of colonial and post-colonial research the question of colonial culture and *mentalité*, it has also brought vivid criticism of the lack of consideration of other historical readings and economic perspectives. It was also criticised for being too centred on European and American perspectives by not developing the existing connections and partnerships with the other populations, or highlighting those who rebelled and reacted against the colonial powers.[3] David Cannadine, well-known for his work on British monarchy and aristocracy, has challenged *Orientalism* with *Ornamentalism*. He emphasised two propositions: that the history of the British Empire is inseparable from the history of Britain, and that the British committed themselves from around 1850 to around 1950 to reproduce in their colonies the same sort of hierarchical society that existed in Britain. The term 'Ornamentalism' describes how this hierarchy was made visible and obvious. The author explains the importance of the 'honours' given to 'natives' from the higher ranks which were modelled on the ones given to British officials. *Ornamentalism* is part of a new wave of studies that began a decade ago and is now integrally part of the new historiography of the British Empire: 'Drawing on precedents established during the period of the Revolutionary and Napoleonic Wars, the British created their imperial society, bound it together, comprehended it and imagined it from the middle of the nineteenth century to the middle of the twentieth in an essentially ornamental mode.'[4] Both *Orientalism* and *Ornamentalism* deal with perceptions from the West and, although they oppose themselves in their approach to those perceptions, both studies demonstrate the importance those perceptions had on the building of the relationship between Britain, its empire and the world. *Experiencing Imperialism* seeks to continue this debate by using experiences at the heart of the creation of those perceptions.[5]

It is with Mary Louise Pratt's *Imperial Eyes* that a clearer dimension can be seen as to how experiences of travel and exploration helped to form

European identities by travellers and explorers defining themselves through their eyes on the world. She presents an interesting spectrum of case studies highlighting scientific purposes and consequences, as well as sentimental writing and also gender determinations. Pratt also succeeds in drawing attention to non-European expression and self-representation that developed in interaction with Europeans. This is what she coins 'transculturation' in order to define her method, a term originally used by ethnographers to describe how

> subordinated or marginal groups select and invent from materials transmitted to them by a dominant or metropolitan culture. While subjugated peoples cannot readily control what emanates from the dominant culture, they do determine to varying extents what they absorb into their culture, they do determine to varying extents what they absorb into their own, and what they use it for. Transculturation is a phenomenon of the contact zone.[6]

Pratt also defines what she calls the 'contact zone' – that is, the space in which colonial encounters occur, and therefore, since there are relations among colonisers and colonised, also relations between travellers and 'travellees' (by which Pratt means 'receptors of travel').[7] Yet, those relationships often show an asymmetrical power relation. Finally, throughout the book, she argues that she is mainly interested in writing 'a study in genre as well as a critique of ideology', but defends herself from defining or codifying travel writing as a genre. Although she uses the study of tropes, she highlights 'its heterogeneity and its interactions with other kinds of expression'.[8] *Experiencing Imperialism* seeks to build on Pratt's work, but by bringing to light a combination of historical cases and perspectives showing this heterogeneity within a selection of different areas in the world through a period – three centuries – that have revealed an evolution of the self-representation of Britain and the world. The concluding chapters of this volume thus show the interconnections of travellers in a 'post-colonial' world with those from the previous centuries. Understanding these interconnections may assist in understanding better the rapport that the British – and Britain as a nation – have with the world.

Experiencing Imperialism self-explanatorily explores the imperial experiences and legacy of those travelling. *At Home with the Empire*, edited by Catherine Hall and Sonya O. Rose, is a very good counterpart. Indeed, it addresses the impact of the British Empire on the metropole, and what were the experiences of being 'at home' with the effects of imperial power. Overall, it argues that the 'empire was, in important ways, taken-for-granted as a natural aspect of Britain's place in the world and its history'; but there was an ' "unconscious acceptance", whether of the burdens or benefits of empire'.[9] Here, as also mentioned in *Experiencing Imperialism*, we need to be aware of 'the dangers of focusing yet again on the British, to the neglect of the lives of colonial peoples across the Empire. Yet our object here is the metropole and the ways in which it was constituted in part by the Empire.'[10] Hall and Rose thus stress that the aim of their study is to focus on British history, but from a transnational perspective, by recognising the ways in which it has been connected to the rest of the world, 'albeit in the context of unequal relations of power'.[11] It is thus along those principles that the present volume – as with *At Home with Empire* – explores the need to broaden the perspectives on national history and the understanding of Britishness to its imperial history.

Stephen Howe has recently demonstrated – in gathering a collection of essays, articles and excerpts from important, influential and controversial works – how the imperial field has become more and more pluralised and creative. In the present volume we contend that that process needs to continue; that more works should be embraced and encouraged that link the various intellectual disciplines outside history itself. What Howe's *New Imperial Histories* stresses – and a point that this volume aims to reaffirm – is to think of different disciplines as complementary, to take into account when one attempts to comprehend the British Empire and British identity the influence of historical and related studies of colonialism and postcoloniality. Barbara Bush rightly pointed out that '*The New Imperial Histories Reader* effectively demonstrates major historiographical shifts away from the old and somewhat stale debates about imperialism. It illustrates how imperialism remains a complex and messy concept that defies historiographical compartmentalisation and will continue to generate historical debate.'[12] Howe has emphasised that nationalist histories have too often been 'emplotted as romance' and that they should now be 'rewritten as tragedy'. Here he poses the question of whether the multiple histories of empire should be 'recast as part of a new, tragic metanarrative'.[13] *Experiencing Imperialism* is therefore part of this debate and consciously reflects this new interdisciplinary approach.

Experiencing Imperialism

This volume is divided into four parts in order to reflect on the experiences from the establishment of British colonial identity through different moments up to the post-colonial British experiences and the new rapports with the world that they have created.

Part I, 'Establishing the Empire', is not about the physical establishment of the British Empire but the way in which it is framed in this volume. It demonstrates first, with Matthew Day, the ways in which eighteenth-century British governments asserted their claims throughout the period. It sheds new light on the reading of early modern books by clarifying the relevance of particular texts to a much later period. It proves that far from being a dilettante habit, the collection and use of old books were an essential part of government. Indeed, Day explains how scientist and architect of empire Joseph Banks is famous for the new knowledge he brought to light as a result of his travels and scientific method. Yet Banks was also a bibliophile, and his library and correspondence attest to the importance to him of older books, especially those published in the sixteenth and seventeenth centuries. Even as those involved in the Republic of Letters discovered and shared new knowledge, so they relied on the publications of an earlier epoch. If this was the case in the field of science, it was even truer of European governments, which wrestled with each other in their claims for territory, trading and fishing rights, especially in North America. The established tripartite process of making claims included an assertion of *res nullius*, a claim to first discovery and taking possession, and continued occupation. In many cases, occupation had not been continued or maintained as colonies failed or 'first discoveries' remained empty. To authenticate their claims, European governments drew on earlier publications to gain legitimacy in the eyes of their rivals. Doing so involved a considerable degree of ingenious and inventive reading, misreading and deliberate non-reading of texts as standard practice. Day highlights the importance for an eighteenth-century diplomat of reading and interpreting (and sometimes misinterpreting, inadvertently or deliberately) earlier period travel documents in order to shape their understanding of the colonised (or those to be colonised) lands and people. The information given, passed on over time, shows the significance of travel writing in the eighteenth century.

Michael Talbot examines the establishment of a British ecclesiastical and political presence in Palestine by the 1840s through the religious ideology of 'Restorationism', the idea that the Jews had to be returned to Palestine to enable the Second Coming. With its roots in seventeenth-century apocalyptic theology and British biblical self-identification, this concept saw two major stages of development, both heavily influenced by British travellers to the Holy Land. It considers British religious travellers in Palestine in the eighteenth century, and how their accounts of an 'empty land' – almost entirely imagined – helped to support biblical prophecy concerning the End of Days: that the land would be barren awaiting the Israelites' return. Then Talbot explains that the British missionaries created a mass movement in support of British-led Restorationism in the nineteenth century, and in many ways this was fuelled by their accounts from their visits to Palestine. These missionaries and their organisations greatly influenced the British political establishment, leading to the setting-up of a British Consulate and the Anglican Church in the Holy Land. In essence, this chapter shows how religiously motivated travel accounts had a profound effect on Britain's relationship with the Holy Land, the effects of which are felt in the Middle East to this day.

In 1914 an employee of the British colonial bureaucracy then ruling the Sudan wrote of Khartoum that it had 'from a mass of ruins and a dust heap become a fashionable winter resort for Europeans...and can boast of a bill of health which proves it to be one of the healthiest towns in the world'. The description was not so much inaccurate as extravagant, and implicitly drew on memories of Khartoum's sensational history, including the self-chosen martyrdom of Charles Gordon in 1885 at the hands of the Mahdi, and the bloody battle of Omdurman in 1898, led by the soon-to-be Lord Kitchener of Khartoum. The cash-poor colonial regime of the Sudan traded on the gains that it could make from publicity opportunities, such as Royal visits. Henrika Kuklick examines how the regime made Khartoum a safe haven in the midst of a territory with chronically insecure borders and minimal government of its subject peoples, and how it cultivated the production of colonial ideology. The public health measures and the architectural designs benefited the city's European residents and created a virtual Mecca for tourists. These measures realised notions circulated in Whitehall and throughout the Empire. The anthropological research conducted there, which built on ideas dear to colonial officials, both connected the Sudanese past with the fabulous history of Ancient Egypt and generated a model of historical change that legitimated the colonial project entirely: C.G. Seligman's 'Hamitic Hypothesis'.

The three chapters of Part II – entitled 'Experiencing the Empire' – focus more on the experiences of individuals as well as their political views, and the cultural and economic production that occurred during a period when the Empire was expanding. Jane McDermid examines the seven-month voyage that Elizabeth Macquarie (1778–1835) made to Australia. Macquarie was the second wife of Lachlan Macquarie, Governor of New South Wales and Van Diemen's Land between 1810 and 1821. The chapter explores their voyage in 1809, focusing on Elizabeth's journal and comparing it with those of her male travel companions. Her journal of the voyage to Sydney, highlights McDermid, is full of vivid detail, her 'imperial eyes' alert to 'foreign' influences. She was a shrewd observer, not simply concerned with the domestic or the position of women, but certainly interested in the practical realities of living in the places that she visited. While Elizabeth did not publish her journal, questions arise as to how far her writing was influenced by the conventions of eighteenth-century travel writing. Did she follow the injunction of Dr Johnson (she was an avid reader of Boswell's biography) that travel journals should reflect the author's own experience and observation? Did she avoid what Ann Radcliffe called, in her *Journey Made in the Summer of 1794*, the 'language of egoism'? To what extent did she take familiar landscapes with her on the journey to Australia? The chapter thus examines how she represented herself, including her relationship to the Empire, and how she viewed non-British, including indigenous and enslaved, peoples. McDermid assesses the role of diplomacy and colonial administration from an individual's perception of their role. It is through the prism of national identity – Macquarie's narrations show the ambivalence of being a Scottish woman and part of the ruling class of the British Empire – often attached to the feeling of duties coming from both a political stance and a gender perspective.

In nineteenth-century travel photography, and writing and historical fictions, the multiple locations of cultural and imperialistic stereotypes interacted through various narrative techniques that enhanced the creation and status of 'truth'. The 'modernising' Victorian travel novel and visual culture in the East saw the establishment of sensational but documentary thrillers, and the depiction of civilisations 'trapped' in their past. Some of the stereotypes considered as facts participated in particular narrative strategies and knowledge paradigms in depicting the violent and erotic 'others' through positivism, empiricism and historicism. Xavier Guégan compares and explores the changing attitudes adopted throughout the long nineteenth century in the context of male and female travel writers in India and the Ottoman Empire. Particular attention is paid to the writers and photographers who represented the 'Orients' through the writing of historical novels, and those who narrated their encounters with the local populations in factual writings and photographs, including Samuel Bourne and Gertrude Bell. A special focus on the difference between male and female discourses is here developed by highlighting that women travelling sometimes had access to some female-only worlds and so conveyed a new discourse that challenged the traditional male view, so this gives an alternative view of how British and Oriental masculinities and femininities have been defined. Guégan explains that the effect of gender perspectives, through some specific writings and photography of countries that were, or had been, part of the Ottoman Empire as well as in the Indian subcontinent, but were now under British rule, brought a more complex – and often contrasting – nature to the way in which the local populations were generally portrayed in the long nineteenth century. The usual creation of colonial stereotypes rested on the representation of the violent nature of the 'barbaric' man and the oriental woman as 'objects' of desire. Although these representations appear somehow in the examples he develops, they were undermined by a more complex dichotomy in the definition of sexuality.

The rapport between Britain, its empire and other countries was twofold: on the one hand there were the general politics and phenomena of certain actions, policies, cultural ideologies and relationships between Britain and those countries and their people; and on the other there was the particular, with individuals who took part in the shaping of those global patterns but also some who disagreed or challenged what has been believed to be the common tropes. John M. MacKenzie reinforces the point that empires' reassurance was created mainly through constructed fantasies. Conceived of as ruling the world, the British fantasy was essentially governmental. Imperial guidebooks became a significant part of the international and colonial travel scene in the nineteenth and twentieth centuries. Some were published by shipping lines; others by major publishers like John Murray or Baedeker. Considering the fact that they appear to have been published in large numbers and to have passed through many editions as they were updated, MacKenzie finds it surprising that they have received so little attention. His chapter therefore shows that guidebooks are in fact redolent of the imperial mind-set, in their approach to the economies of the territories that they cover, the environments, natural histories and historic monuments of such apparently remote and exotic places, and above all to the social mores of colonial settlers and expatriates as well as to relationships with and attitudes towards indigenous peoples. He examines here some of the characteristics of these guidebooks and analyses the insights that they provide into imperial/colonial touring, as well as the manner in which they reveal the ways (mainly bourgeois) in which European tourists envisioned the world in that era. Although usually the guides gave the appearance of being relatively uncommitted, the structure and selection of topics made it apparent that they were indirectly praising the British Empire and its alleged 'progress'. The significance of their 'Britishness' and the delimitation of the British sphere of influence were given prominence by drawing an 'all-red route'.

Both volumes of *The British Abroad – Travellers and Tourists* and *Experiencing Imperialism* – bring to the reader's attention that British travellers explored countries and empires other than their own, and those cases are too often overshadowed by focusing only on the British Empire. Part III, 'Experiencing Other Empires', thus unveils the experiences of British men and women who travelled to territories that were part of other colonial empires. Firstly, Kerry Sinanan investigates the masculinity of an officer, John Stedman – who was hired by the Dutch to help quell the ongoing Maroon uprisings – by examining a journal he kept while in Suriname. Published in 1796, *Narrative of a Five Year's Expedition against the Revolted Negroes of Surinam* was, however, heavily edited and rejected by Stedman. Returning to the original, this chapter engages with a complex travel text that weaves a variety of genres and perspectives, a fascinating and complex representation of the 'experience of empire' that contests many of the apparent dichotomies between coloniser/colonised and slave/master. The versions of self that Stedman constructed emphasised the coincidence of his variegated selfhood drawn from Sterne, Smollett, MacKenzie and other novelists, with the material reality of his role as a colonial agent and slave master. Stedman's text brings us close to the complexities of feeling for slaves and their construction as 'other' in this period. Far from remaining in a position of unselfconscious mastery, he rigorously denounced the violent tyranny of slave masters in an extended satire. His ameliorative position is not incompatible with a sincere sensibility for the slaves who, while ambivalent, were nevertheless part of a wider critique that eventually led to abolition. Stedman's manly pursuits are interwoven with manly sentiment, which was entirely in keeping with a wider cultural view towards the end of the century: forthright, rational and even philistine. Following his culture's modification of the overly sentimental man of feeling, Stedman proposed an entirely masculine man of action, and the chapter emphasises the way in which literary culture affects the representation of a historical experience of empire. Sinanan highlights that some soldiers, despite their love for the military, also felt 'universal goodwill' towards all creatures. They were officers who cared about universal benevolence, representing a regiment as comprising all of the men in it: white, black, free and slave. In the case of Stedman, he believed in his cause and repeatedly argued that, although he was an official enemy of the rebels, he was also sympathetic to their cause and did not consider himself a foe.

The 1840s, a period of extreme economic distress in Britain, marked several imperialist adventures abroad, including the Anglo-French intervention of 1845 in the Rio de la Plata. Steam power played an important part in the conflict. Lord Palmerston viewed the Rio Paraná as an ideal venue to test steamships in war, while some Liverpool merchants dreamt of converting the river into a second Mississippi, and of redrawing the political map of the Plata region, thus reducing the territory of the Argentine Confederation and augmenting that of the Republic of Uruguay. What was a military defeat for the Argentines could be claimed as a strategic victory of sorts as the British subsequently abandoned military and naval action and resumed diplomacy to develop their business interests in Argentina. David Rock analyses the Anglo-French intervention in the light of recent writings in Argentina, focusing on the episode as a stage in the development of national identity. Firstly, he argues that the conflict of 1845 typified the early post-independence period in Latin America, where issues of provincial sovereignty remained primary rather than national identity. Secondly, Rock claims that the British were divided, and when the intervention failed to produce profits from trade, the British government abandoned the intervention. However, while the Argentines opposed foreign intervention, they were prepared to enter into a partnership with the British based on informal imperialism, proposing an association of a type that took shape in the late nineteenth century. In the 1840s, far-sighted liberal intellectuals in Argentina dreamt of forming a republic with similar economic and democratic potential as the United States, but as yet such ideas stood far from the minds and imagination of the popular mass.

Some of the specific cases and experiences explored in this volume thus challenge or refine some knowledge that is usually considered as established. During the last decades of the nineteenth century, the travel of consuls and diplomats to the Maghreb – in particular Morocco – gradually increased. Partly this was due to Tangier's mild climate and the allure of a relatively mild winter, spent in the company of like-minded, socially conservative expatriates. For the more adventurous, the Maghreb offered the stimulation of a fairytale land whose colours, smells and sounds formed a direct link to the land of the Arabian Nights. Admittedly, in the case of Morocco, the country had begun to change with the beginning of the French protectorate in 1912, but its charm and exoticism remained in large measure thereafter. John

Fisher explores diplomats' and consuls' impressions of the Maghreb which have survived among official and private archival collections, as well as in their published memoirs. In several cases, notably successive members of the extended Drummond-Hay family, who served at Tangier and, in one case, at Tunis, officials were inured to their environment by long association with the country and its people. For others this was not the case and they struggled to adapt to their environment, seeking solace in a cloistered expatriate world of picnics and pig-sticking. This chapter documents the challenges of official travel in the Maghreb, through the official lens of late nineteenth- and early twentieth-century imperialism, and considers the extent to which, if any, the experience of travel left a discernible imprint upon the conduct of official duties.

Part IV, 'Experiencing a Post-colonial World', brings the views and perceptions of the British of the post-colonial world and its chapters deal with the construction of memory and the evolution of representation of that world. James Canton first highlights that the romantic vision of Arabia as an exotic, if desolate, desert occasionally peopled by Bedouin tribesmen was one sustained by numerous twentieth-century works, including T.E. Lawrence's *Seven Pillars of Wisdom* (1926) and Wilfred Thesiger's *Arabian Sands* (1959). But then he wonders what happened to that image with the erosion of British colonial power in Arabia, and he asks whether post-colonial writers see the same Arabia. Jonathan Raban's *Arabia* (1979) signalled a decisive challenge to any such colonial visions. When Canton interviewed him in 2007, Raban spoke of his fierce determination to ensure that there were 'no camels; no little brown boys' in his Arabia. This chapter then explores how radical Raban's departure was from the representation of Arabia by earlier British travel writers and how Tim Mackintosh-Smith's work has since played on the imperial nostalgia evident in Thesiger's work. However, is it even appropriate to talk of being in a post-colonial period when British troops have only so recently departed from Iraq? Rory Stewart's *Occupational Hazards* (2006) is an account of governing in post-Saddam Iraq. His work seems to mirror an age when previous British imperial figures, such as Gertrude Bell and T.E. Lawrence, narrated their own colonial experiences of running the show in Arabia. And yet he emphasises that for all those years in southern Arabia, 'the modern British tourist is just another foreign face'. As Mackintosh-Smith asked, what were the British doing there?

An important aspect that this volume also brings in its interdisciplinary approach is a connection between colonial and post-colonial experiences. Anna Bocking-Welch explores another dimension. While professional travel narratives like those of Jan Morris, Eric Newby, Norman Lewis and Patrick Leigh Fermor were significant in shaping (post-)imperial consciousness in Britain, they tell us little about how travel as a leisure pursuit provided the British public with experiences of imperialism and decolonisation. In contrast with the individual attention that professional travel writers receive in scholarship, their amateur and touristic counterparts have almost always been considered collectively. In his 1991 book *In Search of Conrad*, Gavin Young described his travels in South East Asia as a ghost hunt 'among the echoes and shadows of a flickering past'. Ghost-hunting has been a feature of British travel narratives since the interwar period, but the precise appeal of the imperial past to travellers has shifted over time. Bocking-Welch looks at amateur efforts to document travel experiences in the 1960s. She examines which aspects of the 'flickering past' particularly appealed to those travelling at the end of empire and explores the extent to which amateur travellers' experiences abroad enabled them to record the sort of narratives that they wished to tell. Amateur filmic and written accounts can tell us a lot about British responses to decolonisation, revealing a far broader range of attitudes and approaches to the end of Empire than has been found within published travel narratives and television programmes – the focus of most existing research. Not only do they reveal shifting nostalgia for the bygone days of imperial greatness, and for the loss of 'primitivism' in the face of globalisation, but they also make clear that alongside this preoccupation with the past, travellers engaged critically with issues of decolonisation and independence. This chapter argues that the sustained interest in decolonisation shown by some of these travellers substantially undermines the dominant historical analysis of the 1960s as a period of widespread imperial amnesia.

There are evolutions of the different experiences and cases that transform into patterns. Some become generalities, for instance, through the representation of the world with the evolution of the language with its meanings and definition. To conclude the volume, Marc Alexander and Andrew Struan use the newly published *Historical Thesaurus of the Oxford English Dictionary* to provide an insight into the shifting and changing conceptions of the world as experienced by English-speaking peoples. Using the terms coined by Britons onwards to describe those they met while abroad, and the ways in which these foreigners were categorised as 'uncivil', Alexander and Struan focus their analysis on the ways in which the British designated and perceived the world with regard to those seemingly 'uncivilised' peoples encountered through imperial expansions and travel abroad. The *Thesaurus* data used here is unique in both their systematic historical sweep and in the precise information included in their classification; through this, they present the experience of the British as it has been recorded through their language over the past millennium. Using this, the chapter categorises the approximately 50 adjectives used to refer to uncivilised people or places into five significant groups, alongside quotes and illustrations of each from a diverse range of sources, including *Hansard* from 1803 onwards. In this way the use of these terms in context is used to support our main argument: that there are five main 'movements' of the British conceptualisation of the absence of civilisation, which span colonial history and lead into the modern conception of the post-colonial world.

Experiencing imperialism took many forms, as the contributors demonstrate. This volume does not claim to attempt to compile all different sorts of experiences of imperialism through travelling – a task that would probably be impossible – but instead highlights some key examples that can help us to improve our knowledge of the relationship between the British and the world over the last three centuries. There were different sorts of colonial actor, and different types of consequence, in relation both to the individuals and the policy-making, and the creation of stereotypes. The 'imperial gaze' is defined through some of the subtleties behind the shape of those experiences that often lie on the connection between the function and activity of the traveller, the medium of their record of experiences and their relation (or lack of it) with the state. There were evolutions of the different experiences and cases that transformed into patterns, even though some of them remained the exception. Gail Ching-Liang Low once wrote:

> Travel necessitates the interrogation of the cultural travelling self even if only to reinstate a more powerful version of self-identity at the journey's end. Travel writing as a distinct genre developed with the Enlightenment and the gradual secularisation of time and space. Travel was no longer tied to pilgrimages for edification and sanctification, but one travelled from sites of learning and power. Travel was linked to the self-realisation of man; it became the 'temporal/spatial "completion" of human history' and philosophical knowledge.[14]

These chapters in their varying ways address the central theme of the book: the experiences of those Britons who went abroad as part of imperialism. The approach has been to be as interdisciplinary and international as possible, and we hope that these contributions to our understanding of the British abroad will be read equally far and wide; indeed, as far and wide as the British abroad.

Notes

1. The concept of diaspora is indeed important here since it implies that these communities of travellers were, in fact, a minority. Despite their experiencing different parts of the world, they often referred to and compared what they knew from home. Those references were tinged with ideas of Britain that explored varied feelings, from embellishment to rejection. Tanja Bueltmann, D.T. Gleeson, and D.M. MacRaild (2012) *Locating the English Diaspora, 1500–2010* (Liverpool: Liverpool University Press); Robert J. C. Young (2007) *The Idea of English Ethnicity* (Chichester: John Wiley), and especially chapter 7: 'England Round the World'.
2. The question of what Britishness is – what it means and its impact – is today one that is often mentioned in academia and in the media. Among academic writings, L. Colley (1992) *Britons: Forging the Nation 1707–1837* (New Haven: Yale University Press) remains an important contribution to the field; and more

recently the edited volume from A. Gamble and T. Wright (2009) *Britishness, Perspectives on the British Question* (Chichester: Willey Blackwell); P. Ward (2004) *Britishness Since 1870* (London: Routledge); T. Kushner (2012) *The Battle of Britishness: Migrant Journeys, 1685 to the Present* (Manchester: Manchester University Press); K. Darian-Smith, P. Grimshaw and S. Macintyre (eds.) (2007) *Britishness Abroad, Transnational Movements and Imperial Cultures* (Carlton: Melbourne University Press); D. Arnold (ed.) (2004) *Cultural Identities and the Aesthetics of Britishness* (Manchester: Manchester University Press); C. McGlynn, A. Mycock and J.W. McAuley (eds.) (2011) *Britishness, Identity and Citizenship: the View from Abroad* (Bern: Peter Lang).

3. E.W. Said (1978) *Orientalism* (London: Routledge and Kegan Paul). See also J.M. McKenzie (1995) *Orientalism: History, Theory and the Arts* (Manchester: Manchester University Press).

4. D. Cannadine (2002) *Ornamentalism: How the British Saw Their Empire* (London: Penguin Books), p. 122.

5. D. Spurr (1993) *The Rhetoric of Empire: Colonial Discourse in Journalism, Travel Writing and Imperial Administration* (Durham and London: Duke University Press) categorises several tropes in the language of imperialism, and perceptions of them within the historical process of colonisation. He highlights that the colonial discourse was in fact plural. Although marked by internal repetitions, it was not a monolithic system. It is through the exploration of some literary works but mainly non-fictional works – such as popular journalism, exploration narratives, travel writing and memoirs of colonial officers – that Spurr identifies several rhetorical modes of colonial discourses, the ways of writing about non-Western peoples. These modes thus defined the relations of power: surveillance, appropriation, aestheticisation, classification, debasement, negation, affirmation, idealisation, insubstantialisation, naturalisation, eroticisation and resistance.

6. M.L. Pratt (1992) *Imperial Eyes: Travel Writing and Transculturation* (London: Routledge), p. 6.

7. Ibid., p. 242, n. 42.

8. Ibid., pp. 10–11.

9. C. Hall and S.O. Rose (eds.) (2006) *At Home with the Empire: Metropolitan Culture and the Imperial World* (Cambridge: Cambridge University Press), p. 2.

10. Ibid., p. 5.

11. Ibid.

12. B. Bush (November 2010) 'Review of *The New Imperial Histories Reader*', review no. 989, http://www.history.ac.uk/reviews/review/989 (accessed 12 October 2012).

13. S. Howe (ed.) (2010) *The New Imperial Histories Reader* (New York: Routledge), p. 16.

14. G. Ching-Liang Low (1996) *White Skins, Black Masks: Representation and Colonialism* (London: Routledge), p. 135.

Part I
Establishing the Empire

1
The Roots of Empire: Early Modern Travel Collections and International Politics in the Long Eighteenth Century

Matthew Day

Sir Joseph Banks, explorer, botanist, President of the Royal Society and member of the Privy Council, was one of the late eighteenth- and early nineteenth-century architects of empire. Despite the 'extreme aversion' to study that he is reputed to have shown at Eton, Banks was also a great bibliophile. Indeed, his botanic interests may have been inspired by finding 'on his mother's dressing-table an old torn copy of Gerard's *Herbal*'.[1] John Gerard's *The Herball or General Historie of Plantes* was first published in 1597 and, true or not, the anecdote attests to two of the Privy Councillor's life-long passions – botany and books – both of which served the project of empire: the former supporting trade, commerce and scientific knowledge as part of the international rivalry of the Enlightenment; the latter as repositories of information which shaped decisions about voyages of commerce, colonisation, exploration and discovery.[2]

The eighteenth century saw a significant increase in voyage literature, and Banks 'bought every travel publication of any importance' reflecting his own predilection for the subject.[3] Such works sought to be both entertaining and useful, and were appropriated for a range of purposes. They assuaged and roused the curiosity of armchair travellers, were perused by those interested in the advancement of science and natural philosophy, and studied by promoters of, and participants in, further voyaging activities.[4] These intellectual, philosophical, scientific and leisure readings were accompanied by those undertaken by governments and their agents engaged in imperial projects.[5]

The varied contribution of travel writing to imperialism has been well established. Despite detractors' claims about the extent to which the concept of imperialism and the promotion of colonialism were both understood and taken up in early modern England, John Parker's thesis that travel collections

published in the fifteenth and sixteenth centuries sought to promote imperial activities still holds good.[6] As Patricia Seed has shown, the practices
of colonisation – making landfall, claiming possession and establishing a
stronghold – were supplemented, asserted and evidenced by narratives of
the events.[7] Though some texts circulated in manuscript, publication in
print facilitated the dissemination of territorial claims. Such strategies were
successful: explorers, merchants, colonists and those otherwise involved in
promoting imperial ventures, such as investors and government, all used
published narrative accounts, as well as manuscript sources, to plan and
implement their activities.[8] Imperialism was a textual as well as practical
phenomenon.

This chapter explores the role of textual interpretation in the imperialist venture.[9] It moves away from Parker's concern with authorial intention
to look at the way texts from an earlier epoch were used in the long eighteenth century to make territorial claims and to assert navigational rights.
Such an investigation is important for a number of reasons. Firstly, the rapid
increase in the publication of travel narratives in the eighteenth century and
the claims made within them about their currency, importance, novelty and
value support Bourdieu's thesis that a field of cultural production is a com-
petitive environment in which new entrants seek to usurp the hegemony
of earlier products.[10] Yet while authors of travel narratives and compilers
of voyage collections in the long eighteenth century condemned earlier
works in the field, claiming their own to be at its cutting edge, readers, especially those engaged in international politics, valued earlier publications as
they sought to justify their claims to territory, trading and fishing rights.
Bourdieu's thesis is helpful when thinking about cultural production, but
less pertinent when considering consumption. Secondly, an examination of
diplomatic memorials and documents produced by such bodies as the Board
of Trade to assert claims of possession sheds light on the reading practices of
an earlier age. The close reading of texts and their manipulation for imperialist ends has not been examined greatly by historians of the Board of Trade
who have looked more at its structure and *modus operandi* than its role in supporting international negotiations with European rivals.[11] Recent work on
diplomacy has focused on delineating diplomatic procedure and the political
and economic implications of negotiations, rather than the textual practices
of administrators.[12] Moreover, attending to such readings, misreadings and
manipulations of texts helps us to go beyond the theoretical and jurispru-
dential issues delineated by John Juricek, Anthony Pagden and Patricia Seed
to see the processes of international politics at work, disclosing the machina-
tions and rhetorical manoeuvres of government.[13] The focus in this chapter
on the reception studies side of the hermeneutic circle thus distinguishes it
from earlier investigations into the role of texts in the history of imperialism. For, whereas Juricek, Pagden and Seed draw on their understanding of
authorial intention, my approach focuses on what readers actually made of
these texts. In doing so it demonstrates the folly of assuming that because a

text promoted the nation's interests it was received in that way. Indeed, this study demonstrates that although governments did draw on early printed sources to promote imperialist agendas, diplomats from opposing countries frequently sought to use the writings of an enemy nation against itself. This was just one of a number of hermeneutic strategies deployed by governments in their negotiations. For, in addition to disputing the semantic meaning of texts, diplomats attacked each others' choice and deployment of materials, challenged their reading practices and drew on such extraneous facts as the perceived availability of particular sources, their place of publication and language, and the credibility of the author in order to make their case. Ultimately, this analysis of late seventeenth- and early eighteenth-century reading reveals, on the one hand, highly sophisticated interpretations of texts which demonstrate the fissures that could exist even among the procedures and practices delineated so clearly by Juricek, Pagden and Seed, and, on the other, remarkably ill-informed misunderstandings of literature which could jeopardise the imperial enterprise.

The rise of diplomacy in the long eighteenth century involving not only issues of precedence, the increasing use of residential ambassadors and the development of a professional administrative support service to inform negotiations has been well documented.[14] Fundamental to that development is what Jeremy Black has called 'the Information Society' in which knowledge was gathered through diplomats, agents and intercepts and from books and maps, reflecting the fact that, as Anderson has noted, international law at the end of the seventeenth and start of the eighteenth century owed much to antiquarianism.[15] The acquisition of texts necessitated better storage and organisation of documents, and the creation of libraries to support administrative processes was a feature of eighteenth-century government, the French amassing an 8,000-volume library at Versailles by mid-century.[16] The availability of such collections helped to make possible detailed researches and archival work which, in turn, facilitated the close examination of texts.

Two of the most important early collections of travel writing used in eighteenth-century international diplomacy were those of Richard Hakluyt and Samuel Purchas. Hakluyt's *The Principall Navigations, Voiages and Discoveries of the English Nation* (1589) was reissued in a second edition as the much larger, three-volume *The Principal Navigations, Voiages, Traffiques and Discoveries of the English Nation* (1598–1600). Purchas took over the mantle of collector from Hakluyt, acquiring some of his documents and producing a four-volume compilation of travel narratives, *Hakluytus Posthumous or Purchas his Pilgrimes* (1625).[17] Hakluyt's and Purchas's collections provided a convenient means of accessing documents, narratives and (in the case of *Purchas his Pilgrimes*) a number of maps relating to the early periods of English navigation, trade and colonialism, and the works of both were used by British governments in their international negotiations.

Yet the willingness to use these compilations in diplomatic circles contrasts sharply with the perception of them by other eighteenth-century producers of travel collections and readers. It is true that attitudes towards the collections changed and that the two were differentiated – Hakluyt's work often being praised while Purchas's was disparaged.[18] Nevertheless, there were certain grounds on which both were condemned. John and Awnsham Churchill's *A Collection of Voyages and Travels* (1704) lamented their 'great mass of useless matter', including 'articles, charters, privileges, letters, relations, and other things little to the purpose of travels and discoveries'.[19] It was a complaint echoed by the anonymous author of *The Construction of Maps and Globes* who thought the 'Charters, Letters-Patents &c.' were 'the useless Parts' of Purchas's work.[20] The second edition of John Harris's *Navigantium atque itinerantium bibliotheca* described *Purchas his Pilgrimes* as 'a very trifling and insignificant Collection: His Manner, for I cannot call it Method, is irregular and confused, his Judgement weak and pedantick'.[21] John Green, the probable editor of Thomas Astley's *A New General Collection of Voyages and Travels*, complained that Purchas 'maimed' texts rendering the whole work useless.[22] John Reinhold Forster judged the maps in Purchas's work 'wretched' and 'paltry'.[23]

Despite the scepticism of those involved in publishing travel narratives, the British Government approved of both Hakluyt's and Purchas's collections. In 1668 a volume was drawn up entirely of materials from *The Principal Navigations*,

> containing copies and extracts of treatises, conventions, grants, &c. relating to trade and voyages of discovery from the time of Offa, King of Mercia, to the year 1586.[24]

A few years later, in 1676, the minutes of the Committee of Trade and Plantations show that the lordships

> proposed a continuation of Purchas' History with relation to his Majesty's Plantations, but seemed to mention some instruction given already in this matter by the Lords of the Admiralty.[25]

In 1730 the Board of Trade and Plantations asserted that 'Purchas his Pilgrims, [was] the most authentic collection of Travels extant in the English language'.[26] Given the poor opinion of these works in some quarters, why did the British Government esteem them so highly?

One source of interest was the information that such old collections contained about still unfamiliar places. In 1676, when preparing 'An account of His Majesty's Islands of Barbadoes and the Government thereof', the Committee for Trade and Plantations turned to *Purchas his Pilgrimes* to get a sense of the indigenous population and concluded that the inhabitants of the smaller Windward Islands 'have always been very pernicious to the English'.[27] In this case the travel collection helped to shape government opinion and was in effect a status report for British eyes only. More usually, collections of travel narratives were used in negotiations with other European powers in a more public environment.

Documentary evidence was a key aspect of international disputes. This necessitated familiarity with the sources of other countries as well as one's own, and there was an assumption that authors wrote to promote their own national interests. As the British Government wrote in 1730, it was 'natural for the authors of every Nation to extend the territories of their own Prince as far as they can'.[28] The British adopted this approach because they wanted to assert what they regarded as the corollary: that an absence of information in the printed sources indicated a lack of title. Drawing on two French authors' work – Jacques du Tertre's *Histoire Générale des Antilles Habitées par les François* (1667–71) and Jean Baptiste Labat's *Nouveau Voyage aux Isles de l'Amérique* (1722) – the British argued that the French had no right to the island of St Vincent's because 'the first of these writers is entirely silent upon this subject' and the latter declared that sailing by the island

> he found the same inhabited by the savages and fugitive negroes from Barbados only, he says indeed, there was one French Missionary there, but he does not pretend to assert that the French had any manner of title to it.[29]

However, the assumption that the failure of du Tertre and Labat to lay claim to St Vincent's indicated that there was no right to acquisition was an intellectual *non sequitur*.[30] Du Tertre's work combined an historical account of the islands of the Antilles with observations on their natural history based on his visits.[31] Though he claimed that there were few in France who could supply such a well-informed history, he noted that there were some things that he was unfamiliar with.[32] Labat described du Tertre's work as 'admirable dans le temps qu'il l'a écrit' ('admirable in the time that he wrote it') but inadequate because French colonies then were 'si nouvelles, qu'elles n'étoient pas entierement formées' ('so new, that they were not entirely formed').[33] Labat's own account drew on his experiences in the Antilles and comprised *L'Histoire Naturelle de ces Pays, l'Origine, les Moeurs, la Religion & le Gouvernement des Habitans Anciens et Modernes*.[34] Its primary aim was to provide more information about the islands, their commodities and opportunities for trade. Labat's reticence about du Tertre's work did not sit well with the British desire to establish the *Histoire* as an authoritative text. For them it was better to assume that du Tertre's silence about St Vincent's indicated a lack of title to it and it was equally convenient to erase the presence of a French missionary in Labat's account. The British Government thus attributed an authorial intention to both du Tertre's and Labat's books that suited its argument, dismissed evidence which contradicted its carefully constructed rhetorical position, and sought to ascribe authority to the publications even though they were by French authors.

The Memorials of the English and French Commissioners Concerning the Limits of Nova Scotia or Acadia (1755) also demonstrate diplomatic techniques, in this case the use of evidence extracted from travel collections.[35] The dispute centred on the boundaries of Nova Scotia and, as Elizabeth Mancke and John G. Reid observe, 'over few places in the seventeenth century Americas did Europeans contest their claims so repeatedly and inconclusively'.[36] In the mid-eighteenth century, ownership was still hotly disputed, in part because of the scepticism of both parties about the validity of the opponent's evidence. Of French proofs, the British noted dryly: 'As to the Opinion of Historians upon this Point, his Majesty's Commissaries will be able to judge of their Authority when they are produced.'[37] In return, the French charged that no maps existed showing the term 'Nova Scotia' to cover the geographical area which the British claimed. In response, the British referred to the 'antient Map [...] found in *Purchas's Pilgrim*, Tom. 4' noting smugly that it was 'one of those antient *English* Maps, which the French Commissaries [...had] challenged [them] to produce'. They claimed that 'it marks both the Boundaries of every Territory within it, and the Limits of *Nova Scotia* or *Acadia* in every Particular'.[38] Thus travel writing underpinned territorial claims and evidence had to be supplied. Textual scholarship and analysis supported the imperial venture and just as historical scholarship 'served as handmaiden to public law and politics' within the German Empire, so it did in international relations between countries competing for overseas empires.[39]

Yet the production of texts was not of itself sufficient to make one's case. Indeed, although the British were just as likely as the French to produce evidence from old collections of travel narratives, they were at times sceptical of their validity, usually when seeking to undermine their opponents. Thus despite their own use of such documents, the British doubted the French Government's claims to Nova Scotia because

> most Histories of those remote and uncivilised Countries are founded upon very light and inadequate Information, and are often the Product of Imagination, than the Representation of Truth.[40]

It was perhaps this scepticism which encouraged the British to assert, and sometimes seek to explain, the authority of its sources. In 1755, in their memorials to the French Government arguing for possession of St Lucia, the British, alluding to settlements on the island, cited

> *Purchas*, whose Book consists of a Collection of Voyages, most of them written by the very Persons performing them, and was actually published just after the Date of these Settlements [in 1606].[41]

The British defence of Purchas ignored the inherent biases and unreliability of participants, a facet of travel writing which much concerned the eighteenth century.[42] Moreover, the notion that *Purchas his Pilgrimes*, published in 1625, was 'actually published just after' 1606 was a contentious claim. The French were to describe a 17-year period between 1590 and 1607 when the English failed to restart their colonizing attempts in Virginia as 'un temps très considérable'.[43] Attitudes towards time thus depended on one's perspective. Prioritised in the British Government's evaluation of *Purchas his Pilgrimes* as a source were authorship by participants and publication close to the events themselves. Yet both could be overlooked when convenient. Moreover, this antiquarian approach, though it was in keeping with that expressed in *A New Collection of Voyages, Discoveries and Travels* (1767), that Purchas's collection was bought 'rather by the antiquary than the modern reader', revealed a different take on ancient texts.[44] The editor of *A New Collection* deemed Purchas's work more an object of 'curiosity than pleasure' but in international disputes, age and information, not pleasure and modernity, carried credit – when, of course, they suited a protagonist's argument.[45]

If establishing the validity of one's own ancient sources was a prerequisite of international disputes, then there were two correlated moves that could be made in negotiations. The first was to discredit the sources of the opponent. Thus when disputing the boundaries of Nova Scotia, the French government drew on Marc Lescarbot's *Historie de la Nouvelle France* (1609). Lescarbot had himself been to New France staying at Port-Royal in 1606–7 and his *Histoire* had gone through three editions by 1618.[46] It included a detailed history of French settlements in America, and it contained a map which he asserted was drawn from experience and demonstrated that 'neither the Spaniards nor any others before us have ever seen' the country.[47] Lescarbot's map pre-dated by 16 years the one which the British preferred in *Purchas his Pilgrimes*. Keen elsewhere in these negotiations to stress the temporal proximity of travel narratives and maps to the events they recorded, the British now took a different strategy because Lescarbot's work pre-dated Purchas's. They sought instead to dismiss Lescarbot's cartography because

> the very Name of *Acadia* is not to be found, and both the Situation and Names of every Country within that Map, are so ignorantly placed and assigned, that little Authority can be drawn from it in Favour of any Opinion.[48]

Inevitably they argued for the accuracy and reliability of their own source asserting that Purchas's map was the

> first antient Map of this Country which has the Marks of Knowledge and Correctness in it; it was published within about Twenty Years after the earliest Settlements made in this Country by the *English* and *French*, which gave Geographers an Opportunity of getting a Knowledge of it.[49]

Discrediting the ancient resources of one's opponents was as important as demonstrating the validity of one's own. The rhetorical strategy involved a certain amount of double-think. Publication close in time to events on the ground was to be a valid argument when it suited the British Government; it was to be trumped by assertions of accuracy when it did not.

The second implication of a reliance on sources was to turn the texts presented by a country back on itself. Thus the British in their claims about Nova Scotia observed:

> We have produced the Authority of one *French* Historian, *viz.* Mons. *d'Estrades*, who being the Minister of the Crown of *France*, employed at the Court of *Great-Britain*, to demand the Restitution of *Acadia*, his Negotiation led him to make the most accurate Enquiry into the Limits of his Country; and it must be presumed, that he was furnished with the best Lights.[50]

Count d'Estrades had been French Ambassador to England in the reign of Louis XIV and here the British sought to establish his authority from his social and political status, emphasising that he was a 'Minister of the Crown of *France*'.[51] They described his researches as 'most accurate' and their strategy was in sharp contrast with their discussion of the reliability of the maps produced by Lescarbot. Yet, here too, there was a rhetorical spin given to the evidence. The British Government asserted that as an ambassador in a foreign country, d'Estrades must have had access to 'the best Lights', but this belies the British Government's own problems in accessing information. At the start of the eighteenth century, some 50 years after d'Estrades, the British Government was having so much difficulty in obtaining information in England that, with choice irony, it sought to obtain maps and other information about the New World from France, and failed.[52] Thus claims about the availability of materials in Britain when d'Estrades was writing, some 90 years before the publication of the *Memorials,* might then be exaggerated. The rhetorical strategies differ here compared with the treatment of du Tertre and Labat, although in both cases the British sought to establish the authority of French sources. The discussion of du Tertre and Labat's work emphasised the text; the credibility of d'Estrades rested on his status as ambassador, assertions about the thoroughness of his research and assumptions about the availability of sources.

The practice of citing the opposing nation's sources back at it was undertaken by both British and French diplomats in the 1755 negotiations. The French presented the British with evidence from both Hakluyt and Purchas, interweaved with other texts, such as John Smith's *The Generall Historie of Virginia, New-England* (1624). They challenged the British assertions of right of possession and continued occupation in North America, which were predicated on the fifteenth-century voyages of John and Sebastian Cabot and subsequent English visits to North America. Through a careful reading of Hakluyt's and Purchas's collections, the French demonstrated that the earliest English voyages were a search for the North-West Passage, not an attempt at colonisation. They also showed that the narrative of Sir Humphrey Gilbert's 1583 endeavour to establish a colony in America, which did, in fact, make landfall, merely proved that the French were already in the region.[53] The French Government asserted, no doubt with a certain *schadenfreude*:

> La relation rapportée par Hakluyt ne permit pas de révoquer en doute que le Chevalier Gilbert n'ait trouvé des navires François à cette côte, lorsqu'il y aborda pour la première fois.[54]

The French, here, made a case entirely on textual evidence, citing the third volume of Hakluyt's *Principal Navigations* in their 'preuves'. Nevertheless there was a certain degree of interpretative licence being deployed. The passage in question states only that the French were 'not farre off' from the harbour in which Gilbert's ship was moored.[55] The presence of another nation in a region did not necessarily mean that right of possession had been asserted since ships often coasted off the shores of North America with no attempt to establish a settlement.

Perhaps not surprisingly, the practice of using the opposing nation's proofs to refute its case seems to have been carried out with a certain degree of triumphalism. Such a tone was understandable. Both *The Principal Navigations* and *Purchas his Pilgrimes* advocated English colonialism and were published in a context of international rivalry. Hakluyt's work incorporated narratives of Spanish voyages in order, he claimed, to reveal secrets which might avail the English and annoy the Spanish; it also set out accounts of failed French colonial projects so that the English could learn from the mistakes of their European rivals.[56] Yet the inclusion of such narratives merely revealed the early nature of colonial and trading voyages by Continental rivals. Such information was a gift to later diplomats. Thus, in 1686, the Marquis de Denonville, Governor-General of Canada from 1685 to 1689, sent a letter to the Marquis de Seignelay, the French Naval Secretary, concerning the 'Right of the French to the Iroquois country and to Hudson's Bay'.[57] In it de Denonville observed that the French

> took possession of [Canada, Virginia, and Florida] in 1504, 1523 and 1564, which fact the English cannot question, inasmuch as Jacques Cartier visited in 1534 all the coasts of that country; his Relations [...] attest it, and are inserted at length in the Collections of divers accounts which Purchas and Hackluit, Englishmen, have published in London, in their language.[58]

The intellectual double-think inherent in Hakluyt's collection that, on the one hand, early English narratives could support claims of possession while, on the other, publishing accounts of French attempts at colonisation could be of practical use, but not also reveal the early nature of French projects, was exposed by diplomats in the long eighteenth century. Nor did this just pertain to territory. An undated memorandum headed 'Memoir on the French Dominion in Canada 1504–1704' in relation to claims about fishing rights in the Gulf of St Lawrence noted:

> the narratives inserted in the works of Purchas and Hackluyt, English authors, printed at London, and other writers, [show that] the French Basques, Bretons and Normands, went as early as, and even long before, the year 1504, to fish for Cod along the entire coasts of the Gulf of St Lawrence.[59]

Negotiations between countries, therefore, relied not only on familiarity with the ancient resources available in one's own nation but also on those published elsewhere and an ability to read them in detail. While countries inevitably often cited sources printed in their own country and mother tongue, drawing on those of the opposing nation was a powerful rhetorical move. This was strengthened by the ability to demonstrate either a lack of evidence or that the opposing country's own texts supplied evidence which supported a counterclaim. Such strategies were supplemented with contextual information unrelated to the texts. An author's social status, assumptions about authorial intent and the availability of sources could all be deployed in the hermeneutics of diplomacy.

Having established the role of early modern travel collections in the negotiations for empire conducted by European rivals, examining some specific examples of the readings of these books will demonstrate how early modern diplomats interpreted and manipulated texts to suit their imperialist causes. It was not only the content of these texts which contributed to imperialist debate; the very act of reading was a subject for comment. Promoting one's cause relied both on gathering and interpreting information, and on undermining the research skills, reading methodologies and rhetorical practices of opponents. As the *Memorials* of 1755 make clear, governments were alive to the use made of resources. The British complained about the 'very uncommon and broken Manner in which the *French* Commissaries [...] cited [...] Authors'.[60] They asserted rather piously that 'Books may be made to carry any Appearance by being quoted imperfectly' and claimed

> the only conclusive Way of arguing from them, is by taking every Paragraph in question entire, and considering every Passage of the Author, in which he treats of the same Subject, as Part of the same Opinion, and collecting that Opinion from the whole State.[61]

Needless to say, British diplomats were far from being practitioners of their own ideal and like their French counterparts examined texts minutely, exposing the fissures in their opponents' arguments. They also wrested writings from their initial contexts, sometimes in the most extraordinary manner. Though the 1755 negotiations were part of a peace treaty, the use of these early modern sources seems more often to have inspired disagreement rather than promoted concord as politically engaged readers disputed facts, language and interpretations. Ultimately the failure of the 1750–5 Anglo-French negotiations was a contributory factor to the outbreak of the Seven Years War in 1756.[62]

The process by which European countries asserted their rights to territory was complex and involved demonstrating that the European country in question was 'first discoverer', as well as proving continued residence or occupation.[63] Letters patent and royal charters could provide important evidence but were not always readily available. In 1730 the Council of Trade and Plantations opined that 'if the records of this Office had been kept in as good order in former times, as they have been in later reigns' they would have been able to supply a fuller account of the history of St Lucia.[64] As a result, one common use of these sixteenth- and seventeenth-century travel collections in the eighteenth century was for reference to those parts of the work – 'Charters, Letters-Patents &c.' – deemed 'useless' by later editors. In 1719 the Council of Trade and Plantations was doing just this as it attempted to clarify boundary disputes in North America.[65] The Council was seeking information about royal charters granted to Sir William Alexander who had attempted in the 1620s to establish a colony in Nova Scotia.[66] The charter proved highly contentious, even in the early seventeenth century, because the territory that it covered 'had been included in grants issued to others by no fewer than three European governments'.[67] In the eighteenth century with the Nova Scotia question still unresolved, the Council of Trade and Plantations

> read so much as related to the said boundaries in the Charter or Patents of Nova Scotia – Purchas Pilgrim Vol. 4., Fol. 1872. Massachusets Bay – Book of Laws, Fol. 5. Rhode Island or Providence Plantation – Proprieties A., Fol. 137.[68]

In Purchas's work the Council found 'The Kings Patent to Sir William Alexander Knight, for the Plantation of New Scotland in America' and they read it in conjunction with supporting documents.[69] Noticeably, however, they gave the differing types of texts equal weight. A 'Book of Laws' carried the same authority as a collection in which, self-confessedly, 'vast Volumes [were] contracted, and Epitomised, that the nicer Reader might not be cloyed'.[70] There seems to have been little attempt to distinguish between different types of historical document.

This investigation into the availability of texts and the gathering of resources was relatively straightforward compared with the reading of the documents themselves, as the 1755 *Memorials* relating to Nova Scotia reveal. The British Government was again deploying letters patent published in Purchas's collection both those of a 1606 charter issued by James I and the later one to Sir William Alexander of 1621, confirmed in 1625 by Charles I. The French focused on the settlement established in the light of the 1606 charter. Accepting that a lasting colony had been successfully begun, they nevertheless interrogated the specific terms of the grant:

> Par la Charte de 1606, les limites en étoient restreintes à des bornes assez étroites; à 50 milles de distance le long des côtes, nord & sud, du premier lieu de leur établissement, entre le 34.^{c} & le 41.^{c} degré de latitude, & 100 milles dans l'intérieur du pays.[71]

This information was crucial because, by turning on 140 pages in *Purchas his Pilgrimes*, the French diplomats came upon a 'briefe Relation of the Discoverie and Plantation of New England [...] Published by the President and Councell', a document of 1622. It was intended to record English endeavour up to that time and to promote further colonisation. In it, however, the French found reference to the fact that the attempted English colony had returned home and 'Nos gens ayant abandonné la colonie…les François se prévalurent immédiatement de cette occasion pour s'établir dans nos limites.'[72] On the basis of this the French Government argued that the land was not 'res nullius' (land unoccupied by any European nation) as there was already a French outpost within 50 miles of the site of the first English colony. Consequently, they asserted, the British claims on the basis of the charter were invalid. Careful attention to the terms of the charter and juxtaposition of it with an extract from a tract published explicitly to record, justify and promote English colonisation thus enabled the French to challenge British assertions.

Producing a charter or letters patent was one method of claiming title and first discovery but it was not the only one. Through being the first ship to encounter a piece of land whether intentionally or not, voyagers sometimes claimed territory that they deemed unoccupied or previously unclaimed. On other occasions, however, governments sought to exploit narratives of voyages to make claims which had never been made at the time, pushing the available evidence to its limits. Just such stretched interpretation can be seen in the long-running dispute between Britain and France over the island of Dominica.

In 1730, in response to French claims to the island, the Council for Trade and Plantations wrote to George II citing the 1589 edition of *The Principall Navigations*, asserting: 'It appears by Hackluyts Voyages, an Author of good Credit, printed at London in the year 1589, that this Island was discover'd by the Subjects of Great Britain on the 9.th of March 156⁴/5.'[73] Following François de Callières's observations in *De la Manière de Négocier avec les Souverains* (1716) that good diplomatic method was founded on credit, the British asserted, rather than demonstrated, Hakluyt's credit-worthiness.[74] This was probably because the evidence they adduced from it was decidedly shaky. In no way did it suggest that the English were the first discovers of Dominica, nor was it originally intended to do so for the account on which it was based was that of John Hawkins's 1564 slaving venture.[75] Having endured a difficult transatlantic crossing, being initially becalmed before encountering storms, the fleet reached the West Indies desperate for water:

> we came to an Island of the Cannibals called Saint Dominico, where we arrived the 9.th of March [...]; and because it was the most desolate place in all the Island, we could not see no Cannibals, [...], and as it should seem [they] forsook the place, for want of fresh water, for we could find none there but rain water, and such as fell from the hills, and remained as a puddle in the Dale.[76]

There was no claim to first discovery here. No ceremony of possession was recorded nor was there any accompanying charter or letters patent. In short, there was neither 'discovery' nor taking of possession, merely an attempt to find water in desperate circumstances. Indeed, the land in this passage seems so unfruitful that such a claim scarcely seemed worth making. Moreover, the fact that the island already had a European name confirms that the English were not, in fact, the 'first discoverers'. This was reiterated in the final sentence of the paragraph on which the British based their claim. It disclosed that the Spanish were familiar with the island and the ferocity of its indigenous population:

> If we had not lighted upon the desertest place in all that Island, wee could not have missed, but should have bene greatly troubled by them [the indigenous population], by all the Spaniards reports, who make them devils in respect of me[n].[77]

Not surprisingly, despite the British statement in negotiations with the French that 'the only conclusive Way of arguing' was to 'tak[e] every Paragraph in question entire', the sentence which confirmed Spanish familiarity with the island was omitted from the Council's submission. The British Government's reading was adroit, manipulative and incomplete. It took a passage from a travel narrative whose main aim was to show how divine intervention facilitated the slaving voyage by supplying water at an hour of need, and by judicious omission and inventive reading turned the passage into evidence of a claim for first discovery, even though the text itself made no such claim, implicitly made it impossible and represented the land in question as undesirable. As the British knew only too well, 'Books may be made to carry any Appearance by being quoted imperfectly.'

Yet if the Council for Trade and Plantations could be adroit in handling materials, it also misinterpreted texts. In 1733 the British Government objected to the sale of the Caribbean island of Santa Cruz, or St Croix, by the French to the Danish Company of the West Indies. The British believed that they had a right to ownership of the island and searched their records for evidence to establish the claim. Unable to find any, they sought the opinion of the Governors of Barbados and the Leeward Islands but concluded in April 1735 that upon 'the most diligent search in the records of our Office, and in the most authentick authors that have given accounts of these matters', no evidence existed to overturn the Treaty of Breda of 1667 and the Treaty of Neutrality of 1686 with France.[78] However, it is clear that the Council misunderstood information pertaining to Santa Cruz. Two islands in the Caribbean Sea had borne that name, one being the modern St Croix, in the Lesser Antilles, and the other the modern Cozumel off the coast of Mexico. The Council had clearly got them confused. In May 1735, Governor Matthews of Barbados wrote to a friend:

> their Lordships are quite mistaken when they give the discovery of our Sta. Cruz to Grijalva. He indeed discover'd an Island and called it Sta. Cruz then, for the reason their Lordships mention but it lost that name and retains still its own old name Cozumel on the coast of Jucatan above four hundred leagues to the westward of the Carribbee Sta. Cruz.[79]

The extent to which 'their Lordships' had misinterpreted the available information is evident from Governor Matthews's summary of Grijalva's position: he 'was bound from Cuba westward to discover the Continent. How then shou'd he fall in with an Island above two hundred and fifty leagues to eastward of the port he sailed westward from.'[80] Had members of the Council of Trade and Plantations really been familiar with *Purchas his Pilgrimes* they would have found the evidence in a tract written by Antonio Galvano who records that in May 1518,

> Diego Velasques Governour of the Iland of Cuba, sent his Nephew John de Grisalva, [...] to discover the Land of Iucatan. And they found in their way the Iland of Cosumel, [...], and named it Santa Cruz, because they came to it the third of May.[81]

Perhaps perplexed by the gargantuan and poorly organised seventeenth-century work, the Council for Trade and Plantations misinterpreted the information relating to Grijalva. It was not just that 'most Histories of those remote and uncivilised Countries [were] founded upon very light and inadequate Information'; it was also that information was sometimes hard to understand and difficult to use.

Despite, and perhaps in part because of, this, European governments used sixteenth- and seventeenth-century travel collections both to inform themselves about colonial territories and to negotiate rights of possession with rival nations. Their practice showed that they esteemed most highly precisely those aspects of the collections which eighteenth-century producers of voyage collections disparaged. In a period when documents were still not always easy to come by, travel collections supplied a means of accessing the information essential for international negotiations. The diplomat's job was to maximise the use of such textual information, fitting his argument to the available evidence. This might require inventive reading, attributing to texts purposes that they originally lacked, or adapting evidence to support claims to possession. Nor was familiarity with the resources of one's own country enough. The ability to cite back to an opposing nation material written in its mother tongue and published in its country was a powerful rhetorical tool. Though it was customary to seek to invalidate the evidence of one's rivals, at times, if occasion served, it might be better to credit them. Indeed, on occasion, contextual information might be adduced to bolster the authority of a source, if it could be appropriated to strengthen one's own argument. Similarly the diplomat had to judge when information should be suppressed. Yet for all of this sophistication, there were times when texts were inadvertently rather than deliberately misinterpreted and the consequences could be significant. What is clear is that sixteenth- and seventeenth-century travel collections played an important role in eighteenth-century diplomacy and that just as the history of empire is the history of trade, colonisation, war and diplomacy, so, too, it is the history of reading.

Notes

1. J.D. Hooker (ed.) (1896) *Journal of the Right Hon. Sir Joseph Banks*, xxiv.
2. Banks's love of his library is evident from N. Chambers (ed.) (2000) *The Letters of Sir Joseph Banks: A Selection 1768–1820* (London: Imperial College Press), pp. 140, 295. For the link between science and imperialism, see J. Gascoigne (1998) *Science in the Service of Empire: Joseph Banks, the British State and the Uses of Science in the Age of Revolution* (Cambridge: Cambridge University Press), *passim*.
3. P. Edwards (1994) *The Story of the Voyage: Sea-Narratives in Eighteenth-Century England* (Cambridge: Cambridge University Press), p. 8.
4. For the relationship of travel narratives to the *Transactions of the Royal Society*, see M. McKeon (1987) *The Origins of the English Novel 1600–1740* (Baltimore: Johns Hopkins University Press), pp. 100–5; for John Locke's reading of travel narratives, see Daniel Carey (1996) 'Locke, Travel Literature and the Natural History of Man', *The Seventeenth Century*, 11:2, 259–80; J.R. Forster – the naturalist who accompanied Cook on his second voyage claimed to have 'a collection of about 700 volumes of voyages', in J.R. Forster (1786) *History of the Voyages and Discoveries Made in the North* (London), p. 428.

5. L.E. Pennington (1997) 'Samuel Purchas: His Reputation and the Uses of His Works', in L.E. Pennington (ed.) *The Purchas Handbook*, 2 vols, I (London: Hakluyt Society), pp. 12, 19.
6. J. Parker (1965) *Books to Build an Empire* (Amsterdam, N. Israel: Thime-Nijmegen); detractors of this thesis include D. Armitage (2000) *The Ideological Origins of the British Empire* (Cambridge: Cambridge University Press) and J. Knapp (1992) *An Empire Nowhere: England, America and Literature from* Utopia *to* The Tempest (Berkeley: University of California Press).
7. P. Seed (1995) *Ceremonies of Possession in Europe's Conquest in the New World 1492–1640* (Cambridge: Cambridge University Press), pp. 160–78.
8. Generally, see Pennington, 'Samuel Purchas', I, pp. 3–118. For explorers, see L. Fox (1635) *North–West Foxe or Fox from the North–West Passage* (London), sigs B1ʳ-H1ᵛ. For the East India Company's use of early travel narratives, see E.G.R. Taylor (1935) *The Writing and Correspondence of the Two Richard Hakluyts*, 2 vols, II (London: Hakluyt Society), pp. 476–82; for an example of a colonist's request to receive a copy of *Purchas his Pilgrimes*, see *Three Visitors to Early Plymouth*, ed. by S.V. James Jr. (1997) (Bedford, Mass.: Applewood Books), p. 33; for investors and government readers, see Anthony Payne (2008) *Richard Hakluyt: A Guide to His Books and Those Associated with Him 1580–1625* (London: Bernard Quaritch), pp. 43–44.
9. My research on the work of Samuel Purchas in particular draws on the excellent chapter of L.E. and G.Z. Pennington, 'A Secondary Purchas Bibliography', in Pennington, *Purchas Handbook*, II, pp. 574–743.
10. P. Bourdieu (1993) 'The Field of Cultural Production, or: The Economic World Reversed', in R. Johnson (ed.) *The Field of Cultural Production: Essays on Art and Literature* (Cambridge: Cambridge University Press), pp. 29–73.
11. O.M. Dickerson (1912) *American Colonial Government 1696–1765: A Study of the British Board of Trade in Relation to the American Colonies, Political, Industrial, Administrative* (Cleveland: Arthur H. Clark), pp. 285–96; H.L. Smith (1928) *The Board of Trade* (London: G.P. Putnam), pp. 1–53; A.H. Basye (1925) *The Lords Commissioners of Trade and Plantations Commonly Known as the Board of Trade 1748–1782* (New Haven: Yale University Press); I.K. Steele (1968) *Politics of Colonial Policy: The Board of Trade in Colonial Administration 1696–1720* (Oxford: Clarendon Press).
12. D.B. Horn (1961) *The British Diplomatic Service 1689–1789* (Oxford: Clarendon Press); H. Nicolson (1954) *The Evolution of Diplomatic Method* (London: Constable); M.S. Anderson (1993) *The Rise of Modern Diplomacy, 1450–1919* (London: Longman); J. Black (2001) *British Diplomats and Diplomacy 1688–1800* (Exeter: University of Exeter Press).
13. J. Juricek (1970) 'English Claims in North America to 1660: A Study in Legal and Constitutional History' (unpublished doctoral thesis, University of Chicago), *passim*; A. Pagden (1995) *Lords of All the World: Ideologies of Empire in Spain, Britain and France c.1500–c.1800* (New Haven: Yale University Press), *passim*; P. Seed (1992) 'Taking Possession and Reading Texts: Establishing the Authority of Overseas Empires', *William and Mary Quarterly*, 49:2, 183–210.
14. See note 12.
15. Black, *British Diplomats*, 118–45; Anderson, *Rise of Modern Diplomacy*, p. 96.
16. Anderson, *Rise of Modern Diplomacy*, p. 95.
17. R. Hakluyt (1589) *The Principall Navigations, Voiages and Discoveries of the English Nation* (London); 2nd edn (1598–1600) as *The Principal Navigations, Voiages,*

Traffiques and Discoveries of the English Nation, 3 vols (London); S. Purchas (1625) *Hakluytus Posthumous or Purchas his Pilgrimes*, 4 vols (London).

18. Pennington, 'Purchas's Reputation', pp. 3–22.
19. A. Churchill and J. Churchill (1704) *A Collection of Voyages and Travels*, 4 vols, I (London), sig. k4ᵛ.
20. Anonymous (1717) *The Construction of Maps and Globes* (London), sig. Q6ᵛ.
21. J. Harris (1744) *Navigantium et itinerantium bibliotheca*, 2nd edn, 2 vols, I, sig. B1ᵛ.
22. [J. Green] (1745) *A New General Collection of Voyages and Travels* (London: for Thomas Astley), vii.
23. Forster, *History*, p. 356.
24. R. Lemon (ed.) (1865, 1967) *Calendar of State Papers Domestic, Elizabeth 1581–1590* (London: HMSO; repr. Nendeln: Kraus), p. 379.
25. 'America and West Indies: February 1675', in (1893) *Calendar of State Papers Colonial, America and West Indies*, (9: *1675–1676* and *Addenda 1574–1674*) (London), pp. 170–80, available at http://www.british-history.ac.uk (accessed: 31 July 2012).
26. 'America and West Indies: July 1730, 9–10', in (1937) *Calendar of State Papers Colonial, America and West Indies* (37: *1730*) (London), pp. 169–88, available at http://www.british-history.ac.uk (accessed: 31 July 2012).
27. 'America and West Indies: February 1676', in (1893) *Calendar of State Papers Colonial, America and West Indies* (9: *1675–76* and *Addenda 1574–1674*) (London), pp. 345–55, available at http://www.british-history.ac.uk (accessed: 31 July 2012).
28. 'America and West Indies: August 1730, 16–31', in (1937) *Calendar of State Papers Colonial, America and West Indies* (37: *1730*) (London), pp. 237–51, available at http://www.british-history.ac.uk (accessed: 31 July 2012).
29. Ibid.
30. For Du Tertre and Labat, see D. Garraway (2005) *The Libertine Colony: Creolization in the Early French Caribbean* (Durham: Duke University Press), pp. 39–145.
31. See 'Du Tertre, Jacques' in (1968) *Dictionnaire de Biographie Française*, 20 vols, XII (Paris: Librarie Letouzey et Ané, 1933–), p. 899.
32. J. du Tertre (1667–71) *Histoire générale des Antilles habitées par les François*, 4 vols, I (Paris), sig. a5ᵛ.
33. J.B. Labat (1722) *Nouveau voyage aux isles de l'Amérique*, 6 vols, I (Paris), sig. a5ʳ.
34. Ibid., I, title-page.
35. The negotiations and the *Memorials* are discussed in E. Robbie (2003) *The Forgotten Commissioner: Sir William Mildmay and the Anglo-French Commission of 1750–1755* (East Lansing: Michigan State University Press), pp. 210–11; and M. Savelle (1940) *The Diplomatic History of the Canadian Boundary Dispute 1749–63* (New Haven: Yale University Press), pp. 56–85. See also M. Savelle and M. Fisher (1967) *The Origins of American Diplomacy: The International History of Angloamerica, 1492–1763* (New York: Macmillan), pp. 386–435.
36. E. Mancke and J.G. Reid (2004) 'Elites, States, and the Imperial Contest for Acadia', in J.G. Reid, M. Basque and E. Mancke *et al.* (eds.), *The 'Conquest' of Acadia, 1710: Imperial, Colonial and Aboriginal Constructions* (Toronto: University of Toronto Press), pp. 25–47 (p. 25). For the early settlement of Acadia see M. Trudel (1973) *The Beginnings of New France 1524–1663*, trans. Patricia Claxton (Toronto: McClelland and Stewart).
37. (1755) *The Memorials of the English and French Commissioners Concerning the Limits of Nova Scotia or Acadia*, 2 vols, I (London), pp. 65–7.
38. Ibid., I, pp. 267–9.

39. B. Stuchtey and P. Wende (2000) 'Introduction', in B. Stuchtey and P. Wende (eds.) *British and German Historiography 1750–1950: Traditions, Perceptions and Transfers* (German Historical Institute and Oxford University Press: London), p. 6.
40. *Memorials*, I, pp. 65–7.
41. *Memorials*, II (*The Memorials of the English and French Commissaries Concerning St Lucia*), p. 55.
42. P.G. Adams (1962) *Travelers and Travel Liars, 1660–1800* (Berkeley: University of California Press).
43. *Memorials*, I, p. 96.
44. Anonymous (1767) *A New Collection of Voyages, Discoveries and Travels*, 7 vols, I (London), sig. A2^v.
45. Anon. *Voyages*.
46. 'Lescarbot, Marc', in (1966–2005) *Dictionary of Canadian Biography*, 15 Vols (Toronto: University of Toronto Press), I, pp. 469–72; see also B. Emont (2002) *Marc Lescarbot: Mythes et Rêves Fondateurs de la Nouvelle France* (Paris: Harmattan).
47. M. Lescarbot (1907) *The History of New France*, trans. by W.L. Grant, 3 vols, I (Toronto: The Champlain Society, 1907–14), p. 31.
48. *Memorials*, I, p. 267.
49. Ibid., p. 267.
50. Ibid., p. 67.
51. It is not clear what 'Authority' the British had 'produced'. D'Estrades's correspondence had been published through the late seventeenth and early eighteenth centuries and a new volume covering the 1662 discussions about Acadia had been published in 1755 as (1755) *Letters and Negotiations of Count d'Estrades in England, Holland and Italy from MDCXXXVII to MDCLXII* (London). There (pp. 210–19), d'Estrades briefly delineated for his monarch the evidence he could adduce in support of French rights to Acadia. It would be a significant exaggeration to suggest that this was the product of 'the most accurate Enquiry into the Limits of his Country'.
52. As early as 1715–20, the Board noted the need to get surveys of the colonies completed in order to catch up with the French (Steele, *Politics of Colonial Policy*, p. 154).
53. For Gilbert's voyages, see D.B. Quinn (1940) *The Voyages and Colonizing Enterprizes of Sir Humphrey Gilbert*, 2 vols (London: Hakluyt Society).
54. 'The account reported by Hakluyt does not allow us to have any doubt that the knight Gilbert found French ships at this coast when he reached there for the first time.' *Memorials*, I, p. 93.
55. Hakluyt, *Navigations*, 2nd edn, III, sig. N3^v.
56. Ibid., III, sig. A2^v; III, sig. 2B5^r.
57. For de Denonville's time in Canada, see W.J. Eccles (1983), *The Canadian Frontier 1534–1760*, 2nd edn (Albuquerque: University of New Mexico Press), 117–20. More generally, see J. Leclerc (1976) *Le Marquis de Denonville, Gouverneur de la Nouvelle-France 1685–1689* (Montréal: Fides).
58. E.B. O'Callaghan (ed.) (1855) *Documents Relative to the Colonial History of the State of New York; procured in Holland, England and France by John Romeyn Brodhead*, 14 vols, IX (*Paris Documents I–VIII; 1631–1744*) (Albany: Weed, Parsons and Company), p. 378.
59. Ibid., p. 781.
60. *Memorials*, I, p. 283.
61. Ibid., p. 285.

62. Robbie, *Forgotten Commissioner*, pp. 211–13.
63. Pagden, *Lords of All the World*, pp. 63–102.
64. 'America and West Indies: July 1730, 9–10' (1937) *Calendar of State Papers Colonial, America and West Indies*, (37: *1730*) (London), pp. 169–88, available at http://www.british-history.ac.uk (accessed: 31 July 2012).
65. The complex situation in Acadia between 1711 and 1720 is explained in J.G. Reid, 'Imperialism, Diplomacies and the Conquest of Acadia', in Reid *et al.* (eds.), *The 'Conquest' of Acadia 1710*, pp. 101–23.
66. For Sir William Alexander's career as colonial adventurer, see J.G. Reid (1990), *Sir William Alexander and North American Colonization: A Reappraisal* (Edinburgh: University of Edinburgh Centre of Canadian Studies). See also T.H. McGrail (1940) *Sir William Alexander, First Earl of Stirling: A Biographical Study* (Edinburgh).
67. Reid, *William Alexander*, p. 3.
68. 'Journal, August 1719: Journal Book V', (1925) *Journals of the Board of Trade and Plantations*, (4: *November 1718–December 1722*) (London), 88–103, available at http://www.british-history.ac.uk (accessed: 31 July 2012).
69. *Purchas His Pilgrimes*, IV, sig. 7R1^{r-v}.
70. Ibid., I, sig. ¶5^{r}.
71. 'By the Charter of 1606, the limits were restrained to quite narrow boundaries: to fifty miles along the coasts, north and south, of the first place of establishment between the 34th and 41st degrees of latitude and 100 miles into the interior of the country.' *Memorials*, I, p. 98.
72. 'Our people abandoning the Plantation ... the Frenchmen immediately took the opportunity to settle themselves within our limits.' *Memorials*, I, p. 112; *Purchas his Pilgrimes*, IV, sig. 7N3^{v}.
73. National Archives, State Papers 71/5/12.
74. Nicolson, *Evolution of Diplomatic Method*, pp. 62–3.
75. On Hawkins's early slaving voyages, see H. Kelsey (2003) *Sir John Hawkins: Queen Elizabeth's Slave Trader* (London: Yale University Press), pp. 13–33.
76. National Archives, State Papers 71/2/4.
77. Hakluyt, *Navigations*, III, sig. 2T6^{r}.
78. 'America and West Indies: April 1735' (1953) *Calendar of State Papers Colonial, America and West Indies*, (41: *1734–35*) (London), pp. 402–12, available at http://www.british-history.ac.uk (accessed: 31 July 2012).
79. 'America and West Indies: May 1735, 1–15', (1953) *Calendar of State Papers Colonial, America and West Indies* (41: *1734–35*) (London), pp. 412–28, available at http://www.british-history.ac.uk (accessed: 31 July 2012).
80. Ibid.
81. *Purchas his Pilgrimes*, II, sig. 8B2^{v}.

2
Divine Imperialism: The British in Palestine, 1753–1842

Michael Talbot

Religion was, for many centuries, a central part of British identity. Reformed Christianity, through its establishment and its dissenters, influenced and developed Britain's society, economy and politics in profound ways that are perhaps difficult for a largely non-religious twenty-first century audience to comprehend. Even more difficult to appreciate are the less tangible elements of religious belief – that is, the 'religious mind'. The blurred boundaries between the temporal and spiritual realms produced a particularly deterministic outlook on how the universe functioned. For many, daily events, from the rise of a mighty empire to the failure of a farmer's crops, was part of an intricate and often unfathomable divine plan for the world. It would be problematic to argue for a homogenous *mentalité* common to all eighteenth- and nineteenth-century British Christians, yet for many there was a fundamental understanding that God was not simply a celestial observer but a constantly active force in every aspect of life on Earth. The writings produced by theologians, preachers, pamphleteers, self-proclaimed prophets and missionaries all sought, via interpretation of revealed scripture, to understand, examine and explain the various elements of these divine workings and thus discover the fate of humanity.

Travel writing became an important medium through which religious thought could be expounded. Although the genre was popular in the vulgar sense, notorious for its embellishers and downright frauds, it was also popular in terms of audience. Combining the mystique of foreign lands with the messages of religion could prove to be a powerful combination in promoting religious aims and ideas. This is especially true in the case of British travel to the Holy Land in the eighteenth and nineteenth centuries. There was a particular strand of British, and particularly English, theology that created a complex relationship between Britain and Palestine, Christians and Jews. It was above all informed by three key ideas: the first was Britain's attitude towards the Jews, both Biblical and diasporic; the second involved the interpretation of Biblical prophecy regarding the fate of the Holy Land itself; and the third concerned the End of Days, and particularly Britain's role in those last times. It is important, therefore, to examine how these themes shaped the experiences of British travellers and missionaries in Palestine, and how in turn their writings fed into British religion and politics with profound consequences for the region.

This chapter will examine how British attitudes towards the Jews were shaped in the seventeenth and eighteenth centuries, before examining how religious beliefs created idealised images of Palestine. The final section will show how these two constructions coalesced to develop a sort of 'divine imperialism'. This particular phrase is borrowed from the late Balachandra Rajan's study of representations of India in British literature.[1] Divine imperialism essentially refers to the establishment of God's empire on Earth; in the particular context of the British in Palestine, this can mean through the propagation of Christianity throughout the world, or by actively attempting to bring about the fulfilment of prophecy that would speed up the apocalyptic clock ticking towards Christ's return.

The importance of British religion and missionaries to the imperial project in terms of supporting and developing (and, as Gregory Claeys has argued, also criticising) the practice and ideology of empire has been made perfectly clear by historians such as Andrew Porter, David Hempton, Rowan Strong and Norman Etherington in their studies on imperial expansion and consolidation, political discourse and imperial culture.[2] Palestine did not come under British rule until conquest in the First World War and the granting of a League of Nations mandate over the territory in 1922, and so it is generally overlooked by such studies. The limited work on the earlier period of British involvement by Meir Vereté and Mordechai Eliav has considered British involvement there prior to that time to have been primarily within the political context of the 'Eastern Question'.[3] A more recent study by Yaron Perry has put greater emphasis on the role of missionaries and religion in general in British policy in Palestine, and it is particularly the eschatological beliefs – in part developed by travel accounts – that fuelled the missionaries who will be examined here.[4]

The status of the Jews in Britain

Restorationism was (and is today, under the name of Christian Zionism) the belief in a literal return of the Jews to the Holy Land as a fulfilment of Biblical prophecy and a precondition to Christ's 1,000-year rule (Millenarianism). Based largely on the writings of the influential seventeenth-century theologian Joseph Mede, this ideology had two major components.[5] The first concerned British self-representation, in that the British, and specifically the English, were often seen as successors to the biblical Israelites as the new Chosen People. This would lead to the development of movements such as the British Israelites in the nineteenth century. The second, and most important for this study, encompassed apocalyptic eschatology, which saw the end of the world as a very real and very imminent event based on the interpretation of the Book of Revelation.

Early on, Restorationism led its adherents to gaze across the oceans, based on two prophecies from Ezekiel and Isaiah in which God promised to gather the scattered Jews from all corners of the world and return them to the Holy Land.[6] As new peoples were encountered in previously uncharted lands, many Christians in Britain hoped to find evidence of the fate of the ten Lost Tribes of Israel. A hugely popular and influential account appeared in 1650 that purported to demonstrate that some tribes in South America were descendants of the Jews. The story had been told by a Portuguese Marrano called Antonio de Montezinos to an Amsterdam-based Portuguese Rabbi, Menasseh Ben-Israel, who published it in Spanish as *Esperança de Israel* (aimed at Jews) and Latin as *Spes Israelis* (aimed at Christians).[7]

This book caught the attention of many in Britain, and an English translation was quickly produced, with a member of the Westminster Assembly, Thomas Thorowgood, providing a commentary.[8] At the encouragement of the Scottish theologian John Dury, Ben-Israel had dedicated his *Hope of Israel* to the Commonwealth, his rationale being that he hoped to 'gaine your favour and good will to our Nation, now scattered almost all over the earth'.[9] The favour he was trying to gain was the Jews' readmission to England. Ben-Israel could not have phrased his plea better when addressing Cromwell. His book claimed to demonstrate that, in fulfilment of Biblical prophecy, God had scattered the Jews to all corners of the world, including the Americas. However, Ben-Israel noted that they had been scattered 'almost' all over the earth. Isaiah (11:11–12) had prophesied that God would gather the Jews from the four corners of the earth, including its islands. As long as England refused to admit Jews, Biblical prophecy could not be fulfilled.

However, a political recognition of Jews' rights, in the context of fairly endemic anti-Jewish popular sentiment, was impractical. Cromwell, hoping to secure the benefits of Jewish commerce as well as divine favour, therefore declined to decree either in favour of or against Jewish settlement in England, instead opting to turn a blind eye. As a result, after a 365-year hiatus, a Jewish settlement was re-established in London between 1655 and 1656. The Jews remained in political limbo in Britain until a bill was proposed to Parliament in April 1753 to enable their naturalisation. Brought about on the premise that permitting Jewish naturalisation would encourage Jewish trade and capital, this Bill stimulated significant debate.[10] Before its third reading in the Commons, some merchants from the City of London petitioned in favour, arguing that it 'may encourage Persons of Wealth and Substance to remove, with their Effects, from Foreign Parts into this Kingdom, and increase the Commerce and Credit of this Nation'.[11] The third reading was further suspended when another group of merchants petitioned against the Bill's enactment, warning of 'very bad Effects to this Kingdom'.[12]

Although the Jewish Naturalisation Act was passed on 7 June 1753, it continued to attract significant opposition. A wave of pamphlets, sermons, polemics and satire demonstrated the concerns and prejudices of the mercantile and religious establishments at the prospect of integrating Jews into British society. Perhaps the most succinct summary of the many negative attitudes towards the Jews was by 'Archaicus' in a vitriolic pamphlet, *The Rejection and Restoration of the Jews*, which emphasised the need for Jews to convert to Christianity before they could be accepted as Britons, and indeed before they could expect salvation. 'Christians are to be ever ready to receive Jews,' the author declared, 'but not with their Judaism.'[13] Primarily as a result of the uproar among sections of the mercantile and religious establishment, above all in London, the Duke of Newcastle, attempting to limit any damage caused to the Government, proposed a repeal of the Act in late 1753. Noting that 'Discontents have arisen', the Repeal Act received Royal Assent on 20 December.[14]

In the decades following the rejection of Jewish naturalisation in Britain, Restorationist ideology, specifically that linked to Joseph Mede, encountered something of a renaissance in a time of political and social turmoil. Numerous sermons preached in the 1770s, 1780s and 1790s showed that several Anglican and Non-Conformist clergymen had rediscovered Mede's interpretation of the Apocalypse, specifically regarding the Jews. While several theologians considered the Jews' survival as a punishment to remind the world of their sin of deicide,[15] or else argued that their only salvation was spiritual Restoration through conversion to Christianity,[16] Mede's followers took a different approach. An indicative sample of sermons from this period illustrate the popularity of the Restorationist message. In 1770, Rev. Samuel Hardy claimed that the Jews' preservation was a sign of continual divine interposition and favour on their behalf, rather than a punishment.[17] Rev. Thomas Reader's 1788 sermon compared the Jews to the Prodigal Son, who would be brought back to the Holy Land by God in a manner 'perfectly consistent with the former displays of His power and grace in their favour'.[18] Both Joseph Eyre and Charles Jerram claimed that the future Restoration of the Jews was so evident and so oft-repeated in the Bible that there was no reason to doubt its eventual occurrence.[19] This enthusiasm for the Jews' Restoration was articulated by Rev. John Baillie, who declared that following the Jews' Restoration and conversion, all people would 'be enlightened, and acquire life from the dead'.[20] The general theme was that, in accordance with Mede's apocalyptic timetable, the Jews would certainly be converted to Christianity and returned by God to the Holy Land.

It is argued that one of the reasons for this return to Mede's apocalyptic theology concerning the Jews' Restoration was the failure of the Naturalisation Act 1753, which had determined that the Jews could not become British without accepting Christ, and therefore that Britain was only a temporary stop on the Jews' wanderings until they could be returned to their own land via divine conversion. Moreover, the increasing popularity of Mede's thought in the later eighteenth century and an interest in travel accounts concerning Palestine appear to be linked. Travel accounts showed that the land was ready and waiting, according to Biblical prophecy, to receive the Children of Israel once again, supporting Mede's Restorationist eschatology.

Imagining Palestine

The Ottoman region of Palestine was part of the wider provincial region of Syria and was divided into smaller *sanjāk*s around urban centres such as Jerusalem and Nablus. Palestine was ill-defined in political terms, but the name had entered the Arabic and Turkish languages via medieval Islamic geographers as *Filasṭīn*, covering areas of modern Israel, Palestine, Lebanon, Jordan, Egypt and Syria, and this entity was tied administratively to the Ottoman provincial capital of Damascus. The population c. 1800 was between 200,000 and 300,000, mainly agrarian, but with some urban commercial centres and ports. Demographically they were mainly Sunni Muslim, but with substantial Christian and Jewish religious minorities. The Jews were concentrated in their four holy cities of Jerusalem, Hebron, Tiberias and Safed, and were primarily *Mizrakhim*, Jews native to the Arab world, with small but growing numbers of *Ashkenazim*, Jews from Europe who came to Palestine to study and die.[21] Palestine was an integral part of the Ottoman Empire although, as with many of the Ottoman provinces before the reform period of the mid-nineteenth-century increased central imperial control, it was dominated by local urban notables who possessed their own armed forces and collected taxes from the local population. Local identities were to some extent defined by city or locality, but above all by religious confession.

The realities of Ottoman Palestine in the eighteenth and early nineteenth centuries were only selectively reported by British religious travellers, who constructed an almost entirely imagined land. As Gerald MacClean has argued in his fascinating account of the English clergyman William Biddulph's travels in the Holy Land, many travellers may as well have remained at home, as their vision of Palestine was entirely conditioned by their Biblical preconceptions.[22] Indeed, it is difficult to ascertain if some of these travel writers did actually visit Ottoman Palestine, as their descriptions were often lifted straight from how their religious beliefs assured them the land would be. Yet their accounts, however flawed, provide crucial insights into the relationship between Britain, the Jews and the Apocalypse.

The three main travel accounts concerning Palestine written by Britons in the eighteenth century were Charles Thompsons's *Travels through Turkey in Asia, the Holy Land, Arabia, Egypt, and other Parts of the World* (1744),[23] James Haynes's *Travels in Several Parts of Turkey, Egypt and the Holy Land* (1774),[24] and Richard Tyron's *Travels from Aleppo to Jerusalem, and through the most*

Remarkable Parts of the Holy Land (1785).[25] These display remarkable similarities, and all three authors used their travel accounts to expound the truth of Biblical history and prophecy based on their interpretations of the contemporary political and economic landscape. Henry Maundrel's *A Journey from Aleppo to Jerusalem* (1697) noted that 'pilgrims are wonderfully deceived in finding the country so different from what they had expected'.[26] What he meant by this was that Palestine was not the land of milk and honey that some religious pilgrims had imagined. Indeed, to many Restorationists who read the stories of these travel writers, the idea that the Holy Land was so different from the beauty and bounty detailed in the Bible was a crucial one in putting forward their case.

By far the most popular British travel account of Palestine in the eighteenth century, Charles Thompson's work first appeared in print in 1744 and was reprinted several times into the nineteenth century. Its two volumes recounted Thompson's extensive travels in the Ottoman Empire, with notes on Ottoman governance, descriptions of trade and produce, and the customs of the local communities. A major focus was on the shrines and religious activities of the Greek, Armenian and Catholic communities living in the Sultan's realms. Thompson also clearly had extensive training in classical history, providing the Greek or Latin names and stories of the many cities and towns through which he travelled, so that, for instance, Sidon was more important to him for its Phoenician and Alexandrian past than it was as a contemporary Ottoman port. In many ways the reader might simply have consulted their copies of Plutarch, Virgil or Vitruvius.

The primary reason for producing his book, however, was religious. His narrative is interspersed with biblical stories, and the majority of his supporting quotations and footnotes were from the Bible. He also included a long discussion of the history of the Jews from earliest biblical history until their expulsion by the Romans. In this and many other pieces of information, Thompson borrowed heavily from Humphrey Prideaux, author of a polemic against the Prophet Muhammad and the Qur'an,[27] and of an influential examination of biblical prophecies, *The Old and New Testament Connected in the History of the Jews and Neighbouring Nations*.[28] Prideaux had certainly consulted Joseph Mede's work on the apocalypse, and in both Prideaux's and Thompson's work, history served to prove prophecy.[29] At face value, Thompson's account considered the fate of the Jews as one of permanent exile. 'They became', he opined, 'Sojourners and Strangers in all Nations, Fugitives and Vagabonds, throughout the Earth, and to this Day remain as the Monuments of the Just Judgement of God, a scattered and despised people.'[30] Thompson also echoed Maundrel, noting that Palestine 'scarce presented anything to our View but naked Rocks, Mountains and Precipices, which are apt to give Travellers quite different ideas of the Land of Promise from those they had form'd before from the pleasing Description of it in the sacred Writings'.[31]

Yet this text does not present the cursed and desolate nature of the Holy Land as a permanent one, and Thompson saw in the arid landscape around Beersheba both past and future fecundity. After listing the supposed produce those barren hills formerly produced, Thompson explicitly addressed the potential of the land:

> Upon the whole, the Complaints of some Travellers relating to the present Barrenness of the Holy Land, and the Objections that have been raised from thence against the Truth of several Passages of Scripture, appear to me to be entirely groundless: For the Country is far from being naturally unfruitful; but as it wants inhabitants, and the few that profess it are quite averse to Labour and Industry, great Part of it lies uncultivated and neglected; whereas if it were well peopled and husbanded as it ought to be, the Soil is generally rich, and would produce as plentiful Crops as the most fertile Parts of Syria.[32]

Thompson was attempting to prove here not only that the descriptions in the Bible of a fruitful land of milk and honey were correct but also that the land remained innately productive.[33] The lack of produce (which, although perhaps true in the desert, was certainly not the case for the rest of Palestine) signified on the one hand the ineptness of the contemporary inhabitants, and on the other the continuing curse on the land following the expulsion of the Jews. To Restorationists reading this work, it would have been the element of potential that was so important.

The second travel writer under examination here, James Haynes, published his travels in the Ottoman Empire in 1774. A merchant's clerk based in Cairo, Haynes followed a similar route to Thompson, through Anatolia, Syria and Egypt. He provided something more of a travelogue than Thompson's history-dominated tomes. It was also more of a personal pilgrimage, although Haynes constantly reminded his reader that unlike the 'primitive Christians' of Palestine who constructed shrines and memorials at the places significant to the story of Christ, he was there out of private piety and not superficial worship. On visiting the Synagogue at Cana in the Galilee mentioned in John 2:1–11 (the water-to-wine miracle), he wrote that 'no Christian traveller can view these sacred ruins, without feeling indescribable veneration, tho' not to the place, but at the remembrance of its holy and all-merciful former visitor'.[34] This emphasis on internalised rather than external devotion was a key element of British Protestant religious writing. Among Haynes's descriptions of local religious customs and geographical features were some rather dark accounts of the land. The Galilee region was populated with numerous agricultural villages and was a relatively fertile region of Palestine, yet Haynes presented it as an area of intense danger:

The surrounding country swarms with wild beasts, such as tygers, leopards, jackals, &c, whose cries and howling, I doubt not, as it did me, would strike the boldest traveller, who had not been frequently in a like situation, with the deepest sense of horror.[35]

Such dramatic descriptions gave further weight to the proof of Biblical prophecy that the Holy Land was desolate and cursed.

The final eighteenth-century travel account to be examined was Robert Tyron's pilgrimage to the Holy Land first published in 1785. A merchant of the Levant Company based in Aleppo, his writing has some similarity in tone with that of Haynes, but with more of a sense that it was intended to function as a guidebook, with itineraries in various towns and costs of provisions. He also noted the chief economic activities of the region, although describing the local population as very poor and dependent on European trade. As with the other two accounts, Tyron spent many pages ridiculing the religious rites of other Christian sects, commenting on their ostentation and superficiality. He was disgusted by the marble and gold adorning the Holy Sepulchre, and believed that money alone drove the dominance of the Catholics and the Greek Orthodox Church in Jerusalem.[36] He also continued the theme of a cursed land. Instead of tigers, the barren terrain was 'pestered with the wild and savage Arabs...said to be the descendants of Ishmael', claiming this was in fulfilment of prophecies in Genesis (16:11–12, 17:20, 21:10–13).[37] It was because of those wild Arabs that the land was 'now under a curse':

It was undoubtedly a most beautiful and fertile country, [the River] Jordan running southward through it, and forming several pleasant and agreeable lakes, and a vast multitude of brooks and rivulets crossing the country on both sides, and a vast multitude of valleys and hills pleasantly diversified; and when the Almighty, by his seasonable warmth and rains blessed the laborious improvers of the soil, it is not the least incredible how it supported the numerous thousands that once dwelt therein.[38]

The land was therefore currently cursed to barenes and plagued by barbarous tribes, but always retaining a potential to return to its ancient lushness.

These three different travel accounts are notable in three major respects. Firstly, they barely mentioned the Jewish communities of Palestine, and both Thompson and Tyron explicitly claimed that there were no Jews there. Secondly, they all presented the land as barren and even divinely cursed, which, although certainly not the case historically, gave evidence to Biblical scripture concerning the banishment of the Israelites. Finally, the idea was presented that the land had once been fruitful and capable of supporting Biblical populations, and that it was simply inhabited by the wrong people. All three writers favoured their Bibles over their eyes in describing Palestine, and the descriptions they provided formed a corpus of Holy Land travel literature that in the nineteenth century would help to fuel a growing Restorationist movement.

Divine diplomacy

The late eighteenth century saw a great increase in apocalyptic belief, partially as a reaction to ceaseless conflict, and this combined with the humanism of the abolitionist movement to produce missionary movements charged with converting non-Christians and promoting the idea of Christian charity. The first major organisation designed to spread the Gospel was the Church Missionary Society (CMS) founded in 1794, and its missionaries operated across the globe, particularly in India, sub-Saharan Africa and the Pacific Islands. In addition to these rather exotic 'heathens', the CMS also began, from 1804, to preach among British Jews. The mission was not successful, with a report in 1806 noting that its lectures directed at the Jews were 'well attended, but principally by Christians'.[39]

As a result of the CMS's lack of success, the leader of their mission to the Jews, Rev. Joseph Frey, instituted a new society in 1809 called the London Society for Promoting Christianity Amongst the Jews, also known as the London Jews' Society (LJS). The LJS grew rapidly, so that by the time of the fourth report of 1812 it had over 90 auxiliary societies operating across Britain.[40] One telling indication of its popularity was its fundraising, with collections from 435 different congregations between 1809 and 1812 raising £7,400, a substantial sum, which funded pamphlets in Hebrew and German directed towards the Jews.[41] It also recruited some big names to the cause, notably the abolitionist William Wilberforce, who was an early Vice-President of the Society.[42] The LJS's members exhorted each other on their Christian duty to show charity and mercy to the Jews,[43] with some even viewing such benevolence as 'national atonement' for the 'violent and general agitation' that arose after the 1753 Act.[44]

Yet already by around 1810, discontent had been arising within the LJS as to the Jews' reception of their mission. 'The great ignorance [of the British Jews]', the 1810 Report lamented, 'can scarcely be credited.'[45] As a result, the LJS began to look abroad. It was not the first; interest in Restorationism led to the creation of an exploratory society, the Palestine Association, in 1805, the aim of which was to survey Palestine 'with a view to the illustrations of Holy Writings', greatly inspired by earlier travel accounts (Thompson's in particular) and other exploratory societies, such as the African Association.[46] As would later be explained by George Faber, an Anglican theologian, LJS member and Mede follower, 'the converted Jews are destined ... to be the sole, finally successful Missionaries to the Gentile world'.[47] As a result of this belief, LJS missionary posts were established across Northern Europe, particularly in Prussia and Poland, and reports came back noting a positive reception to its efforts.[48]

In the 1820s the Society began to move its attentions to Palestine.[49] An LJS missionary, Rev. W.B. Lewis, travelled to Palestine with a Jewish convert, Rev. Joseph Woolf, in 1824, and there they encountered travel writer John Madox. Madox's *Excursions in the Holy Land* (1834) detailed the geography and customs of the areas through which he traversed, and, as with earlier accounts, emphasised the instability of the land as overrun with marauding Arabs.[50] Interestingly, although Madox did not explicitly discuss the land in biblical terms, he appended a letter from Rev. Lewis that 'will no doubt be perused with interest by the readers of the present work'.[51] In the letter, Lewis complained of the restrictions placed by local officials on distributing religious tracts in Jerusalem and of the 'miserable' state of that city, yet spoke of 'a field ... here opening for the missionary bearing the glad tidings of salvation' for the Jews.[52] Most importantly, Lewis argued for 'the necessity of having a resident [British] consul in the Holy City'.[53]

Such accounts really galvanised the activities of the LJS. In 1825 it established a Palestine Fund to encourage its activities, and by the 1830s the conversion and Restoration of the Jews had become a prominent feature in its rhetoric.[54] The invasion of Ottoman Syria in 1831 by the nominally vassal but essentially independent Mehmet Ali Pasha, Viceroy of Egypt, was also viewed by the missionaries as an opportunity for furthering their aims. Mede had argued that political turmoil, particularly relating to the Ottomans, would indicate the approaching Apocalypse, and the LJS sought to speed up the process by encouraging Jewish migration. Plans were drawn up in 1835 for the construction of a British chapel in Jerusalem, which would 'form the nucleus, round which shall gradually assemble in the Holy Land a Protestant Church'.[55] In 1836 the LJS held discussions with its resident missionary in Palestine, John Nicolayson, concerning the establishment of a church for Hebrew-Christians, and they were confident that Mehmet Ali would view their proposal with favour;[56] in anticipation, the Anglican liturgy was translated into Hebrew.[57]

In 1826, Joseph Wolff, the missionary who accompanied W.B. Lewis to Palestine, wrote to Stratford Canning, the British Ambassador in Istanbul, extolling the successes of the LJS and even claiming that a 'Judeo-Christian Church' had been established in the Ottoman capital with 300 congregants.[58] Wolff's correspondence with Canning, added to Lewis's letter of 1825 emphasising the need for a British consul in Jerusalem, shows that the LJS had a clear aim in lobbying the British political establishment. The image constructed of Palestine by earlier travel writers of a desolate, wild and above all dangerous land provided the basis for their argument. Jerusalem hosted few British merchants, with religious travellers forming the main body of British subjects there, so that consular protection would primarily serve the missionaries and pilgrims. Although John Farren, the

Consul-General for Syria, attempted to appoint an Ottoman-Armenian agent to act for British interests in Jerusalem in 1834 (reversed by the Duke of Wellington), it was only with the return of Viscount Palmerston to the Foreign Office in April 1835 that things began to move forward.[59] Following its discussions with Nicolayson in 1836, the LJS had written to Palmerston requesting his assistance in obtaining permission to establish their Hebrew-Christian Church,[60] and in the same period Palmerston instructed his secretary, John Bidwell, to write to Patrick Campbell, the Consul-General in Egypt, and the British Ambassador in Istanbul, Viscount Ponsonby, to secure the necessary commands to that end from Mehmet Ali and Sultan Mahmud II, respectively.[61] It is notable then that in November 1836 Palmerston wrote that 'it could be Expedient to have an English Consular agent at Jerusalem'.[62]

The diplomatic records show that the proposed church, and its mission to the Jews of Palestine, began to take centre stage. Support for the church, and for the Jews, indeed served a political purpose; in the Ottoman realms, the French had significant rights over Ottoman Roman Catholics as their protector, and the Russians had a similar agreement concerning the Greek Orthodox subjects. The LJS and its church may have provided a convenient excuse for the diplomatic interests of Britain in the Levant, but there is no doubt that in the local context of Jerusalem, the religious imperative was key. This is demonstrated clearly in the selection of William Tanner Young for the new Jerusalem posting. A keen supporter of the LJS, he was suggested to Campbell by Nicolayson in late 1837, and was subsequently appointed Vice-Consul in late 1838.[63] Young was given very precise instructions on his role in Jerusalem by Palmerston, which included cultivating a favourable image of Britain, and, where possible, promoting the consumption of British commodities; yet most notably he was told that 'it will be a part of your duty as British Vice-Consul at Jerusalem to afford protection to the Jews generally'.[64] In this instruction one can see the influence of the LJS. Certainly the British sought to protect the Jewish population of the Ottoman Empire as a measure to compete with French and Russian protection of their respective Christian communities, yet the pressure placed throughout the 1830s by the LJS on various diplomatic figures must have had an effect.

The correspondence between the LJS and the Foreign Office concerning the establishment of a Hebrew-Christian Church, the selection of William Young as Vice-Consul, and the active involvement of major political figures, such as the Earl of Shaftesbury in the LJS, points to the importance of the religious element. Travel writing again provides evidence for the links. In 1838 an account was published on travels in Egypt and Palestine by Lord Lindsay, in the style of letters back to England, yet in the same tone as many of the eighteenth-century accounts; Jerusalem and its hinterland were described as barren and desolate, Nazareth and Galilee as uncultivated.[65] There was a definite Restorationist element in the text – for instance, claiming that the fertility of Lebanon 'had departed from her when Israel rejected Christ ... and blighted she must remain till the second spring ... when, at the voice of God, Israel shall spring anew to life'.[66] Lindsay also included a letter by John Farren, the Consul-General in Damascus, who had attempted to establish a British agent in Jerusalem, which described the political turmoil occasioned by the Egyptian invasion of Syria; political turmoil and the divine curse were thus clearly linked.[67]

Shaftesbury reviewed Lindsay's book in *The Quarterly Review*, using it as an opportunity to provide encouragement for the Restorationist agenda. He spoke of the Vice-Consul in Jerusalem as 'accredited ... to the former kingdom of David and the Twelve Tribes', and noted that British endeavours in Palestine could provide both economic and religious benefits:

> the presence of a British officer, and the increased security of property which his presence will confer, may invite [the Jews] from these islands to the cultivation of Palestine; and the Jews, who will betake themselves to agriculture in no other land, having found, in the English Consul, a mediator between their people and the Pasha, will probably return in yet greater numbers, and become once more the husbandmen of Judaea and Galilee.[68]

Shaftesbury's words were echoed by Palmerston in 1840, who believed that the Jews held a 'strong notion that the Time is approaching when their Nation is to return to Palestine', and that this cause excited 'a very deep interest in the minds of a large number of Persons in the United Kingdom'.[69] Moreover, it is notable that Young took with him a map showing the biblical Holy Land, including the supposed boundaries of the Twelve Tribes.[70] In this diplomatic endeavour, the lines between the Bible and geopolitics were very much blurred.

With the support of Palmerston and Shaftesbury, and Nicolayson and the LJS, Young energetically complied with his instructions to protect the Jews of Jerusalem and Palestine. The LJS's endeavours to establish a Hebrew-Christian Church began to come to fruition when, in 1841, Michael Alexander, a converted Jew, was appointed bishop of the new episcopacy of Jerusalem, although the physical church would not receive permission to be constructed until 1845.[71] Despite the fact that few Jews actually converted to Christianity, leaving the LJS mission with a rather disappointing result for all of its efforts, British protection did in some ways cultivate a favourable attitude towards Britain. Following reports of an assassination attempt on Queen Victoria in 1840, the Jews of Jerusalem wrote a letter to the British monarch thanking God for preserving her, recalling her 'great goodness...toward the House of Israel' and styling her 'Anointed of the Lord'.[72] This may not have made up for the lack of converts from those Jerusalemite Jews, yet the failure of the LJS's evangelical mission should not detract from the centrality of its religious agenda, encouraged by travel accounts, to the establishment of a British political presence in the Holy Land.

Conclusion

The religious aspect of the British project in Palestine in the first half of the nineteenth century had profound effects on the history of the modern Middle East. Young was succeeded by James Finn, another member of the LJS, who made even greater efforts to encourage Jewish settlement of the Holy Land. However, following the emancipation of the Jews in Britain in 1858, negating the need to find British Jews a new home, the LJS lost favour among the political elite and its political influence concerning Palestine was greatly diminished. Yet the British foothold in the Holy Land would continue to be a focus for Restorationist Christians, so that when political Zionism began to be widely articulated in the late nineteenth century, politicians such as Joseph Chamberlain and Arthur Balfour renewed the ties between religion and politics. Balfour's 1917 Declaration expressing British support for a Jewish homeland in Palestine following the defeat of the Ottoman Empire was, of course, a document of political expediency, but it is no coincidence that Balfour, a strong believer in the prophecies of Isaiah concerning the Restoration, willingly signed it off as British policy.

The creation of the State of Israel in 1948, following the withdrawal of the British Mandate over Palestine, has been taken by contemporary Restorationists, particularly in the United States, as the next step in the apocalyptic process. It is, of course, problematic to argue that eighteenth-century travel accounts are the root cause of the troubles in Israel and Palestine today. It is, however, possible to argue for the importance of travel writing in establishing the British image of Palestine that galvanised missionary movements, and which in turn affected British foreign policy in the Holy Land. From the developing association between Britain and the Israelites of the Bible, and continual apocalyptic discourse, a vibrant Restorationist movement had come to the fore in British politics in the nineteenth century. This was in no small measure due to the reports of travellers and missionaries from the Holy Land. Eighteenth-century travel accounts provided the image of a land that was desolate but had much potential, awaiting only the right inhabitants. In the aftermath of the rejection of Jewish naturalisation in 1753, such accounts provided a possible solution to the question of the Jews' itinerancy. When this was combined with the notion of Christian charity in the later eighteenth century, and the increasing sense of the approaching Apocalypse, it is no wonder that the LJS and its aims to restore the Jews to Palestine gained so much popular and political currency.

The LJS failed in its goal of establishing divine imperialism through converting the Jews and sending them *en masse* to Palestine in order to trigger the Apocalypse. Yet in combining long-held eschatological interpretation, British biblical self-representation and Christian charity, it utilised the image of the cursed and desolate land presented in the travel accounts to influence the establishment of a British political and religious settlement in Palestine. That settlement sowed the seeds for future British political involvement in the twentieth century, which would eventually lead to the establishment, so devoutly desired by earlier travellers and missionaries, of a mass Jewish return to the Holy Land under British protection.

Notes

1. B. Rajan (1999) *Under Western Eyes: India from Milton to Macaulay* (Durham NC: Duke University Press), pp. 7–8.
2. G. Claeys (2010) *Imperial Sceptics: British Critics of Empire, 1850–1920* (Cambridge: Cambridge University Press); Andrew N. Porter (2004) *Religion versus Empire? British Protestant Missionaries and Overseas Expansion, 1700–1914* (Manchester: Manchester University Press); D. Hempton (1996) *Religion and Political Culture in Britain and Ireland: From the Glorious Revolution to the Decline of Empire* (Cambridge: Cambridge University Press); R. Strong (2007) *Anglicanism and the British empire, c. 1700–1850* (Oxford: Oxford University Press); N. Etherington (2005) *Missions and Empire* (Oxford: Oxford University Press).
3. M. Vereté (1970) 'Why Was a British Consulate Established at Jerusalem?', *The English Historical Review*, 85, 335, 316–45; M. Eliav (1997) *Britain and the Holy Land, 1838–1914: Selected Documents from the British Consulate in Jerusalem* (Jerusalem: Yad Itzhak Ben-Zvi Press and the Magnes Press, the Hebrew University); M. Eliav, 'Ha-Ḳonsuliyah ha-Briṭit be-Yerušalayim (1838–1914)' in Yehoshu ʿa Šwarẓ, ẓohar ʿAmar and ʿIrit Ẕifer (eds.) (2000) *Yerušalayim ve Erez̄-Yiśra ʿel* (Ramat Gan: Merkaz Inenborg Renarṭ li-Limudei Yerušalayim; Tel-Aviv: Muzei'on Erez̄-Yiśra ʿel), pp. 199–217; I. Friedman (1992) *The Question of Palestine: British-Jewish-Arab Relations: 1914–1918* (New Brunswick: Transaction).
4. Y. Perry (2003) *British Mission to the Jews in Nineteenth-Century Palestine* (London & Portland: Frank Cass).
5. J. Mede (1627) *Clavis Apocalyptica Ex Innaris & insitis visionum characteribus eruta, & demonstrata* (Cambridge: For the Author, T & J Buck.).
6. Ezek 34:11–16; Isa 11:11–12.
7. M. Ben-Israel (1650) *Miḳveh Yiśra'el, Esto es, Esperança de Israel*. (Amsterdam: Semuel Ben-Israel Soreiro, 5410 [1650]); Menasseh Ben-Israel, *Miḳveh Yiśra'el, Hoc est, Spes Israelis* (Amsterdam: unknown publisher).
8. Menasseh Ben-Israel (1650) *The Hope of Israel*, trans. anonymous (London, R.I.); Thomas Thorowgood (1650) *Jews in America, or, Probabilities That the Americans Are of the Race. With the Removal of Some Contrary Reasonings, and Earnest Desire for Effectual Endeavours to Make Them Christian* (London: W.H.).
9. Ben-Israel, *The Hope of Israel*, ii.

10. Parliamentary Archives [PA]: *Journals of the House of Lords, Beginning Anno Vicesimo Sexto Georgii Secundi, 1753*, 28, p. 73.
11. PA: (1803) *Journals of the House of Commons. From January the 17th, 1750, In the Twenty-Fourth Year of the Reign of King George the Second, To April the 6th 1754, In the Fourteenth Year of the Reign of King George the Second*, vol. 26, II (reprinted by Order of the House of Commons), p. 827.
12. Ibid., p. 829.
13. 'Archaicus' (1753) *The Rejection and Restoration of the Jews, According to Scripture, declar'd with Indications of the Means by which, and Nearly, of the Time when, the Latter of These Great Events Is To Be Brought to Pass* (London: R. Baldwin) pp. 22, 30.
14. PA: *Journal of the House of Commons*, 26:2, pp. 852, 855, 856–7; PA: *Journal of the House of Lords*, 28, p. 182.
15. See, for example, 'Philogos' (1755) *A Letter of Thanks to the Rector of St Botolph, Bishopsgate, for the Ingenious Discourse Which He Delivered at that Church on Sunday*, November 24, 1754 (London: M. Cooper), p. 7; R. Clarke (1760) *A Spiritual Voice to the Christian Church, and to the Jews* (London: J. Townsend), pp. 113–4.
16. For instance, G. Swanne (1760) *The Advantage of the Jews under Their Dispensation Set Forth, and the Use They Made of Them Considered in Two Sermons Preached before the University of Oxford, At St Mary's, on Sunday April 27th, and Sunday May 4th, 1760* (Oxford: Clarendon Printing House), pp. 53–4; 'J.S.', (1774) *An Enquiry Concerning the Arguments Which Relate to Our Controversy with the Jews, as They Arise from Prophetic Records* (Dublin: William Sleater), pp. 28, 38; (1779) *A Friendly Address to the Jews in General, in a Series of Letters* (London: unknown publisher), pp. 26–8, 55–64.
17. S. Hardy (1770) *The Principal Prophecies of the Old and New Testaments; Particularly Those in the Revelation of St John; Compared and Explained* (London: unknown publisher), pp. 84–5.
18. T. Reader (1788) *Israel's Salvation: or, An Account from the Prophecies of Scripture of the Grand Events Which Await the Jews, to the End of Time* (Taunton: T. Norris), pp. 32–3, 37.
19. J. Eyre (1771) *Observations upon the Prophecies relating to the Restoration of the Jews* (London: T. Cadell), pp. 116, 123, 127; C. Jerram (1796) *An Essay Tending to Shew the Grounds Contained in Scriptures for Expecting a Future Restoration of the Jews* (Cambridge: Cambridge University Press), pp. 18, 40–1, 44.
20. J. Baillie (1792) *Two Sermons: The First on the Divinity of Jesus Christ; The Second on the Time, Manner, and Means of the Conversion and Universal Restoration of the Jews*, 2nd edn. (London: Minerva), pp. 49–50, 53–5, 67–8.
21. For overviews of the history of Palestine in this period, see G. Krämer (2008) *A History of Palestine* (Princeton: Princeton); Doumani Beshara (1995) *Rediscovering Palestine: Merchants and Peasants in Jabal Nablus, 1700–1900* (Berkeley: University of California Press). For an analysis of archival sources on Ottoman Palestine, see: Y. Sarınay (2009) *Osmanlı Belgelerinde Filistin* (Istanbul: T.C. Başbakanlık Devlet Arşivleri Genel Müdürlüğü).
22. G. MacLean (2004) *The Rise of Oriental Travel: English Visitors to the Ottoman Empire, 1580–1720* (Basingstoke: Palgrave Macmillan).
23. C. Thompson (1767) *Travels through Turkey in Asia, the Holy Land, Arabia, Egypt, and Other Parts of the World: Giving a Particular and Faithful Account of What Is Most Remarkable in the Manners, Religion, Polity, Antiquities, and Natural History of Those Countries, with a Curious Description of Jerusalem, As it now Appears,*

and *Other Places Mentioned in the Holy Scripture*, 3rd edn., 2 vols. (London: J. Newbery).

24. J. Haynes (1774) *Travels in Several Parts of Turkey, Egypt, and the Holy Land* (London: unknown publisher).

25. R. Tyron (1785) *Travels from Aleppo to Jerusalem, and Through the Most Remarkable Parts of the Holy Land, in 1776*,1st edn. (Glasgow).

26. H. Maundrel (1697) 'A Journey from Aleppo to Jerusalem', in (1757) *A Compendium of the Most Approved Modern Travels, Containing a Distinct Account of Religion, Government, Commerce, Manners, and Natural History of Several Nations*, vol. 1 (Dublin: J. Smith), pp. 1–127 at p. 52.

27. H. Prideaux (1708) *The True Nature of Imposture Fully Display'd in the Like of Mahomet*, 4th edn. (London: For W. Rogers).

28. H. Prideaux (1725) *The Old and New Testament Connected in the History of the Jews and Neighbouring Nations*, 2 vols, 9th edn. (London: for R. Knaplock & J. Tonson).

29. For instance, their extensive history of the Jews, Thompson, *Travels*, vol II., pp. 64–114, has many similarities with Prideaux's narrative.

30. Thompson, *Travels*, II. p. 113.

31. Ibid., I, p. 248.

32. Ibid., I, p. 249.

33. For instance, Exodus 3:8, 17, 13:5, 33:3, Leviticus 20:24.

34. Haynes, *Travels*, p. 119.

35. Thompson, *Travels*, p. 118.

36. Tyron, *Travels*, pp. 7–8.

37. Ibid., pp. 19–20.

38. Ibid.

39. British Library [BL]: Church Missionary Society Collection [CMSC] (1806) *Four Sermons, preached in London, at the Twelfth General Meeting of the Missionary Society* (London: T. Williams), p. 27.

40. BL: London Jews' Society Collection [LJSC] (1812) *The Fourth Report of the Committee of the London Society for Promoting Christianity amongst the Jews* (London: B.R. Goakman).

41. Ibid. pp. 61–72. BL:LJSC (1810) *No.2. Education. Le-Benei Avraham. To the Children of Abraham* (London: For the [LJS] Society); BL:LJSC (1810) *No. 11. An Address to the Jews. Le-Benei Avraham* (London: For the [LJS] Society); BL:LJSC (1810) *No.10. Igeret Polos ha-Šaliyaḥ ha-Ḳadoš el ha-ʿIvrim* (London: For the [LJS] Society); BL:LJSC (1810) *Versuch über das göttliche Ansehen des Neuen Testaments* (Basle, unknown publisher).

42. Ibid., pp. 6–8.

43. BL:LJSC, Thomas Scott (1810) *The Jews a Blessing to the Nations, and Christians Bound to Seek Their Conversion to the Saviour* (London: For the [LJS] Society); BL:LJSC (1810) 'A Presbyter of the Church of England', *The Obligations of Christians to Attempt the Conversion of the Jews* (London: For the [LJS] Society); BL:LJSC, Edward Williams (1811) *Apostolic Benevolence Towards the Jews Recommended for Imitation* (London: For the [LJS] Society).

44. BLJSC, 'A Presbyter of the Church of England', *The Obligations of Christians* p. 13; BL:LJSC, Richard Graves (1811) *A Sermon, Preached in St Andrew's Church, Dublin* (London: For the [LJS] Society), pp. 26–7.

45. BL:LJSC, *Report of the Committee to the Third Half Yearly Meeting*, pp. 7–8.

46. BL: The Palestine Association Collection [PAC] (1805) *Palestine Association: Proposal* (London: For the [LJS] Society).

47. G. Faber (1822) *The Conversion of the Jews to the Faith of Christ, the True Medium to the Conversion of the Gentile World* (London: for the [London] Society [for Promoting Christianity amongst the Jews), pp. 13, 16–17.
48. C.S. Hawtrey (1826) *A Summary Account of the Origin, Proceedings and Success of the London Society for Promoting Christianity amongst the Jews* (London: A. Macintosh), pp. 12, 20–1.
49. The CMS had already demonstrated a limited interest in Palestine: BL:CMSC (1816, 1818, 1819, 1820, 1822, 1828) *Missionary Papers for the Use of the Weekly and Monthly Contributors to the Church Missionary Society* nos. II, IX, XIII, XX, XXV, LI (London: For the [LJS] Society); BL:CMSC, W. Jowett (1825) *Christian Researches in the Holy Land in MDCCCXXIII and MDCCCXXIV* (London: For the [LJS] Society).
50. J. Madox (1834) *Excursions in the Holy Land, Egypt, Nubia, Syria &c*, vol. 2 (London: Richard Bentley), pp. 191–258.
51. Madox, *Excursions*, p. 357.
52. Ibid., pp. 356–62.
53. Ibid., p. 360.
54. BL:LJSC, H. Norris (1825) *The Origin, Progress, and Existing Circumstances of the London Society for Promoting Christian Societies Amongst the Jews* (London: For the [LJS] Society), pp. 461–2; BL:LJSC, A. McCaul (1835) *New Testament Evidence to Prove that the Jews Are To Be Restored to the Land of Israel* (London: R. Wertheim).
55. BL:LJSC (1835) *Jersey Auxiliary to the London Society for Promoting Christian Among the Jews, First Annual Report* (Jersey: For the [LJS] Society), pp. 3–6.
56. BL:LJSC (1838) *Hebrew Church at Jerusalem* (London: for the [LJS] Society).
57. BL:LJSC (1836) *Seder ha-tefilah ke-piy minhag Ḳehilat ha-mašiaḥ šel medinat Ingland ve Irland* (London: For the [LJS] Society).
58. The National Archives [TNA]: Foreign Office [FO] 352/14B, Joseph Wolff to Stratford Canning, 8 March 1826.
59. TNA:FO78/243/36, John Farren to Viscount Palmerston, 18 October 1834; TNA:FO78/243/43, Farren to Palmerston, 20 November 1834; TNA:FO78/260/8, John Backhouse to Patrick Campbell, 1 April 1835; TNA:FO78/260/8/A, Memorandum of the Duke of Wellington, undated.
60. TNA:FO78/300/46, Palmerston to Lord Ponsonby, 24 June 1837.
61. TNA:FO78/295/25, Campbell to Palmerston, 7 October 1836; TNA:FO78/295/18, John Bidwell to Campbell, 29 November 1836; TNA:FO78/300/113, Palmerston to Ponsonby, 11 November 1837; TNA:FO78/322/18, Bidwell to Campbell, 18 November 1837.
62. TNA:FO78/260/13/A, Memorandum of Palmerston, 6 November 1836.
63. TNA:FO78/322/28, Campbell to Palmerston, 19 September 1837; TNA:FO78/329/122, Palmerston to Ponsonby, 6 June 1838; TNA:FO78/344/20, Campbell to Palmerston, 20 July 1838; TNA:FO78/329/152, Palmerston to Ponsonby, 26 July 1838; TNA:FO78/340/1, Palmerston to William Young, 19 September 1838; TNA:FO78/344/17, Palmerston to Campbell, 19 September 1838.
64. TNA:FO78/340/2, Palmerston to Young, 19 September 1838; TNA:FO78/368/2, Bidwell to Young, 31 January 1839.
65. Lord Lindsay (1838) *Letters on Egypt, Edom, and the Holy Land*, vol. II (London: Henry Colburn), pp. 60–238.
66. Ibid., p. 213.
67. Ibid., pp. 239–341.
68. Lord Shaftesbury (1839) 'Letters on Egypt, Edom, and the Holy Land by Lord Linsday', *The Quarterly Review*, 63, 125, 166–91 at 188–9.

69. TNA:FO78/390/134, Palmerston to Ponsonby, 11 August 1840; TNA:FO78/391/ 248, Palmerston to Ponsonby, 24 November 1840.

70. TNA:FO78/340/2/A, Mr William Young's Map of Palestine (1836) *Map of Palestine, the Holy Land or Land of Canaan* (London: R.H. Laurie).

71. BL:LJSC, Michael Alexander (1841) *Farewell Sermon* (London: R. Wertheim); TNA:FO78/501/1, Earl of Aberdeen to Young, 3 May 1842; TNA:FO78/501/7&A, Young to Aberdeen, 11 October 1842.

72. TNA:FO368/13&A, Young to Palmerston, 24 May 1840; TNA:FO78/368/21&A, Young to Palmerston, 23 July 1840; TNA:FO78/413/17/A, Young to Palmerston, 23 July 1840.

3
Model City: Fact and Fiction in Early Twentieth-Century Khartoum

Henrika Kuklick

In mid-November of 1909, Brenda Seligman and her husband, Charles Gabriel Seligman, future professor of ethnology at the London School of Economics, stopped in Cairo, Egypt, *en route* to Khartoum, the capital of the Sudan.[1] Preparing for the first of two stints of anthropological research they would undertake for the Sudan government between 1909 and 1912, they met with officials employed by the British regime in Egypt to which the Sudan was formally subordinate. They also mixed pleasure with business, as they did when they revisited Cairo, then a tourist mecca offering the attractions of both high-minded recreation and extravagant consumption. They saw the pyramids; cruised the Nile; heard an opera performed by a Sicilian troupe; shopped for Persian carpets, silver tableware and fine china; visited the field sites of the prominent Egyptologist (later Sir) William Flinders Petrie; and complained about British and American 'tourists of the most virulent type' – intent on frivolous pursuits, with no interest in ancient Egypt.[2]

Once in Khartoum, the Seligmans were swept into a social whirl. Brenda's diaries describe patterns of behaviour familiar to students of life in colonial enclaves – performances of elite British practices by persons who were usually unfamiliar with the metropolitan originals. She reported 'quite quaint' customs, such as 'paying calls in white kid gloves'; formal dinners, including one hosted by the Sudan's Governor, Sir Reginald Wingate, at which he escorted her to the table and Lady Wingate invited her to call of a Sunday afternoon; horseback riding with officials' wives; and the wives' complaints about their virtually obligatory service for Lady Wingate's charities.[3] Happily, the Seligmans met two congenial couples: (later Sir) James Currie and (later Sir) Andrew Balfour and their wives. Currie, the Sudan's Director of Education until 1914, was responsible for the government's invitation to the Seligmans, and attended to their practical needs. Balfour, who between 1902 and 1913 directed the Wellcome Tropical Research Laboratories in

Khartoum, was also Khartoum Province's Medical Officer of Health and sanitary advisor to the Sudan – and believed that anthropological knowledge served medicine.[4]

Once in the countryside to do their research, having travelled there by camel or boat (and occasionally by rail), the Seligmans acquired information from indigenes in exchange for goods and services: salt, pieces of brass and lengths of Liberty silk; and the medical care that Charles, a trained physician, could provide (many anthropologists, regardless of their training, found that the provision of medical care was a means to ingratiate themselves with diverse peoples). Brenda collected genealogies to determine indigenes' understanding of kinship relationships and acquired a working knowledge of Arabic, the language of interpreters in the Sudan (though it was not spoken everywhere; members of the Sudan Political Service, the administrative arm of the regime, were required to learn it). Charles investigated social customs, archaeological evidence and peoples' physical traits.[5] Occasionally the Seligmans encountered a living stereotype – the colonial official determined to uphold proper British standards in the bush – such as the Provincial Governor, whose 'china, silver, rugs and linens [were] of a quality unknown otherwise in the provinces', who gave them 'an absurdly good dinner'. Ordinarily they communicated with officials by mail and dined on game they shot. Sometimes their mailman was a touring member of the Sudan Political Service, such as (later Sir) Harold MacMichael, an accomplished amateur ethnographer and historian (in early 1912 his duties took him to one of their research sites, from which he departed with their letters). But the Seligmans' movements were restricted: they were not permitted to go where colonial rule was insecure.[6]

Thereby hangs the tale: Khartoum was a safe haven. In the roughly 1 million square miles of the Sudan's vast territory – comprised of the virtually distinct Islamised north and the so-called pagan south (increasingly Christianised over time) – were many areas beset with feuds and given to uprisings (often religiously justified). Pacification campaigns were often difficult. The last major campaign, against the Nuer, lasted from 1927 to 1930 and involved air and ground strikes as well as forced resettlement.[7] C.G. Seligman's student, E.E. (eventually Sir Edward) Evans-Pritchard, whose government-financed study of the Nuer was supposed to suggest an administrative order for them, famously pronounced colonial authority fragile at best: officials 'cannot control development to any great extent'; policy was 'an intellectualisation of a process of development and not the cause of the process'.[8] However applicable Evans-Pritchard's generalisations were to other British colonial regimes, they rang true in the Sudan.

Certainly, officials talked a good game. Wingate's administration set a high moral tone – perhaps congenial for the many clergymen's sons in the Political Service. A 1908 visitor felt as if he 'were in the midst of a band of lay missionaries whose object was to secure the peace and happiness of the world', and officials claimed that extraordinary progress had been made throughout the country following Britain's assumption of power in 1898.[9] But the Sudan regime exemplified the type of colonial polity that relied on spectacle because it was 'chronically short' of the material resources needed to effect control.[10] Although Andrew Balfour implemented successful public health strategies, his medical views were arguably at least as significant in symbolic as in practical terms. Likewise, Charles Seligman's ideas hold interest primarily for their ideological import; they were influenced by, as well as contributions to, ongoing conversations in the Sudan, and figured in imperialist thought elsewhere.

In sum, arguments such as Balfour's and Seligman's were important because they circulated far beyond the Sudan's boundaries. They represented both ideological and practical resources for Britons abroad – means for the confident operation of Empire. This chapter centres on the early years of the British regime in the Sudan – between 1898 and 1916, when its governors-general were (briefly) Herbert Kitchener and Reginald Wingate. Then the Sudan had resources that it subsequently lost and it received considerable public attention, not least because of its late nineteenth-century history. The chapter has three foci: Seligman's 'Hamitic Hypothesis'; the planning of the city of Khartoum; and Andrew Balfour's practice of tropical medicine, especially notable because he would achieve international status.

Background: Reluctant imperialism

As a nearly independent state within the Ottoman Empire, Egypt had presided over the Sudan since 1821, governing through mercenaries – often Europeans, supposedly less corruptible than locals – many of them extravagantly self-fashioned figures, such as the British career soldier Charles Gordon. During the reign of the Khedive Ismail (1863–79), Egypt went bankrupt. In 1875, when Britain bought Ismail's shares in the Suez Canal (vital to imperial communications), it acquired the financial stake in Egyptian stability that justified an invasion in 1882. Sir Evelyn Baring (soon to be Lord Cromer) shortly became British Agent and Consul-General – the effective ruler of Egypt – charged with restoring solvency (Britain declared Egypt a Protectorate after the Ottoman Empire joined the Central Powers in the First World War, ending Turkey's remote jurisdiction).[11] Meanwhile, a powerful social movement had swept the Sudan. Its leader, Muhammad Ahmad ibn ʿAbdallah, proclaimed himself the Mahdi (Islamic messiah) in 1881; after his natural death in 1885 he was succeeded by the Khalifa ʿAbdallahi. Ismail's agents had provoked rebellion, not least by attempting to suppress the slave trade, a vital element in the Sudan's economy, outlawed in 1877 by a British-Egyptian convention. But following a military debacle in 1883, British statesmen proclaimed the Sudan strategically worthless and decided to withdraw – a decision disliked by both Queen Victoria and ordinary Britons. The press encouraged public disapproval, deriving sensational copy from Mahdist triumphs. The most sensational of these made a martyr of Major-General Charles Gordon, a fervent Christian who believed himself to be an instrument of God's will. Already a national hero in 1883 when he was sent to Khartoum to assess the British situation there and lead an evacuation if the British presence was untenable (as direct inspection showed it was), he disobeyed orders, entrenching himself in the city as the Mahdists grew closer. Bowing to public demand, Britain organised a military rescue party in 1885, but it was a two-days march from Khartoum when – according to legend – Gordon wore his dress uniform to meet the death he had anticipated.[12] Memorials to Gordon were installed all over Britain, including a statue in Trafalgar Square, but Britain did not undertake to avenge his death until the end of the century.

In September 1898 a force of British, Egyptian and Sudanese soldiers commanded by Sir Herbert Kitchener (soon to be Lord Kitchener of Khartoum) won a major victory in Omdurman, the Mahdist capital, across from Khartoum on the White Nile. Kitchener celebrated with an ecumenical Christian service at Khartoum's Palace, which concluded with Gordon's favourite hymn, 'Abide With Me' (and with many of those present, including Kitchener, in tears).[13] The great public fanfare that greeted news of Kitchener's triumph did not translate into official enthusiasm, however. Britain remained a reluctant presence in the Sudan. Under the Condominium Agreement of January 1899, designed by Cromer to preclude reassertion of Ottoman rights, Egypt and Britain ruled the Sudan jointly – but Egypt had fiscal responsibility without authority (Egypt's influence was deliberately minimised, and occasional subventions from Britain were hard won). In Whitehall the peculiar legal status of the Sudan placed it under the indifferent supervision of the Foreign Office.[14]

The agents of British rule in the Sudan, members of its Political Service, were remarkably independent of Khartoum, not least because they were thin on the ground. Indeed, when Cromer noticed the Sudan's increasing expenditure on stationery, he pronounced in 1901 that its staff were committing 'excessive writing', denoting 'excessive centralisation'; 'administration should be decentralised as much as possible', he said (the historian laments that Cromer's policy made for sparse archives). Moreover, the Sudan was *de facto* two domains – the Muslim-dominated north (where Khartoum is situated) and the animist and (increasingly over time) Christian south, home to black Africans. Moreover, Khartoum officialdom was, in Robert Collins's words, 'completely indifferent to the Southern Sudan', where officials often called 'Bog Barons' acted as dictators of their domains; at the time of Sudan's independence, it was Africa's 'most dysfunctional' nation, and it is not surprising that in 2011 the north and south became the separate states of Sudan and South Sudan.[15] In sum, the Sudan regime had neither the power nor the inclination to implement a rigorous programme of administrative control. Its greatest concern was subversion of any sort, including (but not limited to) pan-Islamism and nationalism, and its most consistent policy was to inhibit the growth of local power centres, which might harbour rebellious movements.[16] Members of the Political Service understood their task in personal terms – to build subjects' trust by attending to 'individual concerns', as Kitchener said; and, accustomed to autonomy, they habitually disregarded the directives they received.[17]

The Sudan Political Service was selective: its recruits were largely Oxbridge graduates with good degrees (second class, at least) and included many 'Blues', who had supposedly learned to exercise initiative from participation in organised games. But its appeal was surely some function of its undemanding work conditions, relative to those of other British colonial services: its officers had time for recreation (improving and otherwise), exceptionally long home leave and retired young, at 48.[18] Indeed, Wingate spent half of the year either at home in Scotland or in a hill station he built, Erkowit, explaining that Khartoum's recurrently unhealthy climate justified his absences.[19] The point is this: British officials in the Sudan had time for scholarship, which could serve ideological purposes. Wingate wrote history. Happily for Seligman, many officials dabbled in anthropology, collecting evidence he could use.

The 'Hamitic Hypothesis'

Sudan officials found peoples they called 'Hamites' in the north; in the south were 'Negroid' peoples, such as the Nuer.[20] And the idea for which Seligman remains best known is his 'Hamitic Hypothesis', specifying traits of a type he (and others) judged to be the 'primitive or modified form of white man'.[21] Why did the administrative culture of the Sudan justify inquiry into Hamite character? Recall the most effective public justification for anthropological inquiry during the first half of the twentieth century: it represented 'practical science', useful to colonial administrators.[22] Hamites' temperament – 'their personal bravery and love of freedom', in the words of the University of London's professor of Hindustani, A. H. Keane – made them simultaneously admirable and dangerous; they had embraced Mahdism, and might prove troublesome under British rule.[23] Seligman's argument was summarised in a passage that appeared in every edition of his *Races of Africa* from 1930 to 1966.

> [T]he history of Africa south of the Sahara is no more than the story of the permeation, through the ages, in different degrees and at various times, of the Negroes and the Bushmen by Hamitic Blood and culture. The Hamites were, in fact, the great civilizing force of black Africa from a relatively early period, the influence of the Semites being late and in

the main confined to the 'white' areas north of the Sahara inhabited by Hamitic peoples.[24]

Hamites were responsible for the civilisation of ancient Egypt, and the least modified descendants of the earliest Hamites were Sudanese, 'physically identical to the pre-dynastic Egyptians'.[25]

Although the 'Hamitic Hypothesis' did not originate with Seligman, his prominence in learned circles enabled him to put it into broad circulation.[26] Indeed, through the early 1960s, the hypothesis persisted in academically respectable African histories, most notably Roland Oliver and John Fage's *A Short History of Africa* (1962). Moreover, the understood association between the hypothesis and a racist justification for colonial rule was straightforward. In 1913, for example, Sir Harry Johnston explained that European powers' move into Africa repeated a familiar pattern: 'Once again, Africa is about to receive a most powerful infusion of Caucasian blood.'[27] It is remarkable that the 'Hamitic Hypothesis' did not receive concerted attack until the end of the colonial era.[28]

Seligman's initiation into anthropology was his participation in the 1898 Cambridge Anthropological Expedition to Torres Straits, and, along with other members of the expedition, he argued that cultural progress could result from diffusion – contact of peoples – as opposed to 'independent invention', nineteenth-century anthropologists' explanation.[29] The 'Hamitic Hypothesis' was a diffusionist argument. But officials in the Sudan accepted it prior to Seligman's arrival, as Harold MacMichael did in 1907, citing works by Keane and philologist Max Müller.[30] Seligman pronounced that MacMichael's research would 'be of the utmost service to administrators and historians of the Sudan' (although he qualified his praise, saying that MacMichael did 'not write as an ethnologist').[31] Moreover, though Seligman questioned details of Keene's narrative, he accepted its general argument: a congeries of African peoples had converged on the Sudan; the impact of Hamitic migrants had been decisive.[32]

What did the 'Hamitic Hypothesis' mean to Seligman? He famously understood theories as ephemeral. As Millville Herskovits observed, Seligman stressed that 'it is the facts on which [theories] are based that will always be of use'.[33] And his generalisations about relationships between physical and behavioural variations were qualified: progress through culture contact need not entail biological transformation since 'a comparatively small number of foreigners carrying a superior culture may impose some at least of the features of that culture on people of inferior race, even though the mass be too large to be influenced considerably in physical characters'.[34] He found correlations between physical traits and personality types – the introverts and extroverts identified by Jung – asserting that populations differed by virtue of their proportions of the two types, but stressed that the correlations were imperfect.[35] Moreover, Seligman pursued dream symbolism to document the universal collective unconscious that Jung postulated.[36] In truth, Seligman was not a rigorous thinker. A man of broad sympathies, he quite possibly did not intend the 'Hamitic Hypothesis' to be used as a racist justification for colonialism. But it was.

Town planning

Architecture had a special place in the late nineteenth- and early twentieth-century British mind: great architecture denoted great civilisation.[37] British architecture 'embod[ied] the traditions and best qualities of our race', said John Burns, the MP who sponsored the Town Planning Act 1909, who boasted in 1910 that Britain was making 'greater strides' in slum clearance and town planning 'than any other country in the world'.[38] Not surprisingly, urban planners understood the built environment as both an expression and a reminder of imperial power. For example, in mid-nineteenth-century Belfast, streets were given the names of colonial cities; and the early twentieth-century buildings of Liverpool's docks celebrated Britain's international trade.[39] The colonies provided work opportunities for British architects and planners, whose achievements were heralded as inspirations for planned urban development at home. Indeed, Herbert Kitchener claimed to have anticipated the Town Planning Act 1909 with the plan for Khartoum's development that he outlined as the Sudan's first Governor-General (which he continued to monitor after he handed his office over to Wingate at the end of 1899).[40]

Throughout the Empire, constructed landscapes were intended to impress upon subject peoples the durability and legitimacy of imperial rule. The British regime's design of Khartoum represented a general pattern. The city was created virtually *de novo*; Kitchener levelled it, save for the principal structures and palm groves of its northernmost portion, which were preserved as urban amenities – and it was built for Europeans; its railroad station, stores and some of its military barracks were in the formally separate area of Khartoum North, where a large population of non-Europeans was anticipated. And its planners anticipated a glorious – unrealised – future: the Sudan would be covered with cotton farms 'capable of supplying most of the cotton that Lancashire can take'; Khartoum would enjoy a thriving economy as the 'centre of an enormous cotton trade', becoming 'the largest town in Africa'.[41] The city's street plan served as a constant reminder of imperial power: over a grid of streets, the major one called Victoria Avenue, was laid a diagonal network of streets, each named after a successful imperial battle. The diagonal network was also practical, intended to facilitate rapid military response to disorder in the city, if suppression of turmoil became necessary. In 1902, planning began for a spiritual centre for Khartoum, the (Anglican) Cathedral Church of All Saints, consecrated in 1912 on the anniversary of Gordon's death, although it took more than a decade to complete, since raising funds for it proved difficult. Built on the putative site of Gordon's death, it was decorated as a shrine to his memory. Its north transept was festooned with large bronze lettering stating 'Praise God for Charles Robert Gordon, A Servant of Jesus Christ Whose Labour Was Not In Vain.' Elsewhere in the church were tablets commemorating soldiers who died with Gordon and in subsequent battles that led to British rule of the Sudan.[42]

Just as important as Kitchener later said (indeed more), Khartoum's reconstruction along 'sanitary lines' would testify to 'the thorough efficiency of the administration of the country' – justifying the imperial mission.[43] Sanitary measures were urgent; before the British conquest, Khartoum was 'dirty in the extreme' and 'very unhealthy'; it was a place of 'miserable mud houses', where during the rainy season 'numerous hollow flats' collected water that stagnated.[44] Elevated standards of public health would make the city a tourist destination, a commercial venue, and a place of long-term residence for Europeans – the intended principal beneficiaries of sanitary efforts throughout the Empire.[45] But as one of Khartoum's planners pronounced, Europeans in the city were 'not in their natural zone and therefore, not in adjustment with their environment'; to live healthfully, they would have to be housed in structures built to protect them from the deleterious characteristics of the tropics.[46] Note that the characteristics of tropical habitats – intense heat, heavy rains, fierce winds and bright sunlight – were thought to make them hazardous environments for all peoples, but that they were believed especially perilous for non-indigenous peoples. Khartoum's climate was inconsistent. During one season, from mid-November to the beginning of March (the time when the Seligmans arrived there), it was relatively free from those 'sudden changes in temperature so liable to induce abdominal complaints and chills', enjoying 'bright sunshine, a dry heat tempered by cool breezes...and comparatively cold nights', as Andrew Balfour said; but it was unhealthy from May through July, plagued by violent sand-storms, 'sometimes followed by torrential rain and accompanied by thunder and lightening', which 'turn[ed] day into night and night into a [sleepless] period of torment', and which swept 'infected dust into food and drink'. Other climatic features – the 'monotony' of conditions in the tropics and 'the action of intense sunlight and heat on the nervous system' – added to the stresses that Europeans suffered, 'play[ing] no small part in producing that nervous irritability so characteristic of the tropics'.[47]

To design buildings suited to its recurrently inhospitable environment, the Sudan found its ideal architects in the Arts and Crafts movement. Participants in this movement – who included Robert Weir Schultz (after 1914, Robert W.S. Weir), the architect of Khartoum's cathedral, and Otto Beeston Hatchard, chief government architect from 1905 to 1910 – were committed to tailoring structures to suit natural conditions: wherever they worked, Arts and Crafts architects looked to vernacular buildings for inspiration, believing that they represented evolutionary adaptation to their environment.[48]

W.H. McLean, Khartoum's Municipal Engineer, also held this view: 'native houses' were exemplary, 'well darkened, with only a few small openings', affording protection from the heat that was needed by all tropical residents; colonists should stop building houses 'only suitable for temperate climates, and in which even a black man would feel uncomfortable'.[49] But Europeans also required protection from the sun's rays, dangerous to humans in inverse proportion to their levels of skin pigmentation; Europeans' houses should be protected by overhanging roofs, oriented to take advantage of prevailing winds, graced with verandahs, surrounded by trees and arrayed on wide streets.[50] Khartoum's cathedral, constructed under McLean's supervision, was an architectural exemplar, designed 'to suit the special needs of a tropical climate'.[51] Built of stone quarried near Khartoum, its outer walls rested on a terrace. Its inner floor was elevated four feet above ground, and its entrances were shelters from sandstorms. Deep stone hoods capped its windows, which were 'thick "bottle" glass of a green specially chosen for the purpose of tempering the strong sunlight' – rendering the cathedral's interior so dark that artificial light was necessary. Its roof, twice as thick as that of a comparable structure built in Europe would have been, cooled its interior and protected it from the Sudan's heavy rains.[52]

In sum, issues addressed both at home and abroad by British architects and planners included matters of health, but these matters were more important in the colonies. Leo Amery (Secretary of State for the Colonies) suggested that living conditions for Europeans in the tropics might be thoroughly transformed if architecture and medicine were properly joined there.[53]

Tropical Medicine

Khartoum possessed a distinctive outpost of tropical medicine, the Wellcome Tropical Research Laboratories, housed in Gordon Memorial College (itself part of Kitchener's plan for Khartoum) a secondary school (headed by James Currie) that trained small numbers of northern Sudanese to work as clerks and artisans for the British regime – and in numbers calculated not to exceed the number of jobs available to graduates, lest it produce a population of unemployed malcontents who would become a force of political agitators.[54] When Kitchener broadcast an appeal for funding for the school, he received a generous cheque from the pharmaceutical magnate (later Sir) Henry Wellcome, who had an avid interest in African affairs. Subsequently, Wellcome visited the Sudan. After observing its diseased peoples, he offered to equip a medical research facility to be housed in the college, on the condition that the government maintain it and pay its personnel.[55] Wellcome's marketing strategies included distributing chests containing his (trademarked) 'tabloid' medicines to imperial adventurers; and the Laboratories' scientists were directed to investigate Sudanese pharmacopeia – 'toxic agents . . . employed by the natives', as well as remedies of 'vegetable origin', cultivated in the Laboratories' 'therapeutic garden' – knowledge of which had potential commercial value. But the Laboratories' primary mission was work that would benefit all inhabitants of the Sudan. Its scientists' duties included assisting the Sudan's medical staff; promoting technical education; and investigating local diseases 'of man and beast', water and food supplies, agricultural and mineral resources, and health factors affecting 'the industrial development of the Sudan'.[56] Its grandiose title (and avowed mission) notwithstanding, it was a modest facility, occupying only a few rooms and never employing more than six scientists full time during its first decade of existence – after which Wellcome stopped supporting it. But he created it with great enthusiasm. He publicised it extensively, ordering many copies of its *Reports* and distributing them to an international congeries of recipients. And he chose Andrew Balfour as the Laboratories' Director, evidently regarding him as his personal employee, whose responsibilities included identifying attractive artefacts and holding them in Khartoum in readiness for Wellcome's inspection.[57]

Trained at the universities of Edinburgh and Cambridge, Balfour specialised in public health, a field predicated on the time-honoured view that states of health derived from interactions between human constitutions and environmental circumstances. In the late nineteenth century the speciality developed rapidly, building on investigative and practical possibilities suggested by then-recent findings – the mechanisms of cholera and typhoid fever transmission among persons and the insect vectors of malaria, trypanosomiasis, plague, yellow fever and dengue fever. Tropical medicine, created at the century's end, derived from public health. And its practitioners appropriated a non-scientific feature of public health reasoning: putatively defective immigrants – such as the behaviourally and racially inferior Irish – could inflict their diseases on host populations. A British-dominated speciality, tropical medicine was first institutionalised in schools founded in 1899 in Liverpool (backed by West African trading interests) and London (established with state support), when its practitioners were growing in numbers; roughly one-fifth of British-trained physicians were then working in tropical places – surely not least for financial reasons (colonial medical officers were permitted to develop private practices to supplement their salaries).[58]

Following his decorated service as a civil surgeon in the South African War, Balfour turned to tropical medicine, mentored by (later Sir) Patrick Manson, founder of the London School of Tropical Medicine, best known for proposing that mosquitoes spread malaria; for confirming Manson's theory experimentally, (later Sir) Ronald Ross won the Nobel Prize in 1902. Balfour was the very model of the ideal Sudan regime employee: he had been a rugby Blue at Cambridge as well as a military hero, and his personal characteristics were likely as significant in his dealings with the government as his scientific credentials and his patron's status. Under his direction the Laboratories became an integral part of the regime: government medical officers used its facilities; officials outside Khartoum sent indigenous remedies (and, in at least one instance, dispatched an experimental subject – an African boy afflicted with trypanosomiasis, who suffered a drug trial); and some government sanitary efforts depended on the Laboratories' assistance.[59] As Medical Officer of Health for Khartoum Province, Balfour imposed what he called a 'sanitary tyranny' on the European city of Khartoum (he ignored the non-white city of Omdurman, although it was part of the province). His sanitary inspectors emphasised mosquito control; but they also monitored the quality of milk and other foodstuffs, destroyed refuse and stray dogs, conducted house-to-house inspections and gave expert testimony in court cases.[60]

By 1906, when the *Second Report* of the Wellcome Laboratories was published, Balfour could celebrate the results of his government-sponsored measures. Although he saw tropical public health schemes as failure-prone because their execution necessarily depended on indigenous personnel – who performed satisfactorily only when closely supervised and threatened with fines for substandard work – the 'mosquito brigade' he organised following Ronald Ross's template proved extremely successful.[61] Comprising two British and seven 'native' inspectors, it used a simple technique to reduce the level of contamination in Khartoum's water supplies from 50.0 per cent to 9.5 per cent during its first six months of operation: all of the city's water repositories save those used for drinking were doused with a mixture of crude and refined petroleum. In addition, a 'special native inspector' monitored boats visiting Khartoum, and a system of sanitary containment for human waste prevented epidemics of dysentery[62] (Balfour also directed a malaria-prevention scheme outside Khartoum, but it was less effective).[63] And improvements in Khartoum attracted attention in the metropole. A writer for the London *Daily Mail* exalted: 'All of Central Africa is going to be made perfectly habitable for the white man. Its agricultural, industrial, and commercial resources will become available... [supporting] a numerous and happy people.'[64]

Balfour's concern with the ecology and demography of Khartoum represented the thinking of his professional generation: he integrated recent models of infection with a time-worn climatic understanding of disease causation.[65] He recognised that human behaviour affected environments – planting gardens, say, both added humidity and lowered temperature – and that effective health management strategies depended on accurate assessments of populations.[66] Aided by his 'Consulting Entomologist', F.V. Theobold, who had surveyed mosquito characteristics worldwide under the auspices of the Colonial and Foreign Offices, Balfour directed a mosquito census that plotted the distribution, habitat and lifestyle of each type of mosquito found in Khartoum.[67] He brought the same approach to his analysis of the city's indigenes: because Khartoum was an urban centre, disease-bearing 'natives [were] continually coming and going and passing through it', and those from the 'humid and typically tropical regions of the Southern Sudan' represented exceptional dangers for city residents (not least because Balfour believed that malaria vectors included people as well as mosquitoes).[68] Significantly, Balfour understood the colonial regime as itself a health risk factor: roughly 3,000 disease-bearing Egyptians and Sudanese were living in Khartoum proper and Khartoum North as members of the regime's army of occupation; and because the Sudan's potential for agricultural development could not be realised without irrigation, new bodies of water would be created that would be contaminated if not properly constructed and monitored.[69]

Europeans could never live completely satisfactorily in the tropics, Balfour said, but they could reduce the risks they took in living there.[70] In addition to his public health recommendations, Balfour prescribed measures that individuals could adopt, incorporating some of longstanding, such as wearing suitable clothing, including black, red, or orange undergarments, which supposedly simulated indigenes' skin[71] (note that concern about clothing's effects on health was also prevalent in Britain at this time).[72] In addition, individuals should douse themselves with mosquito repellent and sleep with mosquito nets, as Balfour wrote in a letter to P.R. Phipps, the Sudan's Civil Secretary, copies of which were circulated to officials all over the country.[73] The tropical resident should take quinine to prevent malaria, and, to ward off chills, should wear a 'cholera belt' (a flannel cummerbund) at night – a somewhat controversial recommendation, as Balfour acknowledged.[74] And individuals should be fined if they did not eliminate stagnant pools of water in their own domains.[75]

At his most utopian, Balfour imagined environmental transformations effected for health reasons. He thought that Khartoum would have been healthier if the British had built it on the site of North Khartoum – 1,269 feet above the level of the Mediterranean – rather than rebuilding it in its original location.[76] But the ecology of Khartoum could still be modified, addressing both present problems and those that would attend agricultural development; the city could be drained or raised, and it could be surrounded by a dry buffer zone at least a mile deep.[77] No crops requiring irrigation, such as sugar cane and rice, should be planted closer than a half mile from 'any' Sudanese settlement, and irrigation channels should be elevated, so that they would drain dry when not in use; the channels should be constructed of leak-proof materials, regularly cleared of vegetation, and, whenever possible, stocked with fish that would destroy whatever larvae grew in them.[78]

Utopian thought was characteristic of public health practitioners in Balfour's era: they thought their research would enable the human species to control its own destiny. Many late nineteenth- and early twentieth-century scientists believed that advances in knowledge had rendered the process of natural selection nearly inoperative among humankind. But natural selection still functioned in encounters between humans and pathogens, and it was especially fierce in encounters effected through migration, such as movement of Europeans into the tropics; populations exposed to diseases to which they had no developed immunities were devastated. Therefore tropical medicine represented the front line of the war against natural selection.[79]

Balfour's achievements in Khartoum led to a series of occupational triumphs. When he returned to Britain in 1913, he presided over the new Wellcome Bureau of Scientific Research. He became a prominent figure on the international health scene after a distinguished career in military medicine during the First World War, and he was appointed by the League of Nations and the Colonial Office to undertake inquiries in a number of tropical territories.[80] He wrote widely read books, such as his 1920 *War Against Tropical Disease*. In 1923 he became the first head of the London School of Hygiene and Tropical Medicine (LSHTM), an institution that expanded the purview of Patrick Manson's School of Tropical Medicine – with Manson's blessing. The LSHTM was funded by the Rockefeller Foundation, and planned by foundation officers in accordance with decisions made by the British Ministry of Health – which appointed Balfour its Director, though the foundation paid his salary. From its inception the Rockefeller Foundation had made international health a central component of its mission; it chose to invest in the LSHTM because foundation officers judged Britain to be the world centre of tropical medicine and predicted – correctly – that the School would draw students from all over the world.[81] And the LSHTM also shaped the practice of tropical medicine in the colonies, since it – along with the Liverpool School – offered the course required of new appointees to the colonial medical services.

Does this story have a moral?

In various ways, architects and planners reason today much as their predecessors did a century ago: they attend to health problems created by built environments, and design buildings to withstand natural hazards – frequent earthquakes, say, or heavy snowfall. The success of Ross-style 'mosquito brigades' in Khartoum and elsewhere heralded a host of water-treatment projects devised to control insect-borne diseases.[82] But sensible lessons that ought to have been learned from Balfour's sermons were resisted. Even during the era of decolonisation, physicians caring for colonial officials were hard pressed to persuade them either to follow well-founded medical recommendations – such as prophylactic quinine use – or to abandon their belief that high altitudes were malaria-free.[83] It was the idea of superior tropical medicine that really mattered to the confident operation of empire – along with the idea of the well-planned colonial city. Finally, elsewhere in Britain's empire, social scientific knowledge of distinctly colonial character was developed and applied – often with unfortunate, long-term consequences.[84] In the Sudan, however, the circulation of the 'Hamitic Hypothesis' apparently served primarily to justify far greater official interest in the country's north than in its south. But there can be little doubt that the idea of superior white races was very powerful for the British Empire as a whole. For the growth of all of these ideas, Khartoum was an exceptionally fertile place in the early twentieth century.

Notes

1. For their comments I thank Edgar Krebs, Erik Linstrum, Ian Petrie, Lyn Schumaker, Amy Slaton, Leila Zenderland and Brian Daniels.
2. Brenda Seligman's journals: 17 and 18 November, 1909, Seligman Papers, London School of Economics (in later notes, Seligman), file 1/4/4; 14 January, 2 February, and 9 February, 1910, Seligman 1/4/3; 2 December 1911, Seligman 1/4/5. In 1921–2 the Seligmans returned for their last research in the Sudan, yielding (eventually) their major work on Sudanese peoples – (1932) *Pagan Tribes of the Nilotic Sudan* (London: Routledge and Kegan Paul).
3. Seligman's, 20 November to 11 December 1909, Seligman, 1/4/4; quotations, 28 November entry. See also 16 December 1911, Seligman 1/4/5.
4. On social activities with the Curries and the Balfours, see Journal, 20 November 1909 and 12 April 1910, Seligman, 1/4/4. For Balfour's interest in anthropology, see, for example, his 'Introduction' (1908) Third Report of the Wellcome Tropical Research Laboratories at the Gordon Memorial College, Khartoum (London: Baillière, Tindall and Cox, for the Department of Education, Sudan Government), 18–19.
5. Journals: 9 January 1910, Seligman 1/4/4; 9 January 1911 and 12 January 1912, Seligman 1/4/5.
6. Journals: 7 February 1910, Seligman 1/4/4; 1–7 January 1912, Seligman 1/4/5.
7. Harold MacMichael (1955) *The Sudan* (New York: Praeger), pp. 91–7.
8. E.E. Evans-Pritchard in 1973, quoted in D. Johnson (1988) 'The Sudan Under the British', *Journal of African History [JAH]*, 29, 541.
9. A.H.M. Kirk-Greene (1982) 'The Sudan Political Service: A Profile in the Sociology of Imperialism', *The International Journal of African Historical Studies* 15, 21–48; quotation, fn. 9, 27; R. Collins (1972) 'The Sudan Political Service: A Portrait of the "Imperialists"', *African Affairs*, 71, 293–303. And see E.A. Stanton (1914) 'Progress in the Sudan', *Journal of the Royal African Society*, 13, 365–8.
10. J. Willis (May 2011) 'Tribal Gatherings: Colonial Spectacle, Native Administration and Local Government in Condominium Sudan', *Past and Present*, 211, 243–68, quotation 245.
11. R.O. Collins and R.L. Tignor (1967) *Egypt and the Sudan* (Englewood-Cliffs, NJ: Prentice-Hall), pp. 59–63, 84–8.
12. The many – popular and scholarly – accounts of these events include B. Farwell (1989) *Prisoners of the Mahdi* (New York: W. W. Norton); M. Asher (2006) *Khartoum. The Ultimate Imperial Adventure* (London: Penguin Books).
13. British victory was complete in November 1899, when Wingate's force killed the Khalifa and defeated his remnant army. Queen Victoria congratulated Wingate by letter, 4 January 1900, Wingate Papers, Sudan Archive, University of Durham (in later notes, WP, SAD), Box 270/1/1-61, Part I.
14. British officials were consulted about such major decisions as large-scale military expeditions and international treaties, but the Sudan government otherwise acted

in consultation with the Consul-General in Egypt, reporting to London after the fact. The Sudan's Governors-General were officially appointed by the Khedive, but were in practice appointed by Britain. The Consul-General and British advisors in Egyptian ministries managed Egypt's role in the Sudan affairs. But officials in the Sudan (notably Wingate) acted to create effective autonomy. The Sudan's dual administration virtually ended after Egyptian independence in 1922 but officially ended in 1953. See, for example, M.W. Daly (1983) 'The Development of the Governor-Generalship of the Sudan, 1988–1934', *JAH*, 24, 77–96; Gabriel Warburg (1970) 'The Sudan, Egypt and Britain, 1899–1916', *Middle Eastern Studies*, 6, 163–78.

15. The last quote is from John Lee Anderson (23 July 2012) 'A History of Violence', *The New Yorker*, 49. In 1930 a border was drawn between north and south, designed to protect the south from subversive influences, which northerners needed visas to cross. The regime's attention to the south grew after the Second World War. H.J. Sharkey (2003) *Living with Colonialism* (Berkeley/Los Angeles: University of California Press), p. 81; Collins, 'The Sudan Political Service', 298.

16. See G.S. Eissa (2005) Review essay on Ahmed Ibrahim AbouShouk and Anders Bjorkelo, 'The Principles of Native Administration in the Anglo-Egyptian Sudan, 1898–1956', *Intellectual Discourse*, 13, 95–9.

17. Kitchener memo of 1899, quoted in H. MacMichael (1934) *The Anglo-Egyptian Sudan* (London: Faber and Faber), p. 73; Collins, 'The Sudan Political Service', 299.

18. See Kirk-Greene, 'The Sudan Political Service: A Profile in the Sociology of Imperialism'; job security depended on passing exams in law and Arabic.

19. Wingate Memorandum to P. R. Phipps, Civil Secretary, 5 December 1905, WP, SAD, Box 277/6.

20. C.G. Seligman (1916) 'Presidential Address', Section H – Anthropology, *Reports of the British Association for the Advancement of Science*, 85th meeting, 1915 (London: John Murray), 651–65.

21. H.H. Johnston, E. Torday, T.A. Joyce, and C.G. Seligman (1913) 'A Survey of the Ethnography of Africa: And the Formal Racial and Tribal Migrations in That Continent', *JRAI [Journal of the Royal Anthropological Institute]*, 43, 375–421, quotation on 405.

22. Henrika Kuklick (1991) *The Savage Within. The Social History of British Anthropology, 1885–1945* (New York: Cambridge University Press), esp. pp. 182–241.

23. A.H. Keane (1885) 'Ethnology of Egyptian Sudan', *J[R]AI*, 14, 91–113; quotation, 101.

24. C.G. Seligman (1966) *Races of Africa*, 4th edn (London: Oxford University Press), p. 8.

25. C.G. Seligman (1913) 'Some Aspects of the Hamitic Problem in the Anglo-Egyptian Sudan', *JRAI*, 43, 593–705; quotation, 595.

26. For just some examples, see H.S. Lewis (1963) 'The Hamites of Africa', *JAH*, 4, 463–65; 1–17; Wyatt MacGaffey (1966) 'Concepts of Race in the Historiography of Northeast Africa', *JAH*, 7, 1–17; E.R. Saunders (1969) 'The Hamitic Hypothesis: Its Origins and Functions in Time Perspective', *JAH*, 10, 521–32. For a useful summary, see Wyatt MacGaffey (2005) 'Changing Representations in Central African History', *JAH*, 46, 189–207. For Seligman's biography, see Kuklick, *The Savage Within. The Social History of British Anthropology, 1885–1945*, 312f.

27. Johnston *et al.*, 'A Survey of the Ethnography of Africa', 391–425, quotation, 410; for Seligman's objections to Johnston's argument, see 419–20.

28. R. Oliver and J.D. Fage (1962) *A Short History of Africa* (Harmondsworth, Middlesex: Penguin), pp. 44–52. The hypothesis was taught in leading universities, as Steven Feierman recalls from his graduate student days at Northwestern University during the early 1960s; personal communication, 30 August 2010.

29. The explanation of innovation by independent invention rested in the axiom that human minds were everywhere the same, meaning that peoples everywhere would follow a parallel course of social evolution. On independent invention and diffusionism, see Kuklick, pp. 82, 125, 257 and 121–33, respectively.

30. Harold MacMichael (September 1907) 'Notes on the History of Kordofan Before the Egyptian Conquest', printed government document, in Seligman 3/4/11.

31. 'C.G.S.', review of *The Tribes of Northern and Central Kordofan* by H.A. MacMichael (1913) *The Geographical Journal*, 42, 388.

32. Keane, 'Ethnology' (cited by Macmichael 'Notes').

33. M.J. Herskovits (1941) 'Charles Gabriel Seligman', *American Anthropologist*, 43, 437–39, quotation 437.

34. Seligman (1913), 679–80; quotation 679.

35. C.G. Seligman (1924) 'Anthropology and Psychology: A Study of Some Points of Contact', *JRAI*, 54, 13–46.

36. E. Linstrum (2011) 'A Dream Dictionary for the World: Charles Gabriel Seligman and the Globalization of the Unconscious', unpublished paper.

37. See N. Pevsner (1976) *A History of Building Types* (London: Thames & Hudson), p. 293.

38. J. Burns (1911) 'Inaugural Address', in Royal Institute of British Architects, *Transactions of the Town Planning Conference*, London, 10–15 October 1910 (London: Royal Institute of British Architects), 62–76; quotations, 63.

39. See, for example, M. Doyle (27 April 2008) 'The Sepoys of the Pound and Sandy Row: Empire and Loyalty in Mid-Victorian Belfast', unpublished paper presented to the Delaware Valley British Studies Seminar; P. De Figueiredo (2003) 'Symbols of Empire: The Buildings of the Liverpool Waterfront', *Architectural History*, 46, 229–54.

40. See Editorial (1913) 'The New Capital City at Delhi', *The Town Planning Review*, 4, 185; see Kitchener's response to discussion of his paper, in *Transactions of the Town Planning Conference*, 596.

41. W.H. McLean, 'The Planning of Khartoum and Omdurman', in *Transactions of the Town Planning Conference*, 585; C. Fergusson to Wingate, 21 May 1900, WP, SAD, Box 270/5/1-60. See also, for example: T.R. Metcalf (1989) *An Imperial Vision. Indian Architecture and Britain's Raj* (Berkeley: University of California Press); T. Mitchell (1989) *Colonising Egypt* (Berkeley: University of California Press), esp. pp. 161–3.

42. See correspondence about the cathedral, G.P. Blyth, Bishop of Jerusalem, to Reginald Wingate, 10 May 1902, WP, SAD, Box 272/3/1-30.

43. Kitchener's responses to discussion of his paper, in *Transactions of the Town Planning Conference*, 596.

44. Intelligence Branch, Quartermaster-General's Department, Horse Guards, War Office (1884) *Report on the Egyptian Provinces of the Sûdan, Red Sea, and Equator* (London: His Majesty's Stationery Office), p. 122.

45. On the long-established fixation of colonial medicine on Europeans only, see, for example, David Arnold (1993) 'Colonial Enclaves: The Army and the Jails', in his *Colonizing the Body* (Berkeley: University of California Press), pp. 61–115; J.W. Cell (1986) 'Anglo-Indian Medical Theory and the Origins of Segregation in West

Africa', *American Historical Review*, 91, 307–35. And for the durability of this view, see, for example, an undated, handwritten memoir by Philip William Hutton, physician in Uganda 1937–61, Mss.Afr.s. 1872, Box XIX, Rhodes House Library, Oxford.

46. W.H. McLean (1913) 'Town Planning in the Tropics, With Special Reference to the Khartoum City Development Plan', *The Town Planning Review*, 3, 226. See also W.H. McLean, 'The Planning of Khartoum and Omdurman', 575–95.

47. A. Balfour (1908) 'Sanitary Notes, Khartoum', in Balfour, *Third Report of the Wellcome Tropical Research Laboratories at the Gordon Memorial College, Khartoum* (London: Baillière, Tindall and Cox, for the Department of Education, Sudan Government), pp. 63–4.

48. Khartoum cathedral's architect, Robert Weir Schultz, was recommended by Ernest Richmond, an architect employed by the Public Works department in Cairo. Hatchard's buildings included law courts, a civil hospital, and government offices; Arthur Butler, Secretary, Society for Architects, to Reginald Wingate, 8 July 1909, WP, SAD, Box 288/1.

49. McLean, 'Dwelling Houses in the Tropics', 68 – incorporated within Balfour's 'Sanitary Notes'.

50. McLean 'Town Planning in the Tropics', 224–31.

51. McLean, 'The Planning of Khartoum and Omdurman', 591.

52. See David Ottewill (1979) 'Robert Weir Schultz (1860–1951): An Arts and Crafts Architect', *Architectural History*, 22, 88–115; Unsigned news story (1912) 'Khartoum Cathedral', *The Architectural Journal*, 19, 3rd series, 231; Robert W.S. Weir (19 May 1916) 'The Cathedral of All Saints, Khartoum, Sudan', *The Builder*, 110, 371–3, quotation on 373.

53. L.S.R. Amery, Secretary of State for the Colonies, to A.J. Balfour (erstwhile Prime Minister and Foreign Secretary, then head of the Committee of Civil Research, which advised the government on the practical use of scientific knowledge), 16 April 1926, Balfour papers, British Library, Box 49775.

54. See Collins and Tignor, p. 124; Sharkey, p. 71. Over time, advanced courses were added and the college became the University of Khartoum.

55. See, for example, A.A. Abdel-Hameed (1997) 'The Wellcome Tropical Research Laboratories in Khartoum (1903–1934): An Experiment in Development', *Medical History*, 41, 30–58.

56. Ryan Johnson (2008) 'Tabloid Brand Medicine Chests: Selling Health and Hygiene for the British Tropical Colonies', *Science and Culture*, 17, 249–68; Andrew Balfour (1904) *First Report of the Wellcome Tropical Research Laboratories at the Gordon Memorial College, Khartoum* (London: Baillière, Tindall and Cox for the Department of Education, Sudan Government), pp. 7–9.

57. The Sudan government supported the laboratories until 1935. See Abdel-Hameed, 'Wellcome'. A memo by C.J.S. Thompson dated 22 April 1913 quotes Balfour's description of several items that Wellcome might find of interest in a letter dated 17 April 1913; Balfour Papers, Wellcome Institute Library, WA/BSR/COR/A, Box 7.

58. An authoritative survey is George Rosen's (1993) *A History of Public Health*, Expanded Edition (Baltimore: The Johns Hopkins University Press). On scapegoating Irish migrants, see Liam Greenslade, Moss Madden, and Maggie Pearson (1997) 'From Visible to Invisible: The "problem" of the health of Irish People in Britain', in Lara Marks and Michael Worboys (eds.) *Migrants, Minorities and Health* (London: Routledge), pp. 147–78, esp. 148–9. On the exaggerated differences between the Liverpool and London schools, see Michael Worboys (1988)

'Manson, Ross and Colonial Medical Policy: tropical medicine in London and Liverpool, 1899–1914', in R. MacLeod and M. Lewis (eds.) *Disease, Medicine and Empire* (London: Routledge), pp. 21–37. On British physicians in the tropics, see an 1897 address by Patrick Manson, quoted in Philip Manson-Bahr (1927) *The Life and Work of Patrick Manson* (London: Cassell and Company), p. 210.

59. A. Balfour (1906) *Second Report of the Wellcome Tropical Research Laboratories at the Gordon Memorial College, Khartoum* (London: Baillière, Tindall and Cox, for the Department of Education, Sudan Government), pp. 10–11. The Government's travelling Sleeping Sickness Commission, for example, could not have proceeded without equipment supplied by the Laboratories; P. R. Phipps to Wingate, 5 July 1905, WP, SAD, Box 277/1.

60. A. Balfour (1920) *War Against Tropical Disease* (London: Baillière, Tyndall and Cox for the Wellcome Bureau of Tropical Research), p. 35.

61. Balfour, *War*, p. 21. See also Balfour 'Sanitary Notes', pp. 62, 66, 72–3.

62. Balfour, *First Report*, pp. 18, 20; Balfour, *Second Report*, p. 15; Balfour, 'Sanitary Notes', pp. 64, 72–3.

63. Balfour, *First Report*, p. 30.

64. News story of 25 September 1906, quoted in Abdel-Hameed, 'Wellcome', 39.

65. See, for example, W. Anderson (1997) 'The Trespass Speaks: White Masculinity and Colonial Breakdown', *American Historical Review*, 102, 1351–5; D.N. Livingstone (1999) 'Tropical Climate and Moral Hygiene: The Anatomy of a Victorian Debate', *British Journal of the History of Science*, 32, 93–110.

66. Balfour, 'Sanitary Notes', p. 64.

67. The same approach was used in plotting mosquito habitats throughout the territory, though in lesser detail. See Balfour, *First Report, passim*.

68. Balfour, *First Report*, p. 14.

69. For example, Balfour, *First Report*, p. 16; Balfour, 'Sanitary Notes', pp. 62 and 67.

70. A. Balfour (delivered 30 September 1926), 'Acclimatization of the White Man in the Tropics', unpublished address, Balfour Papers, London School of Hygiene and Tropical Medicine, Box 1.

71. Balfour, 'Sanitary Notes', p. 67. See Ryan Johnson (2009) 'European Cloth and "Tropical" Skin: Clothing Material and British Ideas of Health and Hygiene in Tropical Climates', *Bulletin of the History of Medicine*, 83, 530–60.

72. Note that the Jaeger clothing firm, founded in 1884, took its inspiration from the German zoologist Gustav Jäger, who recommended wearing woollen clothing close to the skin. Analysing the health effects of babies' clothing made of different fibres, the eugenicist Karl Pearson and his collaborator Mary Noel Karn argued that wool clothing was healthiest; (1922) *Study of the Data Provided by a Baby-Clinic in a Large Manufacturing Town* (Cambridge: Cambridge University Press).

73. Andrew Balfour to P. R. Phipps, 4 December 1905, Wingate Papers, SAD, Box 277/6.

74. Andrew Balfour to Miss E. Gurney Salter, 14 October 1918, Balfour Papers, Wellcome Institute Library, WA/BSR/COR/A, Box 6.

75. See Balfour to Wingate, 25 April 1906, WP, SAD, Box 278/4.

76. Balfour, 'Sanitary Notes', pp. 61–2.

77. Balfour, *Second Report*, pp. 19–21.

78. Balfour 'Sanitary Notes', p. 67.

79. For a specimen and an analysis, see Ray Lankester (1905), *Nature and Man* (Oxford: Clarendon Press); D.N. Livingstone, 'Tropical Climate and Moral Hygiene: The Anatomy of a Victorian Debate', 93–110.

80. See, for example, A. Balfour (1921) *Report on Medical and Sanitary Matters in Mauritius* (London: Waterlow and Sons for the Colonial Office); Balfour (1923) *Report on Medical and Sanitary Matters in Bermuda* (London: Waterlow and Sons for the Colonial Office); Balfour et al. (April 1905) *Further Report on Tuberculosis and Sleeping Sickness in Equatorial Africa*, submitted to the Health Committee of the League of Nations at its Fourth Session.

81. D. Fisher (1978) 'Rockefeller Philanthropy and the British Empire: The Creation of the London School of Hygiene and Tropical Medicine', *History of Education*, 7, 129–43.

82. See, for example, L. Schumaker (2008) 'Slimes and Death-Dealing Dambos: Water, Industry and the Garden City on Zambia's Copperbelt', *Journal of Southern African Studies*, 34, 823–40; A. Spielman and M. D'Antonio (2001) *Mosquito* (New York: Hyperion), pp. 218–20.

83. See R.S.F. Hennessey (who retired as Assistant Research Director of the Wellcome Foundation in 1970) (22 April 1983) 'Learning About Disease in Uganda: 1929–44 and 1949–55', typescript, MSS Afr.s.1872, Box XVIII, Rhodes House Library, Oxford, 5–6.

84. See, for example, H.C. Aspengren (2010) 'Sociological Knowledge and colonial power in Bombay around the First World War', *British Journal for the History of Science*, 43, 1–16; Kuklick, *The Savage Within. The Social History of British Anthropology, 1885–1945*, pp. 182–241.

Part II
Experiencing the Empire

4
A Governor's Wife in the Making: Elizabeth Macquarie's Voyage from England to Australia in 1809

Jane McDermid

In 1809, Elizabeth Henrietta Campbell (1778–1835) embarked from Portsmouth, England, on a seven-month voyage to Sydney. She did so as the second wife of Lachlan Macquarie (1761–1824), a career soldier who was on his way to take up the position of governor of New South Wales (NSW) and Van Diemen's Land (Tasmania) in the wake of a rebellion against the man he was to replace, Captain William Bligh.[1] Elizabeth kept a journal of this voyage. She does not appear to have intended it for publication, but, in line with Mary Louise Pratt's characteristics of imperial travel writing, it abounds with anecdotes as well as detailed descriptions of civic life.[2] Elizabeth Macquarie's journal is that of a 'colonial traveller', one who is indeed 'curious about the other and secure in [her] own superiority'.[3] She wrote vivid but not hyperbolic descriptions of the voyage, including accounts of life on board ship and of visits ashore to Madeira, Rio de Janeiro and Cape Town, and the welcome they received on arrival in Sydney. Yet while the journal is full of the kind of detail – places, people, customs, the weather, landscape, flora and fauna, discomfort and illness – generally found in such travel writings, close reading shows that it is not simply a traveller's tale: it is a record of Elizabeth's conscientious preparation for the role of wife of a colonial governor. Whereas the narrative presented here of Elizabeth's 1809 voyage does not reveal the causes of her actions over the next decade, it highlights impressions which helped to shape the way in which she performed her wifely role by integrating herself into the public world of the colonies governed by her husband.

Read alongside the journal her husband kept of the voyage, Elizabeth's also provides a portrait of a marriage. Moreover, she seems typical of an imperial wife, foreshadowing Mary A. Procida's analysis of gender, politics and imperialism in late nineteenth- and twentieth-century India: 'the wife of an imperial official experienced imperial service through her husband, yet she often felt that she was part of his work'.[4] Indeed, though the Macquarie marriage pre-dated Procida's study by eight decades, it displayed the characteristics she found in the Indian imperial service: it was a 'partnership between men and women as imperialists in the masculine mould, rather than one of antagonistic polarity between adventuresome men and ultra-domestic women'.[5] Whereas Lachlan Macquarie had already travelled widely in imperial service (for example in North America, the West Indies, India and Egypt), this was Elizabeth's first journey outside the British Isles, and the only one in which she kept a journal. The novelty as well as the duration of the voyage may have been one reason for her doing so; there was also the example of her husband who regularly recorded his travel observations, while both would have been familiar with the genre of published travellers' tales. Elizabeth in particular was an avid reader of James Boswell's biography of Samuel Johnson, drawn to his tour of the Highlands and Islands of Scotland.[6]

Before marriage she had journeyed regularly and often alone between the Campbell family home of Airds in Appin, Argyllshire, and her elder sister Jane's home on the Lochbuie Estate on the Isle of Mull, as well as the homes of friends and extended family members in Edinburgh, London and Devon. She generally journeyed with a purpose, such as for her education or to accompany younger family members. She had been travelling unaccompanied just before Lachlan Macquarie met her on Mull in 1804, and she continued to do so during their engagement in London two years later, when he was with the army in India and she took up a post as governess in Devon. The journal reveals that she was a keen traveller, admired by her husband as intrepid; but he had nevertheless delayed the marriage because he did not want Elizabeth to accompany him to India, which he blamed for the death of his first wife in 1796.[7] Within a month of their wedding in Devon in 1807 the Macquaries returned to Scotland and the Perth garrison of the 73rd Regiment with which he had served in India. However, being the wife of an imperial careerist held out the possibility that she could travel much further afield as well as the opportunity to serve as advisor and assistant to her governor husband. That opportunity was provided two years later with his appointment as a colonial governor and the journey with the 73rd to the Australian colonies. His post governing these convict colonies empowered Elizabeth to deploy her talents for the benefit of the Empire as well as her family. Indeed, as will be discussed below, Elizabeth's work in agriculture and architecture, and her active encouragement of her husband's emancipist policy, went beyond the involvement of Procida's Anglo-Indian wives in their husbands' work, suggesting that the horizons for imperial wives had somewhat diminished by the late Victorian period.

Elizabeth's 1809 journal also gives an insight into the making of the British Empire as well as the importance of an individual's and a family's social connections in carving a place in that enterprise. Empire was not only about the colonies and the colonised; it was also about interconnections and adaptation. Elizabeth and Lachlan were brought together by family connections and they maintained those links by seeking to promote the interests of members of the extended family – for example, he took family members into his service. Indeed, Elizabeth's nephew, John Maclaine, travelled with them in 1809 as Ensign to Lachlan. They also forged alliances with non-kin and non-Scots, confirming the significance of networks for getting into and getting on in imperial service.[8] Her marriage and her husband's career, especially in the Australian colonies, confirm that the British Empire gave the chance to poor but aspirational Scots not only to rise in society through service but to realise their own ideas of empire.[9] Both Elizabeth and Lachlan had a strong sense of national identity and expected their Australian-born son to make regular visits to family in Scotland and to tend to his estates there once he came of age; but both parents looked to the Empire for family advancement. Thus, in his will, Lachlan recorded a desire that his son be educated in England and if possible at Eton, which in his experience had educated the sons of the 'greatest men of the present age'.[10]

Elizabeth's journal descriptions convey a strong sense of conviction regarding the superiority of the British Empire, but also show curiosity about and a desire to learn from the places and people she visited. While she had previous experience of travelling by ship, notably between the Scottish mainland and the Isle of Mull, such a lengthy journey accompanied by so many people (personal servants as well as their own cook, butler and coachman, soldiers, other passengers and crew, and a companion vessel) was an adventure of much greater magnitude. The journal shows that she eagerly accepted the challenge, with few serious complaints except for sea sickness and periods of being becalmed or diverted from purpose. Although the vessels were hired for imperial business, the captains of both ships, Pritchard of the *Dromedary* (which carried the Macquaries) and Pascoe of the *Hindostan*, also saw the voyage as providing opportunities to seek bounty: they frequently and enthusiastically went after small ships if they perceived there was gain to be had. Generally she expressed admiration of Pritchard for seamanship and care of the passengers, but Elizabeth was critical of this practice for the inconvenience such chases caused in extending the voyage. She recorded on 4 June:

> we go off our course in pursuit of every sail we see, by which we have lost many a fair breeze, and encounter'd [sic] many a foul one … we have, however, once succeeded in taking a Prize … an American ship which had been taken some days before by a French privateer, by which I am happy to find that Cap^tn Pascoe will derive a considerable sum of money.[11]

That 'we' implies that she saw this act of plunder as justified in depriving the French of such spoils. This may not simply have been because of the war against France: not only had her husband fought against the American revolutionaries, but two of his elder brothers had suffered at the hands of both the French and the Americans during the War of Independence.[12]

However relatively humble her own and her husband's family origins, as wife of an imperial careerist, Elizabeth was both sure of her superiority as a subject of the British Empire and, as evidenced in her 1809 journal, concerned about threats to it, whether from a rival power like France or from internal dissent as had occurred in Sydney and which had provided her husband with such an unexpected late career opportunity. Her marriage to a soldier of the Empire presented her with a chance to throw off the limitations of impoverished spinsterhood and gentry life in Highland Scotland; but her journal showed that the prospect held out by Australia was not simply of escape from those narrow confines. Rather, she saw it as a chance to build on her existing interests and to expand that knowledge during the voyage in anticipation of applying it in the colonies. Like most governors' wives, she was a temporary colonist and the voyage to Sydney was an adventure; but she was less preoccupied with the sensory experience of travel because her curiosity was not simply that of a tourist, reflected in her journal entries about the conversations with Lachlan regarding the political situation which awaited them in the colony. These reveal ambitions on her part to play an active role and both Elizabeth and her husband would go beyond the British government's penny-pinching policies towards, and narrow vision for, the Australian colonies: they were improvers who saw a future for the colonies beyond transportation.[13]

Elizabeth was, as noted above, alert to threats to British imperial power. She observed, indeed shared, the alarm caused by sightings of 'strange sails', and when vessels bearing down on them were revealed to be from the Royal Navy she wrote: 'it is a gratifying sight to every English person to see the ships of their country possess the dominion of the Seas'. Indeed, on leaving Portsmouth on 24 May she had looked back until they lost sight of 'good old England'.[14] That pride in and fondness for 'England' reflected the commitment of both Macquaries to the Union and the Empire: 'England' was 'common shorthand' for the British Empire at this time.[15] The Macquaries, as individuals and as a married couple, confirm the importance of the British Empire for the Scots in the eighteenth and nineteenth centuries.[16] Both Elizabeth and Lachlan had extended families with imperial (mainly military) careers and links, while they shared a profound attachment to Mull: despite spending much of their lives away from it, they built an estate on the island and are buried there.[17] Thus Elizabeth's 1809 journal reveals that she had a layered notion of identity: Highland, Scottish, British and imperial. As Edward Cowan and Richard Finlay have noted, not only did the Scots see themselves as 'natural empire builders' and as an 'imperial race', but they considered that their contribution to the empire was 'the best way to demonstrate what were thought to be Scottish characteristics'.[18] While Lachlan could do that as both soldier and governor, Elizabeth's 'imperial gaze' on this voyage strengthened her determination to participate in his Australian colonial project. Thus the Empire provided her with a means of expressing her national identity through contributing to the smooth running of the Australian colonies. Moreover, as Jane Rendall has argued, 'a culturally superior femininity entrenched in women's domestic power and moral influence would work for the benefit of the Empire'.[19] The time the Macquaries spent in the colony showed that marriage and family were not simply shaped by circumstances but that domestic decisions and relations influenced, as well as being influenced by, the politics and economics of the Empire. As the colonial advocate and driving force behind the early nineteenth-century colonisation of South Australia and New Zealand, Edward Gibbon Wakefield (1796–1862) wrote in 1849: 'a colony that is not attractive to women is an unattractive colony: in order to make it attractive to both sexes, you do enough if you take care to make it attractive to women'. Indeed, Elizabeth epitomised this claim later made by Wakefield for the essential participation of women in the imperial project:

> In trade, navigation, war and politics – in all business of a public nature, except work of benevolence and colonisation – the stronger sex alone take an active part; but in colonisation, women have a part so important that it all depends on their participation in the work.[20]

As we shall see, however, Elizabeth saw her role as moving beyond the narrowly domestic.

Yet as noted above, while committed to and actively engaged in the imperial mission, the Macquaries also saw themselves as rooted in their ancestral home, he on Ulva, an island in the Inner Hebrides off the west coast of Mull, and she both in Argyll, where she was born, and on Mull, where her elder sister was married to Lachlan's uncle, the Laird of Lochbuie, and where Lachlan had begun to buy up land in the mid-1790s.[21] Thus Elizabeth's sense of her 'Scottishness' was rooted in the Highlands and Islands: describing her attempt on 24 September 1809 to climb the 'treacherous' stairs of the pier at Cape Town on all fours, she recorded an amused officer saying that 'he saw I had not been brought up in the Highlands for nothing'.[22] Those roots may help to account for the severe judgment she passed on the elderly uncle of the British consul in Madeira, Henry Veitch (1782–1857), a Lowland Scot who gave them hospitality when they anchored just off the island in early June. Acknowledging the elder Veitch as a 'pleasant' man, she added:

> I am sorry to remark in him what I believe is seldom to be found in a Scotch man, that a long residence in a foreign country seems to have deprived him of that natural love for his Country which I should wish every good man to live and die with.... [H]e has been fourty [*sic*] years

resident at Madeira, and only once during that time at home.... [H]e has now outlived all his very old friends, and seems to have no idea of returning again.[23]

His nephew was similarly inclined: Henry Veitch had only recently (1809) been appointed consul on the island but, unlike Lachlan Macquarie, he was an imperial careerist with no longing to return to the land of his birth. Consul Veitch was to make Madeira his home and he continued to play the genial host to visitors from Britain, such as the writer and traveller Thomas Edward Bowdich and his wife Sarah in the early 1820s.[24] Still, Elizabeth appreciated Consul Veitch's invitation to dine with his family, an act which she saw as a characteristic of the Scottish diaspora. Scotsmen, she remarked, could be found in 'every part of the world' and were always friendly 'to persons from their own country'.[25] Hospitality such as the Macquaries were offered, by colonial officials, military garrisons and wealthy white settlers, is a prominent theme of travel accounts of this period. Yet while Elizabeth appreciated it, she also tired of the social expectations bound up in the formal dinners and balls: she was particularly relieved when the time came in early October to quit the Cape and embark on the last leg of their voyage, having become 'distressed' by the late hours and heavy 'regimental feasts'.[26]

As Mary Louise Pratt has observed of travel writing of this period, Elizabeth's journal also contains criticisms of the work ethic among the non-British people she visited.[27] On the one hand, she considered that first impressions were often correct, but on the other she accepted that such assumptions might be mistaken. Thus when their ship anchored off 'Rio Janeiro' on 7 August Elizabeth commented on the beauty of the harbour, reflecting that though 'the Portuguese have a character for great indolence, no one to see the very many great works which have been carried on at this place could think it justly due'.[28] Still, while willing to make allowances for imperial powers, Elizabeth's journal also reflects the casual racism of empire, for example in her description of the driver of their carriage on an excursion in Rio as 'a monkey looking black man', and in her observations of indigenous people.[29] Thus she perceived the wives and children in a Hottentot camp outside Cape Town to be 'sad-looking creatures' who 'altogether form a most savage like Groop [*sic*]'.[30] The 1809 journal as well as her attitudes and actions as a governor's wife indicate that while she accepted the racial hierarchy, she also saw the miserable condition of indigenous peoples as well as poor settlers to be at least partly a failure of imperial responsibility. In the following decade in NSW, she was often present at Lachlan's regular meetings with the native peoples and her philanthropic efforts were extended to them, though, as the 1809 journal indicates, both the governor and his wife saw a need to 'civilise' indigenous peoples: in Australia they encouraged their education in English and tried to persuade them to adopt settled ways.[31]

Elizabeth does not appear to have regarded proselytism as part of her imperial mission, though the journal shows that she took a keen interest in church buildings and ceremonies. The Macquaries were Episcopalian and relatively tolerant of the Catholic Church, though she expressed alarm on 18 June at the ceremony in a church in Madeira surrounding the induction of a young woman into an order of cloistered nuns.[32] Nevertheless, in NSW she worked on building projects with many Catholic Irishmen who had been transported, both convicts and emancipists, establishing a 'tradition' of St Patrick's Day dinners at Government House.[33] Such relative tolerance, however, had its limits, as reflected in her depiction of Mr Harris, the surgeon-general of NSW and one of the elite settlers involved in the opposition to Governor Bligh whom she met in 1809 on their way to London to defend themselves against the charge of mutiny. Elizabeth recorded an occasion in which Harris had 'dress'd [sic] like a Jew, in a shabby little shop making merchandise of some precious stones he had brought for sale from New Holland'.[34]

Moreover, while her later actions as governor's wife showed that she held a progressive view of transportation as depriving the convicted of freedom and their rights for the term of sentence only, there are hints of ambivalence towards slavery, which Elizabeth never explicitly condemns in the journal. The voyage from Portsmouth to Sydney in 1809 was long, yet it was also a reflection of a shrinking world in which colonies and 'home' were linked. One notable aspect of this was the presence on board of Lachlan Macquarie's valet, George Jarvis. Macquarie and his first wife, Jane Jarvis (1772–96), bought two slave boys in Cochin (Kochi, Kerala) in 1795 and Lachlan formed a 'life-long attachment' to the younger one who was named after his first wife's brother.[35] On Jane's death, Lachlan freed both boys and sent them to school in Bombay. After accompanying Lachlan to Egypt in 1801, George was sent to Scotland to further his schooling until he became head servant to Macquarie back in India in 1805. In the Australian colonies, George accompanied the Governor on all of his tours of inspection, and in 1820 married Mary Jelly, a chambermaid in Government House who had been sentenced in England in 1819 to seven years' transportation. Macquarie granted Mary an absolute pardon in 1821 so that she could accompany her husband and the Macquaries on their return to Britain in 1822.[36]

Whatever the ties that bound George Jarvis to Lachlan Macquarie, Elizabeth's 1809 journal shows that she was certainly alert to the inhumanity of the slave trade. It contains a memorable description for 3 August of coming across a Portuguese Brig on its way to Rio de Janeiro with a load of female slaves. An account written by Lachlan's aide-de-camp, Captain Henry Colden Antill, recorded that 436 women were confined to the hold.[37] According to both Antill and Elizabeth, many of these women had 'an infectious fever', and both expressed profound shock that the slaves were being thrown overboard in an attempt to halt the spread of infection.

Elizabeth, however, claimed that such brutal efforts had not prevented it from affecting the ship's captain, implying that this was his just desserts. While Antill hoped 'for the sake of human nature' that such drastic action was untrue, Elizabeth added that 'we all thought of Mr Wilberforce'.[38] At the same time she saw the conditions experienced by these slaves as extreme. She compared the position of slaves in the places she visited in 1809: slaves in Cape Town had superior (her words were 'wonderfully different') conditions to those in Brazil, whom she acknowledged were in a 'miserable state'.[39] Yet she was also sympathetic to the plight of the former, admitting that whereas the slaves in the Cape 'had every appearance of being well treated, they were respectably clothed, and looked well fed, contented and happy', nevertheless she had to accept that the flight of some to 'the most inaccessible precipices on top of Table Mountain' indicated a lack of such perceived acquiescence to their situation.[40]

Elizabeth travelled as a wife and her journal shows that while she enjoyed stepping beyond the boundaries of the domestic sphere, she never sought to escape it. Yet whereas she accepted her role as complementary to that of her husband, she did not see rigid demarcations between the public and the private spheres. Indeed, she looked on aspects of her husband's command of his regiment on the ship as akin to a woman's domestic duties: he visited every part of the ship regularly, overseeing its cleanliness and good order, insisting that not only the part (around half) of the regiment which sailed with him but all passengers (including over 100 women and children), as well as the crew of 102 men, attended to their personal hygiene. To this she attributed the general good health and lack of infectious diseases: at the end of the voyage, only half a dozen of the 370 soldiers on board were in sick bay, and all for 'trifling' reasons.[41] There were, however, accidents for example, one of the ship's carpenters was swept overboard and drowned on 31 August as he tried, unaided, to mend a leak on the side of the ship; two months later another young man, possibly inebriated, fell to his death from the top of a mast to the deck.[42] She also recorded that even Lachlan's firm regime did not prevent delays due to poor hygiene. Their sister ship, the *Hindostan*, which carried around 400 soldiers and a similar number of women, children and crew to the *Dromedary*, had an outbreak of dysentery in early August which necessitated an unplanned stop to seek treatment ashore in Rio de Janeiro, where Elizabeth was impressed by the medical treatment they received.[43]

While she appreciated her husband's attention to his public role as commander of the regiment, she welcomed the uninterrupted mornings he spent in her company on board ship when they read or wrote 'in a social manner', foreseeing that she would not enjoy this companionable domesticity in NSW where he would have to 'shut himself up alone all the morning' to fulfil his duties as governor.[44] In those private mornings spent together, the couple discussed the condition of the colony to which they were headed and in particular the tension between the elite settlers and the New South Wales Corps, on the one hand, and Governor Bligh, on the other. Elizabeth recorded her husband's concern that he would have to punish men whom he otherwise considered faithful servants of their 'King and Country'.[45] Nevertheless, however well founded their grievances, their actions constituted a rebellion against imperial authority; and though the causes of the NSW revolt were local and related to the personality of Bligh, the new governor and his wife were aware that this was not an isolated challenge.[46]

Besides reviewing with considerable trepidation the difficulties of the situation which awaited them, Elizabeth seems to have regarded the voyage to Sydney as providing her with ideas and examples of how to fulfil her new and unexpected role. The journal records her keen observations of the wives of men in similar positions to her husband, while the following decade saw her attempt to apply those lessons to the colonies for which her husband was responsible. However, she did not simply emulate them but rather considerably expanded the range of activities of such a position. This was particularly the case with architecture and public gardens. Indeed, the Museum of Sydney records that she was celebrated there for her 'unfeminine' interest in architecture, which is reflected in her 1809 travel journal where she frequently commented on buildings and the layout of streets. Thus of the Government House and Gardens in Cape Town she had noted the Dutch influences, especially on the 'ornamental part' of the house; and she wrote of the 'very fine walk' in the gardens, commenting favourably on its length (about three-quarters of a mile) and breadth (between 30 and 40 yards), and that it was 'well shaded by an avenue of oak trees, enclosed on each side by a hedge of cut myrtle'. She described the Government House as spacious and elegant, and recorded in August and September her general approval of the town, both private houses and public buildings, and private and public gardens:

> I had always hear'd [*sic*] said of the neatness and beauty of Cape Town, but indeed I think not more than it deserves, the streets are wide and spacious, the houses all large & handsome buildings, & the town built on a regular plan.[47]

In addition, she recorded on 25 September that Lachlan considered the military parade ground 'the finest he saw in any part of the world, except that at Petersburg'.[48] On the other hand, she noticed the demoralising effect on people of rundown buildings and inadequate provision. The Macquaries did not go ashore at Porto Prayo on the island of St. Jago at the end of June, but she reported the shock of those who did: 'even the military were in rags' while the governor's house was so dilapidated that it resembled more a shack than a building meant to reflect the majesty, solidity and benevolence of imperial rule.[49]

Such observations built upon her existing interests: in her luggage she had packed books on architecture – notably Edward Gyfford's *Designs for Elegant Cottages and Small Villas* (1806) and *Designs for small picturesque cottages and hunting boxes adapted for ornamental retreats for hunting and shooting: also some designs for park entrances, bridges, etc., carefully studied and thrown into perspective* (1807) – which she lent to builders in NSW. Her 1809 journal reveals her interest in the functionality as well as the look of buildings, both interior and exterior, and during her time in the Australian colonies she advised on a variety of construction projects, including government offices, barracks, farms, dairies, stables, schools, private houses, a lighthouse and even churches.[50]

As Grace Karskens has noted, Elizabeth and Lachlan Macquarie were already 'familiar with the language of fashionable architecture and landscape design as a true marker of social standing, taste and gentility' which Elizabeth consciously tried to introduce to the colony.[51] Her curiosity about other peoples and cultures and her interests and preoccupations outside of the domestic and philanthropic duties of a governor's wife may have broadened the scope of what was possible in that role. As an 'amateur architect' she made a significant contribution to the development of the colonial style; and such influences did not stop with this governor's wife. She set a precedent for future governors' wives: both Eliza (also known as Elizabeth) Darling in NSW (her husband Ralph was governor 1825–31) and Jane Franklin in Van Diemen's Land (her husband John was governor 1836–44) took a keen and detailed interest in house design.[52] Indeed, the former's plan for a new Government House won first prize in 1827, though it was not built as designed because the cost (of £30,000) was deemed by the British Treasury as too high.[53] Whereas in architectural history it seems that women get most (though not a lot of) recognition for domestic design, usually of the interiors of houses, this appears to be where Elizabeth Macquarie stands out for her influence on the exterior as well as the interior of public buildings.[54]

However exceptional in some areas, then, Elizabeth was not unique among Australian governors' wives; yet though the colonies gave such women opportunities to act independently, most fulfilled their role according to the expectations of middle-class women in Britain. Elizabeth was one of a few such wives with interests outside those conventions; Jane Franklin was another. Seven years after Elizabeth left Sydney, Edward Gibbon Wakefield described the role of the governor: 'The Governor is King; and a much more powerful man he is in respect to those over whom he rules than the Sovereign of Britain.'[55] One critic of Elizabeth among the settler elite in Sydney 'fancied that she would have preferred being the governor to the governess'.[56] Some 20 years later, Jane Franklin was similarly criticised for exercising 'Petticoat Influence' over her husband in the running of the colony.[57] In both cases, this criticism may have also been due to the closeness of the marriage partners with suspicion among the wider society that some governors paid too much attention to their wives' opinions and advice. Hence, although a predecessor of Elizabeth as the governor's wife in NSW between 1799 and 1806, Anna King, had focused her efforts on philanthropy, she too was thought to have so strong an influence over her husband, Philip, that she was nicknamed 'Queen Josepha'.[58] Still, there was a hint of affection in that sobriquet whereas the criticism of Elizabeth Macquarie and Jane Franklin was more censorious. The intense hostility towards governors' wives whose interests went beyond the domestic and philanthropic was an attempt to keep such women in their place.[59]

Elizabeth's travel journal confirms that her interest in architecture and landscape was serious and one which, as her time in Sydney was to show, was not just a tourist's pastime or a superficial accomplishment with which she filled idle hours. She was determined to apply what she had learned to the shaping of the colony beyond its current status as a penal settlement. Nor did she did simply take preconceived ideas from Britain; she developed her thoughts by observing the practices of others. As already noted, the journal reflects her belief in the superiority of the British Empire; but it also shows an openness, indeed an eagerness, to learn from what other imperialists had done, notably the Portuguese and the Dutch, as well as to see what Britain could and should do better. Thus she admitted that the Government House and Gardens in Cape Town were not as well maintained as they had been under the Dutch, though she considered that that may have been due to the swift changes in control over the colony between the two imperial powers in the period 1795–1806.[60] After setting sail on 13 October and looking back to shore, Elizabeth again commented favourably on the regularity applied to the planning of Cape Town. Lachlan, too, favoured the grid system for laying out towns and he, too, had observed the impact of the ornamental on his travels, notably through Russia in 1806 on his way to marry Elizabeth. Anthony Page has noted the deep impression that St Petersburg made on Lachlan as a 'model enlightenment city: a precarious triumph of science over nature, with geometric planning and architecture, and regulations enforcing westernised cultural practices'.[61]

Both Macquaries were aware of the effect on people's perceptions of well-proportioned buildings and public squares. However, while Elizabeth admired the orderly planning and handsome appearance of the stone buildings in Cape Town, she appreciated that appearance was not everything, having been informed that the practice of white-washing which she found pleasing caused 'a terrible glare in an extremely hot climate'.[62] She sought to avoid such mistakes in the construction of towns in the Australian colonies. She also encouraged road-building, notably in Sydney, where the road she planned around the inside of Government Domain, as well as the point to which it leads, are named after her. As reflected in her observations in the 1809 journal, the buildings, broad streets and public spaces which the Macquaries oversaw in Australia were not envisaged by either of them as merely utilitarian: they were to be decorative as well. Both the British government and the free settlers resisted these improvements because they considered them to be not only extravagant but also unfitting, inappropriate for a penal settlement. But whereas the elite settlers complained of the frivolity of the new buildings and public spaces, the local newspaper, the *Sydney Gazette*, reported on how their beauty and elegance stimulated civic pride, as the Macquaries had intended: hence the Macquarie influence on public buildings was considerable.[63] One biographer of Lachlan observed that Elizabeth 'entered fully into his interests and, in some respects, seemed to go further than he did in promoting controversial policies', so that her encouragement of Lachlan's building programme as well as his emancipist policy during his governorship cannot simply be portrayed as the mark of a loyal wife.[64] She was certainly proactive in both areas, working closely with the ex-convicts he appointed to important positions, such as colonial architect and deputy surveyor.[65]

Aside from architecture, Elizabeth recorded her observations of agriculture and the general provisioning of colonies. When in Cape Town she had noted how plentiful meat, fish and game were, but whereas she admired the countryside which she thought a botanist 'would be lost in admiration for', she judged agriculture to be backward, with vegetables scarce, expensive and of poor quality.[66] She had also noted the poor clothing and housing of the indigenous people. Once in NSW she paid particular attention to the state of agriculture and gardening, and she is considered to have had a significant impact on both as an exemplar and by encouraging others to improve their practices. Thus she superintended the planting of what became Parramatta Park, which had served as the Government Domain from 1788 and was designated as a public park in 1857; she set up a dairy and a farm on the Government Domain; she encouraged the importation and planting of fruit trees; and she helped to develop what became the Botanic Gardens in Sydney.[67] In all of this she was neither alone nor always the initiator, but her 1809 journal confirms her staunch belief in the importance of such public projects.

Although never explicitly stated in the journal, there is an assumption that this voyage was taking them towards the peak of, and probably the final stage in, Lachlan's imperial career, and that they would return to Mull at the end of his governorship. There is one explicit reference to feeling 'homesick' when she wrote on 5 August of coming close to the coast of South America after some days sailing with no other ships in sight:

> I felt quite rejoiced at the sight of human beings again, it gave rise to a kind of feeling new to me till that moment, connected with the idea of being totally seperated [*sic*] from our Country, and the people belonging to it, seeing that we were on another part of the globe, with a new Race of beings, which I could not help regretting were not our own people. So that there was a great mixture of melancholy reflection combined in the satisfaction which I felt.[68]

At the same time, she was confident that they would return to Scotland and looked forward to making their home on Mull. Impressed by the beauty (though not the scent which she found overpowering) of orange trees in August growing below a house she visited in Rio, Elizabeth looked forward to planting a grove of birch trees in front of their house on Mull.[69] Indeed, like the 1809 journal, their time in Australia – they anchored in Sydney Harbour in December 1809 and departed in February 1822 – again points to the multiple meanings of 'home' and the construction of identities noted above, partly through the Governor's practice of naming and commemorating (both the natural and the built environment), often after his wife. This may be seen as reflecting the powerful trope of Mull/Scotland/Britain as 'home' and the Empire as 'away', though Paul Carter is less sanguine: he describes Macquarie's practice of naming as a kind of 'onomastic megalomania'.[70] And however strong the pull of 'home', even after they returned to Mull in 1822 they continued to journey away from it. The Macquaries went on a mini 'grand tour' of Europe in 1822–3. Elizabeth did not keep a journal and seems to have been ill for much of the trip, but Lachlan recorded their six months travelling in southern France, northern Italy and Switzerland, confirming their shared interest in the built environment as well as in landscape, and their appreciation of the picturesque. They were indefatigable visitors at museums, art galleries, theatres and shops which sold local manufactures, as well as castles and churches. They even managed a meeting with the Pope on 8 May 1823 'by special appointment', followed by a walk in the Vatican's gardens.[71]

Nor did Elizabeth's travels end with the death in London of her husband in 1824. She journeyed regularly between Mull and London, where she spent lengthy periods seeing to the education of their son while tirelessly lobbying government to publish Lachlan's refutation of the critical report of the commission of inquiry into his governorship, which he had written on that grand tour during 12 days spent at Fontainebleau in July 1823.[72] In this she was eventually successful. She did not keep a journal of the return voyage from Sydney to London; nor did she ever go back to Australia. She did, however, maintain correspondence with friends in the colony and was gratified to be mentioned in an obituary of another governor's wife published in the *Sydney Herald* on 14 May 1832, which included a review of the wives of previous governors. Of Elizabeth, it noted that she had 'spread abroad everywhere, during her long residence, the marks of her taste and beneficence', and that she 'now witnesses her Australian-born son, "Young Lachlan", an excellent and talented officer in the Scots Greys, imbued with an ardent desire to revisit the land of his birth'.[73] As noted above, the 1809 journal shows that while Elizabeth's taste had been formed before she left Britain, she was receptive to new influences; but she did not consider the land of her son's birth to be his home. For her, Australia was an additional layer to his identity whose foundation was the ancestral land of his parents.

When he decided to follow his father into the army, Elizabeth did not relish the prospect of her son leaving 'home', which seems to have meant leaving her rather than a particular place, but she assumed that he would, as his father had done, combine imperial travel with a dedication to home and the role of a Highland laird.

Thus the 1809 journal suggests that she saw her role as more than that of the dutiful woman supporting her husband in the ways expected of the wife of a public official, through philanthropy for the poor settlers, indigenous people and convicts, and hospitality for the white elite and, to their chagrin, the wealthier freed convicts. As noted above, some of the Governor's critics among the elite settlers complained of Elizabeth's 'avidity for power and her influence over the governor'; others saw her as 'prone to flattery'.[74] Whereas similar criticism of Jane Franklin resulted in her husband appearing to be 'amiable but weak-willed', this did not have the same effect on popular perceptions of Lachlan.[75] The Macquarie governorship of NSW has been described as a 'benign patriarchy', a term which Elizabeth's account of the voyage in 1809 suggests could also be applied to their marriage: she saw herself as his helpmeet in the sense of his partner (albeit unequal), not his servant.[76] Both of the Macquarie journals of the 1809 voyage demonstrate a close harmony of interests and sympathies.

Still, if there is a hero in Elizabeth's journal it is that benign patriarch: she depicts Lachlan as orderly and efficient, martial and domestic, competent and caring, curious and reflective. He confided in her his concerns about the task ahead, appreciated her loyal support and accepted her advice, while she shared his vision for developing the colonies. All of Lachlan's biographers paint him as anxious to use the Empire to improve the standing and fortune of his family; but there is, too, a general acceptance that he had a sincere belief in the public good that his improvements to the colonies in his charge would bring in the long term, which he also considered would be to the benefit of the British government.[77] In this he did not convince either the free settlers or the colonial office, but his wife needed no persuading: as she had observed of Rio de Janeiro, it was 'not only highly favor'd [*sic*] by nature, but also much adorned by the art of Man'.[78] Her 1809 journal shows that she shared his convictions about the relationship between good governance and the fabric in which it was carried out, and that she was determined to play her part in colonial improvement.

Notes

1. H. Dillon and P. Butler (2010) *Macquarie: From Colony to Country* (Sydney: Heinemann), p. 12.
2. M.L. Pratt (1992, 2008) *Imperial Eyes: Travel Writing and Transculturation*, 2nd edn (London: Routledge.), p. 20. Macquarie University, in partnership with the State Library of New South Wales, State Records NSW, the National Library of Scotland, the Historic Houses Trust of NSW, the National Library of Australia and

the National Museum of Australia, has put transcripts of the writings of Lachlan and Elizabeth Macquarie held in the Mitchell Library, Sydney, online: LEMA [the Lachlan and Elizabeth Macquarie Archive], http://www.lib.mq.edu/digital/lema/. In addition, Robin Walsh, Curator of the Macquarie Room at Macquarie University Library, transcribed and edited Elizabeth's writings (2011) *In Her Own Words: Elizabeth Macquarie 1778–1835* (Sydney: Macquarie University), as part of the celebrations marking the bicentenary of the start of the Macquarie governorship: for the 1809 journal, see pp. 51–118.

3. T. Todorov (1996) 'The Journey and Its Narratives', pp. 287–96 in C. Chard and H. Langdon (eds.) *Transports, Travel, Pleasure, and Imaginative Geography 1600–1830* (New Haven & London: Yale University Press), p. 295.

4. M.A. Procida (2002) *Married to the Empire: Gender, Politics and Imperialism in India, 1883–1947* (Manchester: Manchester University Press), p. 1.

5. Procida, *Married*, p.6. For a similar analysis, see C. Samonte (2011) ' "Sympathetic Understanding": Gender, Empire and Representation in the Travel Writings of American Officials' Wives, 1901–1914', *The Journal of Transnational American Studies*, 3:2, 1–13.

6. In 1773, Boswell and Johnson visited Mull where Lachlan Macquarie established an estate and Ulva where he had been born. See J. Ritchie (1986) *Lachlan Macquarie: A Biography* (Carlton, Victoria: Melbourne University Press), pp. 89–90, 219.

7. See L. Cohen (1979) *Elizabeth Macquarie: Her Life and Times* (Sydney: Wentworth Books), pp. 19–20; M.H. Ellis (2010) *Lachlan Macquarie* (Sydney: HarperCollins), p. 132.

8. See, for example, D.J. Hamilton (2005), *Scotland, the Caribbean and the Atlantic World, 1750–1820* (Manchester: Manchester University Press), pp. 5, 27.

9. For two other Scottish imperial families, see E. Rothschild (2010) *The Inner Life of Empires: An Eighteenth-Century History* (Princeton NJ: Princeton University Press) and S. Foster (2010) *A Private Empire* (Millers Point: Murdoch Books).

10. 'Will of Major General Lachlan Macquarie', am baile highland history & culture, http://www.ambaile.org.uk/en/item/item_writtenword.jsp?item_id=16879 (accessed: 16 February 2012).

11. Walsh, *Words*, p. 80.

12. Donald Macquarie spent a year (1778–9) as a prisoner of the French, returning to Mull in poor health; Hector was captured by the rebels in South Carolina and died two years later while still in custody. See R.W. Munro (March 1989) 'Governor Lachlan Macquarie and his Family Circle', *The Scottish Genealogist*, 36:1, 8.

13. See Leonore Coltheart and Peter Bridges (2001) 'The Elephant's Bed? Scottish Enlightenment Ideas and the Foundations of New South Wales' in W. Brest and G. Tullo (eds.), *Scatterings of Empire: Journal of Australian Studies*, pp. 68, 19–33.

14. Walsh, *Words*, p. 80.

15. Michael Fry (2001) *The Scottish Empire* (Edinburgh: Tuckwell Press & Birlinn), p. 160. It became more contentious in the later nineteenth century. See Richard Finlay (Autumn 1994) 'Controlling the Past: Scottish Historiography and Scottish Identity in the 19th and 20th Centuries', *Scottish Affairs*, 9, 131.

16. See, for example, T.M. Devine (2003) *Scotland's Empire, 1600–1815* (London: Allen Lane); Esther Breitenbach (2009) *Empire and Scottish Society: The Impact of Foreign Missions at Home, c.1790–c.1914* (Edinburgh: Edinburgh University Press).

17. Stana Nenadic (April 2006) 'The Impact of the Military Profession on Highland Gentry Families, c. 1730–1830', *The Scottish Historical Review*, 75:1, 219, 75–99.

18. E.J. Cowan and R. Finlay (2000) *Scotland since 1688: Struggle for a Nation* (London: Barnes & Noble), p. 99.
19. Jane Rendall (2006) 'The Condition of Women's Writing and the Empire in Nineteenth-century Britain', pp. 101–21 in Catherine Hall and Sonya O. Rose (eds.), *At Home with the Empire: Metropolitan Culture and the Imperial World* (Cambridge: Cambridge University Press), p. 106.
20. Edward Gibbon Wakefield (1849, 1914) *A View of the Art of Colonization, in Letters between a Statesman and a Colonist* (Oxford: Clarendon Press), Letter xxiv, pp. 155–56.
21. Jo Currie (2000) *Mull: The Island and Its People* (Edinburgh: Birlinn), pp. 249–50.
22. Walsh, *Words*, p. 98.
23. Ibid., p. 82.
24. A naturalist and author, Sarah Bowdich edited (1825) her husband's *Excursions in Madeira and Porto Santo, during the autumn of 1823* (London) after his death in 1824, adding her own experiences of Africa as appendices. See Pratt, *Imperial Eyes*, p. 104.
25. Walsh, *Words*, p. 103.
26. Ibid., p.106. For a discussion of the role of colonial hospitality see C. Petley (2012) 'Gluttony, Excess, and the Fall of the Planter Class in the British Caribbean', *Atlantic Studies*, 9:1, 85–106.
27. Pratt, *Imperial Eyes*, pp. 145–8.
28. Walsh, *Words*, p. 88.
29. Ibid., p. 90.
30. Ibid., p. 104.
31. Cohen, *Elizabeth Macquarie*, pp. 120–1.
32. Walsh, *Words*, pp. 82–3.
33. Ritchie, *Lachlan Macquarie*, p. 135.
34. Walsh, *Words*, p. 96.
35. Jane Jarvis died in Macao in 1796 and was buried in Bombay/Mumbai. See Dillon and Butler, *Macquarie*, pp. 58–60.
36. Lachlan died in 1824, George in 1825; Mary continued in Elizabeth's service on Mull until the latter's death in 1835. See Robin Walsh, 'Jarvis, George (1790–1825)', *Australian Dictionary of Biography*, http://adb.anu.edu.au/biography/jarvis-george-13005 and *Journeys in Time*, http://www.lib.mq.edu.au/all/journeys/people/profiles/jrvis2.html (accessed: 19 February 2012).
37. For Captain Henry Colden Antill's journal of the voyage, see http://www.lib.mq.edu.au/digital/lema/antill1809 (accessed: 19 February 2012).
38. Walsh, *Words*, p. 86.
39. Ibid., p. 107.
40. Ibid., p. 107.
41. Ibid., p. 114.
42. Ibid., pp. 94, 116.
43. Ibid., p. 92.
44. Ibid., p. 109.
45. Ibid., pp. 94–6.
46. For the revolt against Governor Bligh, see A. Atkinson (1997) *The Europeans in Australia: A History* 2 vols, I (Melbourne: Oxford University Press), pp. 280–91; see also R. Fitzgerald and M. Hearn (1988) *Bligh, Macarthur and the Rum Rebellion* (Sydney: Kangaroo Press).

47. Walsh, *Words*, p. 106.
48. Ibid., p. 106.
49. Ibid., p. 84.
50. See, for example, J. Broadbent (1997) *The Australian Colonial House: Architecture and Society in New South Wales 1788–1842* (Sydney: Hordern House).
51. G. Karskens (2009) *The Colony: A History of Early Sydney* (Crows Nest: Allen & Unwin), p. 104.
52. See A. Selzer (2002) *Governors' Wives in Colonial Australia* (Canberra: National Library of Australia), which in addition to Darling and Franklin, considers Mary Anne Broom, Western Australia 1883–9, Elizabeth Loch, Victoria 1884–9, and Audrey Tennyson, South Australia 1899–1903. See also M. Hancock (1997) *Colonial Consorts: Wives of Victoria's Governors 1839–1900* (Melbourne: Miegunyah Press).
53. B.H. Fletcher and J. Kerr, 'Elizabeth Darling's Biography' at Design and Art Australia Online, http://www.daao.org.au.bio/elizabeth-darling (accessed: 18 February 2012).
54. See, for example, Broadbent, *The Australian Colonial House*; Diane Brand (1998) 'An Urbane Gaol: Macquarie's Sydney', *Journal of Urban Design*, 3:2, 225–39.
55. Edward Gibbon Wakefield (1829, 1929) *A Letter from Sydney: The Principal Town of Australasia, and Other Writings on Colonization* (London: J.M. Dent), p. 24.
56. Ritchie, *Lachlan Macquarie*, p. 135.
57. Alison Alexander (1987) *Governors' Ladies: The Wives and Mistresses of Van Diemen's Land Governors* (Sandy Bay: Tasmanian Historical Research Association), pp. 69, 97, 112.
58. Marnie Bassett, 'King, Anna Josepha (1765–1844)', *Australian Dictionary of Biography*, http://adb/anu.edu/au/biography/jarvis-george-13005 (accessed: 13 February 2012).
59. See P. Russell (2010) ' "Citizens of the World?" Jane Franklin's Transnational Fantasies', pp.195–208 in Desley Deacon, Penny Russell and Angela Woollacott (eds.), *Transnational Lives: Biographies and Global Modernity, 1700-present* (Basingstoke: Palgrave Macmillan), p. 197.
60. Walsh, *Words*, p. 108.
61. A. Page (2009) 'Enlightenment, Empire and Lachlan Macquarie's Journey Through Persia and Russia', *History Australia*, 6:3, 70.8.
62. Walsh, *Words*, p. 110.
63. See M. Casey (September 2010) 'A Patina of Age: Elizabeth Macquarie (née Campbell) and the Influence of the Buildings and Landscape of Argyll, Scotland, in Colonial New South Wales', *Journal of Historical Archaeology*, 14:3, 342.
64. F. Marsden (2001) *Lachlan Macquarie: from Mull to Australia* (Tobermory: Brown & Whittaker), p. 16.
65. Ritchie, *Lachlan Macquarie*, p. 140. See also M. Rosenthal (April 2008) 'London versus Sydney, 1815–1823: The Politics of Colonial Architecture', *Journal of Historical Geography*, 34:2, 191–219.
66. Walsh, *Words*, pp. 108–09.
67. Cohen, *Elizabeth Macquarie*, pp. 113–14.
68. Walsh, *Words*, p. 86.
69. Ibid., pp. 91–2.
70. P. Carter (2010) *The Road to Botany Bay: An Exploration of Landscape and History* (Minneapolis: University of Minnesota Press), p. 332.

71. See Lachlan Macquarie's journal of the Grand Tour and the entry for 'Thursday 8. May 1823', http://www.lib.mq.edu/digital/lema/1823 (accessed: 19 February 2012).

72. For the Commission see J.M. Bennett (1971) 'The Day of Retribution – Commissioner Bigge's Inquiries in Colonial New South Wales', *The American Journal of Legal History*, 15, 85–106.

73. As quoted in Cohen, *Elizabeth Macquarie*, p. 221.

74. Ritchie, *Lachlan Macquarie*, p. 135.

75. Russell, ' "Citizens of the World?" Jane Franklin's Transnational Fantasies', 197.

76. Marian Aveling (April 1992) 'Imagining New South Wales as a Gendered Society, 1783–1821', *Australian Historical Studies*, 25:98, 1–12.

77. Besides the previously cited biographies by Ellis, Ritchie, Dillon and Butler, see Marjorie Barnard (1946), *Macquarie's World* (Carlton, Vic.: Melbourne University Press).

78. Walsh, *Words*, p. 88.

5
Against 'the Usual Restraints Imposed upon their Sex': Conflictive Gender Representations in Nineteenth-Century Orients

Xavier Guégan

Defining masculinity and femininity in the representation of the 'Other' in Victorian and Edwardian travel ethnographic writings and historical fictions as well as commercial and governmental photographs is not easy. Moreover, when one attempts to analyse nineteenth-century cultural representation of the orients in a post-Saidian era, the re-evaluation of the locations of colonial stereotypes themselves seem to be challenging. Yet some successful writers and photographers from the long nineteenth century require specific attention to understand that some of the now well-established tropes could – if not entirely, at least partially – be reconsidered. Although Philip Meadows Taylor's *Confessions of a Thug* (1839) was famously considered to be one of Queen Victoria's favourite novels and belongs to an era when travel writing was flourishing, it nonetheless tells another story of the conventional description of the British Empire and masculinities. To a certain extent, Taylor's *Confessions of a Thug*, Sophia Lane Poole's *The Englishwoman in Egypt: Letters from Cairo* (1844), Samuel Bourne's photographs in the 1860s, Lucy Garnett's *The Women of Turkey and Their Folklore* (1890), Flora Annie Steel's *On the Face of the Waters* (1896) and Gertrude Bell's albums of Mesopotamia at the turn of the century participate in a typical scheme of representation of nineteenth-century imperialism and Orientalism as coined by Said, but they also involve ethnographic surveys and artistic features, which give 'nobleness' and 'beauty' to the people or scenes they portrayed.[1] They betray a strange mixture of attraction and repugnance (for some of them), fascination and incomprehension, scientific claims and imagination.

These texts and photographs first seem to differ entirely in their literary and visual forms, geographic spheres and time periods, and yet here gender and the status of 'truth' are the key facets that connect them together. The aforementioned authors used factual and historical re-creation to develop narratives that act as the representation of an oriental world.[2] To that effect, they have indeed 'created' an orient.[3] Nonetheless, the different patterns that they use in their depiction of their characters – memories and psychology of details of past lives, precise descriptions of present experiences, expression of the effect of sensations on the narrator (be it a fictional character or the narration as a first person) – and the visual representation of 'greatness' through the photographic portraiture of indigenous populations, often illustrate a true wish to immerse and attempt to understand a foreign culture rather than just dismiss it as imaginary. The connection of the authors with the representation of those colonised men and women is sometimes surprising because, in the examples that follow, they do not always conform to the traditional and mainstream colonial discourse. Although the following cases are exceptions to the main portraiture of colonial subjects, this chapter brings something new to the study of representation of colonial otherness and gender perspectives. Those cases show a strong connection, and often a critic, to gender relations 'at home'.[4]

Depicting foreign cultures and behaviours

A fascination with historical topics grew in nineteenth-century European cultures, both as a genre and as a way of representing and questioning truth. The texts and pictures here 'convey' history but also 'create' it in their own production. Greenblatt argues that there is no 'fixity' in regard to history, that man himself can alter history in narration because cultural mediums involve a range of overlapping consciousnesses.[5] This is the case with these texts, which are credible historical documentaries in their own right despite having elements of fiction. However, there is an intrinsic bias in the authors' depiction of the foreign cultures: they also create them from a Western perspective. Western representations of the Orient are intrinsically tied up with questions of difference, mystery and fantasy, thus the novels, diaries and photographs are not just oriental historical accounts as they serve a wider, Western purpose. When Steel claims that the writing of her novel is an attempt 'to be at once a story and history, [but] probably fails in either aim', we could actually argue that all of these authors achieve both. They do challenge the traditional Western view of the orient but are still in effect writing a Western history. The line between fiction and reality is blurred by the very concept of the 'historical' description; it is mostly written in narrative form to explain events, rather than to record them, as found in, for example, annals. White describes narrativity as inseparable from morality, and 'it is difficult to think of any historical work produced during the nineteenth century, the classic age of historical narrative, that was not given the force of a moral judgment on the events it related'.[6] The nineteenth century's historical narrative is therefore inextricably linked to the 'moral judgments' of the nineteenth-century narrator. Said advocates that representations should be read as *'representations,* not as "natural" depictions of the Orient. This evidence is found just as prominently in the so-called truthful texts (histories [...]) as in the avowedly artistic'.[7] The narrative techniques of fiction and photographs cannot be removed from works of representation, however 'true' they profess to be. The criticism and historiography reveal the difficulty in ascribing these writings, and accordingly the Orient, to any one description, but acknowledge that the representation of the Orient, whether 'fantastic' or not, is inseparable from the complications of representation itself. 'Aesthetics' appears to be problematic in the narration of the historical novel and ethnographic and commercial photographs. It brings duality between factual and aesthetic judgements, and questions whether History is meant to convey 'beauty'. The uses of aesthetics as the main reminiscence of Orientalism develop a controversial pleasure of curiosity where narratives are exotic displays. These travel writings and pictures highlight the problem of emotions and passions with a factual narration and produce cognitivism through moral realism and moral subjectivism. Travel writings of the 'dying' Ottoman Empire and the 'rising' British Indian Empire here express great emphasis on emotion and sensation, and there is indeed propinquity of the texts to the crime and adventure fiction genres popular in the period. The involvement and description of strong feelings – love, loath, attraction, disgust, doubt and incomprehension – equate the documents with the epic or the romantic novel and painting, and thus alter the apparent purpose of plainly 'documenting' and 'exposing' the Orient.

The definitions of literature in the nineteenth century were similarly fraught with contradictions, including historical fiction. Green explains how Chateaubriand saw 'post-revolutionary historical writing falling into two distinct categories [...] "l'histoire *fataliste*" and "l'histoire *descriptive*" '.[8] This division of historical fiction reveals the difficult relationship of historical novels and imagination. Green describes the 'fatalist' school as wanting to 'present general truths at the expense of colourful details [...] rigour and authenticity' and the 'descriptive' school as 'making history come alive for the reader' with evocative descriptions.[9] The concern for depicting 'truth' as well as being 'sensationalist' brings these writings to work on a dual, but not an obvious segregate, representation of the 'oriental crime' and 'gender condition'. If they somehow create a mirage of a contemporary 'other', they do it through the 'character-isation' of history. Therefore the subjects of their writing become 'humanised' heroes – or anti-heroes– instead of the traditional 'mystified' ones; and historic narration is written through the combination of the epic and romantic characteristics. The authors here use different techniques in their historical or factual portrayal, whether a vivid and highly descriptive language in Poole's *The Englishwoman in Egypt: Letters from Cairo* and Garnett's *The Women of Turkey and Their Folklore* allowing the reader to experience an extremely distinctive culture, or a simpler and uncomplicated style in Taylor's *Confessions of a Thug* and Steel's *On the Face of the Waters*, achieving a notable intimacy to understand events and characters, or again familiar signs that do not seem to be too difficult to read in Bourne's and Bell's collections of portraitures. Through gender perspectives in the representation of customs, violence and sexual images, these written and visual texts bring a binary division in the representation and exploration of the Orient throughout the nineteenth century, a confirmation of stereotypes by highlighting 'immobility' and an expression of changes and 'mobility' in criticising a colonial discourse to the benefit of native populations' ends, and also the British 'at home'.

Philip Meadows Taylor and Flora Annie Steel

Taylor and Steel, respectively, described a pre- and post-Mutiny era where violence is at the centre of the discourse.[10] They both wrote their historical novel with the 'descriptive' method, and both challenged in their own way the colonial system and the representation of sexuality.

After originally being sent to India at the age of 15 to become a clerk to a Bombay merchant, Philip Meadows Taylor (1808–76) soon accepted a commission in the service of the Nyzam of Hyderabad. During his career he acquired different civil functions, and a knowledge of the languages and the people of southern India. He wrote several novels highlighting the interaction between the Anglo-Indians and Indians; *Seeta* (1872), for example, depicts a romantic portrayal of the marriage between a British civil servant and a Hindu widow just before the Indian Mutiny. His first, and most famous, work was *Confessions of a Thug*, where Taylor documents the notion of terrorism through a depiction of the Thuggee, a religious practice or cult in which murderers – of both Hindu and Muslim background – pronounce their devotion to the goddess of destruction, Bhowanee or Kali, through the ritualised strangulation of travellers. The murders take place using what they deem a holy symbol of their profession, a white handkerchief – the roomal – containing a silver coin, which they employ inconspicuously to strangle to death innocent travellers. The murders are 'instances of sacred terror' – they are always preceded by a ceremonial procedure, which includes the use of daily prayers and oaths, and attention to omens.[11] The process of the murder is also extremely efficient, well organised and timed. Taylor's claims are to expose the tales he came to learn about the Thuggee from his 15 years of experience in India, and are 'almost all true'. His key motive is a true and accurate portrayal of oriental crime, yet he admits to the use of fiction 'only to connect the events'.[12] Taylor claims that he was personally acquainted with the 'real' Ameer Ali – who would become the main character of his novel – in 1832, and his sources are transcripts of interviews that he conducted with captured Thugs and some information from Colonel William Henry Sleeman's book *Ramaseeana*, published in 1836. In addition, to add more credibility to his narrative, he highlights the intervention of British officials and officers of the East India Company who were key actors in the suppression of the Thuggee, Governor General Lord William Bentinck, Colonel Sleeman and Captain Reynolds.

The British methods to capture the Thugs are described as 'silently yet surely' striking 'at the power and confederacy of the Thugs a blow as severe, nay more so, as being more lasting, than any they had yet experienced'.[13] The 'system' represents India under the British control, and yet the Thugs could recover from such a system, and so the Orient is not without its own power. Statements of British dominance are also undermined; not through direct criticism of the Company but by implied similarities between the Thugs and the East India Company. The Thugs use the discourse of business and transaction, and call themselves a 'company'.[14] A murder is referred to as 'business' as the Thugs appropriate the language of the system; 'blood gushed from the wound and his mouth [...] you have settled his business nobly'.[15] The representation of the Orient is not one of opposition, but the similarities between the British and the Thugs are subtly suggested. Ameer Ali simultaneously represents an epic and recognisable figure, representing an Orient that engages the reader. The narrator suggests: 'although the mind would ordinarily reject sympathy with the joys or sorrows of a murderer like Ameer Ali [...] the death of his favourite child could so much affect him, even to tears, and they were genuine'.[16] Although the narrator feels that it is natural to separate the figure of the murderer from 'joy' and 'sorrows', Ameer Ali transcends this division, and becomes a murderer and a grieving father at the same time. Poovey suggests that 'passages that encourage the reader to view the two narrators as similar depart from the narrator's explicit norms because the English narrator specifically tells us that Thugs are unlike the English in every way'.[17] The narrator explains his position on the 'murderer' Thugs before undermining it by exploring their similarities.

The practical descriptions of the murders and Ameer Ali's dismissal of omens also prevent any supernatural force from overriding his actions, and so he remains accountable.[18] Ameer Ali is, nonetheless, defined as a 'fantastic' figure by the scale of his crimes. He gained great booty, 'dollars, gold mohurs, and rupees, to the value of sixty thousand rupees in all; and there were also six strings of large pearls';[19] the quantities of gold and pearls form a discourse of the fantastic because it requires a suspension of disbelief and the hesitation of the reader, and the Orient becomes a place filled with treasure and crime. The murderer Ameer Ali aligns with the concern of the nineteenth-century public with criminality and the psychiatry of the criminal mind. Foucault explains that the developed 'literature of criminality' transformed 'the criminal mind into a hero, perhaps, but equally the affirmation that ever-present criminality is a constant menace to the social body as a whole.'[20] The fascination with criminality creates a mythical figure, the 'criminal', and the 'constant menace' is as a result of fear and fascination. *Confessions of a Thug* is concerned with the criminal behaviour and motivation of Ameer Ali; the fictional representation concerns the current interest, combining the epic with contemporary concerns. Ameer Ali is a complex hero or anti-hero, both guilty and heartless; Indian, yet similar to the narrator and most certainly a criminal, an incredible figure both attracting and repelling the reader. *Confessions of a Thug*, whether read as propaganda, a critique or a popular Victorian crime novel, represents an ambiguous scene of violence. If read as propaganda, it could be a representation of a barbaric Orient, and justification for the British presence in India, but the novel can also be read as an assimilation of the British fascination with crime and a recognisable figure of a murderer. The representation of the Orient becomes at once extraordinary and familiar. Throughout the narrative, Taylor tries to give a representation of Indian customs. We become familiar with aspects of life in India at the time: various styles of dress reflecting different social hierarchies, medical treatments, different foods and traditions, the landscapes, and Indian entertainment and etiquette.

Confessions of a Thug was influenced by contemporary sensibilities. Although not under direct British rule, the Nyzam had to comply with the East India Company. Poovey suggests that 'as an English servant of an Indian prince, Taylor self-consciously positioned himself somewhere between the Indians and the English'.[21] Taylor's 'in-between' position allows him access to the Company while maintaining a detached position. The Company demanded an end to the Thuggee, and officer Sleeman was the first who brought the 'Thugs' to the attention of the British people. Taylor therefore wrote for an audience who were aware of the cult. Poovey argues that they regarded the novel as a truthful account, and 'as proof that the English presence in India was fully justified', although this is not to suggest that it was intended this way or always read as such. She dismisses this argument, as the novel can be read 'certainly not as an unequivocal justification for British rule in India – but as an oblique critique of the East India Company' and assumptions about racial superiority.[22] Taylor expresses criticism of numerous characteristics in the novel, namely the widely held Western belief that Christianity is the only true religion. She also suggests that Taylor is highly critical of the general imperialists' sense of racial superiority; the author achieving this through proximity of the Thugs to the Company in the novel, for instance, and the fact that they can disguise themselves as merchants. Taylor does seem to equate the Thugs with Company representatives, as Poovey explains, for example, in Ameer Ali's 'particularly martial appearance' and his exterior of 'respectability'.[23] The Thugs also adhere strictly to a set of laws, and more importantly a private set of laws, suggesting that the East India Company is unjust and is founded on corruption, yet masks itself as something professional. Here the novel serves as a strong statement, communicating powerfully a political history. There is a clear message that the Thugs – to read the Indians – are not afraid of the 'English' but cannot get rid of them:

How many of you English are passionately devoted to sporting! Your days and months are passed in its excitement. A tiger, a panther, a buffalo, or a hog, rouses your utmost energies for its destruction – you even risk your lives in its pursuit. How much higher game is a Thug's! His is man: against his fellow-creatures in every degree, from infancy to old age, he has sworn relentless, unerring destruction![24]

Alongside Taylor's *Confessions of a Thug*, Steel's *On the Face of the Waters* offers another representation of violence and gender from the usual tropes. From the end of the nineteenth century, Flora Annie Steel (1847–1929) established herself as the only serious rival to Rudyard Kipling. Although most of her novels describe contemporary Anglo-Indian life in the transition from the end of the nineteenth century to the first decades of the twentieth, she also wrote five historical novels. Steel represented both the Anglo-Indian and the Indian interests, and her novel on the Indian Mutiny received for that reason some criticism for not 'leaving the natives in the background';[25] indeed she was famous for having interacted with local Indian women and learned their language. As with Taylor, Steel's experience of living in India influenced her description of historical events. *On the Face of the Waters* is based on the experiences of those who lived through the Indian Mutiny of 1857 and Steel uses primary sources, government archives and personal interviews. Although written over 40 years after the revolt itself and with fictional characters, the novel conforms to many records of the events.[26] Steel claims that all incidents related to the Mutiny are entirely factual, 'scrupulously exact, even to the date, the hour, the scene, the very weather'.[27] The use of fiction does not detract from the historical account; rather, it adds to it, allowing the story more coherently to flow.

In *On the Face of the Waters*, Steel expresses the influence of colonialism in India through her representation of Indian culture. For instance, the recreation of a home as a hideaway highlights the conflict between coloniser and colonised. It is also expressed through description of indigenous landscapes, which become almost tainted or degenerated by colonialism:

> The English [*sic*] flag drooped lazily in the calm floods of yellow light. For the rest, were dense dark groves following the glistening curve of the river, and gardens gravely gray in pillars of white chumbaeli creeper and cypress.[28]

The image of the flag starkly contrasts the two cultures, emphasising the foreign and unknown to the Western reader and distinguishing it evocatively as something obviously and powerfully emblematic of British culture. Later, Steel writes that Lucknow is deprived of its 'profligacy' merely by 'one stroke of an English pen',[29] which sets up imperialists as powerful and oppositional to indigenous society and custom. It also suggests that England is active in the defilement of extravagance and indulgence in sensual pleasure. Mallonee in her essay on 'hybridity' in Steel's novels argues that the author destabilises the notion of the self and the other by actually demonstrating proximity between the coloniser and the colonised.[30] In this sense the novel can be read as a hybrid colonial discourse. Looking again, the flag 'droops' in the sky, the term 'droop' having connotations of something tired, disintegrating and on the brink of collapse. This perhaps foreshadows the instability and volatility of the colonial government's authority. There is no palpable opposition here; rather, a hybrid description of colonial existence.

Steel thus represents the hybridisation of cultures when she depicts a scene unfamiliar to British culture and juxtaposes it with Britishness; 'nothing there to prepare him for finding an Englishwoman within [...] busy Heaven save the mark! In sticking some disjointed jasmine buds into the shallow saucer of a waterpot.'[31] The character is equated with the native culture by the fact that she is using jasmine in her cooking, and thus part of the oriental scene and in some way hybridised with native culture. This stresses the fluidity of colonial experience as outlined by Bhabha. Steel, through her use of hybridity, renders the text rather complex, highlighting the difference between coloniser and colonised and their roles, yet underlines the complexities and intricacies of colonialism, and evident amalgamation of culture. It can therefore be read not as a mere categorisation of self and other, and East and West, but more as an interlaced changing and merging society.

Sophia Lane Poole and Lucy Garnett

Poole and Garnett, respectively, described the beginning of the British influence in Egypt and a collapsing Turkey at the end of the century where Oriental woman attracted much interest and created a phantasm within the Western world. They both wrote their factual narrations following the 'fatalist' method, and both challenged in their own way the colonial system and the representation of sexuality.[32]

The sister of the famous Arabist Edward William Lane, Sophia Lane Poole (1804–91) visited Egypt and wrote a book – *The Englishwoman in Egypt: Letters from Cairo* – that was intended as a companion to her brother's *Manners and Customs of the Modern Egyptians* (1836).[33] Her writings were meant to supply 'the female, personal and the domestic' to the academic work of Lane.[34] Although Poole's accounts of an Englishwoman's life in Egypt were an immediate success, the fact that a Christian Western woman wore Turkish trousers and the veil in order to gain access to harems, bathhouses and other 'women-only' areas caused some sensation. Poole's *Englishwoman in Egypt* is a series of letters, which, as she writes what appears to her, forms a type of travelogue.[35] She uses the present tense, which creates a sense of the Orient that is immediate, as if Poole is writing as she travels. Her account is removed from overtly fictional techniques, although she presents a highly personalised Orient, stating that she 'must observe, and admire all that is admirable, and endeavour to forget what is objectionable in the state of Eastern society'.[36] Watt suggests that 'the travelogue allowed for selective factual description, rational or motional reaction, personal experience, and any number of digressions'.[37] Poole has the power to be selective and often selects events that enable her to make comparisons on moral grounds. '[P]erhaps a hundred voices, in solemn, and indeed harmonious, concert' she hears during an evening fast, 'and oh! as their voices are borne on the night-wind, let the silent prayer of every Christian who hears them ascend to a throne of grace for mercy on their behalf.'[38] Poole creates an opposition between the religious, because of the dichotomy between the noise of the 'hundred voices' and the 'silent prayer'. Her description is evocative of a missionary, helping the Orient by asking for 'mercy on their behalf', consistent with the contemporary paternalistic ideas of 'saving' the Orient. To some extent Poole is representative of the role of the reader within the text, integrating with the Egyptian women; the reader has a recognisable figure to follow, and to explore, for them, the 'hundred' voices in the night.

The higher-class women are represented by visual descriptions, noting their clothing, make-up and etiquette. Very little else is revealed. Poole notes of one that 'she was in one respect strangely disfigured; her eyebrows being painted with kohl [...] in a very broad and unbecoming manner [...] her other feature were deprived of their natural expression'.[39] The woman, as 'disfigured' and 'unbecoming', reveals what Poole believes is unnatural in a woman's appearance, and therefore what Englishwomen should look like; by describing what is unattractive, Poole implies what is aesthetics and what convention. Her personal opinions create a representation of the Orient that also defines the Englishwoman, because she presents the Englishwomen as opposite to the Eastern women. Abdel-Hakim stresses that Poole 'commodified the women by posing and sketching them to be consumed by the reading public'.[40] In the physicality of the representation, the women are 'commodified' because they appear as nothing more than their jewellery and make-up. However, while they may be 'posed' for the reading public, they are not limited to the sexual representation that preceded Poole's writing, to be found in the writings of Edward William Lane and his contemporaries. The description of the women breaks from a traditional representation of the Orient, disregarding the erotic fantasy of the harem. Poole realises another image, as removed from perversions and desire. Her relationship with the Orient – witnessing it with her female position, and realising and destroying stereotypes – creates a varied description based on grounded exploration. Her writing is personal and uniquely feminine; it does not present the Orient as a 'fantastical' exotic and erotic East created by the writing of a male-dominated society.

Alongside representing the Orient in need of saving, Poole also creates a representation of the Orient as oppositional: 'the perfect contrast which the

customs of Eastern life present to the whole construction of European society [...] these people which have no parallel in the West'.[41] The East and
the West are thus distinct and separate, a recognisable presentation of the
Orient in the nineteenth century; as Said suggests, 'it was a world elsewhere,
apart from the ordinary attachments, sentiments and values of *our* world in
the West'.[42] Said's statement reflects Poole's representation of the Orient as
'apart' and 'elsewhere'. This 'otherness' extends to the representation of the
women. The stereotypical image of the 'eastern women', which begins as
a curiosity for Poole, is 'observed'. Her beliefs are realised during her visit,
and so become knowledge, which she shares with the reader, reinforcing a
representation of the 'oriental' woman. Bhabha explains that a stereotype
is a 'form of knowledge and identification what vacillates between what is
always "in place", already known, and something that must be anxiously
repeated'.[43] Poole provides a 'repetition' of the stereotype; it becomes as an
essential idea, at once recognisable but never proved, and occupies a position of ambivalence because it is constructed as a 'probabilistic truth', and
so not in need of proof.[44] While the women become a representation of the
'other', it is a complex, and not simply negative, or singularly sustained,
image. While her own superiority is never questioned, she does acknowledge the power of the 'eastern woman' over her husband, who, rather than
the 'lord and master' imagined in the West, in fact 'may be excluded for
many days from his own harem'.[45] Poole changes the 'eastern woman' from
a submissive figure into one who can command. However, the women do
not appear dominant in relation to Poole; rather, they become almost props
for the clothes and jewels that she describes. She undermines one representation of the Orient as 'submissive', but realises another – the representation
of the Orient as inferior.

Garnett's observations of Eastern women are more nuanced and sympathet-
ically supportive. Lucy Garnett (1849–1934), a traveller and folklorist, was
granted in 1893 a civil-list pension for services to literature for her achievement in the documentation of the customs of the people among whom she
lived during her trips in the Balkans and the Middle East.[46] Garnett was
particularly interested in the lives and status of women, and *The Women of
Turkey and Their Folklore* diverges from male writers first from their erotic
creations of the harem and the area, and also from the generalisation of the
harem as a singular system which identically works in every ethnic group.[47]
Rather, Garnett bases her descriptions on laws and historical comments, and
she is meticulous in her attempt to understand how the different systems
in fact function and fight certain Western stereotypes. Because Muslim law
required maintenance, 'none but the wealthiest can, and few of them care
to, indulge in a polygamy, or even bigamy, which is practically found to be
more of an inconvenience than a luxury'.[48]

Her analysis also appears to be often active rather than passive in her
understanding of the politics and geopolitics of the region. She mentions

the influence of European opinion on the Porte to close the slave-market in Constantinople and formally prohibit the slave-trade, but also explains how in reality no material change, so far as slave women are concerned, has taken place in this respect. Garnett does not try to legitimate the European morals, nor the local ones, but instead assesses the fact that the West wants the East to change according to its ideologies as proving to be everything but positive and constructive. She then explains that since the institution of slavery is indispensable to the social system of the Osmanlis, its total abolition would also involve the abolition of the harem, 'a revolution for which they are as yet by no means prepared'.[49] Therefore their demand for slave women is undiminished, and that prohibition merely served 'enormously to increase the horrors of the traffic in its initial stage by increasing the difficulties under which it is carried on'.[50]

Additionally, Garnett clearly aspires to give an account of all social status and classes of the societies that she encounters and describes. Throughout her narration it becomes apparent that she wants first to draw attention to societies and conditions in which Eastern women live, and then to highlight, more generally, the condition of women within a male world. So, daughters of the Sultan, in consequence of their rank, take precedence over their husbands, and 'consider themselves exempt from many of the usual restraints imposed upon their sex'. However, this exemption has unfortunate consequences and prevents these high-rank women, who are above the common restrictions that usually work against women, to acquire the esteem of society and the affection of men. This exemption leads them to be 'wayward and extravagant in their habits, tyrannical, and sometimes even guilty of great cruelty'.[51] Garnett seems to make the case that they become so 'tyrannical' because society – men – have created gendered rules that, once broken, bring extremes. She also makes the point later that there were some of these ladies who were 'still remembered with affection by the numerous dependents of their respective establishments, no less than by their friends in higher ranks'.[52] Garnett proves to be highly involved with the countries and people that she encounters; for example, 'I was in intimate relations with the Albanian Chiefs during their Revolt, and admitted to their Councils as an affiliated member of the Albanian League.'[53] She not only highlights the harmful actions of the West and how the East fought against its rule and moral values, but also reveals herself as a Western woman who lives among the local societies, has 'intimate relations' with local men, and is fully accepted and highly regarded by them.

Unlike many women who travelled to the Orient, Garnett does not have an evangelical 'mission' or think of her travel as a religious journey.[54] In fact, she is extremely critical of Christianity and its repercussions on women's status. Here she compares Muslim and Christian marital laws, and concludes that women – particularly extraconjugal women – are more contented and have more rights within a Muslim system since women, whether slave or free, have enforceable legal rights against men. She states that the distinctive principle, on the other hand, of the Christian Marriage Law is entirely based on an indissoluble monogamous marriage. While Turkey displays and has legitimated polygamy, and therefore protected women's rights, what is upsetting for Garnett is that Christian values reside in 'hypocrisy' where women are at the mercy of men's rules.

> Monogamy has, in Christendom, been a conventional fiction rather than a social fact...the Social Evil has, in no Civilisation whatever, been so hideous in its degradation and misery as in Christendom. But as the existence of this Evil is the necessary correlate of the rightlessness of women under the Christian Law, so the absence of this Evil is the necessary correlate of the rights of women under the Moslem Law.[55]

Samuel Bourne and Gertrude Bell

Bourne and Bell each explored through their travel the visual representation of the populations that they were encountering. Photography was their means of expression and also how they wanted to portray reality, yet with an aesthetic system of depiction. Bourne portrayed and categorised a fair range of tribes in post-Mutiny India; Bell described throughout her surveys a variety of archaeological sites alongside local populations in early twentieth-century Greater Syria, Turkey and Mesopotamia. They embraced visually the British colonial fashion of categorising the world, but they also challenged in their own way the representation of 'greatness' that was usually the antithesis within the colonial ideology of representation.[56]

Samuel Bourne (1834–1912), one of the most prestigious Victorian English commercial photographers to have worked in British India, is best known for his photographs of the Himalayas and the Indian peoples from many locations on the subcontinent. Bourne was in India initially from 1863 to 1870, thereby establishing his career as a professional photographer. Within a few years, the firm of Bourne & Shepherd became recognised as being a directing influence over British-Indian photography. The photographs were taken either in a studio or on location, and included individual and group portraits of both British and Indians, topographical images in which peoples were incidental, as well as a range of representations of Indian life, customs and types. These images were informed by, and in turn contributed to, an expanding body of photographic practice that mixed, to varying degrees, authenticity and aesthetic style. Placed in the context of the development of photography as a medium of record and representation, Bourne's work is a significant historical source for understanding British cultural presence in post-Mutiny India.

The depiction of some Indian tribes stresses the image of nineteenth-century India as Europe's opposite. The subcontinent was represented as a multitude of villages where the communities were idealised and codified; Metcalf speaks of an Indian present meant to symbolise Britain's past.[57] In the post-Mutiny era, although the superiority of British culture and character was not brought into question, the emphasis on an oriental and traditional society in some parts of India was reinforced.[58] The romanticised vision of the tribal village was strong throughout the nineteenth century, and 'the aesthetic practices, philosophies, cosmologies, customs, visual art forms' dismissed by the utilitarian-minded as 'wasteful, deluded, or even repulsive', Inden writes, the Romantics found 'worthy of study and perhaps even of praise'.[59] Moreover, the mid-nineteenth century saw the resurgence of the image of the so-called 'Noble Savage' through the framework of anthropology. The romantic version of the noble savage was more positive, and Samuel Bourne drew on this in his imagery of the Todas and Lepchas. The image of the tribe emphasises a community closer to nature, closer to the state of 'primitiveness', where they do not need others to do their work, stressing thus the concept of equality as part of this community; this idea of communal self-sufficiency was reinforced in post-Mutiny India. *Toda Mund, Village and Todas* (Figure 5.1, 1869), *Lepcha Man of Sikkim, Darjeeling* (Figure 5.2, 1860s) and *Lepcha Woman of Sikkim, Darjeeling* (1860s) convey the image of primitive communities and individuals. Those images represent indigenous shepherds, but following a classic Christian depiction of God's shepherds from the Old Testament, introducing an ideal of primitive life that once again links back to established iconography. Although Bourne in his writing is often negative in his description of indigenous villages, his visual representation of tribal men and women reflects a sort of 'idyllic' village society, which was seen as 'the irreducible unit, the "atom" of the state in the nations and empires of Asia'.[60]

The photograph of the Todas, taken in the midst of their environment, accentuates the idea of harmony between these people and their relation to nature. There was a growing interest in the production of photographic portraiture of the Nilgiris inhabitants (southern part of India) from the 1860s onwards. This attention was on the part of photographers and scientists but also very quickly on the part of tourists who became one of the tribe's main sources of revenue.[61] The Todas were seen as a 'curiosity' – Bourne's photographs catered to this fascination. *Toda Mund, Village and Todas* (Figure 5.1) is one of Bourne's finest and best-known photographs. This small tribe of buffalo pastoralists living in the forests on the Nilgiri Hills in Ootacamund, south India, were regarded at that time as 'aboriginal' (pre-Indo-Aryan), and as a hill and forest population they occupy an 'ambivalent place below, outside or parallel to [the] varna'.[62] Bourne took this ethnographic portrait with his usual stylistic devices that both attract curiosity by virtue of the unusual scene and draw the viewer's eye to the aesthetic features (Figure 5.1).

The people of Sikkim (the smallest Himalayan kingdom) – the Lepchas – were often represented by the British as a majestic and strong tribal people,

Figure 5.1   Samuel Bourne (1869) *Toda Mund, Village and Todas, the Neilgherries*
[Rubenstein Library, Duke University – Image 1907].

and this depiction is also found in the portraiture of a half-naked man and woman in Bourne's *Lepcha Man of Sikkim, Darjeeling* (Figure 5.2) and *Lepcha Woman of Sikkim, Darjeeling*. As Ollman has pointed out, Bourne's depiction of each figure emphasises their 'noble' character by drawing on the conventions of European portraiture – where a royal subject was shown leaning forward with a foot resting on an item of furniture. Bourne shows his subjects supporting themselves on a natural feature, a rock.[63] *Lepcha Man* and *Lepcha Woman* are two unusual portraits. They are dissimilar from other portraits by Bourne, which are of groups, and the firm's studio portraits, which were taken with Victorian décor and conventional postures. In contrast these photographs show two single portraits in a natural environment. Although these portraits have similarities with pictures taken by anthropological photographers such as Watson and Kaye and Sergeant Wallace, they do not apply the traditional nineteenth-century models of anthropological photographic representations. Bourne positioned his subjects with an artist's eye that provides an appeal and a distinctiveness for the viewer: the natural environment which occupies a sizeable space in the proportion of the framing, the models who sat in a relaxed ordinary position, the sharpness of the

Figure 5.2 Samuel Bourne (1869) *Lepcha Man of Sikkim, Darjeeling*
[Rubenstein Library, Duke University – Image 2020].

Lepchas contrasting with an 'out of focus' background that softens the pictures. Bourne 'flatters' his subject and this attracts the viewer's curiosity and imagination. His portraiture of the Lepchas appears to accord with a more general approach to the tribe during that period. In 1869 the first superintendent of Darjeeling described their strength and nobility, qualifying them as 'the most interesting and pleasing of all the tribes around Darjeeling' and 'always continued to be the most liked by the Europeans'; comparisons showing an affinity between the British society and the Lepchas', unlike the Hindoos.[64] Lepchas were thus considered less dirty than Tibetans, taking care of their body, and especially their hair, which they washed, oiled and plaited.[65] As with most of the tribes of India, they did not follow the apparent distinct caste system of the vast subcontinent and thus did not conform to the general Indian imagery, but somehow represented the primitive state of humanity as a whole, including Western societies: an appealing dichotomy to the British (Figure 5.2).

Born into a wealthy family and having lost her mother when young, Gertrude Bell (1868–1926) was from an early age independent-minded.[66] She received a university education not at all common for women, and became one of the leading female travellers of her lifetime, famous for her intervention in the Middle East as an archaeologist and diplomatist. Throughout she produced diaries, writings and a vast correspondence with members of her family, friends, academics and politicians, including David Lloyd George, Winston Churchill, Richard Doughty-Wylie and T.E. Lawrence. Her photographs are also an important part of her work, and she took numerous portraits of local populations, and pictures of archaeological sites, monuments and landscapes of Greater Syria, Mesopotamia, Asia Minor and Arabia.[67]

Bell is now well remembered for her unusual and extraordinary life, but also her relations with local men and women in the countries she visited in the 1900s–1920s. Although regularly mentioned in her correspondences and in studies of her, not enough attention has, however, been given to Fattuh, her Armenian companion in travelling and 'the best servant I have ever had'.[68] Fattuh originally came into Bell's service in April 1905 on the recommendation of George Lloyd, and remained until her death. Bell spoke and wrote very highly of Fattuh, who 'met all her boats, put up all her tents, measured all her churches, and whom she cared for when ill as she would have cared for a member of her family'.[69] He is present in her photographs of monuments, archaeological sites and local landscapes (for instance, *Karaman (Laranda)* [Figure 5.3, 1905]) but he is also portrayed on his own (*Diyarbakir (Amida)* [1909]) or standing next to an artefact (*Konya (Iconium)* [Lion statue from Alaeddin Cami and kiosk, with Fattuh standing next to it] [1905]), or again while cooking or resting at the camp (*Untitled* [Fattuh at Gertrude Bell's camp] [Figure 5.4, 1905]).[70] But there also some portraits of Fattuh and Gertrude Bell together (for example, *Deghile* [Gertrude Bell and Fattuh standing in front of tent at camp] [cover image of this book, 1907]). Bell's evident rapport with him reveals that that in the solitude of her travelling, Fattuh became not only an important part of her work but also of her life (Figure 5.3).

   The companionship between this upper-middle-class British woman and her Caucasian male servant is somehow comparable to Garnett's friendships described in her writings. The prominence of Fattuh suggests how a different relationship between independent Western women, travelling far away from home in lands traditionally 'orientalised' by Western men, and Eastern

Figure 5.3   Gertrude Bell (1905), *Karaman (Laranda)*
[Gertrude Bell Archive, Newcastle University – D_103].

men was being made possible at the turn of the century. Bell opposed the extension of the franchise to women because she believed that until they became truly independent, socially and professionally, their political views would always be attached to those of men. By travelling to distant lands, where senses of class, race and gender blurred, Bell found herself to be equal to men (Figure 5.4).

Figure 5.4   Gertrude Bell (1905) *Untitled* [Fattuh at Gertrude Bell's camp]
[Gertrude Bell Archive, Newcastle University – D_073].

Bending colonial discourses about gender

The contemporary exploration of aestheticism in the Orient stemmed from
fascination and served the purpose of enjoyment. In some ways it was
the supposed violence and sexuality of the East that made it so alluring.
Here these texts and pictures partially contradict the usual image of oriental sexuality within the colonial discourse. In *Empire and Sexuality*, Hyam
argues how 'Empire provided ample opportunity for sexual indulgence.'[71]
He draws particular comparison with a Britain of 'frigid wives' and 'desex-
ualised children'.[72] Furthermore, DelPlato, by drawing on Foucault, shows
that 'sex in the nineteenth-century was understood not simply as pleasure
of the experience but as pleasure enhanced by telling and recreating it'.[73]
Here the actualities of Empire were retold, and often with more realistic
consequences. We understand that the nineteenth-century readership had
a particular aesthetic interest. Depictions of oriental cultures were, at the
time, primarily for the enjoyment of Europeans, but here also to challenge
gender relations and conformity in Britain via the depiction of those different 'orients'. Representations of gender roles and sexual desires inevitably
open on to questions of the readership. The plot of *Confessions of a Thug* for
Rushby 'is simple: a murderous anti-hero strangles his way to fortune and
fine women, some of whom he loves and some of whom he kills'.[74] Women

are actually rarely mentioned, and when they are, it is with familiar representations of oriental grace and sexualities; they are often 'dancing girls'.[75]
Ameer Ali particularly describes the dancing-girl Zora as 'exquisitely formed',
with dress 'of the richest description'; she is said to dance 'like the full
moon emerging from a cloud, sailed towards [him] with a slow and graceful
motion', which leaves Ameer Ali's soul 'fairly entranced'.[76] The novel is really
about the portrayal of Indian men and particularly Ameer Ali, the 'male odal-
isque'. Pal-Lapinski stresses the homoerotic desire that is nearly constant in
the narration and how it acted as 'a radical critique of Victorian domesticity'.
She also argues that *Confessions of a Thug* complicates Spivak's definition of
the 'native informant' since in the novel 'the identities of both native informant and ethnographer are called into question as each seems to collapse
into the other'.[77] It is indeed obvious that a close relationship between the
narrator and Ameer Ali is developing, leading to numerous signs of affection
between the two, and attraction of the narrator towards the Thug. It is not
dissimilar to the relationships between Garnett and the Albanian chiefs, and
Bell with Fattuh.

One of the main foci of these writings centres on religious practices.
Here the varied oriental cults disguise symbols of 'primitiveness', but also
conflicts and opposition to the West. The narrations and descriptions first
indulge a prim reaction to oriental rituals and customs, but the dramatic
and epic heroes and characters – be they fictional or real – present different forms of morals. Is the 'roomal' an instrument to free the Indians from
the Europeans? Is the apparent female submissive fate a symbol of archaism,
another understanding of the different power relation in the Eastern domestic sphere or just the acceptance of another system? Moreover, the attraction
to portray a violent 'Other' finds its origins first in the fact that nineteenth-
century British society was far from tranquil. Public debates between 1808
and 1835 distinguished between violent and non-violent offences as a principle upon which to ground the criminal law; 1862 saw a 'garrotting' panic;
and the era ended with much excitement about 'serial' killers. This violence was transcribed in crime and gothic novels, and helped define an
industrial society creating a new system of hierarchies. Exacerbating the constant violence enabled fear to spread and conferred the power to produce
disorientation, beyond or within rational comprehension. The significance
of the Indian Mutiny perhaps lies less in what it was and more in what
commentators professed it to be.

The effect of gender representations in these writings adds a more
complex – and often contrasting – dimension to the ways in which local populations are portrayed. The usual creation of colonial stereotypes lies in the
representation of the violent nature of the 'barbaric' man and the oriental
woman as 'object' of desire. Although these representations are sometimes
reflected, they are undermined by a more ambiguous dichotomy in the definition of sexuality. Rather than the more typical scheme – Western men

writing about Eastern women and Western men writing about disregarded or feminised Eastern men – these texts and photographs are from Western women describing Eastern women and men and Western men fascinated by Eastern men. The 'Oriental' woman becomes less alienated; the 'Other' male becomes less dissimilar and negative. The picturesque elements remain, but the definition of masculinity and femininity becomes less 'dichromatic', and more diverse and confused.

Notes

1. All of them are recognised as influential British travellers, whose writing and photographic productions were well known in the long nineteenth century via the sales of a large number of copies and through several exhibitions.
2. See also A. Sanders (1978) *The Victorian Historical Novel, 1840–1880* (Basingstoke: Macmillan); and D. David (2002) 'Empire, Race and the Victorian Novel', Chapter 5, and J. Bowen (2002) 'The Historical Novel', Chapter 14, in Brantlinger and Thesing (eds.) *A Companion to the Victorian Novel* (Oxford: Blackwell).
3. See E.W. Said (1978) *Orientalism* (London: Routledge and Kegan Paul).
4. For further details about this debate, see M. Anderson (2006) *Women and the Politics of Travel 1870–1914* (Cranbury: Fairleigh Dickinson University Press); T. Ballantyne and A. Burton (2005) *Bodies in Contact: Rethinking Colonial Encounters in World History* (Durham: Duke University Press); D. Birkett (2004) *Spinsters Abroad: Victorian Lady Explorers* (Stroud: Sutton); A. Blunt (1994) *Travel, Gender and Imperialism: Mary Kingsley and West Africa* (New York: Guilford Publications); J.F. Codell and D.S. Macleod (eds.) (1998) *Orientalism Transposed, The Impact of the Colonies on British Culture* (Hants: Ashgate); A. McClintock (1995) *Imperial Leather: Race, Gender and Sexuality in the Colonial Context* (New York: Routledge); and R.J.C. Young (2011) *Colonial Desire: Hybridity in Theory, Culture, and Race*, 2nd edn (London: Routledge).
5. S. Greenblatt (1991) 'Resonance and Wonder', in Karp and Lavine (eds.), *Exhibiting Cultures: The Poetics and Politics of Museum Display* (Washington: Smithsonion Institute Press), pp. 42–56.
6. H. White (2001) 'The Value of Narrativity in the Representation of Reality', in Rice and Waugh (eds.) *Modern Literary Theory* (New York: Arnold), p. 271.
7. Said, *Orientalism*, p. 21.
8. A. Green (1982) *Flaubert and the Historical Novel: Salammbô Reassessed* (Cambridge: Cambridge University Press), p. 18.
9. Green, *Flaubert*, pp. 19–21.
10. See E. Thornton (1837) *Illustrations of the History and Practices of the Thugs: and Notices of Some of the Proceedings of the Government of India, for the Suppression of the Crime of Thuggee*; P. Roy (1998) 'Discovering India, Imagining *Thuggee*' in *Indian Traffic: Identities in Question in Colonial and Postcolonial India* (Berkley: University of California Press), Chapter 2; A.L. Macfie (2008) '*Thuggee*: An Orientalist Construction?', *Rethinking History*, 12:3, 383–97; M. Sinha (1999) 'Giving Masculinity a History: Some Contributions from the Historiography of Colonial India', *Gender & History*, 11:3, 445–60; and G. Chakravarty (2005) *The Indian Mutiny and the British Imagination* (Cambridge: Cambridge University Press).
11. D.C. Rapoport (1984) 'Fear and Trembling: Terrorism in Three Religious Traditions', *The American Political Science Review*, 78:3, 659.

12. P.M. Taylor (1839, 1998) *Confessions of a Thug*, introduced and edited by P. Brantlinger (Oxford, New York: Oxford University Press), p. 5.
13. Ibid., p. 492.
14. Ibid., p. 244.
15. Ibid., p. 277.
16. Ibid., p. 334.
17. M. Poovey (2004) 'Ambiguity and Historicism: Interpreting *Confession of Thug*', *Narrative*, 12:1, 5.
18. Taylor, *Confessions*, pp. 56, 82, 413.
19. Ibid., p. 333.
20. M. Foucault (2003) 'About the Concept of the "Dangerous Individual"', in Rabinow and Rose (eds.), *The Essential Foucault* (New York: The New Press), p. 221.
21. Poovey, 'Ambiguity', 10.
22. Ibid., 4.
23. Taylor, *Confessions*, p. 102.
24. Ibid., p. 16.
25. A. Lyall, Review on *On the Face of the Waters* in *Edinburgh Review* (October 1899).
26. A. Thorpe (2007) 'Introduction', *On the Face of the Waters* (Dorset: Traviata Books), xvii.
27. F.A. Steel (1896), *On the Face of the Waters* (London: William Heinemann), xvii.
28. Ibid., p. 6.
29. Ibid.
30. S.M. Mallonee (2003) *Exploring Hybridity in Flora Annie Steel's* On the Face of Waters *and* The Law of the Threshold (unpublished master's thesis, University of Florida).
31. Steel, *Face of the Waters*, p. 243.
32. See also S. Foster (2004) 'Colonialism and Gender and Gender in the East: Representations of the Harem in the Writings of Women Travellers', *The Yearbook of English Studies*, 34; Nineteenth-Century Travel Writing, 6–17; and B. Melman (1992) *Women's Orients: English Women and the Middle East, 1718–1918: Sexuality, Religion and Work* (London: Macmillan).
33. Edward William Lane was also famous for his new translation of *One Thousand and One Nights* (1840).
34. S.S. Abdel-Hakim (2002) 'Sophia Poole: Writing the Self, Scribing Egyptian Women', *Alif: Journal of Comparative Poetics*, 22; The Language of the Self: Autobiographies and Testimonies, 3.
35. S. Poole (1844, 2003) *The Englishwoman in Egypt* (London: American University in Cairo Press), p. 14.
36. Poole, *Englishwoman*, pp. 215–16.
37. H.S. Watt (1991) 'Ida Pfeiffer: A Nineteenth-Century Woman Travel Writer', *The German Quarterly*, 64:3, 339.
38. Poole, *Englishwoman*, p. 109.
39. Ibid., p. 213.
40. Abdel-Hakim, 'Sophia Poole', 111.
41. Poole, *Englishwoman*, p. 215.
42. Said, *Orientalism*, p. 190.
43. Homi Bhabha (1994, 2004) *The Location of Culture* (London: Routledge), pp. 94–5.
44. Bhabha, *Location*, p. 95.
45. Poole, *Englishwoman*, p. 23.

46. R. Fowler, 'Lucy Mary Jane Garnett', *Oxford Dictionary of National Biography*.
47. Melman, *Women's Orients*, pp. 59–63.
48. L. Garnett (1890) *Women of Turkey, and Their Folk-lore* (London: David Nutt), p. 449. Here see also S.K.K. Khattak (2008) *Islam and the Victorians: Nineteenth Century Perceptions of Muslim Practices and Beliefs*, (London: I.B.Tauris); P.P. Laisram (2006) *Viewing the Islamic Orient: British Travel Writers of the Nineteenth Century* (London: Routledge); R. Lewis (2004) *Rethinking Orientalism: Women, Travel and the Ottoman Harem* (London: I.B.Tauris).
49. Garnett, *Women*, pp. 382–3.
50. Ibid., pp. 382–83.
51. Ibid., p. 393.
52. Ibid., p. 393.
53. Ibid., p. 452.
54. Melman, *Women's Orients*, pp. 165–69.
55. Garnett, *Women*, pp. 450–2.
56. For further reading on Samuel Bourne, photography in the British Empire and in British India, see X. Guégan (2014) *The Imperial Aesthetic: Photography, Samuel Bourne and the Indian Peoples in the Post-Mutiny Era* (Aldershot: Ashgate); X. Guégan (November 2011) 'Visualising Racial Alienation: Duality and Symbols in Bourne's India', *Visual Culture of British India*, in *Visual Culture in Britain*, special issue, 12:3, 349–65; C. Pinney (2008) *The Coming of Photograph in India* (London: British Library Publishing); J.R. Ryan (1997) *Picturing Empire, Photography and the Visualization of the British Empire* (London: Reaktion); G.D. Sampson and E.M. Hight (eds.) (2002) *Colonialist Photography, Imag(in)ing Race and Place* (London: Routledge).
57. T.R. Metcalf (1995) *Ideologies of the Raj* (Cambridge: Cambridge University Press), pp. 68–80.
58. F.G. Hutchins (1967) *The Illusion of Permanence: British Imperialism in India* (Princeton: Princeton University Press), pp. 153–85.
59. R. Inden (1990, 2000) *Imagining India* (Oxford: Blackwell Publishers), p. 67.
60. Ibid., p. 131.
61. R. Desmond (1982), *Victorian India in Focus: A Selection of Early Photographs from the Collection in the India Office Library and Records* (London: British Library Press), p. 54.
62. S. Bayly (1999) *Caste, Society and Politics in India from the Eighteenth Century to the Modern Age* (Cambridge: Cambridge University Press), p. 9.
63. A. Ollman (1983) *Samuel Bourne: Images of India* (California: The Friends of Photography (no. 33)), p. 20.
64. A. Campbell (1869), 'On the Lepchas', *The Journal of the Ethnological Society of London (1869–1879)*, 1:2, 145–57.
65. G. Gorer (1938) *Himalayan Village, an Account of the Lepchas of Sikkim* (London: Michael Joseph), p. 277.
66. L. Lukitz, 'Bell, Gertrude Margaret Lowthian', *Oxford Dictionary of National Biography*.
67. See E. Al-Yahya (2006) *Travellers in Arabia: British Explorers in Saudi Arabia* (London: Stacey International); and K.S. Howe (1997) *Revealing the Holy Land: The Photographic Exploration of Palestine* (California: Santa Barbara Museum of Art).
68. Gertrude Bell to H.B. Bustbirklisse, 24 April [13 May], 1905, in G. Bell (1927) *The Letters of Gertrude Bell*, Vol. I.

69. E. Moore (1980) 'Gertrude Bell (1868–1926)', *Bulletin (British Society for Middle Eastern Studies)*, 7:1, 12.

70. For her safety, Bell also had local soldiers who accompanied her but even though they sometimes appear in her writings and her photographs, it is only occasionally.

71. R. Hyam (1990) *Empire and Sexuality: The British Experience* (Manchester: Manchester University Press), p. 7.

72. Hyam, *Empire*, p. 58.

73. J. DelPlato (2002) *Multiple Wives, Multiple Pleasures: Representing the Harem, 1800–1875* (Cranbury: Associated University Press), p. 46. See also I. Grewall (1996) *Home and Harem: Nation, Gender, Empire, and the Cultures of Travel* (Durham: Duke University Press).

74. K. Rushby (2002) *Children of Kali* (London: Constable & Robinson), p. 8.

75. Taylor, *Confessions*, p. 103.

76. Ibid., pp. 105–7.

77. P. Pal-Lapinski (2005) *The Exotic Woman in Nineteenth-Century British Fiction and Culture* (Lebanon: University of New Hampshire Press), p. 31.

6
Empire Travel Guides and the Imperial Mind-set from the Mid-Nineteenth to the Mid-Twentieth Centuries

John M. MacKenzie

Empires throughout history have sought self-confidence and reassurance through erecting a sequence of fantasies designed to justify their existence and seek intellectual and ideological consolation. Their governmental and administrative elites fabricate such notions; their intellectuals, writers and educators develop and disseminate them; and the populace, more or less, accept them as evidence of their superiority. Such fantasies include the fantasy of global government and the related concept of universal monarchy, global and universal defined according to the world view of the Empire concerned. The British fantasy was primarily governmental, based upon culturally specific concepts of 'freedom' and administrative and legal arrangements that supposedly set them apart as incomparably capable of world rule. But they also indulged in the fantasy of global monarchy, evidenced by the raising of Queen Victoria's status to that of Empress (albeit theoretically solely in respect of India) and the appearance of her material presence in statuary throughout the Empire, not to mention on coinage and postage stamps. The second fantasy is the notion of a uniquely superior civilisation, one so distanced from the Empire's neighbours or, in modern times, overseas 'others' as to render rule both inevitable and morally appropriate. The corollary of this is the demarcation of all others as 'barbarians'. The British elite, deeply influenced as they were by ancient Greece and Rome, as well as by Edward Gibbon's *Decline and Fall*, extensively adopted this binary between 'civilisation' and 'barbarism'.[1] Taken together, these fantasies promoted the notion that the allegedly superior standards and ideas of the rulers conferred freedoms and liberty upon subject peoples in ways that had been unknown before. By the later nineteenth and twentieth centuries, freedom and liberty were seen to have been enhanced by modern scientific and medical ideas. Imperialists carried with them a new portmanteau of disciplines, theories and practices which included microbiology, germ theory and natural taxonomies of all global phenomena, as well as the new technologies of steam, electromagnetism, the telegraph and, in the twentieth century, electricity and all of its related media developments.

All of these concepts fed into the fantasy of free movement, of travel, which has received less attention than the others. Like all fantasies, this tends to be class and ethnically specific, though theoretically it contains within it the fantasy of ready availability. Of course the concept of free movement had not always been dependent on the provision of what were perceived as forms of good government – as pilgrimage throughout the ages and in so many societies had demonstrated – but particularly in modern times the two were seen to go inseparably together. Imperial rule offered unprecedented possibilities for movement, for officials, traders, the military and even those seeking forms of pilgrimage and leisure. We now know that opportunities for travel were viewed as one of the attributes of Roman rule. Roads, the provision of inns, forms of cartography and distance measurements, even accounts of such travel designed to encourage and help others, something akin to the 'guide book', obviously limited by problems of reproduction until the era of printing, all made their appearance in the ancient empires.[2]

But if travel has been for some time a major subject of modern scholarship, historical, literary, geographical and also economic, the fantasy of imperial free movement not least as expressed through its associated guide books has received very little attention.[3] Where guide books have been subjected to intensive study – for example, by Parsons – the principal focus has been on Europe.[4] The 'Grand Tour', with its origins in the late 1600s, massively developed in the eighteenth and early nineteenth centuries, has been subject to scrutiny by historians, art historians and those interested in the development of architectural and aesthetic styles in those eras.[5] The Grand Tour was, of course, an aristocratic and upper middle-class phenomenon, a means of socialising (and often also of corrupting) the young from these social classes, educating them in the history of the ancient world, in art and architecture, in concepts of cultural decline (the contrast between ancient splendours and modern realities) and even in forms of ethnography. The tutors of the grand tourists were invariably middle class, clergymen and aspiring intellectuals, and they often attempted to capitalise upon their experiences by producing accounts and guides for those who followed.[6] But it was with the great enlargement of the bourgeois classes in the nineteenth century that such notions of travel freedoms began to percolate down the social scale. Such 'bourgeoisification' of travel coincided with – and in some respects was consequent upon – the great expansion and technical improvement of print capitalism. Guide books were now published and printed in large numbers, designed to be easily carried from place to place and act as handy print 'tutors' for the tourists. If the abiding image of the

Grand Tour is of a sprig of the nobility (though aristocrats may actually have been in the minority on the Grand Tour) accompanied by his older and highly serious 'bear' or tutor, then that of guide book tourism is of the middle-class tourist in the midst of some great European or imperial site with his or her nose stuck in the pages of the informative guide book. That 'her' is important for while the Grand Tour was almost exclusively a male phenomenon, bourgeois tourism included women in increasingly large numbers.

This chapter is designed to take us out of the Eurocentric bias of most of those who have written about travel and its associated guide books, unveiling journeys in time as well as in space. Thus to a certain extent the Grand Tour constituted guided explorations of ancient empires. But from the middle of the nineteenth century, such space became global while the time dimension embraced Middle Eastern and Asian pasts, as well as more recent, though highly resonant, imperial events. Thus the British Empire came to constitute a prime location for the fantasy of free movement (a reality for some privileged people) expressed through travel. Genuinely worldwide in extent, with major possessions on all five continents, accessible by steamships and railways, offering a common language, familiar urban environments set in exotic natural contexts, as well as many familiar institutions, the British Empire seemed to offer the ultimate fantasy of such free and protected movement. As the nineteenth century progressed, it became increasingly comfortable and largely danger-free, offering the pleasurable sensation of global travel in new geographies and among strange and intriguing peoples, without in a sense leaving one's own country. Thus contact zones could be accessed by the extension of the comfort zones of one's own culture. The exotic could be explored in contiguous space to the familiar, with railway stations and Western-style hotels used as jumping-off points into the historical sites, bazaars, native or 'black' towns and villages of a tamed indigenous culture. As General Keating VC, a hero (for the British) of the Indian Mutiny or revolt, and Sir George Forrest put it in their introduction to the 1891 Murray's *Handbook* for the Indian subcontinent and adjacent territories, 'a trip to India is no longer a formidable journey or one that requires very special preparation. The Englishman who undertakes it merely passes from one portion of the British Empire to another' or, as we might put it today, from one part of the British world to a more distant one.[7] What follows is an examination of the considerable range of guides which are much less well known than European equivalents, and scarcely noticed by imperial or travel historians. Such guides exist in a number of forms. Murray, Baedeker and Macmillan were the leaders in the field and concentrated on what might be called pure tourism, but with a strong cultural slant. Shipping line guides had a tendency to be much more commercial in tone, as though they were explicitly operating as helps to the businessman as well as guides for tourists. The third category embraces guide books issued by colonial administrations, though their tone and objectives seem little different from those emanating from private enterprise. The fourth category might be described as 'personal' – that is, guide books which bore the stamp of a single author, illustrating individual prejudices and interests. What follows will mainly examine the mainstream guides of the principal publishers, with a briefer examination of some others.

John Murray (1808–92), the third of seven of that name who ran the remarkably durable family publishers between 1768 and 2002, had himself set out on a late version of the Grand Tour in 1829, a date which may be seen as constituting something of a watershed between the aristocratic Grand Tour and middle-class travel.[8] Perhaps it was his encounters with bourgeois travellers that led him to recognise that there was a market for such informative, handy-sized guide books. Murray's was prominent as the publisher of literary travellers and explorers of all sorts, and such travel and exploration would become one of the publishing phenomena of the century. The house was already famous as the publisher of Byron and would soon publish David Livingstone, perhaps regarded as the most heroic traveller of the times.[9] The guide book part of the business thus fitted the general thrust of Murray's interest and was able to capitalise on the developments in printing technology that helped to bring down unit costs. The number of guide books published ensured that this part of the business was extremely important until the early twentieth century, when Murray's detected a decline in the market and sold its 'guides' to Stanford (interestingly, with the exception of the handbook to India).[10] There must, indeed, have been a circular effect in this publishing activity. Once Murray's had provided them, the guide books became sufficiently popular that their very existence helped to prompt further tourism to territories that were so agreeably and helpfully described. The descriptive texts were written by authorities on the countries covered and the handbooks were organised into a section of preliminary information, followed by a whole succession of journeys from one point to another, usually following railway routes, with descriptions of places, people and antiquities encountered. Each section was headed by a general description with historical, geographical, ethnographic and other information. Thus the very organisation of the guide was redolent of travel.

Murray's first *Handbook* (after a preliminary testing of the market) had been one covering several European countries, issued in 1836.[11] This was swiftly followed by a plethora of individual country guides, including those for the British Isles. The one for Scotland clearly capitalised upon the expansion of Romantic travelling to that country, encouraged by Sir Walter Scott's writings and famous travellers such as the composer Mendelssohn. But even as this great European expansion took place, Murray had already set his sights upon a wider world. Murray's and their successors would be distinguished by their global reach, something absent from all of the proto-guidebooks written earlier. The *Handbook to Egypt and the Sudan* was issued as early as 1847, only 11 years after the publication of that first

European guide book. This illustrates the fact that the antiquities of the Nile Valley were beginning to be accessed by increasing numbers of tourists. Napoleon's invasion with his savants and their subsequent books had firmly put Egypt on the map of travellers and artists. The journeys of the artist David Roberts and his magnificent lithographs (with reproductions still sold to tourists in Egypt today) and, for example, Amelia Edwards had produced growing interest in the monuments of ancient Egypt.[12] Murray now described such antiquities in considerable detail. Moreover, the Nile had further patriotic resonances for the British. Napoleon had been defeated in 1798 in Nelson's naval action at Aboukir Bay, the Battle of the Nile, an iconic moment in the history of empire later mentioned in imperial textbooks and every 'guide' to the eastern Mediterranean.

Murray soon extended his coverage in the Middle East, demonstrating his taste for elaborate titles as he did so, such as *Murray's Handbook for Travellers in Turkey in Asia, including Constantinople, the Bosphorus, Plain of Troy, Isles of Cyprus, Rhodes etc., Smyrna, Ephesus, and the Routes to Persia, Bagdad, Moosool etc with General Hints for Travellers in Turkey, Vocabularies etc.,* with the three etceteras providing hints of the extensive information to follow. Thus even the title seemed to offer the image of a journey. This *Handbook*, first issued in 1847, had already reached its fourth edition (revised) by 1878. Here, Murray's not only served up much of one empire, the Ottoman, for penetration by the citizens of another, the British, but also neatly delineated some of the principal places for travels into ancient 'heritage', such as Troy and Ephesus. The title also conveyed to the knowing reader the fact that the Ottoman Empire was already in decline, since the British were even then acquiring the island of Cyprus. Meanwhile debates and conflicts relating to the Bosphorus, access from the Black Sea to the Mediterranean, to Persia and to potential railway construction to Bagdad were major issues in European diplomacy and would continue to be so up until the First World War. Thus travel and its accompanying guide clearly represented both aspects of the designs of one empire upon another and some of the diplomatic tensions and conflicts of the era.

1878 was, indeed, a pivotal year and this remarkable guide book duly reflected this. It was quick to note the British acquisition of Cyprus at the Congress of Berlin, ending the Russo-Turkish War. This allowed Murray's to dilate on some of the significance of these events (p. 175):

> [Cyprus's] position is thus central and commanding, making it to a large extent the key to the commercial and military supremacy of the East. In the hands of England, and garrisoned by a large force of English troops, it will effectually control the turbulent tribes of Syria and Asia Minor; while it will at the same time, by the establishment of law and order, and the encouragement of native industry, tend to develop the enormous resources of those rich and fair countries. The enterprise of resident

English merchants, and of natives who follow their example, have hitherto been the chief sources of wealth and progress in the great cities of the
Levant; but their efforts have been largely neutralised by a corrupt government and local disturbances. Now the presence of English troops in
Cyprus, and the general exercise of English superintendence, will enforce
reform and give security to all classes. Christians of every sect will attain
and hold their rightful place, and will ere long gain a power and an
influence that must give new life to the whole of Asiatic Turkey.

This is a perfect expression of the fantasies of empire. The global reach
of government; 'pacification' by British troops; the enlightening effects of
trade; and the inevitable advance of Christianity are all here. The clear implication is that the acquisition of Cyprus would aid the spread of civilisation
over barbarism, the 'turbulent tribes'.

Moreover, this advance of the British Empire in the eastern Mediterranean
would extend the civilising effects of the new technology into more areas
of the Middle East. Later in the *Handbook* (p. 384) the question of Cyprus
returns:

The occupation of Cyprus by England will probably tend to revise the
project of a railway from the shore of the Mediterranean along the
Euphrates valley to the Persian Gulf, as a through route to India.
It may therefore be interesting to describe the intervening country, the
difficulties to be surmounted, and the objects to be attained.

In fact, these high hopes for Disraeli's acquisition of Cyprus did indeed
turn out to be fantasies. Cyprus never fulfilled the role hoped for it by the
British and by Murray's *Handbook*. Instead it became virtually a forgotten
possession.[13] Nor did the British manage to build the Euphrates Valley railway; instead, German ambitions to build the Bagdad railway became a major
source of tension between Britain and Germany before the First World War.
Indeed, the British, in the shape of T.E. Lawrence, spent more time blowing up railways in the Ottoman Empire than building them. In short, the
Suez Canal constituted the only 'through route' to India that the British
needed. But it is indicative that a tourist handbook of 1878 was, in effect,
issuing British propaganda for Middle Eastern ambitions.

Egypt was by this time a major tourist destination, having developed considerably since the 'attention of the civilised world was directed to Egypt'
by Napoleon's invasion.[14] Many more guide books were issued and Thomas
Cook organised his popular tours. As is well known, Cook's even provided
the steamer services on the Nile, the attractively advertised 'Nile Flotilla'.
Baedeker's Guides to Egypt were compiled by Professor Georg Steindorff of
Leipzig, the city where the publisher was located. Interestingly, Baedeker's
texts were much 'cooler' in their approach to imperial rule; they also

provided more historical and technical detail. So far as Egypt was concerned, Baedeker restricted its imperial content to a very brief description of the events of 1882 (the defeat of Urabi Pasha at the battle of Tel-el-Kebir) and simply remarked that 'since then British influence has been paramount' (p. c). Nevertheless, a positive comment was added: 'In Egypt itself numerous reforms were accomplished by the British administration, and in especial, much was done to further agriculture by the building of light railways and the extension of the irrigation system' (p. ci). Perhaps this acknowledgment of British achievements was a nod to the British tourist market. In the case of the Sudan, the 'sixth remodelled edition' of Baedeker's *Handbook for Travellers to Egypt and the Sudan* (1908), published just ten years after the British defeat of the Khalifa (the Mahdi's successor) and reconquest of the upper Nile could not fail to mention the rapid remodelling of Khartoum, the heroic status of General Gordon and the founding of the Gordon Memorial College (pp. 412–13). Indeed, Baedeker also described travel in Egypt and the Sudan through the connections formed by the steamers on the Nile. For example, the description of the temple of Dendera was restricted to what could be taken in during the hour allowed by the visit of the mail steamer (p. v).

Egyptian tourism built up to such an extent that another celebrated publisher, Macmillan, joined in the provision of a travel guide. This was first published in 1901 and included Palestine, as did the second edition of 1903. From 1905, however, the guide was restricted to Egypt and the Sudan. Further editions were published in 1907 and 1908, the latter with the extensive title *Guide to Egypt and the Sudan including a Description of the Route through Uganda to Mombasa*. The further extension of the British Empire in the space of only a decade (with the confirmation of protectorates over Uganda and Kenya and the reconquest of the Sudan) now rendered an 'all-red overland route' from North to East Africa a possibility (Gondokoro to Mombasa briefly described on pp. 165–8). Macmillan's 1908 guide asserted that the 'increasing importance of the Sudan has led us to enlarge the section dealing therewith', as well as extend much of the guide's preliminary information (p. v). Both Baedeker and Macmillan adopted the role of protecting the traveller 'against extortion' (Baedeker on the first page of the preface). Macmillan proclaimed that 'bakshish would seem to be the first word the Egyptian child learns so great is the cupidity of the tourist-spoilt Arab' (p. 5). Inevitably, Macmillan was a great deal less reticent about British rule. In describing the events of 1882, the guide asserted that because 'the country was unable to govern itself, it was natural that England should dictate a policy to Egypt, and take every legitimate means to see it carried out. English officials were placed at the head of departments' (p. 13). As a result, 'under English control, the rapid recuperation of Egypt was complete' (p. 14). Hence a combined Anglo-Egyptian force had not only retaken the Sudan but had also pushed the French out of Fashoda (Kodok). Soon Khartoum was being laid out with squares and wide streets, symbolic of its new civilised town planning.

Government offices were removed from Omdurman; buildings were generally built of stone; and a beautiful oasis of gardens and trees (though still 'very young') was created. It is noticeable that while Baedeker referred to 'Britain' throughout, Macmillan used 'England'. Moreover, Baedeker's attention to detail ensured that the stone of the buildings was identified as Kerreri sandstone, while considerable botanical detail was added to the descriptions of Khartoum's gardens (p. 412).

Thomas Cook also issued a *Tourist Handbook to Egypt and the Sudan*, priced at ten shillings in 1913. Most of Cook's handbooks related to European countries (there were at least 15 by the twentieth century), but handbooks were also issued for more exotic destinations. As well as Egypt and the Sudan, there were Algeria and Tunisia, Palestine and Syria, Lower Palestine, Galilee and Syria and – the only one to break out of the Mediterranean and Middle Eastern worlds – Burma. In 1913 the latter was priced at a mere shilling. But Cook's seem to have recoiled from moving into other imperial destinations, even though they conducted many tours to India and other parts of the Empire. Piers Brendon suggests that these guide books (collectively) sold some 10,000 copies a year, but that the company never succeeded in developing them into a major reputable series.[15] It is indeed noticeable that Brendon himself seems to show very little interest in them, following the tradition of ignoring this important source of travel literature.

By the twentieth century, one of the most extensive and, in a sense, monumental of all guides was Murray's classic description of India. In fact, the publisher had created its own 'through route' to India at a surprisingly early date. It is fascinating that the first Murray's *Handbook* on India (in one volume) appeared in 1858, just a year after the 1857 revolt. It was presumably in preparation before the notorious Year of the 'Great Fear', but its publication coincided with the transfer of India from the East India Company to the Crown and Queen Victoria's declaration on the principles by which India would be governed. But tourism to India inevitably made a slow start, with the necessity of the land crossing of Egypt from the Mediterranean to the Red Sea, and only fully took off after the opening of the Suez Canal in 1869. Moreover, the amount of information available had grown to such an extent that Murray's was soon issuing guides to the different regions of India: Madras (1879), Bombay (1881), Bengal (1882) and the Punjab (1883). They were restored into a single volume from 1891, when the elaborate title indicated the full geographical scope of the enterprise: *The Handbook for Travellers in India, Burma and Ceylon, including All British India, the Portuguese and French Possessions, and the Protected Native States*. The 'protected native states' were better known as the princely states, those extensive areas of India not ruled directly by the British but over which they exercised suzerainty through powerful 'residents' positioned at each court.

The handbooks became massive compendia of information and travel guidance. They were presumably bought by officials, army officers,

journalists, educationalists, some missionaries, travellers and visitors, including those seeking commercial opportunities, and were repeatedly reissued. The ninth edition, running to 726 pages plus 175 numbered in roman numerals for the preliminary information, appeared in 1918 at the end of the First World War, though in many respects it followed the pattern of earlier editions. Although the guide gave the appearance of being relatively uncommitted, its structure and the selection of topics made it apparent that this was a restrained paean of praise to the British Empire and its alleged 'progress'. The preliminary pages laid out the route to India, embracing Gibraltar, where the significance of its 'Englishness' and its key strategic history were described, as was that of Malta. From there, ships continued through the British sphere of influence in Egypt, the Suez Canal and Aden before arriving in Bombay (Mumbai). Even the sea lanes were thus seen as an 'all-red' route. After the exposition of the journey, the *Handbook* laid out the findings of the 1911 Census of India, suggesting that there were over 244 million Indians in the territories directly administered by Britain, that the princely states and agencies contained 70 million and that commanding all of this there were no more than 123,000 British people, two-thirds of them soldiers. The population of each of the many territories of British India appeared in extensive tables, as did the statistics of the ethnic and religious make-up of the subcontinent. Thus a fundamental justification for British rule – that India was immensely heterogeneous, so fragmented that foreign overrule was essential – was implied in these pages of statistics. This was also implicit in the historical sections, emphasising the diversity of indigenous polities and the internecine strife that allegedly preceded the British arrival.

A lengthy passage followed on Indian ancient monuments and the establishment and development of the Archaeological Survey by the British (starting in 1860 under the Viceroy Canning, developed in 1878 under Lytton, and particularly forwarded through the genuine interest of Curzon at the turn of the century). This suggested that it was through foreign rule that the great heritage of India could best be preserved, that much conservation work had been effected and that 'wise and comprehensive reforms' to the whole system had been accomplished in the previous quarter-century. A notable section followed on the 'industrial arts' of India, something that had been much emphasised in the great exhibitions in Britain during the previous decades, arts and craft products that included painting, metalwork, wood-carving, box-making, jewellery, silk, damascening and much else. But an indication of the peace brought by British rule, an essential aspect of imperial propaganda, lay in the decline of the crafts of the armourer's because the incidence of warfare had been in abeyance. There followed passages on irrigation, sanitation, the Lady Dufferin Fund (established in 1885 for female medical education), Lady Hardinge's Medical College for women, statistics of massive Post Office and telegraphic activity, the extent of railways and their continuing extension, commerce and trade, and the situation of 'native Christians'. The general thrust of all of this preliminary information was provided in a ten-page description of the Indian Mutiny of 1857, 'the most important episode in the whole history of British rule in India' (p. cxlv). The conclusion was that 'Both races have learned their lesson. The best proof of this is that, whereas formerly sepoy mutinies were of frequent occurrence, no single example has occurred in the space of sixty years to revive memories of the great tragedy of 1857' (p. clv). In such passages, the *Handbook* clearly expresses the British imperial mind-set.

A timeline of events in the history of the contact between Europeans and India from the sixteenth century to 1917 covers a number of pages and inevitably concentrates on the era of British rule and the years of authority of each viceroy. A glossary of 'native terms' is followed by a good deal of information about the several steamship companies (including those of Italy and France) by which the European traveller could access India, Ceylon and Burma, including the frequency of their sailings. The central meat of the *Handbook*, characterised by the Arabic numeral pages, kicks off with an account of Bombay and its environs, its buildings, facilities, places of recreation, clubs and much else. Thus Bombay is highlighted as the 'gateway of India', the name given to the triumphal arch and gateway built in Bombay Harbour commemorating the visit of George V and Queen Mary for their Durbar in 1911.

As with most nineteenth-century guide books – a pattern clearly established by Murray and Baedeker in their respective publications – the formula is then to take the tourist on a succession of 'routes' around the country, progressing by easy stages from point to point. In the India section of the guide there are no fewer than 36 of these 'routes' before it offers guidance for travelling in Burma and Ceylon. In following these routes it is striking that the tourist and traveller is expected to be interested in war and battlefield tourism – long before it became such a characteristic of Europe in the twentieth century – in the many campaigns through which the British asserted control of the Indian subcontinent. There are frequent diversions to describe both such campaigns and battles, and the redoubts of the Marathas and other Indian peoples. But the most significant aspect of this battlefield tourism relates yet again to the 1857 'Mutiny'. In the 1918 guide, at a time when heightened Indian nationalist activity might have been expected to cause the toning down of such material, Murray's devoted (in addition to the preliminary pages mentioned above) no fewer than six pages to the revolt in the section on Delhi, five in the pages relating to Cawnpore (Kanpur) (including a sketch map of the Cawnpore entrenchment) and nine pages under Lucknow.

Under Delhi we hear of the exploits of Sir John Lawrence, Major General Barnard and 'one of the best soldiers that India ever produced', Brigadier General John Nicholson. Statistics are offered for the Siege of Delhi, which is summed up as follows: 'no more marked display of endurance and steady courage than that shown by the Delhi Field Force during the summer of 1857 can be found in the whole splendid record of the British and Indian armies' (p. 258). At Cawnpore we hear of 'the cowardly massacre of a large number of women and children' (p. 407), of General Wheeler's entrenchment, and of all the commemorative plaques and sculptures to be found in the Memorial Church, together with the considerable cost of its erection (p. 411). When the traveller reaches Lucknow there are references to the various iconic places which should be visited (pp. 387–96). The siege of the residency, together with its relief, was perhaps the most famous event of the revolt, much celebrated in plays, paintings and novels set in India. 'The residency is the spot which all Englishmen will wish to visit first in Lucknow' (p. 395). It is a place of memories and of memorials, the latter carefully recounted, a central symbol of 'sacrifice' in the alleged advance and progress of British rule in India, constituting the key moment in the consolidation of British power. The 'heroes', generals Sir James Outram, Sir Colin Campbell and Sir Henry Havelock, are duly extolled. In the copy of Murray's *Handbook* owned by myself, it is clear that the former owner (possibly called C.A. Gawith) either visited Lucknow or intended doing so. In the list of hotels in the town, the Carlton is described as 'good' and has been duly ticked.

While it is not the exclusive concern of the *Handbook* – there is a good deal about temples, mosques, palaces, fortresses, caves and sculptures from the Indian past – much of the content constitutes an unveiling of the sites of memory of British rule, as well as the military contact zones (in this case invariably internal rather than on frontiers) between dominant and subordinate peoples, and what may be called the 'places of immortality' associated with imperial heroes. Empire is justified not only by the alleged achievements (as in trade and post office statistics, irrigation works and Western medicine) but also in terms of a sort of sanctification by past events. Thus the Murray's *Handbook* unconsciously reveals its affinities with the European pilgrim guides of the past. Imperial travel was a sort of 'pilgrim's progress' in which the traveller charted the historical journey from a form of political and cultural 'darkness' into light. If the horrors of the First World War would seem to have made such an optimistic progression more difficult, particularly as it had helped to stimulate much resistance and turbulence in India itself, nonetheless imperial optimism seemed to survive at least in the pages perused by the bourgeois traveller.

These guides were the classics of the imperial genre. The second category, those provided by shipping lines, included a number of popular examples. Perhaps the most notable was the *Castle Line Guide to South Africa* 'for the use of Tourists, Sportsmen, Invalids and Settlers'. It may be that the inclusion of 'businessmen' in this list would have exposed imperial money-making too openly, but there can be little doubt that it was intended for them too. This guide was inseparably associated with flamboyant and wealthy Scottish ship-owner Sir Donald Currie. He had issued the *Handbook and Emigrants'*

Guide to South Africa in 1888, no doubt to increase the number of emigrant passengers using his already considerable fleet.[16] But he later heard of the existence of *Brown's Guide to South Africa*, first issued in 1893. This had been produced by two brothers of that name and it is an indication of its great popularity that the first edition, of 2,000 copies, was sold out within weeks of its first appearance.[17] South Africa was in the midst of a gold boom and Currie was not to be outsmarted. He swiftly bought the brothers Brown out and the guide was reissued under the imprimatur of the Castle Line. From 1900, when two lines amalgamated, it became the Union-Castle Line guide and continued to be published, virtually on an annual basis, until the 1960s. This Line had an exceptionally extensive fleet serving islands in the Atlantic (such as Ascension and St. Helena), ports in South-West Africa, the Cape, Natal, as well as East African ports accessed by the Suez Canal and Aden, including calls in Somaliland, Kenya, Tanganyika, Zanzibar and Mozambique, with Durban as the terminus. The Browns did well under the aegis of Currie, for they continued to edit the guide for 45 years. It included East Africa from 1910 and ultimately became so extensive that it was divided into two volumes in 1950. It grew from 420 pages in 1899–1900 to a two-volume combined size of some 1,300 pages in 1957, by which time it also included an atlas of 60 maps.[18]

The early guides offered advice about booking coaches to the gold fields, but soon such advice was restricted to railway lines as the network grew. The supposedly health-giving climate of the region was emphasised, particularly for chest complaints, together with the number of spas available. Another environmental concern was the existence of wild animals and opportunities for hunting and shooting, later transformed into concerns with game-watching in national parks. But the prime focus was on economic matters, on mineral resources and their prospects (often highly inflated), on opportunities for farming, both stock-raising and arable (with information about soil types, temperature and rainfall), and on many other employment opportunities for settlers. There was also a fascination with modernity, with the scale and amenities of cities, the grandeur of their buildings, their facilities and their travel infrastructures. Africans, despite their numbers, received relatively little attention except insofar as advice was offered on the advantages and limitations of their employment. Some historical content tended to emphasise African rulers whom the British admired. Early editions revealed prejudice about the alleged backwardness of Boers (Afrikaners) and Portuguese, although this was toned down later, particularly when Afrikaners came to dominate politics after the creation of the Union of South Africa in 1910. Nevertheless, battlefield tourism was a significant theme, relating to both the celebrated campaigns of the Zulu War of the 1870s and of the two Anglo-Boer wars, notably that of 1899–1902.

The emphases on the information about Central and East Africa was somewhat different (South Africa was deemed to include Northern and Southern Rhodesia and Nyasaland), with more on tourism, wildlife and natural spectacles (the Victoria Falls, Rift Valley Lakes and Mount Kilimanjaro). By the interwar years the guides moved into information about roads and the use of 'motors' for tourism. In these guides the practice of dividing the information into a number of routes, common in Baedeker and Murray, was also followed. Extensive historical sections generally seemed free from overt ideological and propagandist intent, though the implications of a notably progressive imperial rule were, of course, pervasive throughout. Sections about missionaries in the region generally extolled their activities in the spread of education to indigenous peoples and in 'the spread of civilisation'. All of these guides contained large numbers of advertisements for hotels, travel and safari companies, clothes and provision suppliers, even pharmaceuticals and much else. The effect of such commercial advertising was to underline the familiar conditions and brands that the traveller would encounter, although the appealing 'wildness' of some safaris was also stressed, as well as the extent to which game laws were relatively ineffectual in more remote districts.

The Union-Castle Line was not, however, alone. The London publisher Allen and Unwin also published the English-language *African Handbook and Traveller's Guide*, edited by Otto Martens and Dr O. Karstedt for the German African Lines. This was originally issued in German in 1930 and appeared in English in 1932. These dates represent the comeback of German shipping lines in the interwar years as well as the renewed interest of Germany in the colonies, which intensified as the 1930s wore on. It was more comprehensive than the Union-Castle guides, containing sections about the Anglo-Egyptian Sudan, East Africa, South Africa, Central Africa, the Portuguese territories, the Congo and all of the West African colonies, from vast ones, such as French West and Equatorial Africa right down to the smaller ones, such as Spanish Guinea. All of these were contained within 950 pages. While sections about history inevitably conveyed the usual progressive biases, political comment was limited – after all, there was an English-speaking market and Germany had lost all of its colonies in Africa in 1919.

Historians have often commented on the category of 'informal empire', territories outside the formal rule of European empires but nonetheless very much part of the imperial economic nexus. Perhaps the most obvious example was South America, where colonies threw off the yoke of Spain and Portugal in the early nineteenth century but, although protected by the US 'Monroe Doctrine' of 1823 declaring them a sphere of American influence, fell into the orbit of the economic interests of the new European empires, notably Britain. Frederick Alcock had first published *Trade and Travel in South America* in 1903.[19] While not a guide book in the true sense, it effectively operated as such, with a large number of illustrations and maps, a good deal about shipping lines, and information for businessmen and tourists. Apparently it sold so well that a second edition at a 'popular price' was issued in 1907. Competition appeared just after the First World War when a journalist, W.H. Koebel, set about issuing handbooks about South America, an enterprise taken over by H. Davies in the interwar years.[20] These stressed the opportunities for British trade and investment as well as the pleasures of tourism in the region. Each of the territories was surveyed in turn, offering an interesting blend of tourist advice with business analysis. As in formal empire, advances in infrastructure and in the 'civilisation' of the cities were stressed, including fine hotels, sporting facilities, railways, river steamers and much else to ease the passage of the traveller. In one glorious passage, British travellers are reassured that although there were many 'primitive touches' in South America, afternoon tea, 'made as it ought to be made', was available in all of the principal cities.[21] Surely nothing could be more calculated to offer reassurance to the British tourist and businessman! Although this work was not directly associated with a shipping line, it is clear that major lines like Royal Mail and Pacific Steam used it extensively, advertising prominently and listing their offices and agencies throughout Europe and South America.

Egypt and the Sudan were, as we have seen, a prime focus of the exotic tourist guide. In 1910 the Sudan Government actually issued its own official guide book.[22] The publication of this guide was an indication either of the popularity of tourism or of the extent to which the administration of the Anglo-Egyptian condominium was eager to encourage it. Purporting to offer information about the Sudan railways and steamers, it actually went much further. Trumpeting the fact that the Sudan could be reached in a mere eight days from London, the guide stressed the excitements of a visit, the glories of its sites and sights, extolling through both text and advertisements the extent to which the Sudan had been pulled into a Eurocentric vision of modernity so soon after its reconquest from the forces of what was seen as Islamic fundamentalism. It was lavishly illustrated with attractive coloured end papers.

By 1925, another country which was issuing lavish guide books was New Zealand, a territory which had begun to encourage tourism, not least through the establishment of a separate government department (the first British colony to do so) from the early twentieth century. This guide was clearly designed not just to hymn the great beauties of the country but also to encourage migration as well as tourism, stressing the reputation of the country as 'The Brighter Britain of the South', the country's transport infrastructure, the grandeur of its cities and its potential in forestry, agriculture, pastoralism, manufactures and much else.[23] One of its objectives was to issue propaganda for 'a self-reliant empire', an empire of complementary economies standing against a hostile world, through protectionism if necessary (at a time when ideas about just such protectionism were advancing towards the Ottawa conference of 1932 in the wake of the great crash in the global economy). Another objective was to emphasise the notion that the Maori were a people of 'high culture' who had won the 'respect and admiration of Europeans', even suggesting that ethnologists believed that they were connected with the Aryan races who had moved eastwards across the globe (p. 108). Thus, unlike in other colonies, the indigenous peoples posed no risk to European settlers, a fact implied in the statistic that there were only 53,000 of them, a figure which included 'half-castes'.

Among more personal works, *The Orient Line Guide: Chapters for Travellers by Sea and by Land* has the appearance of a shipping line guide, but it was by a single author, W.J. Loftie, an Irish clergyman (of the Anglican communion) who stamped his own eccentricities upon it. He was billed as editing it 'for the Managers of the Line' and it was published for the Orient and Pacific Steam Navigation Company by the travel publisher Edward Stanford, first appearing in 1882 in a lavish hardback edition, but priced very reasonably at half a crown.[24] Many editions followed, concentrating on the advanced technology and engineering of the company's ships sailing to Australia and New Zealand. Loftie created a paean of praise to the British Empire, emphasising the ways in which the route to Australia touched on so many British territories and passed through seas made famous by celebrated naval battles of the past which had confirmed British supremacy. As well as exhibiting considerable interests in meteorology and astronomy, he seems also to have been a social Darwinist. For him, the great advantage of the Australian colonies was that their indigenous people were doomed to extinction and that their culture was so primitive that settlers need have no anxiety about dispossessing a people lacking little history or cultural presence. Thus Australia displayed no 'ancient civilisation' and had been wrested from 'barbarism and desolation' (pp. 304, 335). Even the Maoris, who were generally placed higher in the global racial scale, had been defeated in warfare and were in serious decline (p. 347). Thus nothing stood in the way of the forces of modernism, so well represented in the cities of both Australia and New Zealand, as well as in the many economic achievements of their settlers. It is true that some of these pronounced opinions were toned down in the twentieth century, but Loftie's shipping guide represents a relatively extreme form of a highly prejudiced and ideologically slanted form of travel narrative and advice.

Another highly opinionated guide book was Sir Algernon Aspinall's *Pocket Guide to the West Indies*, published by Stanford and first appearing in 1907, shortly after the Jamaica earthquake of that year.[25] Aspinall was a London barrister who established a considerable reputation for himself as a West Indian expert, serving on a number of government bodies. Like Loftie, he emphasised a great imperial past and grand naval successes (Nelson's association with Antigua and with Anguilla were highlighted, pp. 122, 228). Strikingly, the history of slavery and of revolt in the West Indies were ignored. There were only two references to slavery, with the emphasis on abolition (pp. 42–3, 284). The only entries for 'black' related to geographical features given that name. The abolition of slavery was important mainly because of the labour problems that it created, problems that were solved by the introduction of 'coolie' or Indian labour. Aspinall mainly concentrated on the supposed achievements of white settlers and surveyed the economic role of the islands entirely from that standpoint. Many pages were devoted to the ease of reaching the West Indies, the several shipping companies available, the comfort of ships and hotels, the glories of tourism there and the convenience of inter-island connections. The tenth edition, revised by Professor J. Sydney Dash, was issued in 1954 and continued to be reprinted until at least 1960. Astonishingly, even at this late date, the format continued to be the same as in 1907, and blacks continued to be well-nigh invisible.

This final point relating to the Aspinall guide is significant. The shelf life of many of these guides (the Union-Castle one is an excellent example) was extraordinarily long. These imperial guides continued to be published almost down to the appearance of a wholly new breed of guide book of the 'Lonely Planet' and 'Rough Guide' variety.[26] They therefore seem to offer further evidence of the continuation of an imperial mind-set right down to the era of decolonisation. The guides cheerfully sailed on in their old courses ignoring the political, racial and economic storms that raged around them. Unwary travellers setting out on a voyage in the 1950s or even the early 1960s could find themselves reading travel material displaying the same mind-set as that disseminated in the second half of the nineteenth century. Thomas Cook had suggested that his handbooks 'possess three-fold advantage – they excite interest in anticipation; they are highly useful on the spot; and they help to refresh the memory in after days'.[27] This could well be said of all guide books, at any time, and even of aspects of all travel writing. But we should be alert to a fourth and fifth characteristic of advantage to the scholar. They offer an astonishingly clear window into another world, into an imperial landscape and mentality forcibly etched into the ways in which their editors organised them and laid out their material. The fantasies of empire can be found everywhere and their often striking silences speak as loudly as their prolix descriptions. The copies used in this research indicate that they were indeed used, for they seem to have been annotated by their original readers, sometimes bringing statistics up to date. Moreover, their existence and their considerable sales provide evidence of the popularisation of imperial values and alleged colonial triumphs, at the very least among bourgeois travellers. They may also have been used and selectively read by some emigrants and by some servants of elite tourists. They are redolent of an age and they have received far less attention than they deserve.

Notes

1. A. Rogers and R. Hingley (2010) 'Edward Gibbon and Francis Haverfield: The Traditions of Imperial Decline' in M. Bradley (ed.) *Classics and Imperialism in the British Empire* (Oxford: Oxford University Press), pp. 189–209.
2. N.T. Parsons (2007) *Worth the Detour: A History of the Guidebook* (Stroud: The History Press), Chapters 1 and 2.
3. J.M. MacKenzie (2005) 'Empires of Travel: British Guide Books and Cultural Imperialism in the 19th and 20th Centuries' in J.K. Walton, *Histories of Tourism: Representation, Identity and Conflict* (Clevedon: Channel View Publications), pp. 19–38 was a first attempt at such a study. See also L. Withey (1998) *Grand Tours and Cook's Tours, a History of Leisure Travel, 1750–1915* (London: Aurum Press) for a brief overview.
4. Parsons, *Worth the Detour*.
5. From an extensive literature, the most accessible are J. Black (1992) *The British Abroad: The Grand Tour in the Eighteenth Century* (Stroud: The History Press); J. Black (2003) *France and the Grand Tour* (Basingstoke: Palgrave Macmillan) and (2003) *Italy and the Grand Tour* (New Haven, Conn.: Yale University Press); and C. Hibbert (1987) *The Grand Tour* (London: Methuen Publishing).
6. Parsons, *Worth the Detour*, Chapter 7.
7. J. Murray (1891) *Handbook for Travellers to India* (London), xv–xvi. The 'British World' is a concept much used by imperial historians in recent times. It was used as the overall title for a series of conferences, held in Britain, Canada, South Africa, Australia and New Zealand, in the first decade of the twenty-first century.
8. For the history of John Murray, see Parsons, *Worth the Detour*, pp. 180–4. Murray's published a history of its handbooks: 'The Origins and History of Murray's Handbooks for Travellers', *Murray's Magazine*, 6 November 1889. The Murray archive is now deposited in the National Library of Scotland.
9. J.M. MacKenzie (1990) 'David Livingstone: The Construction of the Myth' in G. Walker and T. Gallagher (eds.), *Sermons and Battle Hymns* (Edinburgh: Edinburgh University Press), pp. 24–42; MacKenzie (2000) 'The Iconography of the Exemplary Life: The Case of David Livingstone' in G. Cubitt and A. Warren (eds.) *Heroic Reputations and Exemplary Lives* (Manchester: Manchester University Press), pp. 84–104.
10. At this time, Stanford also issued attractive hard-bound maps – for example, *Map of The Nile from the Equatorial Lakes to the Mediterranean embracing the Egyptian Sudan (Kordofan, Darfur etc.) and Abyssinia* and the (more snappily titled) *Map of Ceylon*.
11. The last Murray's handbook was, interestingly, for New Zealand. It was published in 1893 and seemed symbolically to take imperial travel to its outermost limits.
12. See, for example, text by Fabio Bourbon, Photographs by Antonio Attini (1996) *Egypt Yesterday and Today, Lithographs and Diaries by David Roberts RA* (Shrewsbury: Stewart, Tabori & Chang); A.B. Edwards (1877) *A Thousand Miles up the Nile* (London). Edwards was one of the founders of the Egyptian Exploration Fund, created to help finance Egyptian excavations.
13. A. Varnava (2009) *British Imperialism in Cyprus, 1878–1915: The Inconsequential Possession* (Manchester: Manchester University Press).
14. K. Baedeker (1908) *Egypt and the Sudan, Handbook for Travellers* (Leipzig), p. v.
15. P. Brendon (1991) *Thomas Cook: 150 Years of Popular Tourism* (London: Secker & Warburg), p. 272.

16. M. Murray (1953) *Union-Castle Chronicle 1853–1953* (London), pp. 311–12.
17. Murray, *Union-Castle*, pp. 311–12.
18. The Union Castle Line guides used for this survey date from 1899–1900, 1911–12, 1930, 1948 and 1957.
19. F. Alcock (1907) *Trade and Travel in South America* (London, second edition).
20. W.H. Koebel (ed.) (1921) *The South American Handbook*; H. Davies (ed.) (1930) *The South American Handbook*. These were published in London by Trade and Travel Publications.
21. Davies (ed.), *South American Handbook*, pp. 9–10.
22. (1910–11) *Sudan Government Railways and Steamers* (Khartoum).
23. (1925) *New Zealand, An Illustrated Description of the Natural Wealth, Conditions of Life, Industries, Trade, and Opportunities for Advancement in 'The Brighter Britain of the South'* (Wellington).
24. W.J. Loftie (ed.) (1882) *Orient Line Guide: Chapters for Travellers by Sea and by Land* (London). Other editions used were 1888, 1889, 1890, 1894 and 1901. The frequency of new editions, as with other guide books, seems to demonstrate the scale of sales of such works.
25. A.E. Aspinall (1907) *The Pocket Guide to the West Indies* (London). Once again, it was frequently reissued, reaching its sixth edition in 1931 and its tenth in 1954, reprinted as late as 1960.
26. The first Lonely Planet Guide was published in 1973, the first Rough Guide in 1982. The shift from imperial to more modern guides (controversial as they are) took place in little more than a decade.
27. Quoted in Brendon, *Thomas Cook*, p. 37.

Part III
Experiencing Other Empires

7
'The Feelings of an Officer': John Stedman in Suriname

Kerry Sinanan

In the Preface to the 1790 manuscript for his 'Narrative of a Five Year's Expedition, Against the Revolted Negroes of Surinam', John Stedman introduces his complex travel text with several references to Laurence Sterne and to the sentimental aspects of his writings. Claiming to 'write from the feelings of an officer',[1] he alludes to Sterne's sentimental soldier, Uncle Toby, in *Tristram Shandy* (1759–67) and he ends by asking his reader to feel along with him: 'at intervals throw down the Book – & with a sigh exclaim in the language of Eugenious – Alas poor Stedman –'.[2] This latter reference invokes Sterne's sentimental traveller, Yorick, in *A Sentimental Journey* (1768) and clearly casts Stedman as a contemporary man of feeling. The influence of Sterne on the 'Narrative' goes beyond character, though: throughout, Stedman makes use of dashes, apostrophes and Shandean turns of phrase, highlighting, as Sterne himself does, his 'disconnected method'.[3] Thus Stedman's 'experience of empire' is rendered through a form of Sternean sentimentalism, offering his readers a real-life narrative cast in the mould of the early novel. This chapter explores in depth the impact of the sentimental novel on Stedman's history, showing the ways in which he utilises the mode to ensure that his text has a reforming impact: the reader must 'feel' with the empirical hero, and this sympathy is a crucial element of Stedman's argument for the relief and better treatment of the slaves of Suriname.

Hired by the Dutch in 1772 to help to quell the ongoing Maroon uprisings, Stedman later worked on his original journal kept while in Suriname and he handed it over for publication to the radical publisher Joseph Johnson in 1791.[4] The relationship between the two men was fraught as Stedman continually disagreed with Johnson's edits as his writing was 'corrected' and potentially offensive language or scandalous passages, detailing Stedman's own rather bawdy behaviour, were erased or rewritten. In 1796 Johnson released a very popular but heavily edited text and Stedman utterly rejected it, writing to his wife: 'My book was printed full of lies and nonsense, without my knowledge. I burnt two thousand vols., and made them print it over again, by which they lost 200 guineas.'[5] Returning to the 1790 manuscript of the 'Narrative' that he intended to be published, we engage with a complex travel text that weaves a variety of genres and perspectives: history, geography, natural history, military journal, satire, *bildungsroman*, picaresque novel, abolitionist sentiment and pro-slavery political economy all jostle together. In this document, transcribed in full by the historians Richard and Sally Price, we find a fascinating and complex representation of the 'experience of empire' that relates many details about Suriname, the slave system there, its flora and fauna, and modes of governance, but through a unique style that owes much to the novelistic genre and its sentimental and satiric foundations. Only by reading the original manuscript can this style be fully appreciated.

Such a multifaceted text demands a multidisciplinary approach. To date, Stedman's work has indeed attracted a range of commentary from various fields. Mary Louise Pratt discusses Stedman's representation of his relationship with a slave girl, Joanna, in *Imperial Eyes*, as does Jenny Sharpe in *Ghosts of Slavery*.[6] Both of these works read Stedman's work as a travel narrative comprising several elements, including this 'romance plot'. In *Slavery and the Romantic Imagination*, Debbie Lee considers the relationship between William Blake and Stedman, and the ways in which Stedman's drawings of what he saw in Suriname were reinterpreted by Blake, whom Johnson commissioned to work on the published editions.[7] In *Slavery, Empathy and Pornography*, Marcus Wood focuses on Stedman's representation of slaves in what he reads as a historical text.[8] This chapter seeks to highlight what has hitherto been neglected – namely, Stedman's reliance on fiction as he weaves his complex tale.

In what follows, Stedman's 'Narrative' will be read as a journal begun within a specific historical context, that of the Boni-Maroon wars, and written within a specific literary domain, a particular strand of eighteenth-century sentimental satire, that Stedman consciously draws upon and alludes to as he weaves his account. Richard and Sally Price offer detail on how Stedman actually maintained a detailed daily journal in difficult circumstances: 'Faithfully, he kept on-the-spot notes – sometimes jotted down on cartridges or even on "<u>a Bleached bone</u>" when writing paper was not available', and he gathered all of his pieces of paper and notes into a small green journal that he wished to expand later.[9] When he returned to England he worked on his journal, as well as on some retrospective diaries, detailing his life in his entertaining and rollicking style from the quiet of his Tiverton home. The content of Stedman's report on the infamous Suriname slave colony cannot be separated from the novelistic language, register and form through which he renders it. In this way the 'Narrative' challenges us to read this history as both factual and fictional, and to consider the ways in which the latter mode enhances the former. What Stedman tells us can be relied upon as much as any contemporary accounts of the slave colonies, but his use of the novel is designed to make the reader 'feel' the truth of what he writes.

Stedman's published *Narrative* has been a valuable historical account of the Boni-Maroon Wars that persistently destabilised the most productive of the Dutch colonies, and its combination of history with travel, romance and adventure meant that it became 'the most famous book on Suriname that has ever been published'.[10] Between 1796 and 1838, during the period of slave abolition and emancipation, 18 editions including translations and abridgements of the *Narrative* were published in Italian, Dutch, French, Swedish and English. Despite the fact that Stedman was not a fully fledged abolitionist, his persistent critique of 'abject Slavery' and his insistence that the Maroons through 'bad usage were provoked to break their Chains and shake of[f] the Yoke to seek revenge and liberty' meant that the 'Narrative' was very easily read as an abolitionist text of the early 1790s.[11] It would also be easy to place Stedman's text within the genre of contemporary histories of the colonies, such as Edward Long's *History of Jamaica* (1774), yet, unlike such texts, which purport to be objective, learned and comprehensive, Stedman draws on the emergent fiction genre for his form, style and language to mediate a personal account, rather than an encyclopaedic overview. Like the contemporary novels on which he draws, his very first page in his first chapter emphasises that his work is not artful but truthful: 'Then let Truth, Simple Truth alone be my Apology,' he claims as he begins his tale.[12] The claim to truth had been the ironic premise of fiction since Swift and Defoe, so Stedman immediately prioritises his own individual perceptions as the hub of his story: what we read has been experienced by him. Thus Stedman becomes our central character and he relates what he sees, feels and learns. In this way we shall see that literature and history cannot easily be separated in his case. This is not to say that Stedman's work is not a history, but, rather, that it is a history forged within the intertextual culture of travel writing and the very new genre of the novel.

The interplay between eighteenth-century literary culture and representations of empire has been examined by others. As Beth Fowkes Tobin writes in her introduction to *Colonizing Nature*, 'popular forms of eighteenth-century art and literature played an important role in developing eighteenth-century ideas about land, labour, and natural resources in the tropical regions of the world'.[13] Tobin's core argument is that the formal properties of genre determined how the tropics were both perceived and represented by imperial Britons. Such an approach to reading travel writing places aesthetics in a central position: in this chapter, we see that sentimental literature deeply affects Stedman's representation of himself in the tropics, producing a highly charged experience of a contemporary slave colony that surrenders the kinds of claims to objectivity that his fellow historiographers, such as Edward Long, assumed.

While Stedman has been the subject of a certain amount of critical debate, not enough attention has been paid to the ways in which his account of his expedition explicitly draws on a contemporary literary culture that linked sentiment and satire with travel and picaresque. Other commentators have noted Stedman's representation of himself as a man of feeling but have not attempted to analyse the peculiar model of the man of feeling that he forges by blending satire and sentiment from a variety of sources.[14] Moreover, critics tend to focus on the heavily edited, and therefore less representative, published 1790 narrative. Stedman's account cannot be read independently of its many influences, such as Laurence Sterne, Tobias Smollett, Henry Mackenzie, Henry Fielding and other novelists. While Mary Louise Pratt notes that Stedman 'worked hard at fashioning himself on Roderick Random, Tom Jones, and Bamfylde Moore Carew an English boy who ran away with the gypsies', she does not further reflect on or consider in detail the implications that such models have for how we read the 'Narrative'.[15] Stedman's historical account of the material reality of his role as a colonial agent and queller of slaves is inextricably linked with experience as mediated and constructed by a wide range of literary sources that themselves play with the boundaries between fiction and reality.

John Stedman's early life and career was, like his writing, varied, and his decision to join the Dutch campaign against the slaves emerged out of a life of general misdirection. His retrospective diary begun in 1785, by which time he had settled in Tiverton, Devon, shows Stedman's deliberate interaction with popular literary sources: he represents his youth as a series of chaotic and violent adventures, resembling those of heroes from novels by Smollett and Fielding: 'Joseph Andrews, Tom Jones, and Roderick random [were] heroes I resolved to take for my models.'[16] This intertextuality is also part of the warp and weft of his 'Narrative'. Perhaps the urge to think of himself in literary terms came from the fact that he did share experiences in common with both the authors and haphazard heroes whom he admired. Stedman's father, like Laurence Sterne's, was a military man, a lieutenant colonel in the Scots brigade, which was a mercenary regiment that had been set up to defend the Netherlands since the sixteenth century. As a child, Stedman moved from post to post throughout the Low Countries, with his father's regiment defending against French attack and general turbulence during the War of the Austrian Succession.[17] At the age of ten, in 1755, he was sent back to the family's home in Fife, Scotland, to be tutored by his uncle, Dr John Stedman. This was a singular failure: neglect and mistreatment spurred him to extravagant misbehaviour and he was sent back to Holland. Despite his misbehaviour his parents recognised his considerable talents as a painter and he was to be sent to be an artist's apprentice, but he refused 'from merely a motive of pride – scorning to be instructed by blockheads'.[18] This talent for painting, however, is part of Stedman's craft in the 'Narrative' and he kept a visual record of his tour in Suriname composing over a hundred sketches and watercolours that were transformed into engravings, including 16 by the poet and engraver William Blake with whom he became friends.[19]

It is interesting to note that Stedman casts his interest in joining the war against the Maroons as that of an objective (if acquisitive) explorer and traveller, for he was about to enter a military reality that would involve him in a vicious and fatal campaign. In 1760, needing a profession, he joined as ensign in the Scots Brigade but noted that 'a military life without either money or interest was my antipathy'.[20] As a result of their relentless guerrilla warfare, both Maroon groups, the Saramaka and the Djuka, had won their independence in 1760s. As Stedman observes, the treaty with the Maroons in the 1760s did not prevent war: instead, new groups of rebel slaves formed and these small bands became very effective at raiding plantations. In his desperation, by the early 1770s, Governor Nepveu asked for more troops. It is perhaps little wonder that when another war with Maroons broke out in 1772, Stedman jumped at the chance for both adventure and wealth to be one of the recruited volunteers: 'impress'd by the Prospect of Preferment usually annext to so Hazardous a Service & in the hopes of Gratifying my Curiosity in exploring a Country so Little known-I offered myself to be one of the party'.[21] He was promoted to rank of Captain to fight in 'The First Boni War' (1765–77) and, following the fate of another of his fictional counterparts, Voltaire's *Candide*, arrived in Suriname in early 1773. As the historian Wim Hoogbergen writes,

> Around 1765, however, the planters discovered that another Maroon tribe had been formed east of the plantation area … From then on, the Boni-Maroons were systematically pursued. The number of military patrols was steadily increased and the Boni-Maroons, for their part, reacted by attacking the plantations with much more verve than they had ever done before. They also attempted to persuade plantation slaves to join them. Thus the beginning of the Boni-Maroon Wars.[22]

Stedman arrived at a guerrilla war in which '[r]aids on plantations, carrying off slaves, murdering supervisors and owners without prior notice' characterised the tactics of the elusive Maroons. In response, '[m]ilitary patrols were very regularly sent off to the jungle' to track them but, because the rebels avoided contact, troops 'were left wandering around and were seldomly attacked'.[23]

The Maroon wars in Suriname had been a thorn in the Dutch side for decades when the British ceded it to them in 1667. In her famous novella *Oroonoko* (1668), Aphra Behn had bemoaned the exchange of the colony for New Amsterdam. From its initial establishment, the colony had lost slaves to the dense forests that surrounded the cultivated areas, and organised groups of Maroons frequently attacked plantations with devastating effects. Yet in the midst of this constant state of war, by the mid-eighteenth century, Suriname had become productive under the 'tolerant and representative regime of the Chartered Society of Surinam', which allowed planters 'a large measure of internal self-government in co-operation with the West India Company'.[24] It is, in part, this semi-autonomy of the Suriname planters that prompts Stedman to denounce their 'luxury and dissipation' as well as their excessive violence.[25] From the moment of his arrival in Suriname, Stedman is simultaneously a participator in and harsh critic of the Dutch regime and, in particular of their treatment of slaves. As he writes his history, the sentimental mode, which also enables satire, becomes indispensable for this complex representation and he casts himself as a man of feeling but also of action, poised between the realm of the literary and that of material reality.

In the Preface to his 'Narrative', Stedman is self-conscious about the contradictions of being a feeling officer and initially prioritises his identity as a man of action: 'A Soldier or Sailor ought to be a man of Courage' and so, he tells us, he will be brave in the face of the criticism that he expects his narrative to receive as, like *Tristram Shandy*, it 'has neither stile, orthography, order, or Connection'.[26] He also follows Sterne stylistically by breaking up his writing with frequent dashes. Indeed his Preface draws attention to the unreliable elements of the 'Narrative': It is 'Patcht up with superfluous Quotations – Descriptions of Animals without so much as proper names – Trifles – Cruelties – Bombast &c. to all which Accusations I partly plead Guilty –'.[27] Just as, in *Tristram Shandy*, Tristram tells us to check Yorick's history in '*saxo-Grammaticus's* Danish' history', Stedman tells us to look up Linnaeus for ourselves if we want to know the proper names of the plants that he will describe. The frequent use of aposiopesis and a disclamatory stance undermine the authority of both his narrating voice and of Stedman's authority in the theatre of war in which he finds himself. In explicitly Sternean mode, the text emphasises its limits, its arbitrary selection of facts and, crucially, includes the narrator himself in the satire. In his mode as a feeling officer, then, Stedman combines action and writing, yet the context of slavery makes this an especially fraught combination, for his feelings for the slaves, as he proclaims them, are in direct opposition to the action he must take against them.

It is through his experience as a man of action that he garners the necessary authority to narrate his expedition. Carrying his 'sheets' 'through Danger-Disease, Famine, water, Smoak & Fire ... ought fully to account for the want of Stile and Elegance'.[28] But this action is swiftly balanced with sentiment and he claims to 'write from the feelings of an officer', informing the reader that their narrator is at once a man of some sentiment but also a 'manly', active and nationally loyal figure.[29] His use of this model is complex and diverges from – as much as it draws upon – the classic man of feeling, Harley, as forged in Henry Mackenzie's novel of 1771. As Dror Wahrman points out, in *The Man of Feeling*, Harley is feminised by Mackenzie in order to be a man of true sensibility.[30] Stedman's narrative, in contrast, is full of manly pursuits recording arduous military campaigns in the depths of the rainforest, as well as his relationship with a mulatto slave, Joanna, with whom he has a son. Wahrman notes that Harley's 'alternative ideal of masculinity was driven home in a scene in which he converts a military officer to feeling, moving him to tears as he drops his sword'.[31] Stedman, however, must wield his sword while still feeling for his enemies, and so satire and sentiment become an inevitable dynamic in his writing. This mutation of manly sentiment was, as Linda Colley observes, entirely in keeping with a wider cultural shift towards the end of the century when 'the British conceived of themselves as an essentially "masculine culture" – bluff, forthright, rational, down to earth to the extent of being philistine'.[32] Following his culture's modification of the man of feeling into a 'cry-shy epigone', Stedman proposes a feeling man of action entirely masculine in his correct feelings, ultimately concluding that manly feeling will cure Suriname's ills.[33] Thus the culmination of his 'Narrative' is to propose a new order for governance: 'Let the Governor & Principal magistrates be Chosen in Europe, let them be Gentlemen of Fortune and Education & above all men of liberal ideas... whose Passions are bridled by Sentiment and manly feeling.'[34] This conclusive statement is the core of Stedman's argument: feeling is vital but must go beyond crying and sympathy to become the basis of a benevolent imperial order and strong, but measured, governance.

Stedman's eighteenth-century models enable him to navigate the inevitably ambivalent and compromised position in which he finds himself – an officer, sympathetic to the Maroons' cause who must, nevertheless, quell their rebellion. In the opening chapters of his 'Narrative', Stedman describes months of inaction as the rebels had been pushed back deep in the jungle. In his five years he took part in seven forays into the forest to engage the Maroons and only encountered them once. As the Prices observe, '[t]he war, then, was characterised by the colonial troops criss-crossing, more or less blindly, vast expanses of treacherous forests and swamps, with the Maroons... almost always remaining at least a step ahead.'[35] It is thus crucial to note that the mechanics of the war Stedman fought in were characterised by this destabilisation, compromise and the interdependence of white European troops upon former slaves and their free black soldiers, the Rangers. This context conditions Stedman's view of himself as part of a coalition to bring peace rather than as an armed enemy of the rebels. Stedman argues that it was the planters' own 'Vice and Debochery'[36] that encouraged slaves to rebel after the peace treaty of 1760 leading to the creation of a '*white* and *black*' army:

> In this dilemma of affairs the inhabitants were now obliged to come to the distracted resolution of *limiting the Game upon itself*, that is to say of forming a regiment of *Manumitted-Slaves* to fight against their Countrymen thus set Negro to battle against Negro.[37]

The Dutch dependence on slaves and free blacks, then, was born out of their own excesses and, ironically, their unlimited wielding of power eventually undermined their position. Stedman continually stresses that such internal ambivalence is at the heart of the Dutch (mis)management of its colony and the fissures in colonial control extend to the composition of the very troops who fight the enemy.

Within this context, Stedman frequently expresses sympathy and pity for the slaves within his regiment. Upon an outbreak of disease within the regiment, Stedman pays particular attention to the slaves' suffering:

> The poor Slaves were peculiarly unhappy who/as I have said getting but half allowance/lived mostly upon the produce of the Cabbage tree, Seeds, Roots, Wild-berries &c...they were so Starved that they tied *nebees* or ropes about their bodies in the vain hopes of thus alleviating their cruel hunger –[38]

Understanding how and why, as a paid mercenary, Stedman chooses to portray himself as a sentimental traveller, a feeling officer, in such moments requires us to be familiar with the literature through which he represents his experience. In this moment, and many others like it, I would argue that Stedman's identity as a feeling officer is based upon the sentimental soldier Uncle Toby in Sterne's *Tristram Shandy* who, despite his love for the military, feels 'universal good-will' to all creatures.[39] Stedman writes from the 'feelings of an officer' who cares about universal benevolence, representing his regiment as comprising all of the men in it: white, black, free and slave. He can therefore express his pity for the slaves without being a hypocrite.

That this relationship to Uncle Toby was deliberately constructed can be seen in his autobiographical journal when Stedman relates an incident when, as a young cadet, he caught a mouse:

> I was ordered immediately to drown [it]. I let the poor little creature escape, supplying its place with a dead one I had just found, in which, being detected, I was miserably whipt for telling a lie without the least mitigation for my sensibility, which I cannot help thinking ought to have counter-balanced my fault, since it proceeded from pure generosity. But no!, I was teached blindly to obey, without consulting either my feelings, or my senses.[40]

Whether or not this incident actually occurred becomes secondary to the sense that Stedman is representing this as a Sternean moment: it clearly recalls the famous incident in *Tristram Shandy* when Uncle Toby releases a fly that has been pestering him, assuring it 'I'll not hurt a hair of thy head...This world is surely wide enough to hold both thee and me'.[41] We also note Stedman's readiness to defy authority and to rail against the suppression of individual feeling by institutional regimes. In this he is very much a man of his age, reflecting the importance placed on the minute sentiments of the individual by the period's own genre, the novel.

The philosophy of universal benevolence expressed by Uncle Toby underpins how Stedman represents his encounters with the creatures and people of Suriname in the 'Narrative'. In the following passage, Stedman has shot a monkey to try to feed his men and, as a feeling officer, he describes his horror at having shot and fatally maimed the animal:

> but may I never again be more Witness to such a Scene, the Miserable Animal was not dead but mortally Wounded, thus taking his Tail in both my hands to end his torment, I swong him round and knock'd his head against the Sides of the Canoo with such a force, that I was covered all over with blood and brains; but the Poor thing stil continued alive and looking at me in the most Pitiful manner that can be conceived, I knew no other Means to end this Murder than by holding him under Water till he was drown'd, while my heart felt Seek on his account... never Poor Devil felt more than I on this occasion, nor could I taste of him or his Companion when they were dress'd, who afforded to some other a delicious repast and which ended the Catastrophe –[42]

Here the final Sternean dash aptly signifies the death of the monkeys as well as the end of this vignette. But by also injecting a tone of reluctant acceptance – we almost sense Stedman turning away from the dead monkeys in resigned disgust – the aposiopesis registers the awareness in Stedman's narrative voice of the problem of being a man of feeling in a situation where hardened pragmatism is needed and survival must be prioritised. Stedman shot the monkey deliberately to feed himself and his troops in one of their treks through the jungle, and yet he finds that on this occasion his manly action exacts a cost from his own feelings that is hard to pay. The dash therefore also lends a self-satirising tone to this very affecting passage: Stedman is deliberately forcing us to confront the reality of war, even if the casualty is a monkey and, as he stands, covered with 'blood and guts', he exposes himself as a guilty figure who, despite his best intentions, literally has blood on his hands.

In his discussion of this passage, Marcus Wood argues that it is a deeply unconvincing representation of Stedman as man of feeling in which 'Stedman is seeking to reconcile the irreconcilable, the world of macho, mercenary, and military violence with sentiment'.[43] While Stedman is clearly invoking sentiment, I would argue that he is drawing explicitly on the inherent contradictoriness of Sterne's Uncle Toby. The 'grotesqueness' that Wood objects to in Stedman's implicit comparison of the 'tortured animal body with tortured slave body' can be read not as a sign of hypocrisy caused by an insincere gloss of sentiment but as an effect that Stedman creates by highlighting his compromised position. What he is writing about here is a model of universal benevolence that is vital to the ethical dimensions of his satire for, just as Toby understands that the fly's feelings are important in a system in which all beings are connected, so Stedman believes that slaves' feelings, both physical and emotional, must be regarded. What may, perhaps, come across as a form of proto-racism that disturbingly relates slaves to monkeys can also be read as an expression of the period's system of the Chain of Being, linking all living creatures. While the hierarchies are inescapable, Stedman emphasises these for satiric effect: his message is that we should still feel for those subordinate to us as their feelings and capacity for suffering is what joins us. Moreover, Stedman is himself exposing the ironic contradictions of his position for he may feel for slaves yet he must shoot and kill the maroons when he encounters them.

Uncle Toby offers just this combination of 'military violence' with 'empathy' which, as many critics have noted, results in Sterne's creation of an 'aesthetic experience of the grotesque'.[44] His very contrariness is precisely what makes him, for Madeleine Descargues, perfect for Sterne's satiric ends as he becomes 'a particular literary item in a series of sentimental soldiers, emblematizing man's folly in the satirical discourse from the Antiquity to the... Augustan age'.[45] To the contemporary reader, Stedman's combination of devotion to his military duty with a continually reiterated sense of feeling for the sufferings of slaves and Maroons would have reminded them of the ambivalent Uncle Toby who, while he feels the 'drum beat' in his own chest, also feels an 'ache for the distress of war too'.[46] And Stedman's sentimental feeling for the plight of fellow humans' suffering goes beyond mere stylised feeling: it is fundamental to his political assessment of the causes of the crisis in Suriname:

> That best of all was never to have drove these poor Creatures to such extremities by constant ill treatment Speaks of itself – while at the same time it is certainly true that to Govern the Coast-of-Guinea Negroes well, nay even for their own benefit – the strictest discipline is absolutely necessary, but I ask why in the Name of Humanity should they undergo the most cruel racks and tortures entirely depending upon the despotic Caprice of their Proprietors and overseers.[47]

Such a statement epitomises Stedman's ambivalent position as he bemoans the colony's loss of control by berating its agents' tyrannical wielding of that power. Running alongside Stedman's humane injunctions against causing suffering is his absolute belief that governance and therefore slavery is necessary. Thus his feeling becomes manly and his role as an officer is not undermined by his sentiment.

While the 'Narrative' therefore becomes a strong political critique, its force is also underpinned by the fact that, unlike his novelistic inspirators, what

Stedman has to say is truly real, not merely realistic, and so the effect of showing things as they really are is even greater. In the satire *Candide*, Voltaire brings his quixotic hero to Suriname to expose the brutal abuses of slaves by planters but, as the Suriname historian Richard Price points out, this attempt at satire is perhaps undermined by the fact that the descriptions by contemporaries of punishments meted out to rebel slaves were much more lurid and horrifying than what Candide observes. These mutilations and maimings are represented for us in words and images by Stedman, who also tells us that what he sees, 'verifies what *Voltaire* says in his Candide'.[48] It is typical of Stedman to think of the novel as a touchstone of experience and as a repository of the real. He wants his readers to approach the 'Narrative' as based in a reality already imagined by fiction. And his powerful sketches supplement this realism. In the famous engraving by Blake entitled *A Negro Hung Alive by the Ribs to a Gallows*, based on a sketch by Stedman, we can see why the 'Narrative' was easily co-opted by the abolitionist camp. Stedman presents this plate alongside his proclaimed horror at the punishments given out to slaves: 'I was hurted at the cruelty of the above execution.'[49] Such sentiment is not appropriation but articulates a vital sympathy that underlies Stedman's role as critic and observer. A contemporary pronouncement of the punishment to be given to a rebel Saramaka Marron, Joosie, in 1730 shows that, even when phrased in the 'objective' language of the law, the horror of slave punishments is manifest:

> [he] shall be hanged from the gibbet by an Iron Hook through his ribs, until dead; his head shall then be severed and displayed on a stake...As for the Negroes Wierrie and Manbotem they shall be bound to a stake and roasted alive over a slow fire, while being tortured with glowing Tongs. The Negro girls...will be tied to a cross to be broked alive.[50]

With such accounts abounding, it becomes difficult to accuse Stedman of sensationalising in any way the suffering and torture that he witnessed: his sentiment is based on reality. In these ways, Stedman's role as a feeling officer becomes a way of proving what fiction has proposed and his empirical experience intensifies his sentiment as necessary, rather than merely stylistically modish, in the real, brutal world of slavery.

Maintaining his focus on individuals and their feelings, Stedman's harshest criticism is directed at the dissipated and corrupt slave owners who wantonly indulge their barbaric appetites. The facts of slavery that Stedman details exceed even the most grotesque iniquities with which the satiric novels he draws on are concerned:

> This day I was also informed of some Cruelties which I must still relate before my Departure, as motives to deter others from the abominable

Practices. Some at which Humanity must Shrink and Seeken – what Reader will believe that a *Jewes[s]*from a Motive of *Groundless* Jealousy/for such her Husband made it to appear/-I say who can believe that this unprecedented Monster put an end to the Life of a young and beautiful Quadroon Girl, by the infernal means of plunging a red hot Poker in her Body, by those parts which decency forbids to mention... Another Young Negro Woman having her ancles chained so close together, that she could hardly move her feet, was knocked down with a Cane by a Jew, till the blood streamed out of her head, her arms and naked Sides.[51]

With the authority of a reporter, duty-bound to relate what he has experienced, Stedman presents details of abuse that exceed the boundaries of acceptable information. Drawing attention to the extremes of reality that he is relating, he notes the potential incredulity of his reader twice. Yet this grants his account that very credence for no novel would go quite so far. The slant towards anti-Semitism forges a link between Stedman and his audience, and his satire unmasks the women planters of Suriname as 'monsters' while, at the same time, trading on the sentimental portrayal of the young women slaves as helpless victims. Thus the sentimental is stretched to the visceral, and the emotional pain we may feel at contemplating suffering becomes an imagined physical pain that participates, albeit to a small degree, in the suffering of the tortured slave. It is these readerly responses, also cultivated by the sentimental novel, that Stedman deliberately creates as a reforming impulse. Here, Stedman's feelings for slaves in no way compromise his manliness, and his role as an officer of honour is sustained.

Throughout the 'Narrative', Stedman's reliance on Shandyism persists and his 'disconnected method' mitigates against a sustained focus on any given topic. Following this shocking scene he reminds his reader that reading his diverse 'Narrative' means that they will not have to endure such misery for long:

Enough – of Cruelties, but which I am obliged to relate, and which I hope will make it the more excusable when I introduce Sometimes Scenes of a more lively Nature however inconsistent with either natural History or the account of a Military Expedition-I wish to diversify the Sable Scenes of Horror, by the more cheering Sunshine of Content, And to variegate this Work in such a manner/if possible/ as to make it please both the Stern Grim Philosopher, and the Youthful, the beautiful and innocent Maid; This shall ever by my desire and my Study.[52]

The above interjection reiterates Stedman's Preface at the end of which he appeals to the 'enlighten'ed understanding & Tender Sensibility' of the female reader in an open declaration of the sentimental thrust of his 'Narrative'.[53] His variegated work includes many readers and, without apologising for the tales of horror he must relate, he appeals to the very feelings that may be offended to excuse them. If we accept that Stedman sees himself to be, like Tristram, a 'world changer', then his disconnected method, conveying violence and torment, love, exploration, adventure and philosophy, becomes necessary to convey the full sense of what his expedition to Suriname involved.[54] This interjection and statement of intent about style also mirrors the novelistic narrator, perhaps modelled most explicitly on Henry Fielding's, who constructs his reader as he addresses them. Thus in the Preface to *Tom Jones*, Fielding conjures the 'candid reader' and, in *Joseph Andrews*, the Author's Preface describes in some detail for the reader what to expect in this novel mode of 'comic epic-poem in prose' while also asserting the form's realism; 'everything is copied from the book of nature'. It is the empiricism of the novel mode and the shared community of feeling that Stedman is exploiting.

Notwithstanding the diversity of topics covered or the recognition of his own compromised position, Stedman believes in his cause and repeatedly argues that although he is an official enemy of the rebels, he is sympathetic to their cause and does not consider himself a foe. Thus, upon seeing captive Maroons at the fort in Zeelandia he has a Dante-esque vision in which the prisoners appear as 'so many hellish fiends in the shape of African slaves, tormenting the souls of their European persecutors (*in which number those in the navy or army ought with justice not be included, as they come not to inspire revolts, but to quell them)*'.[55] This remark is at the heart of how Stedman views himself in his engagement with slaves and Maroon rebels: he is there to restore peace for the good of the colony and for the welfare of the slaves. But the feeling for slaves is also there, and here we can see how Stedman's use of sentiment often creates a sense of 'ironic distance' which Lynn Festa notes is central to another crucial Sternean influence, the traveller Yorick in *A Sentimental Journey*. Festa reads sentiment in colonial texts as a literary consequence of empire, and highlights its formal structures to examine its effects on the feeling subject, noting the inherent ambivalences: '[I]n the case of sentimental fiction, the gap between the feeling self (absorbed in another's emotion) and the detached spectator (that part that does not identify)...can generate additional displacements of the self and produce irony.'[56] We see this ironic distance often in *A Sentimental Journey*. On one occasion, Yorick feels that he has not time or space to respond fully to a mourner's tale retelling his love for his faithful ass who has died. 'The thirstiest soul in the most sandy desert of Arabia could not have wished more for a cup of cold water, than mine did for grave and quiet movements,' laments Yorick as his postchaise gallops at pace and prevents him from feeling full empathy with the grieving man. Here Yorick feels sentiment and distance, and this is vital to

Stedman's depiction of himself as a feeling officer whose position will always be attended by irony.

In his concluding pages, as Stedman moves to end his story, the ironic distance is palpable:

> The Above *Skeaches*, together with those Acts of Barbarity I have so frequently Related through out this Work, are Assuredly Sufficient to melt the Heart of the most unfeeling with Compassion, nor is it to be Wondered that Armies of Rebels at every Hazard Assemble in the forest to Seek Revenge & Liberty[.][57]

It was because of the powerful, if extreme, sentiment of such moments that Stedman was lauded by the *Analytical Review* as an abolitionist, 'inciting in the breasts of his readers a degree of indignation, which will stimulate vigorous and effectual exertions for the speedy termination of the execrable traffic in human flesh'.[58] Such a reception was inevitable given Stedman's insistence that the suffering of slaves must end. Yet these proclamations of sympathy for suffering slaves and Maroons sit uneasily for current commentators with his insistence that, even after amelioration, 'Negroes' in the colonies be kept '*dependent*, & under proper restrictions...not so much for the Sake of the European as for that of the African himself, with whose passions, debauchery and indolence, I am perfectly acquainted'.[59] Inevitably such sentiments, interwoven with a proto-racism typical of his age, mean that recent critical assessments of Stedman's work are less sure either of his sympathetic stance towards the slaves, or of his abolitionism.

We can only make sense of Stedman's position and his sentimental satire if we understand his eighteenth-century literary sources and, in particular, the forms and modes of the novels that he draws on. As Ronald Paulson notes, satire in the eighteenth-century novel had necessarily to move away from being concerned primarily with the 'satiric object – the culprit – to the satiric observer, either to the observer as observer or to the observer as a satiric object himself'.[60] Stedman's novelistic inspirators emphasised the nature of man as ambivalent and mixed, forged of sin and glory, a message that ultimately returns us to one of Sterne's most important sources, *Hamlet*. Such a view of humans as a composition of the corrupt and the divine is emphasised by corporal Trim in *Tristram Shandy*, whose love for mankind acknowledges 'this delicious mixture'.[61] Thus paradox, irony, conflict and unease are all part of the aesthetic of the 'Narrative'. In fully engaging with these complexities we have seen that, far from remaining in a position of unselfconscious mastery, Stedman rigorously denounces the violent tyranny of slave masters in an extended satire that gains its force from the juxtaposition of slavery with sentiment. As the Prices observe, Stedman's 'positions were well within the mainstream of contemporary educated British opinion – ambivalence and equivocation about slavery combined with genuine compassion for oppressed humanity'.[62] While we may find it hard to stomach his belief in continued slavery, read in its own time, this ameliorative position is not incompatible with a sincere sensibility for the slaves that, while ambivalent, was nevertheless part of a wider critique that eventually led to abolitionism.

As we have seen, in his Preface the feelings of an officer are what give Stedman a claim to 'sincerity'[63] and to presenting 'simple truth unmask'd'.[64] And in his concluding paragraph he shows that this role as a feeling officer has been maintained right to the end:

> And now farewell my Patient Friends who have been pleas'd to peruse this Narrative of my Sufferings with any Degree of Sensibility, particularly those whose Simpathetick Feelings have been Rous'd by the Distressing Scenes they may have met with in reading, & whose good nature is ready to forgive the inaccuracies annext to the pen &pencil of a Soldier debar'd from his youth from a Classical Education.[65]

In his closing words, then, Stedman's identity as a feeling officer is finally emphasised. He addresses his constructed readers as people of benevolent sensibility and common sense, and implies that he has been utterly truthful precisely because he has learned from the popular novel, rather than from the classics. His readers are now his friends because they have felt along with Stedman, and their better natures have been appealed to. Such sympathy and fellow feeling is powerful and should lead to change for, unlike other travellers of his era, Stedman's quest has been not just to inform but, like his fellow writers of novels, to reform.

Notes

1. In my discussion I rely on the full transcription of Stedman's manuscript. J.G. Stedman, *Narrative of a Five Years Expedition Against the Revolted Negroes of Surinam*, R. Price and S. Price (eds.) (1988) (Baltimore and London: Johns Hopkins University Press). To distinguish between this published manuscript and the 1790 edited version, I refer to the former as the 'Narrative'. See Stedman, lxxiii–lxxxii for a full publishing history, p. 9.
2. Ibid., p. 11.
3. Ibid., p. 128.
4. When speaking of the country myself, I will use the current spelling of Suriname; when quoting Stedman and older sources I will follow the older spelling of Surinam.
5. Stedman, 'Narrative', L.
6. M.L. Pratt (1992) *Imperial Eyes: Travel Writing and Transculturation* (London and New York: Routledge); J. Sharpe (2002) *Ghosts of Slavery* (Minneapolis: University of Minnesota Press).
7. D. Lee (2002) *Slavery and the Romantic Imagination* (Pennsylvania: University of Pennsylvania Press).

8. M. Wood (2002) *Slavery, Empathy and Pornography* (Oxford: Oxford University Press).
9. Stedman, 'Narrative', xxvii.
10. W. Hoogbergen (1990) *The Boni Wars in Suriname* (Leiden and New York: E.J. Brill), xiii.
11. Stedman, 'Narrative', p. 68.
12. Ibid., p. 27.
13. B.F. Tobin (2004) *Colonizing Nature: The Tropics in British Arts and Letters, 1760–1820* (Philadelphia: University of Pennsylvania Press), p. 12.
14. See T.G. (Fall 1998) ' "Scenes of Horror," Scenes of Sensibility: Sentimentality and Slavery in John Gabriel Stedman's *Narrative of a Five Years Expedition Against the Revolted Negroes of Surinam'*, *ELH*, 65:3, 653–73. And Wood, *Slavery, Empathy and Pornography*. Gwilliam notes to Stedman's 'self-portrait as father and as man of feeling' (667) and critiques his use of sentiment but does not fully consider the literary models that inform the *Narrative*, and Wood simply notes that Stedman uses this model.
15. Pratt, *Imperial Eyes*, p. 91.
16. Stedman, MS diary, 1786, 15. Cited in Stedman, 'Narrative', p. xix. Stedman kept a series of diaries and journals, including the one kept in Suriname on which he bases his 'Narrative'. For a full discussion of these, see Stedman, xxvi–xxxvi. Stanbury Thompson edited and published these diaries and memoirs in consecutive order in 1962. While this edition is not entirely reliable in its transcription of the Suriname diaries as the Prices demonstrate, I use it occasionally as a source for details from Stedman's retrospective diary, which retells his early life.
17. The Netherlands were attacked and occupied by the French, who were fighting Austrian interests there. The French were anti-Austrian and the British in favour of the Hapsburg Maria Theresa of Austria. This was resolved by the Peace of Aix-la-Chapelle in 1748.
18. S. Thompson (ed.) (1962) *The Journal of John Gabriel Stedman, 1744–1797, Soldier and Author, Including an Authentic Account of His Expedition to Surinam, in 1772* (London: Mitre Press), p. 20.
19. See Stedman, 'Narrative', xxxix.
20. Thompson, *Journal*, p. 21.
21. Stedman, 'Narrative', p. 29.
22. Hoogbergen, *Boni Wars*, xiii.
23. Ibid., pp. 15–16.
24. Robin Blackburn (1997) *The Making of New World Slavery* (London and New York: Verso), p. 501.
25. Stedman, 'Narrative', p. 49.
26. Ibid., p. 7.
27. Ibid., p. 7.
28. Ibid., p. 8.
29. Ibid., p. 9.
30. D. Wahrman (2004) *The Making of the Modern Self: Identity and Culture in Eighteenth-Century England* (New Haven and London: Yale University Press), p. 38.
31. Wahrman, *Making*, p. 38.
32. Linda Colley (1992) *Britons: Forging the Nation 1701–1837* (New Haven and London: Yale University Press), p. 252.
33. Wahrman, *Making*, p. 40.
34. Stedman, 'Narrative', p. 593.

35. Ibid., xxvi.
36. Ibid., p. 80
37. Ibid., p. 81.
38. Ibid., p. 220.
39. L. Sterne (1759–67, 2003) *The Life and Opinions of Tristram Shandy, Gentleman* (London: Penguin), p. 100.
40. Thompson, *Journal*, p. 23.
41. Sterne, *Tristram Shandy*, p. 100.
42. Stedman, 'Narrative', p. 141.
43. Wood, *Slavery*, p. 104.
44. M. Descargues (2006) 'Tristram Shandy and the Appositeness of War', in T. Keymer (ed.) *Laurence Sterne's Tristram Shandy: A Casebook* (Oxford University Press), p. 247.
45. Descargues, 'Tristram Shandy', p. 247.
46. Sterne, *Tristram Shandy*, p. 415.
47. Stedman, 'Narrative', p. 68.
48. Ibid., p. 246.
49. Ibid., p. 103.
50. R. Price (1983) *To Slay the Hydra: Dutch Colonial Perspectives on the Saramaka Wars* (Michigan: Ann Arbor Press), p. 9.
51. Stedman, 'Narrative', p. 115.
52. Ibid., p. 116.
53. Ibid., p. 11.
54. R. Paulson (1967) *Satire and the Novel in Eighteenth-Century England* (New Haven and London: Yale University Press), p. 252.
55. Stedman, 'Narrative', p. 102 (my italics).
56. L. Festa (2006) *Sentimental Figures of the Enlightenment in Eighteenth-Century Britain and France* (Baltimore: Johns Hopkins University Press), p. 31.
57. Stedman, 'Narrative', p. 533.
58. *Analytical Review*, September, 1796, 225–6. Cited in Stedman, lxv.
59. Stedman, 'Narrative', p. 172.
60. Paulson, *Satire and the Novel in Eighteenth-Century England*, p. 6.
61. Sterne, *Tristram Shandy*, p. 329.
62. Stedman, 'Narrative', lxi.
63. Ibid., p. 7.
64. Ibid., p. 9.
65. Ibid., p. 626.

8
British Communities and Foreign Intervention in Nineteenth-Century South America: The Rio de la Plata in the 1840s

David Rock

European naval and military intervention in the Rio de la Plata in 1845–8 led to forms of 'experiencing imperialism' in South America, an area almost devoid of formal colonialism after the early nineteenth-century wars of emancipation. The British hesitated to use force in Latin America, realising that it would meet sharp resistance and that its material costs likely outweighed its probable gains.[1] From the 1890s, the rising power of the United States became an additional deterrent to the use of coercion by European powers, including Britain.[2]

The 1845 intervention, an exception to the general rule, was carried out jointly with France. Comparisons between the two countries illustrated the way in which commercial interest and rivalry with the French dominated British policy, although in some respects they operated in similar ways. The Orleans monarchy shared with the British governments of the time the habit of sending out diplomats to the Plata with personal agendas. William Gore Ouseley, in particular, who served in Buenos Aires and Montevideo in 1845–6, practised free enterprise imperialism. 'You have merged the mediator in the partisan', complained Foreign Secretary Lord Aberdeen as he chided Ouseley for his conduct.[3] Predictably, in Argentina, the nationalist writers known as the Historical Revisionists denounced the intervention repeatedly. Having peaked in 1955–75, their critiques disappeared for years but recently revived with the support of the government of Argentina. In 2010 the Fernández de Kirchner administration instituted 20 November, the anniversary of the battle of Vuelta de Obligado fought between Argentine and Anglo-French forces, as a national holiday. In 2011 the Argentine government promoted 'revisionist' writing by subsidising a study centre in Buenos Aires.[4] The writings of the Argentine nationalists had a counterpart in a French study of the 1990s by Jean-David Avenel.

Although he wrote from an opposite position, Avenel's book contained chauvinistic strands resembling those in a book recently published in Argentina by Pacho O'Donnell.[5]

British historians writing after 1950 treated the episode in light of the concept of informal empire, which some supported and others opposed.[6] Informal empire – a long familiar paradigm – meant the willingness of the major powers to trespass on the sovereignty of weaker countries outside Europe for economic gain without reducing them to colonial status. Removing the constraints on commerce became the overriding purpose of informal empire. In their classic text of the 1950s, Gallagher and Robinson emphasised how free trade could be combined with external domination.[7] In a more recent study, David McLean analysed the intervention in the Rio de la Plata from this perspective but raised doubts about how to classify it because it proved unsuccessful. How could the episode be seen as a case of 'informal empire' or 'free trade imperialism' when it so conspicuously failed?[8] Despite its military defeat in November 1845, the government of Buenos Aires refused to bow to European pressure to open the rivers of Argentina to foreign trade. When 'free navigation' was finally accepted in the 1850s, its adoption occurred for reasons other than external intervention or gunboat diplomacy.

This discussion focuses mainly on British communities resident in the Plata during the intervention era. The Britons living in the region comprised two groups, one in Buenos Aires in the Argentine Confederation and the other in Montevideo in the Republic of Uruguay (an area then known as the Banda Oriental). Although merchants dominated both British communities, they differed in size and outlook. The much larger community in Buenos Aires preferred to uphold very loose ties with Britain. In sharp contrast, the smaller Montevideo community campaigned for British military and naval intervention, and to establish a British protectorate. Gallagher and Robinson considered 'free trade imperialism' as a distinctive feature of the early and mid-Victorian period that contrasted with the 'formal imperialism' of the late Victorian period. In the Plata region in the 1840s, the two subtypes of imperialism coexisted to exemplify, to quote John Darwin, 'the chaotic pluralism of British interests at home and of their agents and allies abroad'.[9] Far from being passive recipients of orders issued in London, the expatriate communities interacted with and at times shaped or almost determined metropolitan policy; they also connected in various ways with indigenous political forces in the Plata; they served as a bridge between British and South American commerce; and finally, the government of Buenos Aires fought to preserve local sovereignty while supporting close collaborative ties with Britain. For Latin Americans, 'experiencing imperialism' implied ambiguity towards the British, a complex mixture of attraction and repulsion, that ranged from general resistance to participatory acquiescence.

In 1845, Britain and France deployed naval power against Governor Juan Manuel de Rosas of Buenos Aires, the 'Tyrant Rosas', one of the most colourful and contentious figures of nineteenth-century Latin America. Rosas grew most notorious for his use of repression. Stories abounded about the Mazorca, a shadowy quasi-police force ('goon squad' might be the best contemporary expression) that assassinated enemies of the regime by cutting their throats. This reputed method of execution lived up to European stereotypes of the Rio de la Plata as a land of knife-wielding gauchos. Cattle slaughtered for hides became the usual targets of the gaucho throat-cutters, but under Rosas their techniques were sometimes applied against people. Europeans were affronted to learn that people had to display the scarlet emblem of Rosas's followers, the Federales, in the streets of Buenos Aires. They risked the unwelcome attentions of the Mazorca if their personal correspondence failed to proclaim the regime's slogan. It exhorted long life to Rosas and death to his enemies: '¡Viva la Federación! ¡Mueran los Salvages Unitarios!' Many of the most damning stories about Rosas contained more fiction than fact and derived from his enemies' propaganda.[10]

In the 1840s the Europeans were not attempting to open up Buenos Aires to trade: revolutionaries who had overthrown the Spanish colonial regime instituted free trade in the city in 1810. They were more concerned about the smaller city of Montevideo across the Rio de la Plata estuary, which was currently under siege by Rosas's allies. In 1845, Lord Aberdeen authorised intervention to pressure Rosas to abandon the siege. He was applying the principle formulated by Lord Palmerston (his predecessor and successor), who held that 'the duty of government lay in opening channels for the merchant'.[11] By the 1840s, British trade with the Rio de la Plata had reached substantial but not massive levels. Currently (during an exceptionally unstable period) its value stood at around one-third of trade with Brazil and Canada, respectively, and one-tenth of the United States.[12]

The year 1845 marked the midpoint of a long civil war in Uruguay known as the 'Guerra Grande'. Montevideo became famous as the site of a siege lasting nine years, which leading French novelist Alexandre Dumas dubbed 'The New Troy'. During the war, Rosas was backing the Blancos (Whites), a rural-based armed faction in Uruguay under ex-president Manuel Oribe. They were fighting the Colorados (Reds) based in Montevideo. The Colorados enlisted numerous European mercenaries, including Giuseppe Garibaldi, who fought for several years in Uruguay before returning home to Italy in 1848 to lead the struggle for unification. Underlying the conflict in the Plata lay historic rivalry between Buenos Aires and Montevideo to dominate foreign trade: in attempting to subdue Montevideo, Rosas intended to seal definitively the commercial supremacy of his own city-province.

Foreign intervention took the form of an Anglo-French blockade of Buenos Aires. As preceding blockades in 1826–8 and 1838–40 had shown, this form of external pressure had serious effects. Blockades throttled foreign trade in a city highly dependent on commerce. Since four-fifths of revenues derived from tariff duties, the disruption of foreign trade threatened to bankrupt the government. Blockades provoked unrest among rural producers who exported cattle goods and wool, and among consumers who relied on imported manufactures. Secondly, the Anglo-French intervention of the 1840s extended into an attempt – quite illegally under international law – to open up the Rio Paraná by force to 'free navigation'. This meant ignoring the sovereignty of the Argentine Confederation over the Rio Paraná in an effort to promote commercial ties between the port of Montevideo and the Argentine interior. Although the envoy, Ouseley, and not the minister, Aberdeen, authorised the forcing of the river, Aberdeen shared the outlook of the time that navigable waterways like the Paraná ought to be open to foreign trade. His opinions reflected those of Richard Cobden and his followers, the ideologues of free trade who claimed that free trade (or free navigation) benefited everyone and provided the key to world peace. If the Latin American republics adopted free trade, they would escape the instability that had plagued them since emancipation. In his instructions to Ouseley, Aberdeen wrote that

> The opening of the great South American arteries to the free circulation of goods would not only provide vast benefits to European commerce but also a practical and perhaps the best guarantee for the preservation of peace in America itself.[13]

As partners in the intervention, the French were attempting to protect about 15,000 French citizens, mainly artisans and peasants from the Basque country, living principally in or near Montevideo.[14] Rosas and Oribe threatened the settlers by overrunning their homes and farms and occasionally taking them hostage. The French wanted to improve the lot of French artisans and shopkeepers in Buenos Aires against whom Rosas occasionally expressed animus because of their previous support for his political enemies. As governor of Buenos Aires he refused to extend to the French the favours and privileges that the British had obtained in 1825 through the Treaty of Amity, Commerce and Navigation. The treaty granted the British the standing of most favoured nation in trade (meaning that no other country could be offered better conditions). They were permitted to build their own churches and worship freely, and exempted from forced loans and military service.[15] Deprived of comparable privileges, French settlers faced inconveniences and the potential horror of military conscription, a virtual death warrant under the harsh conditions in which the men were forced to serve. In 1830–45 the French population of the Plata grew rapidly to prompt speculation in Britain that Uruguay could become a French colony. Under Palmerston, who served as foreign secretary before 1841 and after mid-1846, the British government manoeuvred to weaken the standing of the French.

In the interim period of 1841–6, however, Sir Robert Peel's ministry adopted a less anti-French stance that provided an opportunity for Anglo-French cooperation.

Throughout this period, British merchants held salient positions in the commerce of both Buenos Aires and Montevideo. The 'Anglo-Porteños' of Buenos Aires enjoyed a larger share of the region's foreign trade. Content with their privileges under the 1825 treaty, they wanted to retain the status quo. They urged the British government to maintain amicable relations with Rosas and turn a blind eye to his designs on Montevideo. The 'Anglo-Uruguayans' argued that trade between Britain and Montevideo was increasing rapidly. They claimed that Montevideo possessed far greater future potential for British trade than Buenos Aires and pressured for metropolitan support to enable them to seize supremacy. Some Anglo-Uruguayans supported a plan to annex the Rio Paraná provinces of the Argentine Confederation to Uruguay. They wanted to establish a federation of Greater Uruguay headed by Montevideo and extending to the Republic of Paraguay in the far north. They dreamt of bringing the federation under British imperial protection. The Anglo-Uruguayan plan lay in seizing control over the hinterland from Buenos Aires in order to establish Montevideo as the new commercial metropolis of the region.[16] These British merchants aspired to redraw the political map of South America.

The 1825 treaty created a system of interdependence between the governments of Buenos Aires and the resident British merchants. The government provided security to the merchants while the merchants generated the trade revenues to support the government. Only a handful of Catholic clerics, objecting to the presence of 'Protestant' interlopers, wanted to disrupt or terminate a relationship that benefited both sides. After his election as governor in 1829, Rosas divested foreign merchants of their previous partial control over the National Bank, leaving it still more a mere paper money printing instrument. In all other respects he tolerated and supported the British, along with everyone else not overtly opposed to him.

After more than 30 years of commercial contact and residence, by the 1840s the British were well established in Buenos Aires. Merchants with access to overseas credit, shipping and goods made fortunes by importing manufactures and exporting cattle goods.[17] Trade expanded rapidly during the early 1820s under Bernardino Rivadavia, an Anglophile liberal.[18] In proposing the commercial treaty of 1825, Foreign Secretary George Canning intended to establish a commercial 'colony' in Buenos Aires like those in ports such as Lisbon and cities of the Baltic and Mediterranean. Members of the merchant colony would sell British export goods wholesale and act as trend-setters or role models for local consumers of British goods, but live under the authority of an independent state. One clause in the 1825 treaty went largely unnoticed until the Anglo-French intervention specified that British merchants or residents could continue to live, subject to good behaviour, in Buenos Aires during a blockade, even if diplomatic relations with Britain were suspended or broken.

In the late 1820s, British settlers spread into rural Buenos Aires led by cattle ranchers, sheep farmers and tenants who became wool producers. The ranchers included city merchants seeking protection against economic instability by investing in livestock and by buying (but more commonly renting) land. Some merchant-ranchers set up *saladeros*, the meat-salting plants of nineteenth-century Buenos Aires, in which gauchos slaughtered thousands of cattle for hides, tallow and salted beef. Sheep farming started to expand in the 1820s and came to dominate many parts of the province until around 1880. By the 1840s, Scottish rural communities were appearing south of the city, although Irish shepherds who settled mainly in the west and north-west outnumbered them. Hundreds of tenants and labourers of British and Irish origin lived in the settled areas of rural Buenos Aires.[19] In another significant process of this period, settlers and ranchers, including some of the British and Irish, were expanding across the local frontier into areas occupied by indigenous peoples.

The Anglophone population of the early nineteenth century contained interesting figures. William Henry Hudson, the eminent nineteenth-century Anglo-Argentine author, was born in 1841 in a hut on a tenancy known as Los Veinte Cinco Ombúes about 25 miles south of Buenos Aires. The farm lay on an estancia (ranch) owned by a Scottish family located near the former Scottish settlement at Monte Grande.[20] Hudson's family formed part of a small English-speaking tenant class of very modest means in rural Buenos Aires. He had Welsh and Scottish ancestry although his parents were New Englanders, members of a small migrant group of ex-Bostonians.[21] Hudson's veneration for the wildernesses and rural spaces of La Plata hinted at his American background. His mother fostered a bond between her son and England by schooling him in English literature using a painstakingly collected home library. In 1874 at age 33, Hudson left Buenos Aires for London where he remained until his death nearly 50 years later. He became known in Britain and the United States during his literary career as someone who wrote mainly about the natural world. He was less well recognised as one the greatest writers about the mid-nineteenth-century rural society and rural culture of the Rio de la Plata.

In old age, Jane Robson (born Jane Rodgers) recounted her life as mother, pioneer rancher and sheep farmer on the pampas. She belonged to an older generation than Hudson, having arrived in Buenos Aires in 1825 from Scotland at age three aboard the *Symmetry*. As a child in the small Scottish colony at Monte Grande, she witnessed the destruction of the settlement in 1829 when her father barely escaped being murdered by insurgent Federales. At a young age she learnt how to cross swollen rivers by horseback and to navigate thickets of giant thistles covering much of the terrain where she lived. She developed a bold and forceful personality. She recalled how she once risked being murdered when she rode through a military encampment of the Federales wearing light blue, the forbidden colours of the hated Unitarios. When a British hospital was founded in Buenos Aires in 1844, she criticised its administrators' refusal to treat women patients. Robson and her husband began married life in 1840 as tenants like Hudson's parents but soon became owners of a large flock of sheep. In the mid-1850s the couple acquired an estancia near Chascomús, a village about 60 miles south-east of Buenos Aires. This district, in which a Presbyterian church was founded in 1857, contained a small, closely interconnected population of Scottish sheep farmers. Like other local landowners, the Robsons profited from the railroad connection to Chascomús built in the 1860s. They amassed camp, flocks, herds and children. Jane Robson died a widow in 1910 at age 88 with an enormous family and as owner of nine square miles of prime grazing and farmland. 'With the passing of the years', she commented modestly, 'we had gradually bought a good deal of land around our house'.[22]

Hudson and Robson and their families shared a tie with sheep farming, which divided rural Anglophones into two social groups of unequal status. The minority, to which the Robsons belonged, joined the gentry while the majority, including the Hudsons, belonged to a much poorer population of semi-itinerant tenants. Jane Robson's situation contrasted with that of the Hudsons by her prominence in a closely knit ethnic community linked by language, religion and intermarriage. Writing about such communities in the mid-1840s, a visitor noted how their members retained

> Their distinctive British habits and institutions... Scattered widely apart though they are over an extensive surface, they maintain by intercourse with one another the feelings and habits of a home community. They educate their children to the extent they are able in the home principles and manners, and they come together at stated times from a circuit twenty or thirty miles in diameter for the purpose of divine service.[23]

Robson and Hudson interacted in contrastive ways with the surrounding Hispanic populace, the peons, gauchos, 'natives' or *chinas* as poor rural women were known.[24] For outdoor work like sheep-shearing or ploughing, the Robsons worked for themselves or hired Europeans, who were housed during the shearing season in communal sheds near the estancia house. Jane Robson viewed the South American peons with mistrust and aversion. Her use of the word 'native', ordinarily an English equivalent of *nativo*, meaning locally born, had the pejorative edge of Anglophone usages in other parts of the world. Her negative view derived from her childhood in the Scottish colony when gaucho soldiers destroyed the Scottish settlement, attacked her father and killed the brother of the man she later married. She contended dogmatically that the 'taking of life and property was held very lightly' by peons; she viewed them all as threatening, 'untrustworthy... worse than useless', and minimised her contact with them.[25]

The negative outlook did not extend to everyone, including some of the visitors to the area from Britain. The exceptions included Charles Darwin, who disembarked at various points along the coasts of the Plata and Patagonia in 1832–3 during the voyage of HMS *Beagle*. Darwin's diaries included a description of a group of local men whom he encountered in the Banda Oriental:

> They are a singularly striking looking set of men-generally tall and very handsome, but with a most proud, dissolute expression. Their politeness is excessive, they never drink their spirits without expecting you to taste it; but as they make their exceedingly good bow, they seem quite ready, if the occasion offered, to cut your throat.[26]

Of the range of attitudes and forms of contact with the Hispanic rural population, Hudson's were by far the most intriguing and appealing. Despite his long residence in England, his writings betrayed his links with the pampas and his upbringing in two cultural worlds.[27] Late in life in the early 1920s, he retained traces of sympathy with the rural Federales of his youth and of his respect for Rosas who had died almost half a century previously. He called Rosas 'certainly the greatest and most interesting of all the South American Caudillos'. In his autobiography, *Far Away and Long Ago*, he recalled that

> [Rosas] was abhorred by many, perhaps by most; others were on his side even for years after he vanished from their ken, and among these were most of the English residents of the country, my father among them.[28]

Hudson grew up in close proximity to the rural Hispanic populace. He knew not only their language but also their cultural and religious codes. In youth he listened to fireside tales that he later wrote up and published. In some of these writings, Hudson's polished English prose contains echoes of the longer cadences of *rioplatense* Spanish. An example appears in a statement by one of his characters arguing that social differences did not count in rural areas:

> Here the lords of many leagues of land sit down to talk with the hired shepherd, a poor bare foot fellow in his smoky rancho, and no caste or class difference divides them, no consciousness of their widely different position chills the warm current of sympathy between them.[29]

Hudson grew famous later in life for his writings about nature – birds, flora and landscapes. A recent study has redefined him as a pioneer environmentalist.[30] His best works relating to the Plata included his description of rural Buenos Aires in *Far Away and Long Ago* and his idiosyncratic account of Uruguay in *The Purple Land*. The latter book narrated the adventures of a young Englishman in a 'country bloodstained with the blood of her children', and therefore known as 'the purple land', where Hudson lived for a time in the late 1860s. As once noted by another great Argentine writer, Jorge Luis Borges, *Purple Land* provided a cross-cultural view of the life of an Englishman in the libertarian world of the rural Rio de la Plata.[31] The book pretended sympathy with imperialism. Hudson initially lamented the failure of the British to conquer the area, to reduce it to order and propel its progress, but he concluded his book with a ringing paean to independence. He extolled the licentious anarchy of a 'perfect republic, [where] freedom of intercourse [was] tempered only by that innate courtesy and native grace of manner peculiar to Spanish Americans'.[32]

He possessed an extraordinary ability to capture the cultural and spiritual outlook of the gauchos. In his short stories, such as *El Ombú* and *Marta Riquelme*, and in passages of *The Purple Land*, he replicated the narrative techniques of gaucho storytellers and balladeers. He was describing himself when he told his fellow writer, Robert Cunninghame Graham, 'Certainly, you are unique among English writers [because] you identify yourself with those who are most unlike us.'[33] He claimed his own efforts to portray the culture of the gauchos had failed because of the limitations of the English language: 'Unfortunately, in converting these old memories to English, the primitive grace of the gaucho narrative [has] disappeared.'[34] More subtly and elegantly than other writers, Hudson recreated the invisible, supernatural world of the gauchos. He illustrated forms of animism, such as snake worship, to denote the linkages between the natural and supernatural worlds in gaucho eschatology.[35] In *Marta Riquelme*, a fantasy set in Jujuy, he deployed animism once more in a story centred on the mysterious bird-woman who played a recurrent role in gaucho legends.

After 1825, amidst recession, political strife and sporadic civil war, conditions in Buenos Aires became much less favourable to the Anglo-Porteños. The collapse of the currency bankrupted numerous merchants, who were paid in depreciating paper money but had to settle their debts abroad in hard currency. In rural areas, bouts of pillage affected the Anglophone settlers, as occurred in the Monte Grande colony. In a period of weak government that preceded the consolidation of power by Rosas in the mid-1830s, Britons attempted to leave the country or sank into poverty. In Britain itself the enthusiasm of Canning's day for Buenos Aires and South America at large waned. The hopes enshrined in the 1825 treaty were apparently being dashed. 'We have long ceased to pay [the area] the attention it deserves,' declared *The Times*. Emancipation from Spain after 1810 'was supposed to have opened [the country] to liberty and civilisation...but the rank native growth of the soil has choked the seeds we hoped to plant there'.[36] In the

1830s, British governments ignored the distant ethnic community in Buenos Aires. A sense of isolation and abandonment among the Anglo-Porteños became manifest in their deferential attitudes towards Rosas. From 1835 when Rosas won re-election as governor of Buenos Aires with unlimited personal power, the community events of the Anglophones concluded with toasts to him in Spanish. Their expressions of regard mingled fear with respect for his ability to impose order.[37]

Montevideo, the second city of the Rio de la Plata, long commanded more interest from British military officers and naval skippers than from merchants. Soldiers commented on its potential as a defensive stronghold, calling it a second Gibraltar on account of its Spanish-built citadel on the peninsula adjacent to the harbour. Sailors preferred the deep-water port of Montevideo to that of Buenos Aires because of its location east of the treacherous shallow waters of the Rio de la Plata. When commerce in Buenos Aires declined in the late 1820s, British merchants in Liverpool began to size up Montevideo as an alternative commercial base. George Canning envisaged setting up an independent city state in the Banda Oriental 'in a position somewhere similar to the Hanseatick Towns in Europe'.[38] Montevideo would become a model beacon of free trade in South America, a 'free port for all nations', whose neutrality was acknowledged and guaranteed by its neighbours.

Under the city-state project, however, Montevideo remained excluded from the main commercial circuits of the region. Exports of wool, cattle goods and, by the late 1820s, dwindling quantities of Bolivian silver passed mainly through Buenos Aires. Most European goods arrived in the Plata on order from Buenos Aires. When disembarked in Montevideo, they were reshipped along the Uruguayan coast in small shallow craft to the port of Colonia del Sacramento (a former Portuguese smuggling depot) and then taken across river to Buenos Aires. In order to prosper independently of Buenos Aires, the Montevideo merchants had to capture the flow of trade from the Argentine interior. The way to help Montevideo lay in stopping up trade in Buenos Aires. When the French imposed a blockade on Buenos Aires in 1838–41, the population of Montevideo suddenly boomed but then fell away sharply from 1843 when Rosas turned the tables and laid siege to Montevideo.

In the 1830s and early 1840s, mercantile firms operating in Montevideo increased to almost 150, of which around a fifth were British and a fifth French (most others were Uruguayan and Brazilian). Several British firms had close ties with Samuel Fisher Lafone, a British merchant and a Liverpool-born migrant to the Rio de la Plata in the mid-1820s. Lafone began his career in Buenos Aires but moved across river to Montevideo in 1833. His departure reflected the impact of a deep commercial recession. It also followed the scandal of his clandestine marriage the year previously to a Creole woman in a Protestant service. Persecution by the Catholic priesthood left him embittered towards Buenos Aires and encouraged him to move elsewhere.

During his near-50-year career (which ended in his death from yellow fever in 1871), Lafone remained at the heart of nearly every leading business venture in Montevideo. His ties in Britain centred on Liverpool, where he possessed an extensive family network with multiple business and political connections. In Montevideo his main activity derived from his *saladero*. It consisted of exports of hides to Europe and of beef (salted beef and 'jerky') exported to Rio de Janeiro and Havana for consumption by African slaves; he also exported tallow used in Europe to manufacture candles and soap. In ways that were typical of the merchant entrepreneurs of the era, he created or dabbled in many other enterprises. These included a scheme to bring migrants from the Canary Islands to Uruguay and to promote trade and settlement on the Falkland Islands, which became a British colony in 1833.[39] Lafone's fortune from exporting cattle goods during the French blockade of 1838–40 illustrated how the merchants of Montevideo profiteered from any disruption of trade in Buenos Aires. His road to wealth lay in obstructing Rosas at every opportunity and he therefore became a prominent backer of the Colorado faction in Montevideo fighting the pro-Rosas Blancos. He took a prominent role in the Sociedad Compradora de los Derechos de la Aduana, a tax farming scheme founded in 1844 in which foreign merchants advanced funds to the cash-strapped government of Montevideo in return for the right to collect customs revenues. The association would profit handsomely if trade through Montevideo increased, as it probably would if another blockade closed access to Buenos Aires.[40] Lafone disseminated a plan to establish a federation in the Uruguay-Paraná region as a British protectorate. William MacCann, his well-informed friend and sympathiser, identified him as the leading proponent of extending the territory of the Republic of Uruguay north-west into the Rio Paraná region.[41]

Lafone's ties in Britain extended to the Association of Mexican and South American Merchants, a pressure group based in Liverpool. In 1842 the association successfully lobbied the Foreign Office to conclude a commercial treaty between Britain and Uruguay, replicating the 1825 agreement with Buenos Aires. *The Times* reproduced in translation the propaganda attacks on Rosas originating among the Unitarios, his Argentine-born opponents, some of whom were currently exiled in Montevideo, and publicised Anglo-Uruguayan claims that stressed the superior commercial potential of Montevideo compared with Buenos Aires.[42] The impact of the publicity on the British government appeared from comments by Lord Aberdeen. In his view, '[o]ur commerce with Montevideo is rapidly increasing and is very much more considerable than with Buenos Ayres...Our trade with Montevideo is very important and it is through the liberal policy of that republic that we may hope for its extension in South America.'[43] Such claims were false. Trade in Montevideo exceeded trade in Buenos Aires only when the latter fell under blockade; similarly, the epithet 'liberal' applied to Montevideo by Aberdeen appeared misplaced in light of the illiberal restrictions that the Anglo-Uruguayans were urging against their cross-river rivals.

Rosas began threatening Montevideo in 1841 when the French blockade of Buenos Aires was terminated. He was anxious to root the Unitarios out of their refuge in the city and to help his client Oribe to regain office. He wanted to increase trade in Buenos Aires to reconstruct the finances of the province after the blockade, and he attempted to restrict trade in Montevideo in much the same way as the Anglo-Uruguayans were trying to restrict it in Buenos Aires. With these objectives he began blocking access to the Rio Paraná and his men eventually sank a line of hulks connected by chains at Vuelta de Obligado, a point at which the great river turns and narrows. The siege of Montevideo began in 1843, following an invasion from the west under Oribe, which John Mandeville, the British minister plenipotentiary, struggled unsuccessfully to avert. Mandeville threatened Oribe with British intervention and later faced some of the blame for committing the British to action.[44]

Negotiations with Rosas over several years failed. In early 1845, Aberdeen appointed Ouseley as the new minister in Buenos Aires, ordering him to make a last attempt to persuade Rosas to terminate the siege. If he failed, as a last resort, Aberdeen authorised him to join the French in a blockade of Buenos Aires. The envoy spent months attempting in vain to persuade Rosas to abandon the siege. In July 1845 he gave up. He crossed the river to Montevideo and in agreement with his French colleague, Baron Antoine Louis Deffaudis, instated the blockade. At least initially, neither European power was prepared to invade Buenos Aires. Aberdeen explicitly prohibited Ouseley from landing troops. The British Government had 'no intention of carrying on any operations by land', except on the small island of Martín García, which dominated access to the interior rivers. He emphasised that the policy aimed to protect the sovereignty of the Republic of Uruguay, not to threaten that of the Argentine Confederation.[45] The Foreign Secretary maintained this position. In March 1846, Ouseley appealed for more troops but Aberdeen refused to send them 'to foment disaffection and disturbance in a country with which we are not at war'.[46]

Reliance on naval power and refusal to engage in a land war partly marked the realisation that the very shallow water adjacent to Buenos Aires would make it difficult to protect and supply troops from the river. The European commanders feared that once ashore, troops would be forced inland for supplies and become vulnerable to attack. Rosas emphasised these hazards in warning against attempts to land troops. He was confident that the interlopers would not invade because of 'the physical impossibility of approaching town or coast with such vessels as those of which their force is composed'. He would use his cavalry to defeat the Europeans and warned that if necessary he would turn the Mazorca loose against British and French residents in Buenos Aires.[47]

Showing no sympathy for Ouseley, local British residents were apprehensive about Rosas's reaction but never panicked or displayed any inclination to flee. When Ouseley departed for Montevideo, he invited the Britons in Buenos Aires to follow him in order to escape. Some poorer people, mostly recently arrived Irish, left but the wealthy Anglo-Porteños stayed in Buenos Aires.[48] They were far more concerned about losing their wealth and property than about possible reprisals by Rosas. Leading merchants and cattlemen drew up a petition to the Foreign Office, noting their opposition to Ouseley. If they left Buenos Aires, they would forfeit their homes and all of the money that they were owed for the goods they had imported:

> It is utterly impossible for us to leave the country ... Many of us who are engaged in trade with Great Britain hold large stocks of British goods consigned to us for sale. [We] have heavy outstandings in a paper currency daily depreciating ... Others have their entire fortunes in [Buenos Aires] and the country districts.

The petition claimed that the Rosas government was meeting its obligations under the terms of the 1825 treaty to provide them with security. They cited its Article XI, which specified that they could remain in Buenos Aires in the event of a blockade 'so long as they behave peaceably'. They underlined the extraordinarily favourable treatment they received under the treaty:

> The privilege we have in commerce, pastoral or agricultural pursuits, inland navigation or any other brand of industry ... places us on a better footing than the natives themselves since we enjoy all the best rights without any of the serious burthens.[49]

This statement encouraged Rosas to believe that he could defeat the blockade. In his view, 'the great mercantile and other interests of Europeans [in Buenos Aires were] opposed to any rupture [with his government]'.[50] He believed that the British Government would soon realise that British interests had far more to lose from a disruption of commerce in Buenos Aires than they would ever gain through promoting trade through Montevideo.

His assessment proved correct. Ouseley backed away from a fully fledged blockade that would pose a greater threat to Rosas but also stifle British trade. He and Deffaudis instituted a hybrid half-measure. Incoming ships had to halt in Montevideo where they would pay duties twice, on entering the port and on leaving; their goods would then be allowed to cross the river to Buenos Aires. Since they collected the customs duties in Montevideo, the members of the Sociedad Compradora including Lafone enthused about a plan that 'forced a sort of spurious commerce through Montevideo ... to the advantage of a few persons'.[51] When goods finally arrived in Buenos Aires, they became liable to a third round of duties imposed by Rosas. The blockade failed to achieve its desired effect of hurting Rosas without affecting foreign trade. The extortionate level of duties in the two ports combined prompted overseas shippers and merchants to curtail their business. When trade in the Plata fell sharply, the British government faced pressure to rescind the blockade.[52] Aberdeen complied. His relations with Ouseley grew tense. He refused to send out more troops or endorse the Sociedad Compradora, as the envoy requested. When Ouseley tried to convince him that Rosas had been struck by madness, Aberdeen retorted that the governor stood out in 'favourable contrast to much that has been reported of him'.[53] Aberdeen turned against the Anglo-Uruguayans, whom he now considered to be the main instigators of the blockade and of the entire campaign against Rosas purely in their own interests: 'We have been a great deal misled. The agents of Montevideo have been indefatigable... while the merchants of Buenos Ayres have been quiescent'.[54]

Following Aberdeen's lead, the ministry formed in mid-1846 under Peel and Palmerston renewed negotiations with Rosas. Lord Howden, a diplomat despatched to Buenos Aires in 1847, characterised the Montevideo merchants as 'unprincipled villains, mere speculators in war... powerful in England from having so much of the Press under their orders and in their pay'.[55] In Parliament, Benjamin Disraeli denounced the intervention as a waste of public money that had stirred pointless conflict with a country he characterised as a 'second rate revolting colony of Spain'.[56] The French upheld the blockade for a time but it no longer affected British trade. When the artificial diversion of trade to Montevideo ceased, the French had to finance the entire local administration as well as the armies fighting Oribe. Soon after the downfall of the Orleans monarchy in the 1848 revolution, the new republican governments withdrew from the Banda Oriental, handing over all responsibility for Montevideo to the Empire of Brazil.[57]

Enthusiasm for steamboats during the 1840s reflected pressure in Britain for new markets and ongoing efforts to develop new sources of raw materials. Steamboats were also considered to be important new weapons of war as demonstrated in a book by Lauchlan Mackinnon, a naval officer who served in the Rio de la Plata during the intervention. In *Steam Warfare on the Parana*, Mackinnon claimed that in 1845–6 'the wonderful power of steam was fully demonstrated not only in warfare but also in speed of transit'. As he discovered, steamboats reduced the time to proceed upriver from the Plata to the distant city of Corrientes bordering Paraguay from three months to around two weeks.[58] Another book published in 1845 by Thomas Baines, a publicist for the city of Liverpool, claimed that steam power would soon convert the Rio Paraná into a second Mississippi River. According to Baines, riverboats built on the River Mersey would soon slice open South America; tropical regions deep in the interior accessible only by river would develop cotton, tobacco and timber plantations; steam power would link the Andes with the Atlantic and the Paraná with the Amazon, and Montevideo would become 'as flourishing as New Orleans'.[59]

The passion for steamboats took root in Montevideo. *El Comercio del Plata*, a periodical published by Florencio Varela, a noted Unitario journalist, argued that they were the key to the future to bring isolated areas like Paraguay into contact with markets and capital, and to encourage them to develop agricultural exports.[60] Lafone linked the opening of the Paraná by steam with his plan to annex the region to the Republic of Uruguay. The protectorate that he envisioned would be enforced by steam-powered gunboats patrolling the river.[61] Attracted by these visions, in late 1845, Ouseley endorsed an armed expedition upriver from Montevideo although in doing so he ignored Aberdeen's categorical prohibition. 'You would have done better not to authorise the expedition', Aberdeen told Ouseley when he heard about it, describing it as 'an act of aggression upon the territory of the Argentine Confederation'.[62] The objective of the expedition lay in destroying the obstructions imposed by Rosas at the Vuelta de Obligado. Beyond that, Ouseley intended the expedition to support anti-Rosas military forces fighting in Corrientes and to establish contact with the government of Paraguay. He was aiming to forge a grand alliance in the upper Paraná to include Paraguay, whose armies he hoped would march south against Rosas.

In the battle of Vuelta de Obligado on 20 November 1845, Anglo-French forces pierced the boom across the Rio Paraná. A score of European marines perished in the combat but the Argentine dead, at ten times the European casualties, totalled around 250. After the battle a British officer reported a 'horrible and disgusting scene... Hundreds [of Rosas's troops] lay about cut in two, arms and legs cut off, and dreadfully mutilated... the woods are literally strewn with the dead'.[63] The naval expedition then vanished upriver for several months, pursued by a flotilla of slow-moving merchant vessels. Their ports of call extended as far as Asunción, the capital of Paraguay, 1,000 miles north of Buenos Aires, although none of the places they visited ranked much beyond the level of a village. The overwhelmingly rural population of the Paraná region – gaucho herdsmen to the south and Guaraní Indian peasants to the north – remained scattered and poor. The south in particular contained large cattle herds, a source of hides and tallow widely sought by European traders, but yerba mate, the locally consumed herbal beverage traditionally traded downriver to Buenos Aires, represented almost the only cash crop of the north. None of the goods produced in the north commanded the interest of European exporters.

The Paraguayans declined to embark on war with Rosas, and the river expedition's strategic and political objectives failed. As a business venture too, it achieved very little. In this very limited, underdeveloped economy as one observer commented, 'the idea of foreign trade [is] entirely chimerical'.[64]

'One Liverpool cargo would suffice to supply all [its] wants for an entire year,' declared another commentator referring to Paraguay. Trade would never flow down the Rio Paraná unless Englishwomen were persuaded to 'sip yerba mate instead of drinking tea'.[65] A small group of British merchants in Corrientes declared that the upper Paraná had commercial potential but chronic civil war had destroyed it:

> The state of continual warfare in which the province has existed for more than seven years has impoverished the people generally; add to this the absence in the army at present of many of the most industrious labouring classes, whose families depended entirely upon them for subsistence has increased their poverty to such a degree as to paralyse all mercantile transactions, since they are destitute of money to purchase the necessaries of life.

In their view it would take up to 18 months to sell any new cargoes brought upriver from Montevideo.[66]

At most the expedition enabled the resumption of a small trade flow that Rosas's closure of the river had bottled up, but its meagre level fell far short of the expectations of the Merseyside steamboat pioneers. Any stimulus to trade was confined to the province of Entre Rios in the extreme south bordering Buenos Aires. Soon after the expedition, Governor Justo José de Urquiza of Entre Rios began to recognise the potential benefits to his native province of opening the rivers. In the late 1840s he swung in favour of 'free navigation' and gradually withdrew from his previous longstanding alliance with Rosas. As his change of outlook occurred, Urquiza formed a new alliance with the exiled Unitarios of Montevideo and with Rosas's other enemies.[67] To this limited extent alone – by contributing to Urquiza's defection and to the break-up of the polity dominated by Rosas – the Paraná expedition helped to build the scenario for transition in the 1850s. When change occurred, its chief stages included the fall of Rosas in 1852 and the promulgation of the Constitution of 1853, which enshrined a commitment to 'free navigation'. These conditions in turn set the stage for the formation of the national state in 1862, known formally as the República Argentina.

In the late 1840s before Urquiza's rebellion had materialised, Rosas continued to ignore the European diplomats urging him to abandon the siege of Montevideo. For him, the failure of the intervention marked the defeat of imperialism. He would accept 'nothing [that would] savour of a [European] protectorate [in the Plata], nor detract one iota from the liberty and national independence of which [we] are very jealous'. He had demonstrated that '[w]e are not Algeria or India'.[68] As the defender of local sovereignty, Rosas merits recognition as a precursor of Latin American nationalism, yet he had no intention of limiting British trade or quashing all British influence. He endorsed both: while opposing British (and European) military and naval power in Latin America, he supported the expansion of foreign trade.[69] Rosas's views of the relationship he wanted appeared in an article published in 1847 in the *British Packet and Argentine News*, an English-language newspaper in Buenos Aires widely known and recognised as a mouthpiece for his government.

The anonymous author of the article, who signed himself 'Anglo-Porteño', typified the pro-Rosas outlook of the hybridised, well-rooted Britons in Buenos Aires opposed to the intervention. The article blamed the Lafone clique in Montevideo for instigating the intervention. It argued that no self-respecting British government should attempt to reduce Buenos Aires to the same base level as Montevideo, which had become a citadel of colonialism defended by European mercenaries. The British should stop worrying about Montevideo and turn their attention to their real interests in the region – namely, their future trade with Buenos Aires. As they faced up to reality, they should once more encourage the Anglophones of Buenos Aires to function as role models and intermediaries in the ways intended by the 1825 treaty:

> The mass of British settlers are the true pioneers of British commerce. More permanently fixed in the country and mixing more freely with the native population, we are in reality diffusing British tastes and habits; in other words paving the way and creating a demand for British manufacture.

Peering into the future, Anglo-Porteño prophesied a leading role for Buenos Aires as an agrarian exporter closely tied to Britain. He emphasised the potential importance of the Argentine pampas to Britain in the event of future foreign wars affecting supplies of food and raw materials. He foresaw conditions during the American Civil War in the early 1860s when wool from the province of Buenos Aires provided a partial substitute for cotton imported into Britain from the American South. He looked much farther ahead to the First and Second World Wars when Argentina provided Britain with vital supplies of meat and grain. He condemned any attempt to impose colonial rule over Buenos Aires but left the way open for a relationship typical of informal empire. As he claimed, future ties between Britain and the Confederation would provide the British with all of the benefits of colonial rule but eliminate the costs of colonial administration.

> By a little indirect encouragement to voluntary emigration, Great Britain might reap here all the essential benefits of a colony without cost or responsibility, without shedding a drop of human blood, or encroaching on a single right of the native population. Their real and effective independence, their peace and prosperity are elements essential to the success of the plan we advocate ... We condemn the whole system of conquest

and colonisation as based on violence and outrage as always hurtful and frequently ruinous to the mother country herself.[70]

Anglo-Porteño picked out the essence of relations between Britain and Rio de la Plata. Complementary economic interests rendered colonial domination superfluous; blockade, invasion, attempted conquest or occupation would forever prove counterproductive.

Throughout the 1840s the British admiralty conducted naval patrols in the Rio de la Plata and the lower Paraná to protect the independence of Uruguay. Despite such activities, the British government stopped short of endorsing a formal protectorate. In 1841–4, Aberdeen attempted to steer away from embroiling the British in the ongoing strife ashore. Swayed by press propaganda and pressure groups, he eventually authorised intervention by blockade in 1845 but then swung to and fro between the two Anglo factions in the Plata region. At first, by allowing Ouseley an opportunity to impose the blockade against Buenos Aires, he supported the Anglo-Uruguayans. When the blockade damaged British trade, he altered direction to favour the Anglo-Porteños.

Steamboat technology shaped the conflicts of the mid-1840s by encouraging the attempt to open the Paraná to foreign trade. For a brief time it appeared that steamboat technology would serve the aspirations of the Anglo-Uruguayans to annex territory along the Paraná. The failure of the river expedition helped to discredit the intervention and strengthened the view in Britain that British interests lay in abandoning the use of force against Rosas.[71] Overall, the intervention of 1845 demonstrated that a combination of free trade and local sovereignty best served British interests. Adhering to the treaty of 1825 enabled the British to retain a strong presence in the Rio de la Plata for the next century. 'Experiencing imperialism' in the Rio de la Plata became a leading paradigm of 'informal empire'.

Notes

1. My thanks to Colin Lewis for comments on a draft of this chapter. The assessment of costs versus benefits in Spanish America first occurred in the Castlereagh Memorandum of 1807. See C.K. Webster (1908) *Britain and the Independence of Latin America, 1812–1830. Select Documents from the Foreign Office* (Oxford: Oxford University Press), p. 9; W.W. Kaufmann (1951) *British Policy and the Independence of Latin America 1804–1828* (New Haven: Yale University Press), p. 44.
2. M. Hood (1975) *Gunboat Diplomacy 1895–1905: Great Power Pressure in Venezuela* (London: Allen and Unwin).
3. Aberdeen to Ouseley, 2 July 1846, FO 6/114.
4. Instituto Nacional del Revisionismo Histórico Argentino y Latinoamericano. (The National Institute of Argentine and Latin American Revisionism). See *Clarín* (Buenos Aires) 22 November 2011.

5. J-D. Avenel (1998) *L'Affaire du Rio de la Plata (1838–1852)* (Paris: Economia). The author described this battle, a stereotype of nineteenth-century imperialist warfare, as 'un fait, le plus glorieux de l'histoire de la Marine sous le règne de Louis-Philippe', p. 73. From the *revisionista* perspective, Pacho O'Donnell portrayed the battle with similar hyperbole as 'a great epic'. P. O'Donnell (2010) *La gran epopeya. El combate de la Vuelta de Obligado* (Buenos Aires: Editorial Norma). Vuelta de Obligado may be translated as 'Obligado's Twist'.

6. Opponents of 'informal empire' included H.S. Ferns (1960) *Britain and Argentina in the Nineteenth Century* (Oxford: Clarendon Press), a book that mentions the intervention of 1845 only in passing.

7. J. Gallagher and R.E. Robinson (1953) 'The Imperialism of Free Trade', *Economic History Review*, 6:1, 1–15.

8. D. McLean (1995) *War, Diplomacy and Informal Empire. Britain and the Republics of La Plata, 1836–1853* (London: British Academic Press). For the informal empire paradigm applied more widely to Argentina, see David Rock (2008) 'The British in Argentina: From Informal Empire to Postcolonialism', in M. Brown (ed.) *Informal Empire in Latin America. Culture, Commerce and Capital* (Oxford: Blackwell Publishing), pp. 49–77. For a still valuable narration of the intervention, see J.F. Cady (1929) *Foreign Intervention in the Rio de la Plata 1838–1850. A Study of French, British, and American Policy in Relation to the Dictator Juan Manuel de Rosas* (Philadelphia: University of Pennsylvania Press).

9. J. Darwin (2009) *The Empire Project: the Rise and Fall of the British World System* (Cambridge: Cambridge University Press), p. 3.

10. J. Lynch (1981) *Argentine Caudillo. Juan Manuel de Rosas* (New York: Oxford University Press) remains the best biography of its subject in English. A balanced view of the Mazorca appears in G. Di Meglio (2007) *¡Mueran los salvajes unitarios! La Mazorca y la política en tiempos de Rosas* (Buenos Aires: Sudamericana). The Mazorca may have assassinated about 50 people. By comparison, the military regimes of the 1970s killed, by the most conservative estimate, 10,000.

11. Quoted in P.I. Cain and A.G. Hopkins (2002) *British Imperialism, 1688–2000*, 2nd edn (Edinburgh and London: Longman), p. 100.

12. Trade estimates based on British Board of Trade data applied to Buenos Aires and Montevideo combined appear in *El Comercio del Plata* 19 February 1846. The British contributed about 40 per cent of total trade in the region. See *British Packet and Argentine News* [subsequently *British Packet*] 1 January 1842.

13. Aberdeen to Ouseley 20 February 1845, in *Instructions to Mr. Ouseley for His Guidance in the Anglo-French Intervention in the River Plate*. From the Archivo Americano. Montevideo: South American Print Office, 1845, 6. Aberdeen warned explicitly against attempting to open the Paraná by force. His successor, Palmerston, admitted that the British had no right to treat the Rio Paraná as an open waterway except by the consent of the Argentine Confederation. Outsiders 'cannot claim any right with regard to the navigation of that river'. Palmerston to Ouseley No. 5, 4 November 1846, FO 6/114.

14. Jürgen Schneider (1977) 'Le commerce français avec l'Amérique Latine pendant l'âge de l'independance', *Revista de Historia de América*, 84, 63–87.

15. A text of the 1825 treaty appears in Sir Woodbine Parish (1839) *Buenos Ayres, and the Provinces of the Rio de la Plata; Their Present State, Trade, and Debt; with Some Account from the Original Documents of the Progress of Geographical Discovery in Those Parts of South America During the Last Sixty Years* (London: J. Murray), p. 396 *passim*.

16. See 'From Lord Sandon', 26 July 1842. 'Requesting an Interview for a Deputation of Liverpool Merchants Trading with Montevideo'. *Index and Register* FO 605.

17. V.B. Reber (1979) *British Mercantile Houses in Buenos Aires, 1810–1880* (Cambridge: Harvard University Press).

18. D. Rock (2013) 'Porteño Liberals and Imperialist Emissaries in the Rio de la Plata: Rivadavia and the British', in M. Brown and G. Paquette (eds.) *Connections after Colonialism: Europe and Latin America in the 1820s* (Alabama: University of Alabama Press).

19. W. MacCann (1853, 1971) *Two Thousand Miles' Ride Through the Argentine Provinces* (New York: Ams Press), Vol. I, pp. 6–100.

20. Maxine Hanon places Los Veinte Cinco Ombúes on land owned by John Davidson, a Scots immigrant who arrived in 1832. M. Hanon (2005) *Diccionario de britanicos en Buenos Aires. (Primera epoca)* (Buenos Aires), p. 256. The ombú is the large evergreen bush of the Argentine pampas.

21. The ratio of Americans to Britons stood at 1:10. The national census of 1869 shows about 1100 *norteamericanos* in urban and rural Buenos Aires compared with almost 11,000 *ingleses*.

22. J. Robson (2000) 'Faith Tried Hard', in I.A.D. Stewart (ed.) *From Caledonia to the Pampas: Two Accounts by Early Scottish Emigrants to the Argentine* (East Lothian, Scotland: Tuckwell Press).

23. Enclosure in Ouseley to FO 30 May, 1845 FO 6/123. The anonymous memorandum to the British envoy is reproduced in Wilbur Devereux Jones (February 1960) 'The Argentine British Colony in the Time of Rosas', *Hispanic American Historical Review*, 1, 90–7.

24. *Peón* is a social label denoting a rural worker and *gaucho* a cultural marker visible in mode of dress, outlook or way of life.

25. Robson, 'Faith Tried Hard', p. 32.

26. R.D. Keynes (ed.) (1988) *Darwin's Beagle Diary* (Cambridge: Cambridge University Press), p. 88; (also 171, 205 for Darwin on Rosas).

27. F. Arocena (2003) *William Henry Hudson: Life, Literature, and Science* (Jefferson, North Carolina: McFarland and Co.), p. 8 refers to Hudson living on 'cultural frontiers'.

28. W.H. Hudson (1945) *Far Away and Long Ago.* Foreword by John Galsworthy (London: T.M. Dent and Sons), pp. 112, 126.

29. Quoted in D. Miller (1990) *W.H. Hudson and the Elusive Paradise* (New York: St Martin's Press), p. 108. Expressions anglicising *platense* Spanish are 'no caste or class difference divides them' and 'warm current of sympathy'.

30. Dennis Shrubsall and Pierre Coustillas (2007) *W.H. Hudson. The First Literary Environmentalist: 1841–1922. A Critical Survey* (Lewiston: E. Mellen Press).

31. J.L. French ' "Literature Can Be Our Teacher?" Reading Informal Empire in *El inglés de los güesos*', in Brown, *Informal Empire*, p. 78.

32. W.H. Hudson (2002) *The Purple Land. Being the Narrative of One Richard Lamb's Adventures in the Banda Oriental, in South America as Told by Himself* (Madison: University of Wisconsin Press), p. 244.

33. R. Curle (ed.) (1941) *W.H. Hudson's Letters to R.B. Cunninghame Graham* (London: The Golden Cockerel Press), p. 71.

34. Jurado, *Hudson*, p. 161.

35. Hudson, *Far Away and Long Ago*, p. 178 (on snakes); p. 194 (on animism, defined as 'the tendency or impulse or instinct, in which all myth originates, to animate

all things; the projection of ourselves into nature; the sense and apprehension of an intelligence like our own but more powerful in all visible things').

36. *The Times*, 8 January 1845.
37. On one St. Andrew's Day, the Scots toasted Rosas as *La Estrella de Esperanza*, 'The Star of Hope' *British Packet*, 19 December 1835.
38. Canning to Ponsonby 28 February 1826, FO 6/12.
39. On Lafone, see Hanon, *Diccionario*, pp. 492–4; Peter Winn (1994) *Inglaterra y la Tierra Purpúrea 1806–1880* (Montevideo: Facultad de Humanidades y Ciencias de la Educación), pp. 66–70.
40. P. Sims (2001) 'Crisis and Speculation: British Merchants and the Uruguayan Civil war, 1839–1851', Paper presented at the European Historical Economics Conference, Dublin.
41. MacCann, a former Liverpool merchant, recorded his conversations with Lafone in the 1840s in his book *Argentine Provinces*, Vol. II, pp. 218–87.
42. *The Times*, 17 February 1845 reproduced the Unitario propaganda known as the *Tablas de Sangre* (*The Annals of Blood*). The newspaper claimed that Rosas had cost British exporters č5 million, equivalent to around seven years' exports – a highly exaggerated claim.
43. Quoted in McLean, *War, Diplomacy*, p. 201.
44. See Anon. (1847) *British Diplomacy in the River Plate* (London: Whittaker and Co.), pp. 14–15; also Index and Register 3 May 1843 FO 605, in which the Foreign Office disapproved of Mandeville's warning to Rosas and Oribe of the imminent arrival of an Anglo-French naval squadron.
45. *Instructions to Mr. Ouseley*, p. 8.
46. Ouseley to Aberdeen, 29 March 1846 FO 6/116; Aberdeen to Ouseley 5 May 1846. FO 6/114.
47. Ouseley to Aberdeen, 4 August 1845. FO 6–104.
48. For discussion of the Irish, see Fahy to Wilfrid Latham 27 August 1845 FO 6–104.
49. Petition from Merchants and Landowners to the Foreign Office, 31 July 1845. FO 6–108. Signatories included some of the best-known British (mostly Scots-Argentine) ranchers and *saladeristas* in Buenos Aires. Article XI of the 1825 treaty stated that if trade were disrupted, 'the subjects or citizens of either of the two contracting parties ... shall have the privilege of remaining and continuing their trade, without any manner of interruption, so long as they behave peaceably, and commit no offence against the laws'.
50. Ouseley to Aberdeen 4 August 1845. FO 6–104.
51. U.S. Consul William A. Harris, 1 July 1847. Quoted in G.D.E. Philip, K. Bourne and D.C. Watt (1991) *British Documents on Foreign Affairs, Reports and Papers from the Foreign Office. Confidential Print Part 1. From the Mid-Nineteenth Century to the First World War* (Bethesda, Maryland: University Publications of America), p. 74.
52. In London, the *Morning Chronicle* for the Whig opposition denounced 'War by England and France against the British merchants of the River Plate' (Quoted in *British Packet* 2 February1846).
53. Aberdeen's exchanges with Ouseley are contained in FO 6/114 and 118. Support in Britain for Buenos Aires mostly surfaced after the blockade was imposed. The Anglo-Porteño outlook is best set out in the anonymous essay, *British Diplomacy in the River Plate*, published in 1847. The end of the British blockade is conventionally dated July 1847, but it ceased in practical form about 18 months previously.
54. McLean, *War, Diplomacy*, p. 80.

55. On Howden, see McLean, *War, Diplomacy*, p. 190.
56. *British Packet* 7 April, 1849.
57. On Montevideo in the late 1840s as the French scaled down their subsidies, see José Luis Bustamante (1849, 1942) *Los cinco errores capitales de la intervención anglofrancesa en el Plata* (Buenos Aires: Solar).
58. L.B. Mackinnon (1848) *Steam Warfare on the Parana: a Narrative of Operations, by the Combined Squadrons of England and France, in Forcing a Passage up that River* (London: Charles Ollier), Vol. I, p. 1.
59. T. Baines (1845) *Observations on the Present State of the Affairs of the River Plate* (Liverpool: Liverpool Times Office), pp. 9–10. On Merseyside steamship building, see K. Warren (1998) *Steel, Ships and Men: Cammell Laird, 1824–1993* (Liverpool: University of Liverpool Press), pp. 30–1. In the 1840s the Laird company, an early developer of iron steamships, was 'ahead of the market, especially in building in iron' and actively seeking foreign markets.
60. *CP* 4 October 1845; on the expansion of steam shipping in Britain as measured by horse power, 5 March 1846.
61. 'A British war steamer should continually ascend and descend these rivers, giving to English merchants the countenance and protection they so absolutely need', MacCann, *Argentine Provinces*, Vol. II, p. 292.
62. Aberdeen to Ouseley 14 February 1846, FO 6/114.
63. Captain Reginald Levinge, cited in *The Westmeath Guardian and Longford News-Letter*, 26 March 1846.
64. *British Diplomacy in the River Plate*, p. 38.
65. *British Packet*, 16 July 1842.
66. Merchants to Ouseley, 27 January 1846, FO 6–117. Further details of conditions in the upper Paraná following the expedition appear in *British Packet*, 6 February 1847.
67. On the impact of the intervention on Urquiza, see B. Poucel (1864) *Les Otages de Durazno. Souvenirs du Rio de la Plata pendant l'Intervention Anglo-Française de 1845–1851* (Paris: Achille Faure), p. 68; Cady, *Intervention*, p. 208; T. Whigham (1991) *The Politics of River Trade. Tradition and Development in the Upper Plata., 1780–1870* (Albuquerque: University of New Mexico Press), p. 62; B. Bosch (1970) *Urquiza y su tiempo* (Buenos Aires: Editorial de la Universidad de Buenos Aires).
68. MacCann, *Argentine Provinces*, Vol. II, p. 27.
69. *British Packet*, 15 January 1848.
70. The article, compiled as a memorandum to Lord Howden in 1847, appears in *British Packet*, 3 July 1847.
71. The view presented here opposes the claim that trade from the upper Paraná (Corrientes and Paraguay) 'increased' in the aftermath of the forcing of the Rio Paraná. For that argument, see D. McLean (September 2007) 'Trade, Politics and the Navy in Latin America: The British in the Paraná, 1845–1846', *Journal of Imperial and Commonwealth History*, 35:3, 351–37.

9

'The Bible Dream': Official Travel in Morocco, c. 1845–1935

John Fisher

Travel to Morocco burgeoned in the late nineteenth century.[1] Steamships offering superior comforts crossed from Gibraltar to Tangier, often calling at Morocco's coastal towns before returning to British and Continental ports. The General Treaty of 1856 between Britain and Morocco permitted the appointment of British consuls in towns in the interior as well as on the coast. It also allowed British subjects to travel or live in any part of the Sultan of Morocco's dominions. But until, and even for some time after, the French protectorate commenced in 1912, travellers portrayed Morocco as a timeless, fairy-tale land, whose colours, smells and sounds formed a direct link to the *Arabian Nights*. Thus, in 1845, the Political Agent and Consul-General at Tangier, John (later Sir John) Hay Drummond Hay, observed that Morocco resembled the land of the Scriptures. 'The Bible and the "Arabian Nights" are your best handbooks, and would best prepare you for the scene.'[2] To Arnold Robertson, British Agent and Consul-General at Tangier (1921–4), Morocco was still a 'Bible dream' in 1922.[3] But in and around Tangier, the juxtaposition of East and West was also manifest. The MP David Urquhart noted this when visiting Miss Duncan's house there in 1848. Shortly, he was seated at a table, before a roaring fire. 'On the table stood cruet-stand, knife and fork, Staffordshire plates, and Scotch broth.'[4]

Most British consuls-general and some diplomats, who at various times were stationed in Morocco, were also inclined to travel and to explore. Importantly, they had to seek an audience with the Sultan and his court at Fez. Also, they nurtured expatriate British colonies and their business interests. British missions to the Moroccan court were long-established. Edmund Hogan recorded his journeys as Queen Elizabeth I's sworn esquire to the Emperor of Morocco in 1577. Further official missions followed during the seventeenth century and after.[5] John Russel was one of many to travel there on an official basis during the eighteenth century in order to liberate Christian slaves. More routinely, in Morocco as elsewhere, British consuls travelled within their districts. Many had a keen interest in travel and were adept at recording detail, some of it destined for the Foreign Office.

For politicians also, as for many Britons of a certain class, temperate Tangier offered a wintertime escape, just as it offered refuge to many fugitives from justice and Victorian and Edwardian respectability. Whether the 'Sodom' of North Africa or not, it continued to attract visitors, such that British expatriates there bemoaned the increasing congestion in the Anglican cemetery, on account of deaths among these winter migrants.[6] The focus of this chapter is thus the interface of British officials and politicians, and travel in Morocco. Literature on the subject is scant.[7] Indeed, historians have only recently begun to address travel and the official mind at all.[8] Some discussion is provided of various kinds of official travel: official perceptions of what was, and remains, a unique country. Specifically, how did officials perceive the prevailing political disorder? Connected with this, how did they perceive Moroccans? Was travel, of various kinds, important in official dealings in Morocco? How accessible was it to official travellers and what dangers did it present?

The instigation of the French protectorate began to make Morocco accessible. Prior to this, as John Drummond Hay found to his cost in 1846, when visiting Sali, *en route* to Fez, when his party was attacked by a mob, travel was dangerous.[9] In fact, Hay was an inveterate traveller and sportsman who documented Moroccan life.[10] This volatility persisted when Henry Colvile travelled in Morocco in the late 1870s. He had hoped to proceed under the War Office Intelligence Department's aegis. It welcomed any information that he might provide but it would not endorse his journey due to the dangers involved.[11] According to one authority, Sir Robert Playfair, who was Consul-General at Algiers (1867–97, and non-resident consul-general for Tunis also, for part of that period), by the early 1890s, Morocco remained largely unexplored. Much of it had not been accurately surveyed, and Europeans abjured travel in many areas.[12] As Playfair noted in 1892, entry into some Moroccan cities by an unwary traveller would mean certain death.[13] Official peregrinations along the coast and inland towards Fez and Marrakesh were permissible, and had allowed intelligence gathering, to supplement that obtained from camel-drivers, pilgrims and traders, 'But the fanaticism of the people, the jealousy of "Christians", and the passive obstruction of the Government' had effectively closed to Europeans non-coastal areas and those beyond the routes to the capitals.[14] As Playfair noted, the holy town of Wazan was closed until recently. Just 50 years earlier, Fez and Marrakesh could only be visited with the Sultan's permission, though British subjects had lived and traded there long before. Made roads were unknown outside towns, and bridges and ferries were rare. There were no hotels in the interior and tents were preferable to the 'rude caravanserais of the towns', fear of robbery or molestation notwithstanding. Permanent villages were frequently built in secluded places to avoid government exactions or hospitality demanded by privileged travellers. Playfair judged it a 'crumbling empire, physically, politically, but not religiously'. The 'Berber villages with their fences of prickly pear, and the castles which have not been bombarded in the endless civil wars', were the only signs of stability.

The risks entailed in official travel were manifest. Lieutenant William Boulnois's ceaseless intelligence gathering when accompanying Sir William Kirby-Green, Minister at Tangier (1886–91), on his mission to Fez and Marrakesh in 1887, induced a fever.[15] The strain of Green's mission to Fez in 1891, and an altercation with the Sultan, induced a fatal cerebral haemorrhage.[16] Political instability also made travel difficult. In the late nineteenth century, international rivalries increasingly afflicted Morocco, as successive sultans failed to unite it. Until the early twentieth century, Britain was the predominant power in political and commercial terms, its right embodied in various capitulations. The April 1904 Anglo-French Entente Cordiale conceded this dominance to France but France failed to impose order for several years. Spain acquired rights also, but the shortcomings of its administration were manifest. These, together with other factors, periodically made travel beyond Tangier dangerous. Thus a sizeable French zone emerged; two Spanish zones, one in the north and one in the south; and a nominally international zone, which included Tangier and its environs.

Was there anything unique about Morocco's geography and its conjunction with the official mind? In one sense there was. Sir Arthur Nicolson, later Lord Carnock, Minister at Tangier (1895–1905), noted that in Morocco, 'to the smallest detail, one lives in [sic] Eastern life of three centuries ago'.[17] In geostrategic terms also it was unique. Like Egypt, Morocco was not a colony but it had some of its characteristics and it was important to the Empire. Unlike Egypt, however, which occupied a partly analogous strategic position, at the opposite end of the Mediterranean Sea, athwart key trading routes, the scramble for Africa had left Morocco untouched. Imperial eyes, as they traversed it, noted administrative chaos and 'backward' habits. Officials inevitably commented in Orientalist terms on the prevailing chaos, and upon the lack of education that might remedy it.[18] The large retinues of the kaids that Kirby-Green encountered between Mazagan and Fez in 1887 reflected the 'half feudal half Oriental institutions which still distinguish... [Morocco's] military organisation... an organisation infinitely more picturesque and interesting than efficient'.[19] Some were covetous: travel in Morocco afforded knowledge with which Britain might maintain its interests. In 1890 a War Office memorandum suggested that British influence might be spread, and the Moroccans' goodwill and affections obtained, by encouraging 'Englishmen, and especially officers, to proceed on shooting and other excursions into the interior'.[20]

For one consular officer, Morocco was a land of colour. Gerald Selous arrived in Tangier just as Louis Hubert Lyautey, Resident-General of the French protectorate, began to transform Morocco. To Selous, Lyautey had dragged medieval Morocco into the twentieth century. Selous's excitement suffused his description of the journey from England. There was 'unholy rapture' as the boat-train departed. The cabin comfort, bountiful food and deck games on the *Ophir*, from Southampton to Lisbon, Gibraltar and then Tangier, fuelled his expectations. Morocco, when he arrived in 1910, resembled medieval Europe. Travel was by horse, donkey or mule, 'with attendant muleteers and mule-trains carrying tent and camp equipment, food, charcoal, barley, [and] luggage'. Tangier presented a 'succession of thrills', as Selous was borne past the swarming outer market.

> I had entered a land where the primitive and the beautiful reigned side by side, and I was in rapture...complexions of olive, copper, black, wheat, and occasionally white; horse, mule, and donkey transportation...the haunting smell of spices in the bazaars...itinerant story-tellers and snake-charmers, squatting money-changers...handicrafts everywhere...chantings from mosque towers, noon-announcing cannon, veiled women, waddling, blanket-swathed bundles, black-scullcapped Jews from the ghetto; what a scene of kaleidoscopic enchantment and diversity under a glorious sun and a cloudless sky stretched out around and before me.

Beyond Tangier the scene had changed little in a thousand years. The farming methods were those of ancient Sumeria: sun-baked soil, wooden ploughs and winnowing shovels, oxen, asses and wild boar. Between polo matches and 'at homes', Selous learnt about Moroccan politics. He also recorded colleagues' exploits as they traversed the Moroccan landscape. 'Bibi' Carleton, the Vice-Consul at Alcazar, 'lived on his horse': shooting, hawking and pigsticking. Sir John Drummond Hay introduced the latter, and its practitioners formed the Tangier Tent Club, a white, chiefly British, preserve. Carleton met his quarry eye-to-eye in pig-runs, in thorn coverts, on moonless nights in the countryside beyond Tangier.[21] The sport involved local beaters, dogs, adrenalin and blood-letting, usually the pig's.

The imperial eyes that observed Morocco were varied. From 1877, consular officials there were drawn from both the General and the specialised Levant Consular Services. For the latter, training in Oriental and modern European languages was followed by a secondment to a consulate-general. Typically, consuls were from middle and upper middle-class backgrounds. Some, especially those of the General Consular Service, who had not expected to serve in a Muslim country, found conditions trying. To Selous, Fez was 'an outer darkness' when compared with Tangier.[22] By contrast, John Dawkins found Tangier cliquey and socially oppressive when posted there in 1913. Listening to story-tellers was frowned upon.[23] Thus consular travel offered a relief from the trials of everyday life. Posts in the interior were generally regarded as unhealthy. Coastal towns presented other hazards, not least the 'relaxing' climate, which encouraged slackness.[24] Accommodation was seldom satisfactory and in one case, Larache, was potentially fatal.[25] Selous's initial captivation was not unusual. Arrival at Tangier by boat frequently evoked excitement. Occasionally it was dangerous. Stormy weather could prevent landings. The Tangerines and the European colony received Arthur Nicolson 'with unwonted enthusiasm' upon his arrival in 1895. But he regarded Tangier as a 'small Spanish town of 5th rate importance'. As he continued, 'there are Moors and there are Jews, but in the streets through which I first passed I saw more Lato than I did turbans and apparently as many scull-caps...Outside the city you might be in the suburbs of a European town.'[26] A cholera epidemic gripped Tangier but Sir Arthur ventured beyond it directly.[27]

To fellow diplomat Richard Onslow, Viscount Cranley, in 1901 Tangier offered a congenial base from which to master Arabic grammar. As he later recorded, he went to Morocco and mixed with Moors in order to study the Oriental mind: the only means of mastering Arabic.[28] When Cranley returned in 1902 he was unpaid attaché at the British Legation in Tangier. Then the unsettled conditions limited travel. A brief foray to Tetuan, on the Atlantic coast in the spring of 1903, which was more Moorish than Tangier, enabled him to inspect its finer houses, including that of the son of Hadj Mohammed Torres, 'full of beautiful things, but spoilt by the juxtaposition of cheap brass bedsteads and hideous mirrors from Birmingham'.[29] Cranley returned to Tangier in the nick of time: a local tribal leader, Moulay Ahmed Raisuni, had blocked the Tetuan road. Travel was unsafe. A spate of robberies and attacks began, including the kidnapping of Walter Harris, *The Times*' correspondent. They persisted until France imposed order, and then resumed during the First World War. These restrictions were disappointing but Cranley found Tangier diverting. As he noted, unlike in other Moroccan towns, the decapitated heads of malefactors were not displayed on pikes but were paraded in the Kasbah. 'The Tangier Moors were in nowise Europeanised in dress, in religion, or in manners and customs; civilisation seemed to have remained stationary for centuries.'[30] A sense of imminent change did not obscure the timeless sounds of Moorish marriage celebrations. Within sight of the legation, in the souk, country Moors on huge stallions raced through the tiny streets, reining their horses onto their hind legs and firing muskets in the air.[31] So, too, there was the curious dance of Hamadsha. Cranley recounted the dancers squatting in the road, talking and smoking in an ordinary fashion. Within minutes, pipes and drums began to play. The dancers swayed and chanted. 'Suddenly, one gashed his bare head, another threw up a cannon-ball and "headed" it like an Association footballer...Soon all the dancers were streaming with blood from head to foot, but their energy did not seem to decrease but to grow as the blood flowed and their knives flashed, and the cannon-balls were thrown higher and yet higher in the air.' Cranley doubted if they were 'drunk with keef', though he suspected that a snake-charmer, a habitué of the souk, who permitted his snakes to draw blood from his tongue, was. The snake-charmer invariably followed this act by the burning and eating of 'straw and filth'.[32] Cranley (later Fifth Earl of Onslow) never returned to Morocco, fearing that progress, so-called, would eviscerate its charms. But like many others who served there, he never forgot it.[33] Sir Ernest Satow, Minister at Tangier in 1894–5, recalled its beautiful skies, and the abundant iris, narcissus and 'fields of copper coloured marigold'.[34]

And yet, while many Europeans wintered in Tangier, its climate was not uniformly congenial. James MacLeod found winter and spring there 'trying', though summer and autumn were 'delightful'. Its fresh breezes, temperate climate and aquatic sports made it ideal 'for those in need of rest and change'.[35] MacLeod occupied various consular posts in Morocco, chiefly at Fez. It was a post of 'exceptional difficulty',[36] not least because few Europeans lived there and because of summer temperatures. Suitable accommodation and other comforts were scarce. MacLeod took solace in alcohol and golf, which he played in the hills surrounding Fez,[37] and sought to establish a British enclave. In June 1897 he recorded the celebrations at the vice-consulate to mark the Diamond Jubilee. They began with a dinner for ten, at which the French Vice-Consul was the only foreigner. There followed an 'at home' attended by Moorish guests, a firework display, tea and the singing of the national anthem. Moors watched the fireworks from neighbouring roofs. The singeing of the spectators and those operating the fireworks marred the event but it helped British prestige.[38] MacLeod and his replacement when he went on leave travelled beyond Fez. Many consuls, MacLeod included, became knowledgeable about their district and Morocco in general. At a time when tribal unrest was expected to provoke French territorial ambitions, he was asked to obtain military and geographical information to update an intelligence handbook on Morocco. For this purpose he acquired a compass and aneroid.[39] Consuls were debarred from covert intelligence gathering but MacLeod was in receipt of secret service funds.[40] His perambulations, golf club in hand, were less innocent than they might have appeared.

Successive consuls-general also travelled beyond Tangier, not least for audiences with the Sultan. Sir John Drummond Hay's missions to Fez and beyond provided opportunity to form a relationship with successive sultans and their advisers, to highlight the extent of British power, and to negotiate favourable conditions for Britons and British trade. Similarly, both he and his successors tried, largely without success, to have the Sultan institute reforms. The party which comprised Hay's 1868 mission was the first to include women. Then they were the object of generally respectful curiosity, but on his 1880 mission to Fez his daughter, Alice, was almost thrown from a rooftop.[41] On his 1873 mission the party had visited the Atlas Mountains, where he enjoyed Berber hospitality. His son reached the snowline but tribal disorder curtailed the excursion.[42]

Philip Trotter accompanied Hay on his 1880 mission, admittedly in a private capacity. Just five miles beyond Tangier the party reached the 'luncheon tent' and that evening their camp comprised 35 tents. The Union Jack was planted before the Minister's tent and a gun signalled reveille. Hay threatened to strike the tent over the head of anyone who slept after seven o'clock in the morning.[43] But there was time for chess and botany, and to visit the village of Beni Aamer, whose inhabitants' unaffected nature charmed Trotter.[44] The slave markets of Fez resembled 'Feeing Fares' in Scotland, where farm labourers were exposed for hire.[45] Such missions also bore upon prestige. Attention must be paid to the warmness of the reception accorded to rival missions. Kirby-Green on his 1887 mission, which was widely publicised, noted that the unusually extravagant welcome was attributable to 'a wish on the part of the Sultan to give me an exalted impression of his strength as well as from his anxiety to mark the importance which attaches to the presence of a Queen's Representative in Morocco'.[46] For Green, as for other consuls-general, these processions helped them to understand Morocco.[47] Abandoning precedent, the 1887 mission did not return from Fez by the most direct route. Instead Green met with British consuls and merchants. In case Lord Salisbury, the Foreign Secretary and Prime Minister, should consider that he had abandoned his duty, the party had marked the Queen's Golden Jubilee on the return journey 'by every available means of rejoicing'.[48] In addition, Green suggested that his journey had demonstrated the accessibility of routes formerly held to be impassable by Europeans.[49]

As previously noted, Arthur Nicolson was determined to explore Morocco. In 1894 the Sultan, Mulay Hassan, had died, leaving his adolescent son, Abdul Aziz, under a Grand Vizier. Nicolson felt unable to advise him, either about French encroachments from neighbouring Algeria or about more generalised lawlessness which was affecting British interests.[50] Early in 1896, Nicolson prepared to visit the Moroccan Court. Camping equipment befitting a British minister was obtained. Archibald Madden, Nicolson's subordinate, fretted about laundry arrangements. Who would wash, starch and iron for the party?[51] Nicolson advised the purchase of presents for the young Sultan: a Maxim gun, 10,000 rounds of ammunition, chessboards and men, mechanical toys and binoculars. Prestige required that Nicolson should be accompanied. Alfred Irwin, the dragoman, George Seymour, the honorary attaché, and Madden would attend. Also there was an imposing cousin of Nicolson's, a guardsman, who might offset his diminutive stature, an officer from the Gibraltar garrison for the Maxim, and a doctor. The Times's Walter Harris completed his retinue.[52] Careful preparation was essential. Attacks on foreigners had occurred and the Moroccan government decreed that until settled conditions returned, no British subjects or protégés should travel by land, and then only if accompanied by a government soldier.[53] In areas without the Sultan's authority a system of protection was operated.[54]

The party arrived by boat in Mogador (Essaouira), where a large crowd of 'ragamuffin soldiers and an excruciating band' waited. Nicolson struggled to retain his dignity as he negotiated a slippery plank. They travelled to Marrakesh, camping *en route* in the verdant Arghan Forest, and were preceded by an escort bearing a silk standard. At each district the local kaid with several hundred followers met the party. The kaid would shake Nicolson's hand, and with his followers would then dash away 'at full gallop chanting and letting off their guns'. Their kindness and attention were unfailing.[55] At Fez, Nicolson met Kaid Maclean, small and rotund 'with a clean little white beard, and the gayest eyes that ever shone above a bagpipe. Arrayed in a turban and a white bernous he would stride along the garden paths blowing into his bagpipes.' Maclean, a stalwart of Tangier's British colony, was Inspector-General of the Moroccan Army and was prone to dramatic entrances on horseback. He was a divorcee and a British spy, whose position at the court afforded information for successive consuls-general. Nicolson's own entrance into Fez, astride a huge black stallion, was a magnificent occasion. On either side of the road, several miles from the city, were thousands of horsemen and soldiers, banners drawn, 'a brilliant mass of colours ... My tail swelled and swelled as I advanced till I led a whole army ... We suddenly dived into a gate in to the town wall and found ourselves in the most lovely garden ... a mass of large orange trees with the fruit and blossom on them – huge olive trees – shady walks – birds singing and a most delicious perfume – a real paradise of rest and coolness.' Nicolson found the Sultan 'podgy and puffy', but his delight at the gift of the Maxim, and his insistence that they must arrange another 'happy day' shooting bottles together, amused him. Nicolson loved Morocco, riding through fields of iris and narcissus, and 'the pungent hubbub of the little market place', but he despaired of the political chaos.[56] And he resented the Sultan's manipulation by his advisers, who indulged his passion for 'useless extravagances'. Such travel had political importance. Nicolson studied the Sultan's character and authority, his relationship with the Vizier and the state of Moroccan government. Soon after arriving in Fez he had plumbed its depths: 'It is all rapacity, treachery, intrigue, and misgovernment ... I have been in most Oriental countries and I have never seen such complete darkness as reigns here.'[57]

In the spring of 1907, the Minister at Tangier, Gerard (from June 1907, Sir Gerard) Lowther, travelled to Fez. To his wife, Alice, who accompanied him, there seemed little to distinguish those who, approaching death, were abandoned in the gutter, and hamstrung bullocks left for carrion. But her impressions were otherwise favourable. Fez was 'Marvellously African', untouched by Europe for hundreds of years: 'Europe, which we ... imagine is the earth!'[58] Lowther's successor, the Hon. Reginald (later Sir Reginald) Lister, travelled to Fez in the spring of 1909. Mulay Hafeed had displaced his brother, the Sultan, and Lister was to negotiate the terms of his recognition. Lt Colonel Edward Gleichen, who was attached to the mission, recorded the trip. Gleichen noted the indignities when boarding the Tahaddart ferry: a large punt. Upon arrival at their first night's camp the servants had dropped the party's spare clothes into the river. Their night baggage was lost and the only comb was located in the first secretary's wife's hair. Gleichen laid the camp out with due regard to precedence and privacy. It included a 'drawing-room tent, a vast circular blue and white arrangement with a big silver ball on top', at the centre of the first line of tents. Sir Reginald's large tent was to its right. Next to it was Irwin's 'Moorish marquee'. The Moors' tents were at the rear, close to the horses. As Gleichen recorded, 'These frightful hardships, however, produced no depression on the party, and after a capital dinner we turned in and spelt the sleep that the righteous are entitled to after a ride of nearly thirty miles.'[59]

Gleichen's travelogue, in asserting the superiority of English values, also demeaned some Moroccans. Though 'picturesque', Alcazar had 'dirty narrow streets…Jews swarm everywhere: whining, cringing, begging Jews in the gutter, and unshaved, fat, greasy, Jews in the shops.'[60] At Fez the Sultan's band rendered 'God Save the King' with euphoniums, bombardons and bass drums.[61] His bodyguard, though intelligent, were 'barbaric-looking'.[62] The Sultan paid little attention to their gifts, a silver gilt *jardinière* and stand, two silver gilt jugs and a gold mounted revolver, but instead stroked his feet, played with his rosary and launched into high politics.[63] While at Fez, Walter Harris acted as guide, providing a buffer between the party and the Moors. Gleichen distanced himself further by portraying the journey in *Boy's Own* fashion. Each member of the party, or *dramatis personae*, had a soubriquet. Lister was the 'Bashador', Irwin the 'Khalifa' and William Rattigan, the Legation's First Secretary, the 'Naib'. Of the food, Gleichen was more positive, though the 16th and final course of a dinner hosted by a Moroccan merchant was a 'sort of orange hair-oil in tumblers. Extraordinarily nasty'.[64] Though critical of the Moors, Gleichen was captivated by Fez:

> one does not need to have the soul of an artist to appreciate the great beauty of the city and its fair surroundings. The huge crumbling, golden-brown walls, the pale, small-handed, grave-faced people in their silent bazaars, the picturesque corners which meet one at every turn in the narrow streets, the strangely-harmonious grouping of natural colours…the tall, rectangular minarets crowned nearly every one with its stork's nest, the luminous white of the town as seen in the evening from the surrounding hills, with the clouds of swifts, pigeons, bluejays and hawks darting through the poplars and over the olive gardens and ancient walls – all combine to form a picture and an impression which will not fade. It is a vision from the past…[65]

Lister, like Nicolson before him, was impressed by the southern kaids' power, notably that of El Glawi, Aissa-Ben-Omar, 'Mtougui and Kaid Anflus.[66] It was fitting that Lister's party, when debarred from hunting in the mountains beyond Fez due to unsettled conditions, shot pigeon and asserted their martial prowess from the relative safety of Dr Egbert Verdon's roof.[67]

Lister toured Morocco's southern towns in the autumn of 1910 in order to assess their strength. When writing to Sir Edward Grey, the Foreign Secretary, in August 1910, he requested the use of a British cruiser. The notion that he might have to await a chance steamer on his return to Tangier was unthinkable. His French, Spanish and German counterparts were transported on men-of-war.[68] Money and time would be saved. Above all, his prestige 'would not be made to suffer...as it undoubtedly would were he after all the honours paid to him by the great officials of the South, to conclude his journey on board a tramp steamer'.[69] So effusive was Sultan Abdelhafid's welcome that Lister suspected that he was angling for an invitation to the coronation. His 'proud and rebellious spirit' was broken, he was compliant towards the French and his energies were now focused upon 'love and the bottle'.[70] From Fez, Lister toured neighbouring areas, addressing issues bearing upon British interests, and found time to shoot an abundance of wildlife. In late October the party reached Marrakesh, where they enjoyed the view from the top of the Djibilat. Below

> the vast plain, with its groves of palm trees, was slightly shrouded in mist, above which the outline of the peaks of the mountains rose hard and glittering against the cloudless sky. As we approached, the shaft of the Kutubia [Mosque] loomed through the mist, dominating the expanse of low, red walls, roofs, and towers of the city.[71]

Haj Thami, the beautifully mannered Grand Vizier's brother, greeted Lister. Kaids of the neighbouring tribes with their warriors, wearing brilliant colours, lined the approach: 'the wildest men I have yet seen, with large tufts of hair sticking out on each side of their heads, slung with weapons'. In Marrakesh were juxtaposed the Kutubia's beauty, areas given over to refuse, and countless fountains and beautiful gardens. From Marrakesh the party traversed the Atlas, which crawled with Berber warriors, to the kasbah at Telouet, a red stone and baked mud building with crenellated towers. A dance was held in Lister's honour and a huge bonfire 'threw weird lights and shadows on the painted faces and brilliant head-dresses of the women and on the wild excited faces of the men'. The rhythmical swaying of the dancers, the monotonous chanting, and the tambourines and pipes conveyed a disconcerting sense 'of some awful incantation or the last solemn rites before human sacrifice. We all felt slightly nervous as to what might happen next and what part we might be called upon to play.'

British diplomats based in Spain also travelled to Morocco. During the First World War, Spain's pro-German neutrality encouraged fact-finding visits. Sir Arthur Hardinge, British Ambassador in Madrid, visited in the spring of

1916, as did the temporary Military Attaché in Madrid and Lisbon, Captain Josceline Grant. In 1927 Sir Horace Rumbold, Ambassador in Madrid, visited Tangier and the neighbouring Spanish zone. The latter he considered 'sinister and hostile', though Tetuan was scenic. Spanish efforts to pacify it impressed him. Although travelling as a tourist, he was treated 'almost as if I had been King Alfonso himself'. The Spanish authorities felt that his visit might facilitate tourism.[72] He returned to Morocco the following spring, travelling 1,500 miles by car through the protectorate, where he visited the main towns. The unwitting consumption of some tripe, to which the party uniformly objected, alone marred the trip.[73]

Like several of his colleagues who served at the Tangier legation after the establishment of the French protectorate, Jack Garnett, who was first secretary (1916–18), was beguiled by Lyautey. His corresponding disdain for Herbert White, Agent and Consul-General, and for the Francophobe British colony there, meant that he frequently journeyed beyond Tangier. In November 1916 he spent two weeks in Fez during the commercial fair. Besides official engagements and sittings with a Spanish dentist, who also ran the local cinema, he inspected a prison and a lunatic asylum. He was pleased that Lyautey maintained the French residency in 'all the pomp & ceremony of a Vice-Regal Court'. He visited French military posts and delighted in the Duchess de Guise, sister of the Duc d'Orléans, who spoke English with a strong cockney accent.[74] Travel was by steamer to Casablanca and then by car, but German submarines made such movements dangerous. German agents monitored him when he visited Larache in July 1917, in order to check consular arrangements. The agents were inciting tribes in the French protectorate. Then Garnett bemoaned Spanish maladministration, including the demolition of the Phoenician settlement of Lix on the River Luccus. The river valley, Garnett noted (wrongly in Playfair's view), was supposed to be the Garden of Hesperides.[75] He considered such perambulations essential, especially as Herbert White disliked leaving Tangier and its golf course. Returning to Tangier, whether from forays to nearby towns or farther afield in Morocco, or occasionally to Spain, inevitably left Garnett feeling deflated. But if nothing else there was Tangier's luxuriant flora. Its spring-time mimosas, sweat-peas, carnations and freesias were superb.

Garnett, rather like James MacLeod, believed that Britain's commercial prospects in Morocco were good. Official opinion oscillated between this view and the more prevalent notion, which underpinned Britain's signature of the Entente Cordiale, that Morocco had limited potential relative to Egypt. Annual reports recording commercial results and potential, based upon consular tours, had begun during the 1860s and continued for many areas thereafter.[76] During the First World War, pressure mounted among British merchants involved in the Morocco trade to ensure fair treatment of British interests. This provoked official investigations, including a 'semi-official mission' undertaken in the spring of 1918 by Walter Harris and William Cozens-Hardy, ostensibly on behalf of the Bank of British West Africa. Harris's expertise in Moroccan affairs was widely recognised but he was generally a thorn in the side of officialdom. Cozens-Hardy was formerly of Naval Intelligence, to which Harris had supplied information during the war, and was Prime Minister David Lloyd George's confidant. A suspicion remains that with the settlement of Tangier pending, Lloyd George espied an opportunity to have France disgorge some of its gains there. Alternatively, Cozens-Hardy's information would strengthen his position when discussing other places which were more vital to Britain. Both the Harris/Cozens-Hardy investigation and a further Department of Overseas Trade investigation in the autumn of 1918 reported favourably on Morocco's economic future, as well as British participation in it. Such investigations, and further studies undertaken in 1919–20, also depended upon information obtained by consuls travelling in their districts.[77]

By the time that Andrew Ryan was posted to Rabat in 1924, Morocco's political geography had changed again. The Tangier settlement of 1923 had established an international administration for the Tangier zone and Britain's legation was downgraded to a consulate-general. A second consulate-general, which was created in the French zone in the Rue des Consuls at Rabat, was Ryan's home for several years. Though 'still a back-water' and lacking the 'glamour' of its Tangier counterpart, it had some appeal, not least the consulate-general's 'old world charm'. Successive British consuls had lived there for over a century.[78] By the early 1920s, communications in Morocco had improved significantly. Though not overrun by British travellers, an increasing number were exploring beyond Tangier by means of bus services and the expanding French railway system.[79] Ryan confessed that he had not travelled as much as he ought to have done in his district, and Agadir was closed to foreigners until his departure in 1930. He disliked Fez because of the 'sinister mystery' of the inner part of the old town, but Marrakesh was 'more cheerful'. Best of all was Meknes, which reminded Ryan of Istanbul, where he had previously served. Of the coastal towns, besides Rabat, Ryan found Mogador 'derelict', but Safi was the reverse. Nearer to home, Salé's low sea-cliffs and views offered a distraction from official duties, as did the abundant flora for Lady Ryan.[80]

British politicians also travelled in Morocco. As previously noted, David Urquhart had visited coastal Morocco in 1848 but was denied permission to visit Fez. In a lengthy account of his travels he commented widely on Moroccan life, including its customs, dress, food and architecture. There was also a lengthy disquisition on the 'antiquity of the bath in Morocco', as well as a tangential section on the Turkish and the Russian bath: 'A greater comfort there cannot be than a bald pate.'[81] And, Urquhart experimented with Hashish. On the first occasion, 'The impression was that of wandering out of myself.'[82] He then experimented on its effects with several 'patients'. Urquhart also reflected upon the practice of travel: the traveller must combine the imaginative gifts of the poet, the 'scrutinizing eye of a philosopher, [and] the analytical spirit of a metaphysician'.[83]

By the time that Austen Chamberlain arrived in the winter of 1922–3, travel had become easier. According to his widow, Chamberlain felt that his wanderings in foreign countries enabled him to 'read more clearly the thoughts of these nations'.[84] The Chamberlains travelled from Tangier to Casablanca by sea, and thence to Marrakesh. Casablanca was 'Frenchified' and, while 'booming and flourishing', was 'uninteresting'. The onward trip from Casablanca, assisted by an agent and undertaken in comfort, in a 'powerful Renauld', with trailer in tow, averaged speeds of 35–45 miles an hour. It was a curious conjunction of the old and the new. The party's route traversed Chiouia's black soiled plains, and the 'brilliant red marly earth' of the rocky hills. They encountered 'a dozen huge motor diligences crammed full of Arabs and with others thickly perched amidst the baggage on the roof'.[85] Morocco's verdure surprised Chamberlain. Uncultivated sections were covered with palmetto and scrub, and asphodel had begun to bloom. Helianthemum and dwarf orange marigold abounded. Marrakesh's labyrinthine souks and side-streets devoted to crafts were appealing. The Djema el Fna, with its jugglers, acrobats, musicians, snake-charmers and story-tellers, and the Bahia, with its mountain views, were noteworthy.[86] He visited the dyers and the Kutubia. Admiring the city's high, red earth walls on his departure, Chamberlain envied his Conservative colleague Winston Churchill's 'power with the brush'. Marrakesh was 'squalid...but practically untouched'.[87] From Rabat to Salé and then to Fez, Chamberlain declared that the latter place had 'unique character', the ancient, narrow streets of the old town hidden when seen from the surrounding hills, other than by the 'confused murmur as of bees swarming'.[88] From Fez to the ruins of Volubilis and onward to Meknes, Chamberlain was entranced.[89]

Lloyd George, having recently relinquished the premiership, was another winter visitor in 1922–3. He travelled there on board *Narkunda* on Christmas Day.[90] Lloyd George returned when contemplating his final bid for government in coalition with Labour, in December 1935. Then he made for Tangier, where he played golf, and then for Marrakesh, where from his hotel room, facing the Atlas, amid palm orange trees and bougainvillea, he wrote his memoirs, assured his wife that Marrakesh was 'picturesque' and 'definitely *not* smelly', and contemplated the 'frightful shemozzle over Abyssinia'.[91] Dame Margaret Lloyd George's arrival in Marrakesh was preceded by the departure of Lloyd George's long-time mistress, Frances Stevenson, and a further shemozzle was avoided. Like Lloyd George, Winston Churchill delighted in Marrakesh's clean air. In fact, Churchill and his son Randolph joined the Lloyd Georges on that occasion but it was not until 1936 that he painted in Morocco.

The question must arise as to whether the foregoing travel was formative in terms of policy formulation. In the case of the few recorded visits by politicians, this seems unlikely, although one might speculate that it had a subliminal influence. However, in the case of consuls and diplomats it was. John Drummond Hay's willingness to travel extensively on horseback made him a visible and virile symbol of British power and accentuated the effect of his firmness when dealing with the Makhzan.[92] The 1856 Treaty, which he secured, gave Britain an advantage over its continental rivals in allowing the posting of consuls in Morocco's interior. They were the government's eyes and ears.[93] The composite image of Morocco that developed in the minds of statesmen, few of whom prior to the twentieth century had ventured there, largely derived from their reports, and those of successive consuls-general and ministers at Tangier. But as previously noted, practical challenges continued to make travel and information-gathering difficult and dangerous, and some official travel foundered. A case in point was the abortive attempt of the Minister at Tangier, Charles Euan-Smith, to negotiate a more favourable commercial convention in 1892 at the Moroccan Court. The fact that the press grossly exaggerated details of what occurred on that occasion merely pointed to the difficulty of such missions.[94] Concerning dealings with the Sultan, even after the onset of the French protectorate had begun to improve communications, and notwithstanding intelligence provided long before this by Kaid Maclean and Walter Harris, difficulties persisted in obtaining information about events at the court. This afforded importance to official perambulations. Admittedly the significance of such information declined as British political interests dwindled. But for the effective operation of the consular service, the continuation of British commercial interests, the maintenance of British expatriates' morale and the continued well-being of British prestige, travel was essential. When Jack Garnett's successor as first secretary, Archibald Clark Kerr, travelled to the protectorate in November 1920, the British colony there complained that no one from the legation had visited them for 20 years. This had led to further ill-feeling towards France.[95] The information obtained by successive diplomats and consuls was, of course, channelled back to the Foreign Office and clearly did afford essential information with which to guide policy. As previously noted, some officials hoped that such information would limit the cession of British influence to France. However, for various reasons it did not. Forfeiture of primacy to France in Morocco was the *quid pro quo* for ascendancy in Egypt. *Realpolitik* aside, one further factor was that, over time, deep-rooted and frequently negative official perceptions of Morocco and Moroccans outweighed countervailing perceptions and pressures from vested interests. Morocco was undoubtedly picturesque, and its people were no more difficult to deal with than other Orientals, but on balance evidence derived from official travel suggested that the task of restoring political order and unity was too onerous for Britain to undertake. France would do it. Indeed, after the First World War, the French authorities encouraged travel, in the form of tourism, specifically to 'consolidate, reinforce and legitimise French control'.[96]

Notes

1. The closing date is one of convenience, reflecting the research undertaken for this chapter.
2. Hay to the Hon. A. Gordon, 6 November 1845, quoted in J.H. Drummond-Hay (1896) *A Memoir of Sir John Drummond Hay Based on His Journals and Correspondence* (London: John Murray), p. 77. Hay had succeeded his father, Edward Drummond-Hay.
3. Robertson to his mother, 7 February 1922, RBTN 1, Robertson Papers, Churchill Archives Centre, Cambridge.
4. D. Urquhart (1850) *The Pillars of Hercules; or, a Narrative of Travels in Spain and Morocco in 1848* (London: R. Bentley), pp. 51, 277–78.
5. See P.G. Rogers (1977) *A History of Anglo-Moroccan Relations to 1900* (London: Foreign and Commonwealth Office).
6. J. Fisher (2010) 'Keeping "the Old Flag flying": the British Community in Morocco and the British Morocco Merchants Association, 1914–24', *Historical Research*, 83/222, 723.
7. Though see K. Chaouch, 'British Travellers to Morocco and their Accounts, from Mid-16th to Mid-20th Centuries: A Bibliography', Sheffield Hallam Working Papers, http://extra.shu.ac.uk/wpw/morocco/Chaouch/Chaouch.htm.
8. K. Robbins (1996) 'Experiencing the Foreign: British Foreign Policy Makers and the Delights of Travel', in M.L. Dockrill and B.J.C. McKercher (eds.) *Diplomacy and World Power: Studies in British Foreign Policy, 1890–1951* (Cambridge: CUP); J. Fisher (2007) 'Official Responses to Foreign Travel at the British Foreign and India Offices before 1914', *English Historical Review*, 122/498, 937–64.
9. Hay, *Memoir*, pp. 100–01.
10. See J.H. Drummond-Hay (1861) *Morocco and the Moors: Western Barbary; Its Wild Tribes and Savage Animals* (London: John Murray). K. Ben-Srhir (2005) *Britain and Morocco During the Embassy of John Drummond Hay, 1845–1886* (London/New York: RoutledgeCurzon), p. 20.
11. H.E. Colvile (1880) *A Ride in Petticoats and Slippers: An Account of a Journey Through Morocco* (London: Sampson Low, Marston, Searle & Rivington), pp. 10–11.
12. R.L. Playfair and R. Brown (1892) *Bibliography of the Barbary States. Part IV* (London: John Murray), vi.
13. Ibid.
14. Ibid., vi–vii. The remainder of the paragraph is drawn from idem., pp. x–xii.
15. Kirby-Green to Salisbury, 3 August 1887, F[oreign] O[ffice] 99/236, The National Archives, Kew (TNA). All remaining FO references are from TNA. Boulnois reported that in wet weather, camels wore leather boots with spikes.
16. Herbert White to Salisbury, 20 March 1891, enc. Surgeon Major Henry Charlesworth to White, 20 March 1891, FO 99/280. Rogers, *Anglo-Moroccan Relations*, pp. 217–18.
17. Nicolson to Sir Arthur Bigge, 15 April 1896, Nicolson Papers, PRO 30/11/81 f120, TNA.
18. See, for example, Nicolson to Anderson, 22 April 1896, Nicolson Papers, PRO 30/11/81 f126, and F. V. Parsons (1978) 'Late Nineteenth-Century Morocco Through Foreign Eyes', *The Maghreb Review* (MR), 3:5–6, 1–5.

19. Kirby-Green to Salisbury, 18 April 1887, FO 99/235.
20. Memorandum on the Occupation of Tangier, Captain Gleichen, 20 July 1893, in Sir West Ridgeway to the Earl of Rosebery, 19 July 1893, FO 881/6407.
21. G.H. Selous (1956) *Appointment to Fez* (London: Unicorn Press), p. 32.
22. J. Fisher (2009) 'British Consular Representation in Morocco, 1912–24: a Question of Pounds, Shillings and Pence', *MR*, 34:2–3, 141.
23. Ibid., note 51.
24. Ibid., 144. Hyacinth Rabino, Vice-Consul at Casablanca, said this in the autumn of 1918.
25. Ibid., 147–48. A faulty sewer outflow was the problem.
26. Nicolson to Bigge, 16 October 1895, Nicolson Papers, PRO 30/81/11 f13.
27. H. Nicolson (1930) *Sir Arthur Nicolson, Bart., First Lord Carnock: A Study in the Old Diplomacy* (London: Constable), pp. 108–09.
28. Onslow, *Sixty-Three*, pp. 58–59.
29. Ibid., p. 74.
30. Ibid., p. 80.
31. Ibid., p. 81.
32. Ibid., p. 82.
33. He later chaired the British Morocco Merchants Association, formed in 1916 to represent its members' interests to the British Government.
34. Satow to MacLeod, 9 August 1916, Satow Papers, PRO 30/26/85, TNA.
35. MacLeod to unknown correspondent, 22 May 1931, GD 523/1/7, MacLeod Papers, National Archives of Scotland. Further references with this prefix are from this collection.
36. Satow to MacLeod, 19 May 1895, GD 1/8/52. In 1919, after seven years' continuous service in Morocco, several at Fez, John Dawkins was about to resign; Fisher, 'Consular', 146.
37. Fisher, 'Consular', 141, note 53.
38. Programme of Celebration of Diamond Jubilee, British Vice-Consulate, Fez, 22 June 1897, GD 523/1/12/15.
39. B.R. James (War Office) to MacLeod, 3 October and 12 November 1900; Nicolson to MacLeod 15 May and 7 June 1900, GD 523/1/14; Nicolson to Hastings, GD 523/1/18.
40. Herbert White to MacLeod, 23 July 1906, GD 523/1/20.
41. P.D. Trotter (1881) *Our Mission to the Court of Marocco in 1880, Under Sir J.D. Hay* (Edinburgh: D. Douglas), p. 91.
42. Sir John's father had scaled the Atlas in 1829.
43. Trotter, *Mission*, pp. 11–12.
44. Ibid., p. 90.
45. Ibid., p. 169.
46. Kirby-Green to Salisbury, 18 April 1887, FO 99/235.
47. Kirby-Green to Salisbury, 24 June 1887, ibid.
48. Kirby-Green to Salisbury, 25 June 1887, ibid.
49. See Note 43.
50. The material below is from Nicolson, *Carnock*, pp. 111–19, 145, 147, and from Nicolson to Bigge, 15 April 1896, Nicolson Papers, PRO 30/81/11, f120.
51. Nicolson to Kaid Harry Maclean, 11 March 1896, ibid., PRO 30/81/11, f113.
52. On these preparations, see Nicolson to Maclean, 3 and 10 January, 2 February 1896, ibid., fos 70, 76, 86.

53. Britain and other powers, whose subjects were similarly affected, resisted this. See Herbert White to Kimberley, 3 June 1895, FO 97/585. The need to travel with a soldier or with protection was of long standing and was accepted.
54. See Selous, *Fez*, pp. 105–6.
55. Nicolson to Bigge, 15 April 1896, Nicolson Papers, PRO 30/81/11 f120.
56. See, for example, Nicolson to Sanderson, 2 December 1895, ibid.
57. Nicolson to Sanderson, 22 April 1896, ibid., f126.
58. G. Lowther (1907) 'Extracts From a Diary in Morocco', *The National Review*, 49:3, 237, 239, 245.
59. A.E.W. Gleichen (1909) *Journal of Our Mission to Fez (1909). By the Military Attaché* (London: Harrison), pp. 4–7.
60. Gleichen (1909) *Journal*, pp. 15–16.
61. Ibid., p. 32.
62. Ibid., p. 68.
63. This contrasted with the pleasure induced by 'Stoke', an Indian elephant gifted to Sultan Hassan I in 1891. Rogers, *Anglo-Moroccan*, pp. 218–19.
64. Rogers, *Anglo-Moroccan*, p. 55.
65. Ibid., p. 98.
66. Lister to Grey, 18 May 1909, FO 371/698/f18931/19996.
67. MacLeod to Aunt Maggie, 4 May 1909, GD 523/1/12.
68. Lister to Grey, 8 August 1910, FO 371/936/28827.
69. Ibid.
70. Lister to Grey, 4 December 1910, FO 371/936/ F28827/44688, enclosing report.
71. Ibid. Unless otherwise noted, the material below is from this report.
72. Rumbold to Austen Chamberlain, 18 November 1927, FO 371/12691/10843.
73. M. Gilbert (1973) *Sir Horace Rumbold: Portrait of a Diplomat 1869–1941* (London: Heinemann), pp. 314–15, 317.
74. Garnett to his mother, 20 November 1916, Quernmore Papers, DDQ 9/42/8, Lancashire Record Office, Preston.
75. Garnett to his mother, 7 July 1917, Quernmore Papers, DDQ 9/24/27. Garnett subsequently attempted to publicise the matter; Garnett to the editor, *Morocco*, 17 February 1920, 2/69, British Library Newspaper Collections, Colindale. Playfair, *Bibliography*, p. 186.
76. Playfair, *Bibliography*.
77. 'Report on the Trade, Industry and Finance of Morocco', Parliamentary Papers, Cmd. 975 (1920).
78. A. Ryan (1951) *The Last of the Dragomans* (London: Bles), pp. 230–35.
79. Ryan, *Last*, p. 246.
80. Ibid., pp. 247, 249.
81. Urquhart, *Pillars*, Vol. II, pp. 29–88, 56. He famously introduced the Turkish bath to Britain.
82. Urquhart, *Pillars*, p. 129.
83. Ibid., pp. 186–7.
84. A. Chamberlain (1937) *Seen in Passing* (London: Cassell), p. vii.
85. Ibid., p. 155.
86. Ibid., pp. 156–57.
87. Ibid., p. 160.
88. Ibid., p. 163.
89. Ibid., p. 164.

90. After dinner, inspired by a tin whistle in one of the crackers, he suggested a game whereby each of the diners played the national anthem on it. The prize was a book that he had inscribed. *Morocco*, 10 February 1923, BLNC.

91. P. Rowland (1975) *Lloyd George* (London: Barrie & Jenkins), pp. 723–27.

92. Srhir, *Britain and Morocco*, pp. 82–3, 91, 98–100, 103, 106, 110.

93. See, for example, concerning James Mario Matra, R. Danziger (1982) 'The British Consular Reports as a Source for Morocco's Internal History during the Reign of Sidi-Muhamed Ben Abdellah (1751–1790)', *MR*, 7:5-6, 103–7.

94. Euan-Smith allegedly tore up the draft treaty and threw it at the Grand Vizier. The Sultan allegedly seized the mission's horses. 'Latest Intelligence: Morocco', *The Times*, 6 August 1892.

95. Clark Kerr to Lidderdale, 25 November 1920, General Correspondence and Papers 1920, Inverchapel Papers, Bodleian Library, Oxford.

96. F.R. Hunter (2007) 'Promoting Empire: The Hachette Tourist in French Morocco', *Middle Eastern Studies*, 43:4, 579–91.

Part IV
Experiencing a Post-colonial World

10
Oriental Expressions: British Visions of Arabia from a Colonial to a Post-colonial World

James Canton

In 1937, Freya Stark was part of the sizeable British community living in Baghdad. For centuries the British imaginative vision of Baghdad had been one overflowing with notions of genii, golden domes and steep minarets; a collection of imagery carried straight from the pages of the *Arabian Nights*. Stark painted a very much darker impression:

> What you first see of the Caliphs' city is a most sordid aspect; a long low straight street, a dingy hybrid between East and West, with the unattractiveness of both. The crowd looks unhealthy and sallow, the children are pitiful, the shops are ineffective compromises with Europe; and the dust is wicked, for it turns to blood-poisoning at the slightest opportunity, and bears out the old Babylonian idea of an atmosphere inhabited by Demons.[1]

British impressions of Arabia have always altered over time. This chapter will explore the nature of those shifting visions of Arabia from the 1930s when Britain's influence in the Middle East was strongest, through the time of gradual British withdrawal from the region in the 1950s and 1960s, and on to the present day. Stark's experience of Baghdad had drastically tainted those earlier exotic templates of the city of the Caliphs. The landscape magically conjured from an imagined incarnation of Scheherazade's tales had vanished to be replaced by a dry, dusty and dangerous new world. Just as Stark found a Baghdad which diverged far from previous impressions of the city, so too did British visions of Arabia alter radically from the late 1970s onwards as a new generation of travellers ventured to the Middle East and the heyday of imperial activity slipped further away.[2]

Britain's initial imperial thoughts in the colonial history in the Middle East were concerned with the safe passage and protection of British naval and merchant shipping rather than conquering Arabian territories.[3] In 1839 the village of Aden came under British control following military action to control piracy in the region. Aden was Queen Victoria's first imperial possession and would remain a British colony until 1967.[4] Especially important after the opening up of the Suez Canal in 1869, it offered a convenient stopping-off point in southern Arabia for colonial traffic *en route* to India. The gaze from British imperialists stationed in Aden tended not to be inland towards central Arabia but out to the waters of the Arabian Sea in order to maintain a watchful eye on British shipping.

However, Cairo rather than Aden was to become the centre for British imperial administration in the Middle East. On 11 July 1882 a British naval fleet bombarded Alexandria in northern Egypt. The action was the start of a military campaign that would conclude with Britain assuming control over Egyptian affairs for the next 70 years. During the First World War, Cairo became home to the Arab Bureau which, under the controlling hand of D.G. Hogarth, served to help instigate an Arab uprising against the Ottoman Empire. T.E. Lawrence and Gertrude Bell were just two of a band of British figures already well travelled across the Near East who came to serve the British war effort from Egypt.[5] Writing about the collective that formed the Arab Bureau, James Morris describes them as 'mostly men of extreme intelligence but somewhat amateur enthusiasm, fired by the exigency of war and intrigued by the allure of Arabness from across the Arabian Sea'.[6] Priya Satia's *Spies in Arabia* (2008) notes the desire of British intelligence towards a 'political project of *fostering* an Arab unity that remained otherwise inchoate'.[7] In order to achieve such a project, British intelligence officers would be needed to head out into the desert and meet the Arab tribesmen whose rebellion they were to encourage.

Britain's imperial reach in Arabia was extended further during the First World War and the break-up of the Ottoman Empire. By 1917 both Baghdad and Jerusalem had come under British control. With Cairo already occupied, three key cities of Arabia were now in British military hands. Unlike those earlier travellers who forged lone paths into lands rarely seen by British eyes, following the capture of those three cities, an increasingly sizeable British population settled in the region. The following 40 years, from 1917 to the Suez War of 1956, represent the period of greatest British colonial activity in Arabia. Elizabeth Monroe named this era 'Britain's moment in the Middle East', a period that witnessed growing numbers of British travellers who were able to explore the furthest reaches of Arabia.[8]

During this 40-year period there were three central aspects of Arabia which British explorers and travel writers would return to again and again: the desert, the Bedouin and their camels. This chapter looks at three well-known examples of travellers with this vision: Bertram Thomas, Lawrence and Wilfrid Thesiger. Each of these figures can be considered as among an elite few who are the key twentieth-century British travellers in Arabia not only covering thousands of miles across the region but also helping to forge a definitive British colonial vision of Arabia. Lawrence is certainly the best known thanks to his extraordinary exploits in the Arabian desert during the First World War, but he is really the least expansive in an exploratory sense. Each of these travellers also wrote highly considered and popular travelogues of their journeys into Arabia. By examining their writings, this chapter outlines the vision of Arabia which re-emerged in the 1930s of a land composed of desert sands and populated by a hardy, scattered handful of nomadic Bedouin Arabs and their equally hardy camels.

Within the writings of many British colonial travellers to Arabia there runs a nostalgic sense of having missed a time when a pure, essential desert existence was possible, when the Bedouin were untainted by modern ways. This expression of nostalgia is central to both Renato Rosaldo's notion of 'imperial nostalgia' and Ali Behdad's concept of 'belatedness'.[9] Both of these theoretical concepts are employed in this chapter to interrogate the colonial writing of Bertram Thomas, T.E. Lawrence and Wilfrid Thesiger. British colonial travellers in the early twentieth century were exploring a landscape that had only rarely been seen by Western eyes in past centuries. The land held something of a mysterious allure. With the arrival of a British imperial presence in Arabia, that allure soon faded. The First World War in Arabia and modernisation, especially in the form of motor cars, allowed far greater numbers of Westerners access to the desert regions. Though this Westernising presence – the very arrival of British travellers – was the driving force which helped to initiate change, the narratives of British colonial travellers often despair at the ways in which the lands and the Bedouin have altered. If only the traveller could have come earlier, could have seen and witnessed Arabia beforehand – before the true essence of Arabia had been lost to change.

The nostalgia which inhabits these colonial writers had dissipated by the time Jonathan Raban headed to Arabia in the late 1970s and had been radically subverted in the words of Tim Mackintosh-Smith in the 1990s. The cross-over from a colonial to a post-colonial perspective is one that inevitably occurred gradually. When did Britain withdraw from Arabia – with the Suez War of 1956 or with the withdrawal of protectorate relations with the Gulf States in 1971? Though there are difficulties in drawing a single, distinct line in the sand and declaring exactly when British travel writing shifted from a colonial to a post-colonial perspective, in this chapter I shall certainly interrogate the nature of these two narrative forms.

Figure 10.1 shows that familiar Arabian triad of desert, camel and Bedu – with a British interloper on the scene.[10] Bertram Thomas, seated on a camel, was one of the most remarkable of the British explorers of Arabia, spending 13 years acclimatising to life in Arabia following his arrival there as a soldier in the First World War. Unlike many of the earlier British travellers in Arabia, Thomas had risen from humble origins and held no unsettled

Figure 10.1   Bertram Thomas in the Empty Quarter (1931)
[Courtesy of Bertram Thomas's family].

aristocratic desire to explore the lands of Arabia such as had drawn Victorian giants such as Charles Doughty, Richard Burton and Wilfrid Scawen Blunt. Imperial war had allowed Bertram Thomas the opportunity of Arabian travel. By 1918 he was an assistant political officer in the Suq-ash-Shuyukh region of what was then still being called Mesopotamia and a decade later he was still in Arabia, now as the *wazir* or prime minister and financial advisor to the Sultan of Muscat and Oman, having learnt the dialects and ways of many Arab tribes.[11] In early February 1931, Thomas became the first Westerner to cross the *Rub' al Khali* – the Empty Quarter – a vast desert covering much of southern Arabia. The scale of the region is simply vast, measuring some 3 million square kilometres; a space the size of India or the combined area of Germany, France and Spain.[12] In the early twentieth century the *Rub' al Khali* remained one of the few regions of the world virtually unobserved by Western travellers.

When Thomas came to write up the details of what was a remarkable journey, British society had already celebrated his achievement with such accolades as a telegram from King George V and gold medals from the royal geographical societies of England, Belgium and Scotland.[13] *Arabia Felix* was published in 1932 with a foreword by T.E. Lawrence. In the Introduction, Thomas drew a striking portrait of the land that he had traversed:

> The virgin Rub'al Khali, the Great Southern Desert! To have laboured in Arabia is to have tasted inevitably of her seduction ... Yet Arabia has remained the forbidden land. Throughout the centuries scarce twenty European explorers have been able usefully to penetrate to her inhospitable heart.[14]

The desert is portrayed as distinctly feminine – an untouched 'virgin' but paradoxically, and at the same time, a seductress to all Europeans who have ventured into Arabia. Yet the vision of an Oriental beauty soon vanishes from the text. Her allure hides an 'inhospitable heart'. This is a foreign land which does not welcome guests. The lack of European visitors to Arabia has meant that 'among her inhabitants, left so severely to themselves, insularity, bigotry, and intolerance are indigenous growths with a long pedigree. Hence an area equal to half the superficies of Europe had remained a blank on our maps' (xiii). After many years of planning, plotting and patience, Bertram Thomas had finally forged a path through the obstacles of the sands to penetrate the *Rub' al Khali*.

In *Arabia Felix*, Thomas seems to be distinctly ambivalent about his feelings towards those lands of Arabia that he has just crossed. There is a clear sense of wonder at the scale and beauty of these desertscapes but it is accompanied by a concern that this world is not spoiled or tainted. Soon after he draws the picture of the 'virgin Rub'al Khali', Thomas is expressing a concern at the air survey which has mapped the region, noting that 'there seems something indelicate in the intrusion of Western machines into these virgin silences' (xv). Here is the voice of the belated traveller expressing a nostalgic melancholia, a desire to leave the unspoiled world of the Empty Quarter alone. Yet it is a voice expressed by the very first European traveller to successfully traverse this region. In *Belated Travellers*, Ali Behdad examined the complexities in the relationship between late nineteenth-century European travellers and their travel experiences. Many felt a sense of belatedness, such that they felt that they had missed out on the more authentic experiences of early travellers and were disappointed in their 'exoticist desire for a disappearing Other'.[15] In Bertram Thomas's words, a similar belatedness is expressed. The belated concerns which Behdad explored certainly can be seen to extend not only into the thoughts of twentieth-century explorers but to those that have inaugurated European travel into a region. The threat that air surveys have already in some sense disturbed the Empty Quarter serves to disquiet Thomas even in his moment of triumph. He may be the first to cross the Great Southern Desert but the pressing presence of modernisation in the form of aircraft has already threatened to despoil the pristine virginity of this unexplored quarter of Arabia.

In T.E. Lawrence, the second imperial traveller that we shall look at, once more the portrait of Arabia painted is of a land seemingly composed almost entirely of brutal desert inhabited by a smattering of Bedu. The figure of Lawrence is far better known than that of Bertram Thomas but the vision they share of Arabia is often comparable. Lawrence's *Seven Pillars of Wisdom* was first published by the *Oxford Times* in 1922 as five copies of an extensive narrative that depicted Lawrence's experiences, ecstasies, prejudices and exotic pleasures in Arabia during the First World War. By that time the simultaneous creation of a mythological figure called Lawrence of Arabia had already begun. Since then, much of the literary interest in *Seven Pillars* has been dictated by a sense of that mythical figure and an intentionalist insistence on understanding the 'real' Lawrence. The text has become background. Forefront has been biographical enquiry, the search for that essentialist white elephant – the author.[16] Alongside the plethora of works that explore the nature of Lawrence there have been critical attempts to examine the nature of his writing. In Edward Said's *Orientalism*, Lawrence is placed in a list of English writers, each of whom was a colonial player actively involved in shaping the Orient and its peoples into imperial service. Said employs Hannah Arendt's term of 'imperial agent' to define Lawrence's *raison d'être* in Arabia. Consequently, Lawrence is seen alongside 'Edward Henry Palmer, D.G. Hogarth, Gertrude Bell, Ronald Storrs, St. John Philby, and William Gifford Palgrave'.[17] Yet Said does recognise that within this broad spectrum of colonial writing the individual constituents 'brought their private mythology and obsessions' to the study of the Orient:

> Each – Wilfred Scawen Blunt, Doughty, Lawrence, Bell, Hogarth, Philby, Sykes, Storrs – believed his vision of things Oriental was individual, self-created out of some intensely personal encounter with the Orient, Islam or the Arabs.

While each of these particular views 'refined and gave a personal twist to the academic style of modern Orientalism... in the final analysis they all (except Blunt) expressed the traditional hostility to and fear of the Orient' (p. 197). In fact, Lawrence's hostility and fear is rather more ambivalent than Said allows. In the Introduction to *Seven Pillars of Wisdom* (1926), Lawrence details how he saw himself transformed by the very environment of Arabia:

> For years we lived anyhow with one another in the naked desert, under the indifferent heaven. By day the hot sun fermented us; and we were dizzied by the beating wind. At night we were stained by dew, and shamed into pettiness by the innumerable silences of stars.[18]

Lawrence and his Bedouin travellers are depicted as having been distilled into a basic essence, an existential core by a process of weathering in their harsh world. The epic vision of the narrative sees only a collective 'we'. They have been physically welded together by the desert environment. Lawrence's desert-woven unity with the Bedouin has displaced his identity as a British political officer.

In his vision of the desert, Lawrence can often be seen seeking out that same perfect, unspoilt landscape that Bertram Thomas saw in the virgin *Rub' al Khali*. Take the following passage from Chapter 2 of *Seven Pillars*:

The eastern frontier was at first an alluvial plain called Mesopotamia, but south of Basra a level littoral, called Kuweit, and Hasa, to Gattar. Much of this plain was peopled. These inhabited hills and plains framed a gulf of thirsty desert, in whose heart was an archipelago of watered and populous oases called Kasim and Aridh. In this group of oases lay the true centre of Arabia, the preserve of its native spirit, and its most conscious individuality. The desert lapped it round and kept it pure of contact. (p. 13)

On initial reading the scene is typically drawn with a traditional Orientalist vision describing the plains of Arabia. Yet the desert, personified as 'thirsty', encloses a group of oases that are considered to be 'the true centre of Arabia'. These oases contain not only the 'native spirit' of Arabia but 'its most conscious individuality'. Here, Lawrence has found the true heart and soul of all Arabia. It has been hidden far away from prying eyes and yet well protected by the desert that 'kept it pure of contact'. Except, of course, the imperial eyes of the imperial agent have managed to espy and now describe that world for the colonial reader. To a degree, the very act of observation provides an appropriation of that Arabian heart and soul. By the conscious delineation of that land, the knowledge of that place invests the Western colonial reader with an epistemological ownership. The imagery of the passage actively aids such a process. The stylistic devices employed create the sense of a pure essence of Arabianness that is nurtured by the very sands and scrub that form the mass of that vast wilderness landscape.

Lawrence exhibits in this portrait what David Spurr calls the 'idealisation' of Arabia. While the passage is fundamentally a geographical description, its 'rationalised' language contrasts sharply with the ultimate vision of an idealised Arabia in the oases of Kasim and Aridh. Spurr talks of the paralleled combination of a rationalised language with the 'most heightened idealisation of Arab character'.[19] In the above passage, Lawrence extends this idealisation to include a homage to the very lands of Arabia. The narrative style of Lawrence shifts from an Orientalist descriptive tone resonant of Edward Lane and an atavistic echo of a previous colonial discourse, to a depiction of a highly idealised Arabian nirvana tucked away far from all. The presentation of a pure Arabian wilderness recalls those drawn by Charles Doughty.[20] The same technique of idealisation is recurrent when Lawrence describes the character of the Bedouin:

The Beduin of the desert, born and grown up in it, had embraced with all his soul this nakedness too harsh for volunteers, for the reason, felt but inarticulate, that there he found himself indubitably free. He lost material ties, comforts, all superfluities and other complications to achieve a personal liberty which haunted starvation and death. He saw no virtue in poverty herself; he enjoyed the little vices and luxuries – coffee, fresh water, women – which he could still preserve. In his life he had air and winds, sun and light, open spaces and a great emptiness. There was no human effort, no fecundity in Nature; just the heaven above and the unspotted earth beneath. (p. 18)

In this void of nothingness, this absolute dearth of meaning, the Bedouin is free of all, save the literary interpretations of the narrator. The individual Bedouin is depicted as an idealised man standing in an empty world.

David Spurr comments of the passage: 'in this image of the human soul embracing a vast nothingness, we may recognise a version of the modernist metaphysic of existentialism, with its myth concerning the absurdity of human life in the face of an indifferent Nature'. The Bedouin becomes, in Lawrence's vision, the 'existential hero' who by facing up to the absurd world is seen to gain an 'ascetic freedom'. The image that Lawrence's language creates may portray the Bedouin as blissfully unblemished by the wider politics of colonialism, yet Spurr points out that 'the relations of power that exist in the political and economic spheres are buried or contained within the all-embracing myth of the existential void' (pp. 130–1). Placing this existential-metaphysical label upon the Bedouin helps to create an idealised version of the desert man. The rhetoric employed emphasises the existential qualities of the Bedouin while at the same time distancing them from the rest of the Arabian peoples.

In Book V of *Seven Pillars of Wisdom*, 'Marking Time', Lawrence returns to the theme of the idealisation of the Bedouin. Once more the Bedouin are contrasted with the other peoples of Arabia, on this occasion in a dissection of the various inhabitants of Syria. Analysing 'a section across Syria from sea to desert', Lawrence's narrative outlines first the nature of the 'Persian immigrants' of the Ismailiya with their 'beastly opinions' before tracing other discrete groupings of people:

> Beyond them [the 'Persian immigrants' of the Ismailiya] were the strange sights of villages of Christian tribal Arabs, under sheikhs. They seemed very sturdy Christians, quite unlike their snivelling brethren in the hills. They lived as the Sunni about them, dressed like them, and were on the best terms with them. East of the Christians lay semi-pastoral Moslem communities; and on the last edge of cultivation, some villages of Ismailia outcasts, in search of the peace men would not grant. Beyond were Beduin. (p. 258)

The final alliterative statement again depicts a conception of the existential nature of the Bedouin. They are contrasted with all other peoples as being simple 'beyond'. The echo of Friedrich Nietzsche's *Beyond Good and Evil* (1886) rings to remind the reader that the Bedouin are the true metaphysical beings; beyond the 'last edge of cultivation' they exist in an idealised nothingness.

In the 1940s the last of the true imperial travellers arrived in Arabia. Wilfred Thesiger was to add a further nostalgic twist to the vision of Arabia already seen in the writings of Thomas and Lawrence. Born in Abyssinia in 1910, educated at Eton and Oxford, Thesiger spent most his life abroad, largely in Africa. When he flew to Aden in 1945, specifically employed to track the movement of locusts across the desert, his other intentions were to travel those areas of the Empty Quarter which had yet to be walked by Western man.[21] Thesiger would spend much of the next four years doing just that. There followed a period of some ten years after leaving Arabia before *Arabian Sands* (1959) was published after the publisher Mark Longman eventually persuaded Thesiger to write up his Arabian adventures.[22]

Even in the opening of the Prologue, Thesiger draws the familiar vision of Arabia with a bold, literary concern for narrative style:

> A cloud gathers, the rain falls, men live; the cloud disperses without rain, and men and animals die. In the deserts of southern Arabia there is no rhythm of the seasons, no rise and fall of sap, but empty wastes where only the changing temperature marks the passage of the year. It is a bitter, desiccated land which knows nothing of gentleness or ease. Yet men have lived there since earliest times. Passing generations have left fire-blackened stones at camping sites, a few faint tracks polished on the gravel plains. Elsewhere the winds wipe out their footprints. Men live there because it is the world into which they were born; the life they lead is the life their forefathers led before them; they accept hardships and privations; they know no other way. Lawrence wrote in *Seven Pillars of Wisdom*, 'Bedouin ways were hard, even for those brought up in them and for strangers terrible: a death in life.' No man can live this life and emerge unchanged. He will carry, however faint, the imprint of the desert, the brand which marks the nomad; and he will have within him the yearning to return, weak or insistent according to his nature. For this cruel land can cast a spell which no temperate clime can match.[23]

In the opening line the delicate divide between life and death in the Empty Quarter is dramatically drawn. Desert living was austere and brutal, a form of masochism promising oblique pleasure with the pain of daily existence, as Lawrence knew so well. Thesiger, like Bertram Thomas before him, personified the land as a sorcerer. It bewitched. Travellers would be forever enchanted. In the final line, Thesiger echoed the romanticism of Walter de la Mare's *Arabia* (1912) with its lines warning:

> No beauty on earth I see
> But shadowed with the dream recalls

> Her loveliness to me:
> Still eyes look coldly upon me,
> Cold voices whisper and say,
> 'He is crazed with the spell of far Arabia,
> They have stolen his wits away.'

Here was a poem already imbued with a certain vision of Arabia; a poem which had been employed as an exotic epigram in Bertram Thomas's *Arabia Felix*. Thesiger maintained continuity with the sense of an imperial mission of knowledge requisition, of filling the blanks on Western maps. Like his imperial forefathers who had explored Arabia, Thesiger saw a land of sand, inhabited by tough, simple men with whom he passed some five years, trekking and mapping their world, photographing the deserts, the camels and the Bedouin who accompanied him on his journeys.

As Thesiger's tale of his travels unfolds, there is a long digression during which he decants his thoughts on the nature of Arabia and the Bedu. The 'unchanging Bedu' of millennia had been irrevocably altered in the last 40 years. Since the First World War, cars, aeroplanes and radio had opened up the deserts to outsiders. Oil now offered an easy, comfortable life:

> It seemed to me tragic that they should become, as a result of circum-
> stances beyond their control, a parasitic proletariat squatting around
> oil-fields in the fly-blown squalor of shanty towns in some of the most
> sterile country in the world. (p. 96)

Nostalgic expressions are a recurring theme in *Arabian Sands*. Thesiger decries the creeping modernisation and industrialisation of the desert, early on in the text reflecting ruefully that 'the maps I made helped others, with more material aims, to visit and corrupt a people whose spirit once lit the desert like a flame' (p. 82). Here is the obvious truth that Thesiger's very presence in Arabia is a Westernising force. Worse, his mapping of the unknown lands has actively aided the oil-men. Thesiger may not wish to be a harbinger of change and indeed may argue that his ethnographic role is to detail the Bedouin culture before those desert ways are bastardised beyond recognition. Yet he yearns for 'traditional' Bedouin society in that paradoxical position of imperial nostalgia which Renato Rosaldo has described as 'mourning for what one has destroyed'.[24]

The vision presented by these three key figures of British exploration in Arabia is of a tough, inhospitable land populated only by equally tough and hardy camels and Bedouin. There are few comforts to be had. Lawrence, Thesiger and Thomas have each travelled into an Arabia composed of desert and tribesmen, where the bare beauty of the landscape, its emptiness, is the world they see. The cities and civilisations of Arabia have been forgot-ten, erased and replaced by the spectre of a scattered, nomadic population wandering a vast desert wilderness. From 1882 when Cairo was invaded, and certainly from 1917 when Baghdad and Jerusalem were in British hands too, an imperial structure ruled over much of the Middle East, with thousands of troops and colonial administrators ensuring that rule was actively maintained. Britain ran its colonial reign from the towns and cities of Arabia, and yet the overriding image of Arabia was of deserts and tribesmen. The vision derived from Britain's most intrepid travellers was one ever tinged with an imperial nostalgia, with a nagging sense that the land and its peoples had been tainted by the very presence of those British footsteps in the sand.

Wilfrid Thesiger finished his explorations in southern Arabia in 1949. By the time his *Arabian Sands* was finally published in 1959, Britain's grip on Arabia had already started to decisively slip. In January 1952, Cairo rioted, targeting British-owned businesses for burning. Four years later, Nasser announced the nationalisation of the Suez Canal and Britain invaded Egyptian soil once more.[25] During this period the British presence in the Middle East can be seen as starting to shift from a colonial to a post-colonial phase. Britain's moment in the Middle East had come to an end. In 1967 it finally withdrew from Aden and in 1971 terminated the remaining protectorate relations with the Gulf States.[26]

Following Thesiger and the departure of a British imperial presence in Arabia, there was a distinct lull in British travel writing on the region. From the late 1960s right through to the 1990s, very little of note was published – with one important exception. Raban's *Arabia: Through the Looking Glass* appeared in 1979 and represented a decisive break from the colonial vision of Arabia as some kind of exotic desert inhabited by hardy Bedu and their camels. Here was the first post-imperial travelogue written by a British traveller in Arabia. Raban's *Arabia* traced the author's path to discovering a modern, mechanised and oil-rich Arabia of the 1970s, a very different world from that seen by earlier travellers:

> For Lawrence and Thesiger, Arabia was an alternative kingdom; a tough utopia without either money or machines. In the bedu tribesman they professed to find all the simplicity, the powers of personal endurance, the stoic independence, which they feared the Englishman was losing.[27]

On the streets of London, Raban saw a distinctly different Arab from the impoverished Bedouin envisioned by reading Thomas, Thesiger or T.E. Lawrence. Raban headed to the Gulf States. These Arabs 'were a people whom the English thought they knew, and who had suddenly turned into bewildering strangers'. Raban understood that though the image of Arabia portrayed by Thesiger was merely a generation old, the British colonial vision of the Arab was merely a construction, 'a version of the Arabs which was impossibly constricting for the Arabs themselves' (p. 16).

Arabia is the tale of Raban's journey into a post-imperial Arabia on the trail of a new vision. Raban flies off to the Gulf and, in Qatar, heads to the desert to find his own Bedouin, only to mistake the encampment for a 'used car lot'. Undaunted, he draws on the cultural remembrances of his own ancestry, on the experiences of earlier British travellers. 'Remembering Lawrence and Thesiger and the legendary hospitality of the bedu, I stopped the car. From somewhere inside this great scrapheap, dogs set up a ferocious yowling, and a young man waved his fist and shouted at me to go away' (p. 101). The imagined vision of the Bedouin formed by a distant generation of British travellers has been replaced with a modern version. Raban finds the Bedouin of Qatar are a bastardised and brutalised collection of people who have missed out on the wealth of oil.

In Abu Dhabi, Raban makes another attempt to discover the Bedouin, following the footsteps of previous travellers not into untouched desert scenes but into the modern-day dwellings that have replaced the tents:

> All over the emirate, the nomads who had been the companions of Thesiger, Philby and Bertram Thomas now lived on new breezeblock estates in the desert. (p. 134)

At Al Ain, a town on the border of the Empty Quarter, Raban enters an unprepossessing house to find a spacious courtyard with a garland of trees and is quite taken with the graceful beauty of the modern Bedouin abode. The old man of the family explains how life has dramatically altered in six years: 'They had been very poor; there had been no television, no motor cars. Now – he praised Allah and Sheikh Zayed [ruler of Abu Dhabi] – they had this fine house; they had "a.c."; life was very good; they wanted for nothing' (p. 140).

But Raban will not leave them at peace with this idyllic experience of modern existence. Were they not afraid that the evils of the cities, of the urban world, could come to Al Ain? He talks of 'thuggery, isolation and family breakdown' (p. 141). The men and boys of the family listen politely:

> Nothing like that, they assured me, would ever happen here. It was obvious that they thought I was telling improbable travellers' tales. Yet they had come much further than I had. Six years away from being desert nomads, they were talking confidently about careers in engineering and medicine... they gave every sign of having adapted gracefully to a life in which Modern Tissues, the Range Rover, the twin-tub washing machine, two televisions, floral Thermos flasks, air travel and the local Hilton were taken perfectly for granted. (p. 141)

These Bedouin emerge not as figures lost in a modern Arabia but as a people glad to accept the vital improvements in living conditions that petrodollars have provided. In a few years the nomadic realities of hunger and hardship have been replaced by the possibility of life away from the Arabian sands. While Wilfrid Thesiger may have despaired at the changes wrought so rapidly over Arabia, these Bedouin celebrate. Their vision of a pre-oil Arabia is far less tainted with nostalgia. Their memories of desert life recall a more impoverished existence, a far tougher reality.

When Raban came to write *Arabia* in the late 1970s, the break from a Thesiger-esque vision of Arabia was absolute. In an interview I conducted with him, Raban detailed this shift of perspective, explaining figures such as Thomas, Lawrence and Thesiger:

> They were figures to rebel against. I remember I'd just got back from travelling in the Middle East and found myself at dinner one evening in London seated next to an ineffably silly, somewhat upper-class woman who asked me what I was doing and I said I was writing a book about Arabia. She said 'Oh Arabia – I so love the desert; so romantic.' And I thought, 'Fuck it! I'm going to write a kind of 'anti-you' book. No camels; no little brown boys.' ... I always remember reading Thesiger with particular ire when he laments the new riches befalling Arabia. He fears that the people are going to be totally spoiled and cease to be these essentially simple people; tough, hardy, the public school dream. Now that money has fallen on their heads, they're all going to be softened and wet and what a tragedy that will be. I thought, 'Well, fuck that.' My sense of Arabia was shaped by going there but also to some extent formed before I went, as this land of passionate city builders: Alexandria, Jerusalem, Damascus, Aleppo, San'a. These were cities in place when London was just a sort of muddy ford across a rather nasty looking estuary. The way in which the British have been inclined to think of Arabia as an unpopulated land of sand dunes, camels and people living in tents is so far from the actual history of Arabia which is a place of spectacular cities. I wanted to get into that second world, to a large extent the truer one.[28]

The desire to break with the past is central to Raban being able to portray this 'truer' Arabia. Instead of plodding along in the ancestral footsteps of earlier British travellers, he flew around the modern world of Arabia in an effort to redefine their vision. There were to be 'no camels. No little brown boys'. Raban's *Arabia* takes British travel writing a giant stride into a post-imperial world beyond the desert romance envisaged by Thomas, Lawrence, Thesiger and many earlier travellers. Raban's Arabia is a world of cities.

In the late 1990s, the travel writer Tim Mackintosh-Smith offered a further reworking, a further twisting, of the vision of Arabia which had been painted by British imperial travellers. In his book *Yemen: Travels in Dictionary Land* (1997), he tells of the journey he has made from the stuffy confines of Oxford University, of the struggle to learn Arabic and of an escape to the streets of Sana, the capital of Yemen, where he settled to life in Arabia. Mackintosh-Smith writes in a jaunty modern style. He knows his imperial history. The past is always close to the surface in Mackintosh-Smith's text. From the mythological ancient, through the Islamic history of Yemen, the record of the country is retold, detailing the reign of Imam Yahya and the 1905 siege of Turkish-controlled San'a in which 'people were reduced to grinding straw for bread and to eating cats, dogs and rats' (p. 94). He knows that he has a role as the latest incarnation of the British travel writer in southern Arabia, a world from which the imperial British have disappeared.

On an adventure away from Sana, Mackintosh-Smith details a vision of Aden post-1967. It is a surreal world with a strangely British feel, even though the British imperial presence is long gone from Arabia. Aden is 'Coventry in the sun'.[29] But Mackintosh-Smith proclaims that the time has come to set Aden free; 'time to lay the imperial ghosts' (p. 143). Its imperial history is detailed from the first arrival of the British in January 1839 and the variety of imperial detritus that the British left behind in 1967. Alongside the 'right-hand-drive Humbers, Rileys and Morris Minor 1,000s' is a Bedford van from which fish and chips are sold. There are still pillar boxes, 'but with the royal cipher chiselled off' (p. 159). Mackintosh-Smith chats to a local trader, eyeing the Baltic amber:

'How much are they?'
'Nothing. I like to give my best customers a little present.'
It was my first visit and I hadn't bought anything.
'Where did you say you were from? Germany? France? Italy? Belgium?'
Belgium. We were here for 128 years, for heaven's sake. We were the ones who *understood* the Arabs. We gave them pillar boxes, and Coventry.
'I'm British.' (p. 159)

The internal outrage and mock use of the collective 'we' create the humour. For all those years in southern Arabia, the modern British tourist is just another foreign face. Mackintosh-Smith recognises the imperial baggage for what it is but cannot quite take it seriously. The passage provides a peculiar subverting of the Thesiger-esque form of imperial nostalgia. The notion that his people, the British, ran the region of modern Yemen is hard to swallow. The evidence lies scattered all around Aden yet still seems strangely incongruous. What *were* the British doing there? The British colonial presence may have left only 30 years before but already it seems an utterly alien world that they produced in southern Arabia.

The post-colonial writing of Raban and Mackintosh-Smith displaces the vision of Arabia as a place of desert and noble Bedouin which had been conjured in earlier centuries and reiterated in the writings of British imperial travellers such as Thomas, Lawrence and Thesiger. Raban and Mackintosh-Smith's texts both offer an ironic take on the plight of the modern British traveller to the region. Both are aware of the imperial baggage that they travel with, and yet both find that unpacking that past luggage unburdens them. They are able to see the people and lands of Arabia with eyes that are free from any overly romantic lustre. The imperial nostalgia which blighted the sight of their forefathers has twisted into something rather more real, as they envisage a modern Arabia shedding the shrouds of its imperial past.

There is a final coda to this chapter. The invasion of Iraq in 2003 illustrated that Britain's imperial presence in Arabia was not ended with the Suez War of 1956, or with the stuttering withdrawal from Aden in 1967, or even with the termination of protectorate relations with the Gulf States in 1971. Indeed, to delineate the period from the mid-1950s as an era in which Britain's relationship with the Middle East turned from imperial to post-imperial is problematic. Is it even appropriate to talk of being in a post-colonial period when British troops have so recently returned under the US-led coalition to reoccupy Iraq? The reimposition of British control over certain lands of Iraq stirs uneasy echoes from the fall of Baghdad in 1917 and the subsequent Iraqi revolt against the British in 1920.

In *Occupational Hazards*, Rory Stewart provides a retake on the British imperial travel text with his depiction of life as a neo-colonial administrator in Maysan province, Iraq.[30] His text echoes an earlier time of colonial rule. In 1931, Bertram Thomas, who we have seen previously as the first Westerner to cross the Empty Quarter, published an account of life as a district officer in the British army during what was then called the Mesopotamian Uprising in 1920.[31] Stewart's 2006 text can been seen in many ways as an updating of Thomas's narrative. Stewart, like Thomas, is a British colonial administrator in Iraq, sent to oversee the local peoples. In *Occupational Hazards* he details that position as the latest incumbent in the role of colonial overseer across vast stretches of southern Iraq and the difficulties in actually carrying out such a role in the post-Saddam era.

Stewart's vision of the return of Britain to Arabian soils as a neo-colonial force is one that we can learn much from. He is perfectly aware of Britain's imperial history in Iraq and writes of the parallels between his time governing in Iraq and earlier figures, such as Thomas. Raban commented on this parallel with the past, noting:

> In a way, [Stewart's] a throwback to the age of Bell and Lawrence and those people. He seems to have stepped out of the pages of *Boy's Own Paper* in 1920.[32]

In the British media, Stewart is recognised as a figure who understands Arabia and its peoples. Certainly his text provides an informed and honest portrayal of dealing with the Iraqi population whom he is detailed to oversee. What Stewart knows better than most is that the romantic vision of Arabia as a desert world of Bedouin, black tents and camels was one conjured during a previous period of British colonial governance. *Occupational Hazards* is undoubtedly a remarkable retelling of a neo-colonial tale of occupation. But the text is also a vital reminder that Britain did not entirely end an imperial presence in Arabia with Suez or with Aden or with Wilfrid Thesiger; that legacy still lingers.

Notes

1. F. Stark (1937, 1947) *Baghdad Sketches* (London: Guild Books), p. 18.
2. There are a number of excellent books on the nature of British travel writing. M. Cocker's (1992) *Loneliness and Time* (New York: Pantheon Books) is a very readable general introduction. R.H. Kiernan's (1937) *The Unveiling of Arabia* (London: Harrap) details the way in which Arabia was gradually revealed to the West. P. Satia's (2008) *Spies in Arabia: The Great War and the Cultural Foundations of Britain's Covert Empire in the Middle East* (Oxford: Oxford University Press) is an excellent uncovering of British imperial activity in Arabia. See also J. Canton (2011) *From Cairo to Baghdad: British Travellers in Arabia* (London: I.B. Tauris).
3. For a general historical take on British activity in Arabia across the nineteenth and twentieth centuries, see E. Monroe (1963, 1981) *Britain's Moment in the Middle East: 1914–1971*, rev. edn (London: Chatto & Windus); J. Morris (1978, 1980) *Farewell the Trumpets: An Imperial Retreat* (London: Penguin); and S. Searight (1969) *The British in the Middle East* (London: Weidenfeld & Nicholson), which are all extremely readable.
4. D. Holden (1966) *Farewell to Arabia* (London: Faber), p. 18.
5. For a history of the Arab Bureau, see B. Westrate (1992) *The Arab Bureau: British Policy in the Middle East, 1916–1920* (Pennsylvania: Pennsylvania State University Press).
6. Morris, *Farewell*, p. 251.
7. Satia, *Spies*, p. 53.
8. The term was coined by Elizabeth Monroe, based on the calculation that 'forty years is only a moment in the life of a region with a recorded history of four millennia'. See Monroe, *Britain's Moment in the Middle East*, p. 11.
9. See R. Rosaldo (1989) 'Imperial Nostalgia', *Representations*, 26, 107–22; and A. Behdad (1994) *Belated Travellers: Orientalism in the Age of Colonial Dissolution* (Cork: Cork University Press).
10. See R. Trench (1986) *Arabian Travellers* (London: Macmillan), p. 210. The terms Bedouin and Bedu are used here interchangeably, as they were by the British travel writers explored in this chapter.
11. A.T. Wilson (1931) *Mesopotamia, 1917–1920: A Clash of Loyalties: A Personal and Historical Record* (London: Oxford University Press), p. 95 and Appendix IV.
12. Cocker, *Loneliness*, p. 39; and Kiernan, *Unveiling*, p. 312.
13. There is no complete biography of Bertram Thomas yet written. Much of this material comes from Robin Braysher's biographical notes produced in February 2004, a project funded by the Anglo-Omani Society.
14. B. Thomas (1932, 1938) *Arabia Felix: Across the Empty Quarter of Arabia* (London: Jonathan Cape), pp. xii–xiii. Further references are to this edition with page numbers given after the quotations in the text.

15. Behdad, *Belated Travellers*, p. 14.
16. Of the more recent Lawrence biographies, see, for example, M. Asher (1978, 1999) *Lawrence: The Uncrowned King of Arabia* (London: Penguin); and M. Yardley (1985) *Backing into the Limelight: A Biography of T. E. Lawrence* (London: Harrap). For an exploration of T.E. Lawrence's *Seven Pillars of Wisdom*, see J. Meyers (1973, 1989) *The Wounded Spirit: A Study of Seven Pillars of Wisdom* (London: Macmillan).
17. E.W. Said (1978, 1979) *Orientalism* (New York: Vintage), p. 197. Further page references are to this edition and are given after the quotations in the text.
18. T.E. Lawrence (1926, 1976) *Seven Pillars of Wisdom*, Book Club edn (London: Jonathan Cape), p. 8. Further page references are to this edition and are given after the quotations in the text.
19. D. Spurr (1993) *The Rhetoric of Empire: Colonial Discourse in Journalism, Travel Writing and Imperial Administration* (Durham: Duke University Press), p. 130. One further page reference is to this edition and is given after the quotation in the text.
20. E. Lane's (1836) *An Account of the Manners and Customs of the Modern Egyptians* was a precise and elaborate study of Arab ways much referenced in Said's *Orientalism*. Charles Doughty's (1888) *Travels in Arabia Deserta* is an account of the author's two-year adventure wandering the Arabian Peninsula from 1876 as an overtly Christian traveller. Doughty chose to write his travels up in a narrative form strangely redolent of Chaucer. It is a remarkably peculiar telling of an incredible journey, even by the standards of the most eminent Victorian travellers.
21. M. Asher (1995) *Thesiger: A Biography* (London: Penguin), p. 244.
22. W. Thesiger (1999) *Crossing the Sands* (London: Motivate), p. 7.
23. W. Thesiger (1959, 1964) *Arabian Sands* (London: Penguin), p. 15. Further page references are to this edition and are given after the quotations in the text.
24. Rosaldo, 'Imperial Nostalgia', p. 107.
25. For an examination of the changing nature of British-run Egypt, see A. Sattin (1988) *Lifting the Veil: British Society in Egypt 1768–1956* (London: Dent).
26. See G. Balfour-Paul (1991) *The End of Empire in the Middle East: Britain's Relinquishment of Power in Her Last Three Arab Dependencies* (Cambridge: Cambridge University Press), pp. 96–136.
27. J. Raban (1979, 1987) *Arabia: Through the Looking Glass* (London: Picador), p. 15. Further page references are to this edition and are given after the quotations in the text.
28. Author's interview with Jonathan Raban, 12 June 2007.
29. T. Mackintosh-Smith (1997, 1999) *Yemen: Travels in Dictionary Land* (London: Picador), p. 145. Further page references are to this edition and are given after the quotations in the text.
30. R. Stewart (2006) *Occupational Hazards: My Time Governing in Iraq* (London: Picador).
31. See B. Thomas (1931) *Alarms and Excursions in Arabia* (London: George Allen).
32. Raban interview.

11
Ghost Hunting: Amateur Film and Travel at the End of Empire

Anna Bocking-Welch

In September 1965, Charles Chislett, a retired bank manager from the industrial town of Rotherham in Yorkshire, set off from Heathrow Airport for a four-month Thomas Cook tour in East Africa. Travelling with his wife, Grace, and his 16-mm cine Kodak camera, he described his sense of anticipation for the journey ahead:

> Even in the days of jet travel the start of a journey to Africa...is something of an event–at least to the average person. Add to that the fact that I had been brought up on Rider Haggard's African adventure books and a deep desire to experience something of the remoter areas, before civilization, for want of a better term, took over from the remnants of 'Darkest Africa'...and Heathrow...was not just 'another airport'.[1]

Chislett would spend the next four months travelling through former British colonies from Kenya to South Africa, staying in luxurious resorts in national parks, visiting bustling cities and spotting big game on safari, all the while vigilant for any traces of 'Darkest Africa'. Though by far the longest, this was not Chislett's only excursion to the former Empire. In 1962 he embarked on a 1,000-mile cruise up the Nile, through Egypt to Wadi Halfa in Sudan, following this up a year later with an air cruise in the Middle East. In early 1965 he took a boat cruise along the East coast of Africa from Tanzania to Suez and in September of that year left again for Africa on the holiday described above. Finally he spent a month travelling across Asia in 1967, visiting India, Bangkok, Hong Kong, Singapore and Penang in Malaysia.

Although Chislett never conducted a coherent or sustained analysis of either imperialism or decolonisation, he returned from these journeys with hours of film footage, pages of accumulated 'facts' and a collection of experiences that shaped and informed his understanding of the end of the

British Empire. This chapter analyses how his writings and films tapped into overlapping and, at times, contradictory discourses of decline, nostalgia, amnesia, optimism and paternalism. Questions of how, where and for whom the repercussions of British decolonisation have and continue to manifest are at the centre of a growing field of research. Where accounts of British decolonisation once focused narrowly on the political and economic dimensions of the decolonising process, the field has now broadened to consider the cultural impact of the end of Empire, acknowledging its diverse effects on the heartland of Britain. By asking how Britain engaged with its imperial past, these histories have begun to chart the complex interactions between nostalgia and amnesia taking place in cultural as well as political life.[2] Yet existing scholarship has tended to focus on representations of Empire and 'narratives of nation' expressed within cultural products, while overlooking the 'lived experiences' through which individual members of the public engaged with and understood the end of Empire.

In order to fully describe the plurality of Britain's post-colonial experience it is vital to move beyond the 'media archive' to consider the experiences and agency of the public themselves. Scholars such as Mary Louise Pratt, David Spurr and Alison Blunt have emphasised the crucial role played by travel texts in shaping narratives of British identity and imperialism, particularly in the Victorian era.[3] In drawing and building upon this work, studies of travel at the end of Empire have to date focused almost exclusively on the experiences of 'literary adventurers' and their published travel texts or television documentaries.[4] While professional travel narratives, such as those written by Jan Morris, Eric Newby, Norman Lewis and Patrick Leigh Fermor, undoubtedly played an important role in shaping (post-)imperial consciousness back home in Britain, they tell us little about how travel as a leisure pursuit – as opposed to a professional endeavour – provided the public with experiences of imperialism and decolonisation.[5] What interested those who travelled overseas? How did they encounter the outside world? What hopes and expectations did they share with their professional counterparts? And what role did the common tropes of imperial nostalgia and amnesia play within their diverse travel experiences?

In contrast with the individual attention paid to professional travel writers, amateurs and tourists have almost always been conceived collectively. Described as moving in droves, herds and swarms, tourists are repeatedly configured as mass consumers of the commodities provided by the tourist industry; in the words of Jonathan Culler, 'animal imagery seems their inevitable lot'.[6] Although recent work has begun to emphasise the diversity of the tourist experience, the ways in which individuals such as Chislett record and account for their experiences are still understudied, particularly in relation to specific historical contexts, such as decolonisation.[7] This tendency is exacerbated by the comparative scarcity of source material on individual touristic experiences against the published exploits of professional writers. It is unlikely, for example, that Chislett's travel accounts would be available to us were he merely the 'average person' that he purported to be as he set off for Africa. A prolific amateur filmmaker, completing more than 100 film projects in his lifetime and accepting over 900 invitations to screen his films publicly, Chislett cemented his place in the historical archive precisely by extending the personal and private project of travel into the public sphere. It is for these public films that he has attracted the kinds of scholarly attention that has not been given (perhaps cannot be given) to those who kept their travel experiences within the private spheres of friends and family.[8]

The preservation of these private and amateur experiences in the form of the silent films that Chislett shot while travelling, rough notes for lectures he gave at film screenings and articles he wrote for his local Rotary Club magazine offers a rare opportunity to reconstruct some of the neglected experiences of British travel and tourism in the 1960s.[9] This chapter brings these experiences to light, tracing connections with the ongoing processes of British decolonisation. Much of the Empire had already been dismantled by the mid-1960s, but the dust of decolonisation had yet to settle. As the Empire contracted, an equivalent expansion in commercial air travel was taking place, giving affluent members of the British public access to the Empire in its moment of decline.

By analysing Chislett's travel accounts, this chapter reveals the complexity and variability contained within non-professional responses to the end of Empire. In keeping with the thrust of much recent scholarship, it recognises that the shifting conjunctions of remembering/forgetting and the silences that they create ought to be central to any study of post-imperial Britain.[10] But it also shows that there was more to imperial engagements in the 1960s than the commonly identified tropes of amnesia, nostalgia and guilt. New narratives did not replace the old in easy succession, nor did they battle openly for supremacy. What the case of Charles Chislett makes clear is that a number of conflicting, contrasting ideas could be held simultaneously, the anxieties and tensions brought about by the end of Empire producing responses that should not be reduced to easy categorisations – where there was amnesia there was also critical interest; where there was guilt there was also optimism and enthusiasm. Chislett represents an acute problem for the historian of decolonisation; neither a professional literary respondent to a changing world, nor a nameless, faceless consumer of touristic experiences, he occupies an as yet unstudied position within the scholarship of the British abroad. The leisure tourist/amateur traveller, empowered by new technologies of travel and new modes of recording their experiences, simply does not fit into any simple mould. The responses of these tourists to the end of Empire were at least as messy as the end of Empire itself; they should be treated with the same caution.

Touristic opportunities

As Chislett himself emphasised, his faraway holidays took place in the 'days of jet travel'. Commercial airline operations had been established in the 1930s but it was not until the post-war period that aeromobility began to have a significant impact on British travel practices. Commercial air travel expanded throughout the 1950s and 1960s, gradually opening up far-flung and post-colonial destinations to British tourists.[11] Yet despite the increasing democratisation of air travel, the cost of the kinds of trips that Chislett made remained prohibitive for much of the population. Those with whom he and his wife travelled were typically of the same social standing – doctors, dentists, a Classics master at Eton and a 'gaggle of headmistresses' – and, as the local press made clear when it reported that Chislett was 'one of Rotherham's most widely travelled citizens', such extensive travel was unusual enough to be noteworthy.[12]

Chislett shared in the excitement of the Rotherham press and embraced the touristic experience wholeheartedly, making extensive use of Thomas Cook's services to arrange packed itineraries for each of his trips. His films document what on the surface appear to be the typical practices of tourism: the constant and repetitive movement from hotel to hotel and sight to sight in the company of a large group of other tourists. The same sequence of pyramid, camel, man with cattle, desert and Nile dhow repeats throughout footage of his cruise in Egypt, while a similar degree of repetitiveness saturates the two hours of African footage – variation upon variation of the same theme: giraffe, zebra, lion, elephant, dusty road, pristine hotel grounds, sunset. Chislett's 16-mm camera seemed to be the perfect tool for capturing these experiences and he advertised screenings for a number of his travel films on the basis that they would help audiences to 're-live the joys and thrills of past holidays'.[13]

These admissions – celebrations, even – of the tourist experience differ significantly from the disdainful attempts to avoid tourist practices that were so prevalent in travel writing dating from the same period. Many self-styled literary travellers went out of their way to avoid the beaten track and, as Hsu-Ming Teo describes, an astonishing number of travel writers expressed a 'nostalgic sense of loss... for the possibilities of "real" travel' in the decades after decolonisation.[14] Yet for non-professional travellers such as Chislett, who were not constrained by the expected tropes of published travel writing, the increased aeromobility of the 1960s was felt to offer expanding rather than diminishing opportunities to experience and understand the world.

As well as relying on the increasing affordability of jet travel, Chislett's touristic experiences also rode, to borrow Hsu-Ming Teo's phrase, 'on the coat-tails of colonisation'.[15] In many Commonwealth and post-colonial nations the tourist industry was inescapably intertwined with the legacy of imperialism – shaped not only by its organisational infrastructure but also by the fantasies of exotic travel that the industry knowingly tapped into.[16] This interplay is clearly present in Chislett's brief description of his flight to Africa quoted above; the game reserves that he was so keen to see were a legacy of both a nineteenth-century imperial infrastructure and a later boom in conservation practices that tied in with Britain's post-war development and modernisation agenda.[17] As Chislett explained, his decision to travel was also shaped by Rider Haggard's fantastical stories of exotic African adventures, first published in the late nineteenth and early twentieth centuries.

Discourses of expansive adventure have long informed Britain's relationship with its Empire, and Haggard's novels were an influential part of this process.[18] When reviewing Haggard's autobiography in 1926, Horace G. Hutchinson wrote that it was 'not to be doubted that Haggard's South African romances filled many young fellows with longing to go into the wide spaces of those lands and see their marvels for themselves'.[19] A quarter-century on, Graham Greene described how reading Haggard's *King Solomon's Mines* as a child fostered his own 'old African Obsession'.[20] And, as Chislett's enthusiasm reveals, these same narratives continued to be meaningful to a new generation of men in the post-war era of decolonisation. Amateur travellers, while perhaps not wholly confined by the tropes of published travel writing, were nevertheless entwined in the complex intertextual discourses and traditions that shaped stereotypes of travel and tourism. How did these frameworks shape Chislett's touristic engagement with the imperial past?

Imperial relics and nostalgic reveries

As Caren Kaplan contends, 'imperialism has left edifices and markers of itself the world over, and tourism seeks these markers out, whether they consist of actual monuments to field marshals or the altered economies of former colonies'.[21] The period of actual decolonisation has often been described as a time of widespread amnesia about Britain's imperial past, a selective forgetting that endured until the late 1970s and early 1980s when, in the context of the Falklands War, blinkered nostalgia for the golden days of the British Empire boomed.[22] Characterised by theatrical re-enactments of imperial narratives on stage and screen, by the resurrection and restoration of imperial heritage sites and by travel narratives that 'wandered in the wake of Empire', nostalgia for the British Empire certainly gained ground once the political and economic processes of decolonisation were largely complete.[23]

Ian Baucom documents how 'mournful wanderings through the lapsing architectures of England's imperial past' became a significant feature of 1980s nostalgia.[24] This sense of belatedness is particularly explicit in Stephen Weeks's *Decaying Splendours* (1979), which, as Hsu-Ming Teo describes, is a nostalgic and melancholy tour of post-colonial India in which Weeks contemplates what he regards as 'the sunset of an era'.[25] This sense of arriving 'too late on the scene' was shared by other professional travellers, including Philip Glazebrook, who travelled to Kars in the footsteps of nineteenth-century explorers – as he put it, 'in the company of ghosts' – and Gavin Young, who set off 'in search of Conrad' on a trip that he described in his eponymous travel book as a ghost hunt 'among the echoes and shadows of a flickering past'.[26] While there was clearly a burgeoning market for published accounts of nostalgic tours in the 1980s, Chislett's experiences make clear that the ghosts of Empire flickered for amateur travellers long before the nostalgia boom, highlighting the need for a more nuanced consideration of the forms that imperial memory and nostalgia took in the immediate aftermath of decolonisation.

Chislett's experiences offer a window onto the particular aspects of the imperial past that might have appealed to amateurs travelling in the settling dust of decolonisation, as well as allowing us to consider the precise ways in which their nostalgia for these pasts was performed. As Veronica Della Dora describes, 'nostalgia turns the thing into think'.[27] In the context of post-imperial travel, it arises from and draws upon physical fragments of the past preserved in buildings, landscapes and objects.[28] These perceptible fragments of imperial residue – what Starobinski calls 'memorative signs' – then 'act as synecdoches for a whole complex of images, experiences and memories'.[29] What things made Chislett think as he travelled through the former Empire? This section considers his nostalgic engagement with the imperial past at three distinct sites of memory: a ruin in Sudan, an African landscape and a nineteenth-century hotel at Luxor.[30]

Abandoned, desolate and decaying, ruins are a quintessential image of what has vanished from the past. The sense of pathos that they invite can make them evocative sites of memory for those wishing to dwell on what went before.[31] When in Wadi Halfa, Sudan, Chislett encountered a deserted military camp – one of the more common ruins dotted across the former Empire – commenting that it seemed to be a 'ghost town of the British army'.[32] The region had once been a busy component of the British military in the Middle East, initially as the base for British forces during the reacquisition of Sudan in the late nineteenth century and later as a communication base for the Allied Forces during the Second World War.[33] By the time Chislett arrived there in 1963, however, the desert was rapidly reclaiming the area. Reflecting upon the ruins, he conjured up an evocative image of the past in which he described how 'the parade grounds are silent and deserted in the blazing sun, but you half expect to hear the imperative summons of a bugle, or meet a squad of pith helmeted sweat-stained khaki figures arguing about Gordon or Kitchener'.[34] This brief reverie highlights three important and recurring features of Chislett's touristic engagement with the imperial past: the notable absence of melancholy; the vivid reconstruction of a past that he has never experienced; and the temporal location of that reconstruction in the nineteenth century.

Chislett's vision of bugles and pith helmets was sentimental, certainly, yet it was far from sorrowful, expressing little of the mournful longing identified in later professional narratives. Svetlana Boym productively distinguishes between two types of 'performative nostalgia': the 'reflective' – a bittersweet pain of longing and loss that lingers on ruins, absences and silences – and the 'restorative', which acts on a desire to 'return to the original and patch up the memory gaps' through reconstructions of the past.[35] It is clear that Chislett's nostalgia at Wadi Halfa was more 'restorative' than it was 'reflective' – although his reverie was prompted by ruins and silences, these functioned as little more than a trigger, quickly left behind as he worked to reconstruct and superimpose a nineteenth-century imaginary onto the scene.

The absence of loss from Chislett's description is brought into sharp focus through comparison with another more reflective account of a deserted military camp, this time by Archer Cust, the Secretary General of the Royal Commonwealth Society. Cust, who had served in military intelligence during the Second World War, returned to Egypt in 1948, describing a flight over Mena camp and his 'old depot on the bluff' where 'the roofs had been removed from most of the buildings, and soon the sand will blot out all traces of the roads, huts, and tented areas that were familiar to so many tens of thousands of the Empire's forces'.[36] Whereas Chislett appeared remarkably untouched by any sense of pathos, preoccupied as he was with the vibrant imagery of the British Empire of the previous century, for Cust the mournful narrative of British loss was made explicit through the powerful imagery of the camp being blotted out by the desert sand. This difference is partly to do with experience. For Cust, who had his own memories of the depot on the bluff, the loss was personal, tied to a specific moment in the not so distant past; for Chislett, who was seeing the camp at Wadi Halfa for the first time in 1963, the loss could not be more than abstract. This lack of personal connection to the imperial past likely shaped the experiences of many tourists.

Yet while it may have dampened the emotional resonance of the scene, Chislett's lack of personal experience only fired his imagination. The physical remains at Wadi Halfa prompted Chislett to reconstruct a scene from Britain's imperial past that he had not personally experienced but which nevertheless seemed to be vividly available to him. That Chislett was so easily able to access this imperial iconography speaks to the extent to which narratives of British imperialism were embedded within domestic cultural memory. Chislett's reconstruction also reminds us that tourists were not simply passive consumers, spoon-fed by the tourist industry. As Mazierska and Walton suggest, tourists are often construed as 'disempowered addicts or sheep' – as 'consumers of objects and meanings rather than their creators'.[37] While we cannot be sure in what terms Chislett's tour guides introduced the ruins at Wadi Halfa – or, indeed, if they were even an intended 'site' on the tour – Chislett's own reverie clearly marks him as an active participant in the production and interpretation of meaning.

The third important feature of this reverie is its temporal specificity. Chislett drew upon his repertoire of imperial imagery to conjure up a scene from the halcyon days of nineteenth-century high imperialism, replete with period costumes and famous figures – an act of imaginative dexterity that enabled him to overlook the awkward and painful post-war years of decolonisation in the Middle East. When Chislett travelled the Nile in 1963, the Suez Crisis was fixed in the public conscious as an 'unambiguous failure to recover a lost show of strength'.[38] The events of 1956 forced a withdrawal from the region that was hasty, humiliating and almost impossible to assimilate within the preferred decolonisation narrative of a steady march towards democracy and independence.[39]

Yet in his various notes about the trip, Chislett makes no mention of the Suez Crisis or of the significant turning point in the course of decolonisation that it was commonly held to have signified.[40] His silence here should not be read as amnesia about Britain's imperial past, nor as obliviousness to the political present – Chislett revealed an awareness of contemporary politics when he commented that 'Nasser is the brightest star in the Arab firmament and other political set-ups seem to be designed and described according to their relationship to him'.[41] Instead the silence should be read as a selective erasure, an avoidance strategy that sought solace in the comforting imagery of the previous century. Chislett's mobilisation of these particular signs of the past at Wadi Halfa worked, in short, to impose a reassuringly familiar British presence onto the destabilised, decolonised and potentially traumatic present.

These same three features – the notable absence of melancholy; the vivid reconstruction of a past that he has never experienced; and the temporal location of that reconstruction in the nineteenth century – also characterised Chislett's nostalgic response to the African landscape, three years later. Describing the view during his flight to Kenya, he observed

> That mysterious area of the Sudd – reed choked wastes around the Nile still one of the world's unexplored areas . . . We could pick out Jinja and the official source of the Nile, and remembered the courage and the devotion of those early explorers Speke, Grant and Stanley who saught [sic] it in the maze of twisting waterways to the north.[42]

Once again he looked back to the expansive high imperialism of the nineteenth century, peopling the post-colonial landscape with heroes of a bygone Empire and calling on the empowering tropes of exploration and discovery. If, as Martin Green has argued, adventure was the energising myth of the British Empire, Chislett's renarration of Speke, Grant and Stanley's courage in Africa – as well as his earlier enthusiasm for Rider

Haggard – explicitly signals the enduring appeal of these discourses to tourists travelling at the end of the Empire.[43] His descriptions here and at Wadi Halfa illustrate the deep influence of intermedial contexts in inscribing certain landscapes and landmarks with narratives of Empire – narratives, moreover, that could be continually invoked and accessed through travel and tourism in the post-imperial world.

The final reverie took place at the Winter Palace Hotel at Luxor. Built in 1886, the hotel was a living memorial to the grandeur of nineteenth-century tourism and a much more standardised and well-defined 'site of memory' than the military ruins and African landscapes discussed above. In the 1890s, similar grand hotels had been built across the Empire as fashionable destinations for well-to-do travellers.[44] In Cairo, Luxor and Aswan, these new modern hotels were the centres of many tourists' social circles.[45] As travel writer Eustace Reynolds-Ball wrote in 1901, 'from January to April there is one unceasing round of balls, dinner parties, picnics, gymkhanas and other social functions'.[46] Chislett's Nile tour took him to the Winter Palace Hotel precisely because of this history. The hotel was, as he described it, 'an Edwardian museum-piece, which should be experienced' and he recounted that

> you can almost hear the rustle of the long dresses of the stately ladies, suitably escorted of course, who did the Grand Tour of 'Thomas Cook's Canal' in the early days of the century.[47]

This reverie followed the same basic pattern as those at Wadi Halfa and Lake Victoria – a reimagination of a high-imperial scene, lacking in melancholy though vividly described. But Chislett's experience at the Winter Palace Hotel also differed from his other reveries in ways that strikingly prefigured the nostalgia boom to come. The 'restorative nostalgia' evident at the hotel – materialised in its explicit efforts to reconstruct the past – was a precursor to what Lowenthal characterises as the era of 'rampant heritage' in which 'regard for roots and recollection permeates the Western world and pervades the rest'.[48] Cultural heritage projects ranged from the work of the British Association for Cemeteries in South Asia, which began to target decaying colonial era European graveyards in the 1970s, to the Mbweni Ruins Hotel in Zanzibar, where guests could sleep in the first Anglican Christian missionary settlement in East Africa.[49] Between the late 1970s and the 1990s, similar projects of 'cultural salvage' across the former Empire encouraged travellers to indulge in nostalgic colonial role-playing.[50] Cook's advertised their 1997 tours along the Nile as 'a contemporary version of [nineteenth-century] grandeur', promising that the voyage would 'recall the grand opening of the Suez Canal, when Africa became an island and crowned heads of state sailed majestically through the new waterway'.[51]

Perhaps unsurprisingly, Chislett's participation in the public display of restorative nostalgia at the Winter Palace Hotel also prefigured some of the prevailing themes of the later nostalgia boom. His description of the 'long dresses of the stately ladies' matched an enthusiasm for costume drama that peaked in the 1980s with television serialisations such as *The Jewel in the Crown* and *The Far Pavilions*.[52] Stephen Weeks's description of a similar scene for *Decaying Splendours*, written more than 15 years after Chislett's trip, closely echoes Chislett's own reverie while emphasising the movement towards ever more 'restorative' projects of nostalgia. As Weeks, who doubled as a director of television films for the BBC, described, 'It seemed such a short step, especially for someone like myself, so used to peopling film-sets at the drop of a hat with handfuls of fake Dukes or ballrooms of Edwardian ladies, to restore, perhaps, and certainly to regret the loss of, the British Empire.'[53] Whereas in the 1960s Chislett could only people ruins, landscapes and hotels with the ghosts of his imagination, the nostalgia boom made it commercially viable – lucrative even – to people them with costumed actors and actresses. His reveries here indicate a much longer and less broken trajectory of interest in the imperial past than is often attributed to the British public.

Primitivism and modernity in Chislett's travel experiences

In addition to the thrills of the safari and the flickering lure of the imperial past, Chislett's trips offered what felt like a last chance to chase after disappearing traces of primitive life before 'civilisation... took over'.[54] Many safari films in this era – both amateur and professional – capture what Amy Staples describes as a similar quest 'not simply for encountering and documenting the remote and the exotic, but for an experience of difference that is increasingly positioned at the edge of extinction'.[55] It was a paradox that for many former colonies the transition to independence was often also a period of increased 'Westernisation', prompting nostalgia among tourists not only for the heyday of Empire but also for the loss of uniqueness, exoticism and primitivism that Empire had done away with.[56] As Elizabeth Buettner reminds us, calling attention to the work of Fredric Jameson, Renato Rosaldo and Raphael Samuel, 'in deracinated postmodern circumstances the allure of disappearing worlds, environments "at risk," and nostalgia for what has been destroyed can readily become enhanced'.[57]

In his written accounts of his trips to the Middle East, Chislett made clear his desire to experience something of the pre-imperial past, titling the film of his Nile cruise *Egypt 2,000,000 Days Ago*, and later describing how in Jordan '"Old Testament" land and life was [sic] all about [him]'.[58] Through his films, in particular, Chislett also attempted to record a still present but disappearing way of life. Each contained multiple rural scenes in which indigenous men and women – some of them clearly uncomfortable about being filmed – were positioned in the centre of still, lingering shots. In *Egypt*, indigenous people face the camera, grouped as if for a photographic portrait; in footage from Malaysia, topless women and children stand at the roadside, frowning at the camera; and in footage from Africa, women carrying large pots on their heads are again filmed by the roadside, standing as though taking a moment from their daily routine to pose resignedly for the tourist's camera. The regular recurrence of such shots indicates Chislett's participation in what is perhaps best characterised as an informal ethnographic safari in which 'traditional' rural groups were sought out as specimens of 'authentic' culture not yet transformed by the spread of civilisation. In one particularly striking scene from his Africa footage he filmed another member of his tour group standing, knees bent, by the side of the road to photograph an African woman in traditional dress. The shot not only suggests that the practice of drive-by ethnography was a common part of touristic experiences in the former Empire but also raises questions about the assumptions that tourists and travellers frequently made about their right to film foreign peoples.

In footage from his Middle Eastern air cruise, Chislett included a shot of a street scene with two men in the middle distance, clearly signalling to the camera that they did not want to be filmed. Chislett may have made some gestures towards cultural sensitivity, writing that 'you naturally consider the feelings of those who object to being photographed', but he greatly undermined this moral stance by admitting that it was the threat of violence rather than deference to the will of indigenous peoples not to be filmed that prompted him to turn off the camera. As he described, 'When the subjects are intriguing veiled women, complications can arise in the form of male owners... who give every appearance of being ready to emphasise any argument with a knife.' Tellingly, Chislett's response to situations such as this was not to stop filming but to conclude instead that 'the best answer is a telephoto lens'.[59]

In adopting such methods, Chislett reveals how the mind-sets and assumptions that informed earlier colonial photography continued to influence filmmaking practices beyond the formal end of Empire. Through their subject matter, as well as their use of a presentational conception of space and address, these moments in Chislett's films hark back to ethnographic photography of the nineteenth century.[60] Shot in this way, indigenous people were presented as two-dimensional 'primitive' character types rather than individuals with agency. Indeed, such was Chislett's desire to capture the disappearing primitive on film that he was willing to resort to manipulation and, as Heather Norris Nicholson describes, inserted into *Africa Old and New* a close-up still image of a woman and three children standing in front of a hut 'derived from different (possibly commercial) film stock and edited as a repeated single frame'.[61]

In these varied efforts, Chislett clearly mourned the loss of primitive life and yet he repeatedly failed to hold colonialism accountable for its role in this loss. Such an act of oversight closely conforms to Renato Rosaldo's characterisation of 'imperialist nostalgia'.[62] Indeed, we could dismiss Chislett as a blinkered imperial nostalgist were these efforts at ethnographic documentation and the romanticised reveries discussed above his only engagements with Britain's imperial role. In actual fact, his treatment of decolonisation both included and transcended these more typical nostalgias of travel writing. Unlike writers such as Levi-Strauss, whose obsessive preoccupation with the past left him, in his own words, 'groaning among the shadows', Chislett balanced his 'ghost hunting' with a keen interest in contemporary development.[63]

For every wistful comment that Chislett made about the past, he made another that engaged critically with the post-colonial present; for every shot of rural life, he filmed another of a busy city. Juxtapositions between 'traditional' life and bustling modernity were a prominent feature of the appropriately titled *Africa Old and New*, which contrasts shots of unpeopled open plains with footage of cities such as Nairobi and Dar es Salaam where the buildings are decked in advertisements for international brands and modern cars line the curb. Similarly, in *Egypt*, Chislett contrasted dusty footpaths and rural agriculture with new paved roads and large modern buildings, repeating this sequence of comparisons at each new location on his trip. The comparisons drawn between 'old' and 'new' were further emphasised by his use of different filmic techniques. In contrast with the lingering and static roadside portraits discussed above, Chislett was much more inclined to use wider panning shots to film urban life. In this footage, crowds moved through the scene rather than being contained within it. Not subjected to the 'fixing' gaze of a still camera, these 'modern' individuals regularly walk across shots, intent on their business and often oblivious to the camera.[64]

The contrasts that these films drew between old and new were also layered with the binaries of rural/urban and primitive/Westernised. Through these juxtapositions, Chislett offered explicit and implicit commentaries on the economic and cultural changes that these societies underwent in the post-war period. Following the loss of India in 1947, Britain redoubled its efforts in Africa and South East Asia, emphasising social and economic development in order to get the most out of the remaining colonies.[65] The long sequences of city life in *Africa Old and New* show an effort to record the rapid intensification of urbanisation at the end of this 'second colonial occupation'. In Malaysia, where accelerated reforms and social welfare initiatives had been an essential complement to the armed counterinsurgency throughout the 1950s, Chislett's busy port scenes and built-up cities tell a similar story of industrial development. These shots were reinforced by his written claims that it was the British who had brought 'the amenities of civilisation' to Malaysia and that Malaya was 'the richest and most highly developed colony in the Empire'.[66] By the time Chislett travelled to Malaysia in 1967, the former colony had become a success story for trusteeship, remaining firmly within a financial and strategic system that made Britain, Australia

and New Zealand her closest partners.[67] Chislett tapped into the same discourses of development that allowed decolonising imperial powers such as Britain to reconcile themselves to their sudden loss of power.

Chislett clearly found comfort in these frameworks of trusteeship and development, but his enthusiasm for the 'new' was also matched by an interest in the problems that emerging nations faced in independence. He engaged most explicitly with the processes of decolonisation in relation to Africa, one page of his scrawled notes listing what he identified as local and general problems in the post-colonial continent. These included 'chips on shoulder re white help [*sic*]', 'evil propaganda', 'nationalism – often quite illogical', 'power of witch doctors' and 'Africans unwilling to prepare for future', as well as mentioning more specific examples, such as the 1963–7 secessionist Shifta War in Kenya, 'problems in Uganda' (presumably referring to separatist Bugandan revolts) and the Rhodesian Unilateral Declaration of Independence in 1965, all events that occurred either during or immediately before his trip.[68]

On another set of note cards for a lecture he gave to members of the London Missionary Society, Chislett repeated a similarly critical evaluation, writing that the missionary 'has to stay there and ride the tides of anti-European, anti-British, anti-white, anti-Christian feeling' that has been 'whipped up by evil propaganda'.[69] Comments such as this reveal that Chislett did not accept decolonisation with total equanimity. In comparison with his account of Malaysian economic success, in which he was quick to claim British credit for economic infrastructure, this more critical account of Africa entirely overlooks Britain's possible culpability, placing any blame firmly on the shoulders of Africans and propagandising Communists. In conjunction with his conspicuous silence on the Suez Crisis, it shapes his broader commentary on the significance of imperial decline into an account far more inclined to highlight the positive aspects of the experience than the negative.

Conclusion

There was no one single moment in which the British Empire ended. British decolonisation was a complex and overlapping series of processes, driven by a diverse international cast of actors.[70] If Chislett's forays into the former Empire did not furnish him with a particularly sophisticated or internally coherent understanding of decolonisation, this chapter has shown that the impact of British imperial decline nevertheless resonated throughout his touristic experiences – in his nostalgic reveries, in his ethnographic attempts to document disappearing primitiveness, and in his fascination with the physical signifiers of development and modernity. As Angela Woollacott succinctly describes, 'it is now well established that colonialism has been an interconstitutive process that shaped British society and culture'.[71] Empire is no longer treated as just a phenomenon 'out there' but as a fact that registered in 'the social fabric, the intellectual discourse, and the life of the imagination'.[72] By showing how the fact of Empire continued to register in the post-colonial experiences of amateur travellers and tourists, this chapter contributes to the expanding body of work exploring the impact of Empire on post-colonial Britain.

Increased mobility in the 1960s gave a greater proportion of the British population first-hand access to the 'out there' spaces and places of the former Empire. Widespread enthusiasm for touristic experiences – encapsulated in the excited anticipation that Chislett expressed before leaving for Africa in 1965 – offers an important counterpoint to narratives of post-imperial decline and inward-facing parochialism.[73] Chislett was among the many Britons who took new opportunities to look outwards on the changing world; his attitude defiantly not that of the 'Little Englander' so frequently stereotyped in accounts of interwar and post-war identity.[74] The case study of Chislett presented here both complements and complicates existing work on the tourist industry, and on travel film and literature, revealing a broader range of attitudes towards the end of the Empire than have commonly been found within published travel narratives. In his touristic search for Empire, primitivism and modernity, Chislett made clear that individuals could hold potentially irreconcilable views, called into play by different moments of the amateur travel experience. The nostalgia that characterises professional travel writing was certainly present in Chislett's reveries, but any sense of mournful longing was tempered by the parallel enthusiasm that he showed for both the typical practices of tourism and also the discourses of development and trusteeship.

In teasing out the indeterminacies, intricacies and contradictions within Chislett's accounts it becomes clear that tourism and critical engagement were not mutually exclusive practices. If looked at in isolation, Chislett's film footage would seem to suggest that the touristic experience offered little opportunity to engage with the more complex dimensions of imperial decline. Looked at in conjunction with his written accounts, however, it makes clear that although these limited frameworks were the most easily accessible to travellers and tourists, they did not preclude more meaningful engagements with decolonisation. Multilayered responses such as Chislett's show that it is necessary to look beyond the tourist industry, its packaged tours and the frameworks through which it promoted its fare to account instead for the individual agency and interests of its heterogeneous consumers. As Teo argues, for most Britons travelling abroad, the nostalgic colonial experience was but one of many different modes of tourism available. The variability of Chislett's experiences explored in this chapter certainly attests to this, but while, as Teo suggests, many travellers might juxtapose a colonial heritage tour with a shopping trip, Chislett balanced his instead with an effort to find out about the political and economic conditions of post-colonial nations.[75] As he travelled through the former Empire, Chislett was not only hunting for ghosts, sifting through the imperial debris in search of memorative signs, but carefully collecting and piecing together a complex series of impressions of the pasts, presents and potential futures of these far-flung holiday destinations.

Notes

1. C. Chislett (September 1965) 'Africa Old and New', Charles Joseph Chislett Collection, Yorkshire Film Archive, York (YFA), 329.
2. See J. Bailkin (2013) *The Afterlife of Empire* (Berkeley: University of California Press); S. Howe (2003) 'Internal Decolonization? British Politics since Thatcher as Post-colonial Trauma', *Twentieth Century British History*, 14:3, 286–304; R. Rosaldo (1989) 'Imperialist Nostalgia', *Representations*, 26, 107–22; B. Schwarz (2011) *Memories of Empire: The White Man's World* (Oxford: Oxford University Press); S. Ward (ed.) (2001) *British Culture and the End of Empire* (Manchester: Manchester University Press); W. Webster (2005) *Englishness and Empire, 1939–1965* (Oxford: Oxford University Press).
3. A. Blunt (1994) *Travel, Gender and Imperialism: Mary Kingsley and West Africa* (New York: Guilford Press); M.L. Pratt (1992) *Imperial Eyes: Travel Writing and Transculturation* (Abingdon: Routledge); D. Spurr (1993) *Rhetoric of Empire: Colonial Discourse in Journalism, Travel Writing and Imperial Administration* (Durham: Duke University Press).
4. C.J. Christie (1994) 'British Literary Travellers in Southeast Asia in an Era of Colonial Retreat', *Modern Asian Studies*, 28:4, 673–737; B. Korte (2000) *English Travel Writing from Pilgrimages to Postcolonial Explorations* (Basingstoke: Palgrave); R. Phillips (2001) 'Decolonizing Geographies of Travel: Reading James/Jan Morris', *Social & Cultural Geography*, 2:1, 5–24; H.M. Teo (2001) 'Wandering in the Wake of Empire: British Travel and Tourism in the Post-imperial World' in Ward (ed.) *British Culture and the End of Empire*, pp. 163–89.
5. This problem is discussed in relation to the Grand Tour in J. Black (1992) *The British Abroad: The Grand Tour in the Eighteenth Century* (New York: Sutton), iv.
6. J. Culler (1981) 'The Semiotics of Tourism', *American Journal of Semiotics*, 1:1, 127–40.
7. N. Uriely (2005) 'The Tourist Experience: Conceptual Developments', *Annals of Tourism Research*, 32:1, 199–216.
8. H.N. Nicholson (1997) 'In Amateur Hands: Framing Time and Space in Home-Movies', *History Workshop Journal*, 43, 199–212; (2002) 'Telling Travellers' Tales: the World Through Home Movies', in T. Cresswell and D. Dixon (eds.) *Engaging Film: Geographies of Mobility and Identity* (Oxford: Roman and Littlefield) pp. 47–66; Norris Nicholson (2004) 'At Home and Abroad with Cine Enthusiasts: Regional Amateur Filmmaking and Visualizing the Mediterranean, ca.1928–1962', *GeoJournal*, 49, 323–333.
9. These films and papers are held as part of the Charles Joseph Chislett Collection, YFA. The films include *Air Cruise to Lebanon, Syria and Jordan* (1963), *Egypt 200,000 Days Ago* (1963), *Africa Old and New* (1966) and *Malaya* (1967).
10. Schwarz, *White Man's World*.
11. M.L.J Dierikx (2008) *Clipping the Clouds: How Air Travel Changed the World*, (Westport, CT: Praeger), pp. 35–71.

12. Newspaper Clipping c.1967, Charles Chislett Collection, Rotherham Archives and Local Studies Service, Rotherham (RA), 88-Z; 'Middle East Mosaic', YFA, 458.
13. Christies Lecture Service Advertisement, YFA, 331.
14. J. Buzard (1993) *The Beaten Track: European Tourism, Literature and the Ways to Culture* (Oxford: Oxford University Press); Culler 'The Semiotics of Tourism'; P. Fussell (1980) *Abroad: British Literary Travelling Between the Wars* (Oxford: Oxford University Press); Teo, 'Wandering', 172.
15. Teo, 'Wandering', p.164.
16. Teo, 'Wandering', p.166.
17. R.P. Neumann (2007) 'The Post-war Conservation Boom in British Colonial Africa', *Environmental History*, 7:1, 26–30.
18. W.R. Katz (1987) *Rider Haggard and the Fiction of Empire* (Cambridge: Cambridge University Press).
19. H.G. Hutchinson (1926) cited in Katz, *Rider Haggard*, p. 1.
20. G. Greene (1951) *The Lost Childhood* p.14, cited in Katz *Rider Haggard*, p. 1.
21. C. Kaplan (1996) *Questions of Travel: Postmodern Discourses of Displacement* (London: Duke University Press), p. 63.
22. S. Hall (1978) 'Racism and Reaction' in *Five Views of Multiracial Britain* (London: Commission for Racial Equality); C. Hall and S. Rose (eds.) (2006) *At Home with Empire* (Cambridge: Cambridge University Press), pp. 4–5.
23. Teo, 'Wandering', p. 174.
24. I. Baucom (1999) *Out of Place: Englishness, Empire and the Locations of Identity* (Princeton: Princeton University Press), p. 166.
25. Teo, 'Wandering', p. 169.
26. G. Young (1991) *In Search of Conrad* (London: Penguin), p. 3 cited in Teo, 'Wandering', p. 175; P. Glazebrook (1984) *Journey to Kars: A Modern Traveller in the Ottoman Lands* (London: Penguin) cited in H. Henderson (1992) 'The Travel Writer and the Text: My Giant Goes with Me Wherever I go', in M. Kowalewski (ed.) *Temperamental Journeys: Essays on the Modern Literature of Travel* (Georgia: Georgia University Press), p. 239.
27. V. Della Dora (2006) 'The Rhetoric of Nostalgia: Postcolonial Alexandria Between Uncanny Memories and Global Geographies', *Cultural Geographies*, 13:2, p. 212.
28. For a discussion of imperial debris, see A.L. Stoler (2008) 'Imperial Debris: Reflections on Ruin and Ruination', *Cultural Anthropology*, 3, 1–34.
29. Della Dora, 'Rhetoric of Nostalgia', 211; J. Starobinski (1996) 'The Idea of Nostalgia', *Diogenes*, 54, 93.
30. P. Nora (1989) 'Between Memory and History: *Les Lieux de Mémoire*', trans. Marc Roudebush, *Representations*, 26, 7–25. See also J. Winter (1995) *Sites of Memory, Sites of Mourning: The Great War in European Cultural History* (Cambridge: Cambridge University Press); and L. Buettner (2006) 'Cemeteries, Public Memory and Raj Nostalgia in Postcolonial Britain and India', *History and Memory*, 18:1, 5–42.
31. Stoler, 'Imperial Debris', 5.
32. C. Chislett (1963) 'Two Million Days Ago', *Rotary in the Ridings*, 33:5, 18.
33. A. Jackson (2006) *The British Empire and the Second World War* (London: Hambledon Continuum), pp. 116–17.
34. Chislett, 'Two Million Days Ago', 18.
35. S. Boym (2001) *The Future of Nostalgia* (New York: Basic Books), p. 41.

36. Archer Cust, cited in R. Craggs (2009) 'Cultural Geographies of the Modern Commonwealth from 1947 to 1973' (unpublished PhD, University of Nottingham), p. 180.
37. E. Mazierska and J.K. Walton (2006) 'Tourism and the Moving Image', *Tourist Studies*, 6, 6.
38. M. Thomas, B. Moore and L.J. Butler (2008) *Crises of Empire: Decolonization and Europe's Imperial States* (London: Hodder Education), pp. 78, 93; W.R. Louis (2006) *Ends of British Imperialism: The Scramble for Empire, Suez and Decolonization* (London: Palgrave Macmillan), p. 17.
39. Craggs, 'Cultural Geographies', p. 180.
40. Louis, *Ends of British Imperialism*, p. 4.
41. 'Middle East Mosaic' notes, YFA, 458.
42. 'Middle East Mosaic'.
43. M. Green (1980) *Dreams of Adventure, Deeds of Empire* (London: Routledge), xi. See also R. Phillips (1997) *Mapping Men and Empire: A Geography of Adventure* (London: Routledge).
44. J. Whidden (2010) 'Expatriates in Colonial Egypt, 1864–1956, in R. Bickers (ed.) *Settlers and Expatriates: Britons Over the Seas* (Oxford: Oxford University Press), p. 50.
45. D. Gregory (2001) 'Colonial Nostalgia and Cultures of Travel: Spaces of Constructed Visibility in Egypt' in N. Alsayyad (ed.) *Consuming Tradition, Manufacturing Heritage: Global Norms and Urban Forms in the Age of Tourism* (London: Routledge), p. 127.
46. E. Reynolds-Ball (1901) *Cairo: The City of the Caliphs* (London) p. 130.
47. Chislett, 'Two Million Days Ago', 15.
48. D. Lowenthal (1998) *The Heritage Crusade and the Spoils of History* (Cambridge: Cambridge University Press), p. 1.
49. Buettner, 'Raj Nostalgia, 13.
50. Teo, 'Wandering', 168; Stoler 'Imperial Debris', 12.
51. Gregory, 'Consuming Tradition', p. 114.
52. Webster, *Englishness and Empire*, p. 538; E. Buettner (2004) *Empire Families: Britons and Late Imperial India* (Oxford: Oxford University Press), pp. 252–71.
53. S. Weeks (1979) *Decaying Splendours: Two Palaces, Reflections in an Indian Mirror* (London: British Broadcasting Corporation), p. 68.
54. 'Africa Old and New', YFA, 329.
55. A. Staples (2006) 'Safari Adventure: Forgotten Cinematic Journeys in Africa', *Film History*, 18, 407.
56. J. Matos (1992) 'Old Journeys Re-visited: Aspects of Postwar English Travel Writing' in M. Kowalewski (ed.) *Temperamental Journeys: Essays on the Modern Literature of Travel* (Georgia: University of Georgia Press), p. 216.
57. Buettner 'Raj Nostalgia', p. 14.
58. C. Chislett (c.1964) 'Air Cruise to the Lebanon, Syria and Jordan', *Rotary in the Ridings*, 15.
59. Chislett, 'Two Million Days Ago', 11.
60. See Ryan, *Picturing Empire*.
61. Norris Nicholson, 'Framing Time and Space', 205.
62. Rosaldo, 'Imperialist Nostalgia'.
63. Stoler, 'Imperial Debris', 28.
64. For further discussion of the 'Colonial Gaze' see Kaplan, *Looking For the Other*; and Pratt, *Imperial Eyes*.

65. A.G. Hopkins (2008) 'Rethinking Decolonization', *Past and Present,* 200, 217.
66. 'Impressions of Malaya', YFA, 1151.
67. Thomas, Moore and Butler *Crises of Empire,* pp. 60–2; N.J. White (2003) 'The Survival, Revival and Decline of British Economic Influence in Malaysia, 1957–70', *Twentieth Century British History,* 14, 222–42.
68. 'Africa Old and New', YFA, 333.
69. Africa L.M.S. Meeting Notes, YFA, 329.
70. See, for example, J.M. Brown and Wm.R. Louis (eds.) (1999) *The Oxford History of the British Empire,* Vol. IV: *The Twentieth Century* (Oxford: Oxford University Press); and J. Darwin, *Britain and Decolonization.*
71. A. Woollacott (2001) *To Try Her Fortune in London: Australian Women, Colonialism and Modernity* (Oxford: Oxford University Press), p. 9.
72. B. Parry (1993) 'Overlapping Territories and Intertwined Histories', in M. Sprinker (ed.) *Edward Said: A Critical Reader* (Oxford: Blackwell), p. 24.
73. R. English and M. Kenny (eds.) (2000) *Rethinking British Decline* (London: Macmillan).
74. The idea of 'Little England' is explored by Webster in *Englishness and Empire,* pp. 129–35; also R.L. Doty (1996) 'Immigration and National Identity: Constructing the Nation', *Review of International Studies,* 22, 235.
75. Teo, 'Wandering', 168.

12

'In Countries so Unciviliz'd as Those?': The Language of Incivility and the British Experience of the World

Marc Alexander and Andrew Struan

'Civilisation', wrote Arnold J. Toynbee in the 1950s, 'is a movement, not a condition; it is a voyage, not a harbour.'[1] In a similar vein, the ways in which peoples and nations have thought others to be civilised, or uncivilised, have altered and changed over time. This development is true particularly of the contact over the past 1,000 years between the British and those they thought to be, and deemed, 'uncivilised'. The ways in which British writers represented and constructed these 'uncivilised' peoples in their factual narratives and explanations, and the extent to which those writers engaged with shifting and changing conceptions of such people, allow an insight into the reactions and attitudes of the British towards those they encountered through imperial expansions and travel abroad. This chapter therefore seeks to analyse the ways in which the English-speaking peoples have sought to conceptualise those deemed uncivil, through an investigation into the word choices which scholars now know were available to them at each stage in the evolution of the English language.

This chapter therefore demonstrates the ways in which speakers of English have adapted their conceptualisations of 'incivility' through travel and contact with the outside world. We aim to trace in linguistic history the cultural, political and social attitudes towards the concept as it developed over time. As a result, we are able to see the shifts in the way in which Britons and other speakers of English termed people deemed uncivil, from giving them rough, animalistic characteristics (for example, 'crude' or 'rough') towards the later significance of the relationship between the person and the state (for example, the overarching modern term 'uncivil'). Through this type of research a researcher can for the first time see longer-term shifts in attitudes using evidence scattered around the historical record. The concept of civility is an excellent illustrative example of this; it details a contentious and shifting conceptualisation which has developed as the British and other English-speaking peoples have come into contact, through travel, exploration and imperial conquest, with other peoples and cultures. This analysis is now possible following the publication of the *Historical Thesaurus of the Oxford English Dictionary* (*HTOED*) in 2009.[2] Its systematic categorisation of all of the words available to the speakers of English throughout their history allows historians to be able for the first time to analyse the development of ideas through the options available to a writer to realise their conceptualisation of the world. It therefore reveals information about social and cultural change which is otherwise locked within the alphabetical arrangement of dictionaries and encyclopaedias.[3] Based on a semantic rearrangement of the contents of the 20 volumes of the *Oxford English Dictionary* (*OED*),[4] supplemented by a range of other materials, the *HTOED* contains all of the recorded words in the English language, alongside dates of known usage, in hierarchical semantic fields. Therefore all of the words for a particular concept, such as the adjectives used to mean 'uncivilised', are arranged together in a category which sits next to other words concerned with civilisation and its absence. Such categories are important because lists of words for the same concept reveal a form of recategorisation on the part of English speakers across time, where the coining of a new term reflects a shift in the understanding of, or attitudes towards, a particular concept. Key here is the notion that speakers of a language do not develop new words meaning precisely the same thing as existing words; for there to be enough benefit to speakers to learn and spread a newly coined word, it must have a distinct contribution to make to the language.[5] Teasing apart such differentiations in the field of uncivilised persons is the aim of this chapter.

This approach to the study of history is beneficial in a number of ways. It allows scholars to comprehensively see the development of ideas and concepts over broad ranges of time, as their associated terms developed. We can therefore now investigate the full range of options available to any given speaker in history for them to describe concepts (in the present case, incivility); and in so doing we are also able to better use the citations and usage evidence stored in the *OED* and other linguistic corpora. This approach enables us to investigate not only the broader shifts in the attitude of the English-speaking peoples but also areas of particular change or of focused word innovation. These alterations or additions to the collective vocabulary can be used by the historian as a means to understand social and political developments through their implicit, rather than their explicit, discussion.

This type of focus takes into consideration some of the 'controversies about the nature of textual interpretation',[6] and it furthers the 'linguistic turn' in historiography while noting the central significance of word choice in understanding the cultures and politics of past discussions.[7] The approach here used takes both an essentialist and a selectionist approach to understanding word meaning. It argues therefore that word meanings in and of themselves are important but disagrees with full essentialist views that 'the context in which the word appears is irrelevant' by emphasising the importance of wider historical context.[8] This chapter seeks to contribute to the understanding of the role played by 'meaning' in historical investigation and understanding,[9] by providing analysis and description of the ways in which meaning shifts over time. This type of work allows us to overcome some of the issues inherent in the study of the past with regard to misinterpretations of meaning, intention or context, and it works to further our appreciation of the argument that 'there are in fact no such time-less concepts, but only the various different concepts which have gone with various different societies'.[10]

The chapter is an approach to social and political history using the new data and approaches available, but built on historiographical tradition. Writing in 1990, Geof Eley noted Hobsbawm's main thoughts on social history as it then was, commenting:

> In his 1971 essay, Hobsbawm suggested that most interesting social history was clustered around six complexes of questions:
>
> 1. Demography and kinship
> 2. Urban studies in so far as these fall within our field [social history]
> 3. Classes and social groups
> 4. The history of 'mentalities', or collective consciousness, or of 'culture' in the anthropologist' sense
> 5. The transformation of societies (for example, modernisation or industrialisation)
> 6. Social movements and phenomena of social protest.[11]

This present work seeks to engage with a number of these points in social history at once, providing commentary on the ways in which a particular social concept – in this case, incivility – developed and changed over time. As such, the research engages with several of Hobsbawm's key themes above, notably those of classes and social groups, the history of mentalities, the transformation of societies and societal movements.

In order to do this the present chapter takes as its starting point those adjectives which have been recorded in English to refer to the concept of being uncivilised. Of the 42 words in the main *uncivilised* category in *HTOED* (see Figure 12.1), the vast majority follow a particular path of lexicalisation which we describe below, with new terms reflecting the shifting conceptualisation of the uncivil throughout the times when they were coined. To best analyse this shift, and relate it to the contexts within which each term was used, this chapter uses the term 'sense-families' to describe those groups of words which fit into similar conceptualisations and which have similar metaphorical roots. For each family we provide citations of their use in a range of different periods, with these examples being used to describe the changing concept and also to relate it to the English-speaking peoples' shifting conception of the wider world. While discussing each conceptual movement in turn, the chapter will focus mainly on the colonial and post-colonial periods, and on British sources where possible. Although the *HTOED* covers the full history of English, including its roots in the Old English (OE) period from 700 to 1150 CE, the OE material is not discussed in detail here.[12] The examples given as evidence will be taken from *OED* citation files, the House of Commons recorded debates in *Hansard*, major linguistic corpora and sundry other relevant primary sources.

03.01.03.02.01 (*adj.*) *Uncivilized*

bærbære OE · elreord OE · elreordig OE · hæþen OE · ungerad OE · wild<wilde OE; *a*1300– · wildern *a*1300 · fremd *c*1374 · bestial *c*1400–1816 · savage *c*1420/30– · savagine *c*1430–1430/40 · rude 1483– · barbaric 1490–1513; *a*1837– · barbar 1535–*a*1726 · barbarous 1538– · Scythical 1559–1602 · barbarious 1570–1762 · raw 1577; 1847; 1865 · incivil 1586 · barbarian 1591– · uncivilized 1607– · negerous 1609 · savaged 1611 · mountainous 1613–1703 · ruvid 1632(2) · ruvidous 1632 · incivilized 1647 · inhumane *a*1680 · tramontane 1739–1832 · semi-barbarous 1798– · irreclaimed 1814 · semi-savage 1833– · semi-ferine 1854–1858 (*rare*) · warrigal 1855 (*Austral.*)–1890 · sloven 1856 (*US*)–1882/3 · semi-barbaric 1864 · wild and woolly 1884– · woolly 1891– · jungle 1908– · medieval 1917– (*colloq.*) · jungli 1920– · pre-civilised 1953– **01** *and unsubdued* unatemed OE **02** *without intelligible language* ungereord OE **03** *specifically of persons* uncivil 1553–1644 · savage 1588– **04** *pertaining to uncivilized people* savage 1614– **05** *acting/speaking as uncivilized* barbarizing 1662; 1855– **06** *rendering uncivilized* barbarized 1602; 1839 · barbarizing 1809– · decivilized 1831–1892 · barbarianized 1885 · decivilizing 1889 **07** *becoming uncivilized* barbarianzing 1859 **08** *absence of accepted social standards/values* anomic 1950–

Figure 12.1 'Uncivilised' in *HTOED* (p.1235 of Kay et al., 2009)

Sense-families 1 and 2: *Wild* and *Crude*

The first two sense-families both arise in the Middle English period, and, although evidence for the first pre-dates the second, at this stage of the recorded language it is best to treat both as contemporaneous. The first family is that of *wildness* and *savagery*, wherein foreign persons were considered untamed and beast-like, and the second is *roughness*, where those without civilisation were somehow unfinished, lacking smoothness or a 'finish' (such as education). These two provide the groundwork from which the later families grow. The first emphasises the way in which not being part of society is akin to being animalistic, a frequent conceptualisation found in many Western societies, while the second mirrors this with a particular emphasis on what the person (or people) in question does not have. These two ideas, of emphasising and exaggerating the negative features of a certain group of others, and of emphasising what it is that they lack, are a consistent starting place for most privative concepts in *HTOED*.

The first family, then, begins with *wild*, which has a reflex term in OE, and as well as being the oldest term in the category is still in frequent modern use. Its primary and oldest sense refers to the undomesticated state of animals, and so constitutes one of the earliest beast-to-man metaphors recorded in English. Its early use stretches from the early fourteenth-century *Cursor Mundi* through Scottish poetry of the fifteenth century ('Scotland...set throuch with our ennemys wilde').[13] It continues in the same sense to the present day; – for example, George Hadfield, MP for Sheffield, used it in 1860 to refer to the native peoples of New Zealand, with a distinctly religious emphasis on their state of being: 'The duty of the bishops and ecclesiastics was to instruct the wild people of the colony in Christian doctrines, and in the principles of morality.'[14] A similar term is *fremd*, an OE term deriving from the earlier Germanic for *from*, originally referring to one who is a stranger,[15] but later referring to not tame, as can be seen in Chaucer's use 'Al this world is blynd/In this matere, bothe fremed and tame.'[16] The two other major terms here, both of which are from the fifteenth century and still in modern use, are *bestial* and *savage*, easily found in many sources to refer pejoratively to uncivilised persons (for example, in 1908 the Attorney-General for Ireland protests in the House of Commons: 'I never said that the people of Ireland were West African savages'; barely 40 years earlier, a Leicestershire MP expressed the opinion that 'The tendency of Parliament to legislate as if the people of Ireland were a set of the most incapable and helpless savages was to him a matter of regret', and another asked if 'Her Majesty's Government will take into consideration the advisability of discontinuing the use of [the dum-dum] bullet in wars with semi-civilised or savage people, as well as with those nations who are parties to the [First Hague] Conference').[17] Similarly, while travelling through South America in 1826, John Miers commented that 'This post consists of three small huts, horribly filthy; the people were extremely miserable in their appearance, and little, if any, better than savages in their mode of life.'[18] To travel abroad in this instance, and to come into contact with these apparently 'savage' peoples, invited hardship and hostility for the British; they sought to place these people in the context of being 'horribly filthy' and 'savage'. Darwin commented similarly on the peoples he met while travelling on the *Beagle*:

> They passed the night here; and it was impossible to conceive anything more wild and savage than the scene of their bivouac. Some drank till they were intoxicated; others swallowed the steaming blood of the cattle slaughtered for their suppers, and then, being sick from drunkenness, they cast it up again, and were besmeared with filth and gore.[19]

The image intended to be conveyed here, exaggerated or not, is clear: to be savage is to be beast-like, lacking in the control of Darwin and his contemporaries in manners, cleanliness and habits. The family is completed with a series of modified terms – *savagine* (c. 1430–30/40), *savaged* (1611) and *semi-savage* (1833–) – alongside one further term: an Australian Aboriginal borrowing *warrigal* (1855–10), originally meaning a wild dog. It is clear here that during their wide travels, Britons such as those quoted above came into contact with numerous people and practices that they viewed to be savage simply due to the fact that they did not conform to British social norms of the time; as in the way of thinking of this sense-family, the presence of those norms was identified with civilisation itself.

The second family is smaller but contains two major terms used from Middle English to the present day, alongside a third variant. The major terms are *rude* (1483) and *raw* (1577–), both used to indicate roughness or crudeness on the part of the uncivil. Of particular interest here is this sense-family's habit, in attested use, of being employed to highlight that which the uncivil lack in the eyes of the writer, so that in *OED* citation files we find:

> **1577** Harrison, *England* in Holinshed *Chronicles* (1587): Men, being as then but raw and void of ciiuilitie.

> **1586** Hooker *Hist. Irel.* in Holinshed II. 141/2 The rude people he framed to a civilitie, & their maners he reformed and brought to the English order

> **1732** Berkeley *Alciphr.* viii. §15 If we suppose rude mankind without the use of language.

Each of these highlight civility, manners and language as aspects of the uncivilised persons being referred to. These aspects are highlighted in detail in later sense-families which emerge (see 3 and 4 below). In particular, the

British view of such persons is highlighted to the extreme in an example of the other term in this cluster: the English borrowing *ruvid* from Latin (meaning simply *rough*). This ideal example of *ruvid* in context comes from William Lithgow, a Scottish traveller of the seventeenth century, who expressed, in characteristically damning fashion, his opinion of the Arabian Peninsula:

> The people generally are addicted to Theft, Rapine, and Robberies: hating all Sciences Mechanicall or Civill, they are commonly all of the second Stature, swift on foote, scelerate, and seditious, boysterous in speech, of colour Tauny, boasting much of their triball Antiquity, and noble Gentry: Notwithstanding their garments be borne with them from the bare Belly, their food also semblable, to their ruvid condition, and as savagiously tame (I protest) as the foure footed Citizens of Lybia: They are not valourous ... Their language extendeth it selfe farre both in Asia, and Affricke, in the former, through Palestine, Syria, Mesopotamia, Cilicia, even to the Mount Caucasus: In the latter, through Aegypt, Lybia, and all the Kingdomes of Barbary even to Morocco.[20]

Lithgow's use of multiple terms for uncivilised persons here displays a range of harsh views concerning the inhabitants of the peninsula, and forms a marker of values and practices which were seen by him as appropriately civilised, and which the others whom Lithgow encountered on his travels seemingly lacked.

These two sense-families together, their roots in earlier Germanic expressions and metaphors, form a baseline for the ways in which English-speaking travellers and writers conceptualised those they encountered outside their contextual 'civilisation'. Their age makes them a consistent and still-current measure of how speakers explore the identity of others whom they encounter and later discuss among themselves. The following sense-families, however, evolved during the history of English in different directions, and highlight other features which the British began to consider dominant.

Sense-family 3: *Barbar*

While the focus on the above, older families of categorisation of those thought uncivil was on their animalistic or simplistic traits, by the late Medieval period an alternative way of naming such others as a different 'type' of people had started to come to the fore in English. This approach adopted a much older racial method of classification from the Classical period; the word *barbaric* entered English in the late fifteenth century and was derived from the Greek term βάρβαρος, via Latin. This word was initially used to describe the ways in which those who did not speak Greek sounded; it worked, in other words, as a way of defining those who were, and those who were not, Hellenic.[21] (In modern-day English, the equivalent might be the use of *blahblah* to signify meaningless and different-sounding speech.)

The concept behind this original meaning developed over time as it shifted from Greek to Latin to English, but it was the later use in English that gave the word its core meaning as savage or uncivil. The term *barbaric* originally was one of sounding foreign or different. William Bonde's use of this term in the *Pilgrimage of Perfection* illustrates the point perfectly, wherein he noted 'My wyt is grosse... & my tong very barbarouse.'[22] Similar discussions revolved around the use of Old French in law as early as the mid-sixteenth century ('To see al our law... ryten in thys barbaiarase langage') and in the teaching of Latin.[23] The use of this family of words – the *barbar* family – to categorise those who spoke a foreign language (be it originally non-Hellenic, not Latin or not English) was used until the late eighteenth/early nineteenth century.

It is important to note that while the tongues used were foreign, it did not necessarily follow that they were uncivilised, brutish or inhumane, other than the author's pre-existing opinion of foreigners (although this is, of course, frequently negative). This distinction remained as late as 1814 and was used simply to determine the nature of the sounds being uttered. There could be an implied connection, perhaps, of a simpler or more rustic life, but there was no cruelness inherent in the description of 'barbaric sounds'. This led to, for example, the author and Anglican cleric Sydney Smith being able to write about his travels:

> When shall I see Scotland again? Never shall I forget the happy days I passed there amidst odious smells, *barbarous sounds*, bad suppers, excellent hearts, and most enlightened and cultivated understandings.[24]

From the author's point of view here there is no contradiction between 'barbarous sounds' and 'enlightened and cultivated understandings', even though it is surrounded by less than complimentary physical descriptions of Scotland. Yet to a modern-day audience this description may appear contradictory in terms. Only in the context of the sorts of data presented here are we able to see such instances of sense-shifting; and only with an appreciation of the historical uses of terms are we able to gain a full appreciation of the subtler shades of meaning.

Over time, however, this concept behind what it means to be barbaric altered and the meaning of incivility began to become intricately connected, so that by the seventeenth century the word had adopted its current-day definition. Smith, above, was even by his time – and probably knowingly – using or punning on an older sense of the word when he discussed the civil barbarity of the Scots. Instead it became increasingly the case that those who were not Christian were deemed barbaric and outlandish: 'Let vs come to Lawes; for euen the barbarousest people had of them.'[25] This religious definition relied on the older interpretation of those who were, and were not, Latin (or Latinised) and reinforced the relationship between barbarity and incivility. As such, Shakespeare, for example, juxtaposed barbarousness and manners when Olivia dismisses Sir Toby Belch in *Twelfth Night*, saying he is fit only for the 'Barbarous Caues, Where manners nere were preach'd'.[26]

Writing in the 1850s regarding his times in Africa, David Livingstone drew a comparison between the peoples he met in Africa and non-Western Europeans. The Austrians and Russians were used as a point of comparison for readers to understand the supposed barbarity of African tribal society, and the ways in which non-British Europeans held onto unpalatable character traits:

> It is noticeable that the system of espionage is as well developed among the savage tribes as in Austria or Russia. It is a proof of barbarism. Every man in a tribe feels himself bound to tell the chief every thing that comes to his knowledge, and, when questioned by a stranger, either gives answers which exhibit the utmost stupidity, or such as he knows will be agreeable to his chief.[27]

Similarly, this new attitude towards barbarism – the one which still holds currency in the modern world – as something from which we might escape, into civilisation, through concentrated effort was exemplified by the *Washington Post*, which reported an uncomplimentary 1930s remark by an unknown Frenchman as 'Americans are the only race which passed directly from barbarism to decadence without knowing civilisation.'[28]

With this shift in the nature of the meaning of the word, there came a number of variations along the *barbar* theme. The word *barbar* was in recorded use from 1535 to just before 1726. *Barbarious* was used from 1570 to describe 'barbarious and miserable creatures',[29] to 1762, where it described 'barbarious nations'.[30] *Barbarian* similarly entered the language in 1591 and was initially used to discuss the 'broad barbarian sound' but increasingly became a method of discussing lacking civility.[31]

However, by the late eighteenth century a further shift occurred in the classification of barbarity. Qualifiers began to be applied to the depth or extent of barbarity through words such as *semi-barbarous* (in recorded use from 1798 onwards) and *semi-barbaric* (1864). This method of classification denoted a sense of being only part savage, or of being on a path towards full civility. The now-civilised peoples of Britain were classified as 'semi-barbarous' in their past in 1798 ('The ancient Britons were as little acquainted with the art of writing, as any of the rude and semi-barbarous nations of those times') but had, importantly, the chance or ability to move towards full civility.[32] This type of part-civility is one which will be discussed further below.

The idea of barbarity, then, was originally born of the need to classify those by the sounds they made. To be barbaric was not in the beginning to be cruel, inhumane or savage in its core sense, merely to be foreign. However, as the concept developed alongside the other sense-families under discussion here – as, for example, the British peoples came increasingly into contact with those they deemed to be uncivilised – the meaning shifted to encompass a greater degree of negative and judgmental ideology. This pattern is one which is reflected in the final two sense-families.

Sense-family 4: *Civility*

While the above sense-families all relied on definitions based around the characteristics of people, the idea of (un)civilness revolves around, and is based upon, our relationship with the state and what we would now deem 'civil society'. The development of these ideas mirrors the growth in the concept of the state from the fifteenth century onwards. That is to say, with the birth of the modern age came a new understanding of what it meant to be (un)civil in terms of one's position within a state's society.

This definition of incivility is based in large part on acting contrary to accepted civil norms, and being defined outside society as a result. The first use of this term was in 1568 – in the word *incivil* – and spoke of 'Tamburlaine, that sturdy Scythian thief That … Daily commits incivil outrages.'[33] These uses of the basis of civil society can be found in the contemporary political and philosophical writings; the development, in the British Isles primarily with Thomas Hobbes and John Locke, of the state of nature and social contract correspond directly with the development of this sense-category. Locke's *Two Treatises of Government* (published in 1689)[34] detailed the nature of the relationship between the state and its citizens, but also worked to emphasise the importance of those outside the state. The relationship was, thought Locke, one of mutual obligation tied into the idea of a sovereignless state;[35] countries/peoples where this relationship was deemed to function were 'civilised', whereas those not following the European pattern of state formation in this period were deemed uncivil. In other words, according to Locke, in the initial stages of mankind's social development, people lived 'together as free and equal individuals, without any relations of political authority, governed only by the rules and principles of natural law', while in the modern, civilised era, mankind 'relate to one another in a framework of political institutions – legislatures, courts, socially sanctioned property arrangements, and so on – institutions which articulate the natural rules and principles in the clear and determinate form of positive law'.[36] It was with this understanding of the concept of civility that Locke was able to say, for example: 'and amongst those who are counted the civilised part of mankind, who have made and multiplied positive laws to determine property'.[37] It was only with the recent pairing of the concept of civility and the development of the understanding of the relationships between states and citizens that Locke was able to describe people as being civilised in this way.

To be *uncivilised* entered the language in 1607 and developed alongside the other categories here available. Although a later entry into the categorisation of incivility, it has become embedded in our understanding of what it means to be civilised or not. It allowed for descriptions of peoples, and countries, as being uncivilised, as shown in Abraham Cowley's poem from 1647:

> Either by savages possest,
> Or wild and uninhabited?
> What joy couldst take, or what repose,
> In countries so unciviliz'd as those?[38]

As a result, James Cook was able to, for example, describe the apparently uncivilised manners in which the Pacific communities with which he came into contact lived and worked. He commented in 1777 that 'They show as much ingenuity both in invention and execution as most uncivilis'd nations under the same circumstances.'[39] In this eighteenth-century period of colonisation and exploration, Cook reported that

> The beats and iron that were found among the people of the coast must undoubtedly have been derived from some civilised nation: and yet there was reason to believe that our English navigators were the first Europeans with whom the natives had ever held a direct communication.

We see here Cook's surprise at finding the 'people of the coast' with forms of civility which he would have thought to have belonged only to European peoples. The text continues to explain that these people – in North America – must have gained the tools of civility through trade and contact with 'the more inland tribes'. This approach to civility characterises the early modern attitude towards civility: only Europeans can be truly civilised, while the 'savage' peoples can gain civilisation only through the adoption of European norms.[40] This type of attitude continued until the late nineteenth and early twentieth centuries. The noted traveller and whaler Henry Theodore Cheever commented, for example, in his 1855 work on his travels around the Pacific Islands, that over time and contact with Europeans the Pacific Islanders would 'acquire habits of diligence, order, and the improvement of their time, in which Hawaiians, like all uncivilised people every where, are lamentably deficient'.[41]

This colonial expansion, and the increasing contact with non-European societies and peoples, led to movements towards what has since been called a civilising mission.[42] Such attempts to civilise others have been discussed with regard to their successes (or lack thereof); it is a result of this concept that to be *irreclaimed* (1814), or to have slipped back towards 'savagery', began to come to the fore at the start of the nineteenth century ('If the brute Multitude ... Wild as their savage ancestors, Go irreclaim'd the while').[43] This concept has similarly been taken further, as mentioned above, in the concept of what it means to be *pre-civilised*. Here, as with *semi-barbarous*, writers are operating on the belief that people can move out of incivility into civility. As such, authors were able by the late nineteenth century to discuss the ways in which other peoples could travel along the path from barbarity to civilisation, such as Richard F. Burton's observation that 'the land of the Pharaohs is becoming civilised, and unpleasantly so: nothing can be more uncomfortable than its present middle state, between barbarism and the reverse'.[44] No longer was barbarity or civility an on or off state; rather, in the views of such authors, the less civilised people were on a path towards full civility, a path which might sometimes be 'unpleasant'. This concept came particularly to the fore in the period of decolonisation in the 1950s and 1960s as the British Empire, and the other great European empires, were dismantled. It marked a change in perception of the outside world in some respects: no longer were vast swathes of the globe uncivilised, wild, savage lands; instead they were viewed as semicivilised societies moving towards full civility.

This concept of making steps towards full civility developed alongside the post-colonial shift in ideas, where it became increasingly unlikely to find descriptions of peoples as being 'uncivilised' owing to their ethnic, cultural or social background. No longer were peoples classed as 'uncivilised', and the language instead turned to describing characteristics of lands and climates, as something untouched by mankind: 'here is an atmosphere of nature at its untamed, uncivilised best. The wilderness stands on its own: free, not propped by access roads, park rangers, interpretative centres, and regulation on use'.[45] Here, to be uncivilised is to be untouched by man and left to nature in the positive, Romantic light of simplistic non-interference.

This sense-family, while late to the discussion of incivility, is central to our understanding of what it means to be uncivilised. Our modern-day conception of this term – to be without civil society or without the state – has developed hand in hand with political and philosophical debates about the role played by society and its relationship with the state. While this is the predominant conception we now use to judge those thought to be uncivilised, it is important to note that this sense-family is later than others developed earlier. As such, conceptions of civility were before this point based on differing approaches to classifying the 'Other', as is shown above.

Sense-family 5: *The Other*

'There is', said Eric Hobsbawm, 'no more effective way of bonding together the disparate sections of restless peoples than to unite them against outsiders.'[46] In the case of Britain, as Linda Colley has so effectively shown, this was in the creation of a British Protestant identity in contrast with the Catholic (primarily French) 'Other'. British men and women, according to Colley, came to define themselves as Britons – in addition to defining themselves in many other ways – because circumstances impressed them with the belief that they were different from those beyond their shores, and in particular different from their prime enemy, the French. Not so much consensus or homogeneity or centralisation at home, as a strong sense of dissimilarity from those without proved to be the essential cement.[47]

While the French were the main focus of Otherness in the development of Britishness from the eighteenth century, the term has also been used extensively in describing those thought to be uncivil. The concept of Otherness is naturally much older than British identity itself, and as a result the first term used in English to describe uncivilised Others was brought in from abroad. *Scythical* (in recorded use from 1559 to 1602) came from the Greek description of an ancient nomadic people from present-day Iran. These people were classed as barbarous savages by the Greeks who fought them, leading to the conception of them as providing 'Such Schythicall... torturing and massacring of Men.'[48] This classification applied also to race; to be *negerous* at the start of the seventeenth century (1609) implied savage barbarity. This description, a direct connection between being of African race and uncivilised, has left few recorded traces in the English language but demonstrates the importance of the growing Atlantic slave-trade at this time, and the increasingly large role played by Britons in the business.

In addition to categorising others as racially or ethnically different, descriptions of incivility in English have focused on where members of groups inhabit. To be *mountainous* (1613–1851) describes a condition where, as Bacon established, there 'are commonly Ignorant and Mountanous People, that can giue [sic] no Account, of the Time past'.[49] These peoples need not necessarily be truly remote from the metropolitan centre to be considered mountainous. Indeed, at the turn of the eighteenth century amid concerns over the relationship(s) between the Scots and English and with shifting conceptions of Britishness, commentators could write of 'England... bounded on the North by a poor mountainous People call'd Scots', while by the twentieth century the mountainous regions had shifted to Ethiopia where it was described that the country was 'by the end of the nineteenth century... a difficult country to conquer, as its mountainous people were very well armed'.[50] This type of description could also be used to describe a situation lacking refinement or poise; to be *tramontane* (1739–1832) implied a sense not of wild or barbaric incivility, but instead of being uncouth and unfashionable: 'I beg... if these can be your real sentiments, that you will keep them as private as possible. They are totally tramontane in this part of the world.'[51]

By the twentieth century the perception of there being only a few truly 'untouched' or 'uncivilised' places left on earth became reflected in the choice of words available. From 1908, *jungle* came to mean uncivilised or savage ('Torn by the savage jungle-cries of the elemental passions')[52] and it has continued to be an acceptable way to describe something which is untamed or savage. *Jungli* (in recorded use from 1920 onwards) has similar connotations. People can in this case be *jungli*, which includes many of the traits discussed above. As with many of the later ideas of civility, there is an implied sense of movement out of barbarity and into civility in this term, and it shows the continuing fascination with a civilising mission in British imperial attitudes: 'already he ceases to be jungli. Note: Wild and boorish, a clodhopper or uneducated peasant.'[53] Finally, the lack of uncivilised places to be found in the modern age is reflected in the colloquial use of *medieval* from 1917, reflecting a view of the past as severe and brutal.

Conclusion

As can be seen from the above discussion, the ways in which Britons have conceptualised what it means to be uncivilised has gone through five distinct phases and has produced the sense-families discussed above. Rather than a static belief in what deemed one to be civilised or not, the concept shifted as the British explored and travelled the world, and as they developed their understanding of the relationship between the citizen and the state. Such contacts with others created specific and divergent attitudes towards incivility, and they demonstrate the ways in which modern-day conceptions of what it means to be uncivilised are not the same as the ways in which past societies categorised the world around them.

This analysis of the cultural approach of Britons towards others deemed barbaric uses what can be called the 'deficit model' of civilisation, where being uncivilised is a state which exists before one is civilised. Therefore a person or a people can become 'finished' somehow by making the movement from one to another. For the earlier models this was constantly implicit (one who is wild can become tamed, one who is unfinished can be finished, a barbarian can learn another language, or one can learn to enter civil society). In the later examples, with the onset of modernity and the post-colonial period, a less overtly judgemental attitude is found (of people being 'pre-civilised' or 'semi-barbarian'), reflecting the changing attitudes of Britons towards the world around them.

Making use of new data such as that provided by the *HTOED,* alongside established historical and historiographical sources, gives a key point of reference for social and cultural research, by identifying and classifying those ways in which past societies themselves identified and classified the world around them. In the examples above, it has been possible for the first time to show one of the ways in which, over a broad range of time, Britons – as travellers, explorers, philosophers, colonisers and tourists – reacted to the societies that they came in touch with, and the ways in which these foreigners were classified and judged. This research displays in a comprehensive manner the shift towards modern conceptions of societal relations, and makes use of the linguistic history left to us from the colonial and post-colonial experiences of Britons abroad.

Notes

1. A.J. Toynbee (October 1958) in *Reader's Digest*.
2. C.J. Kay, J.A. Roberts, M.L. Samuels and I.A.W. Wotherspoon (2009) *Historical Thesaurus of the Oxford English Dictionary* (Oxford: Oxford University Press).
3. M.L. Samuels (1972) *Linguistic Evolution* (Oxford: Oxford University Press), p. 180.
4. J.A. Simpson and E.S.C. Weiner (2000–) *OED Online*. 3rd edn, rev. J.A. Simpson and others of Murray, J.A.H., and others (eds.) (1989) *Oxford English Dictionary*, 2nd edn, compiled by J.A. Simpson and E.S.C. Weiner, 20 vols. (Oxford: Clarendon Press, http://www.oed.com).
5. See, *inter alia*, J. Lyons (1995) *Linguistic Semantics* (Cambridge: Cambridge University Press); A. Verhagen (2007) 'Construal and Perspectivization', in *The Oxford Handbook of Cognitive Linguistics*, D. Geeraerts and H. Cuyckens (eds.) (Oxford: Oxford University Press), pp. 48–81; and J.R. Taylor (2003) *Linguistic Categorisation*, 3rd edn (Oxford: Oxford University Press).
6. M. Dobson and B. Ziemann (2009) *Reading Primary Sources: The Interpretation of Texts from Nineteenth – and Twentieth-Century History* (London: Palgrave Macmillan), p. 2.
7. See, *inter alia*, Q. Skinner (1969) 'Meaning and Understanding in the History of Ideas', *History and Theory*, 8, 3–53.
8. R. Moxley (1997) 'Skinner: From Essentialist to Selectionist Meaning', *Behavior and Philosophy*, 25:2, 96.
9. See *inter alia*, T. Jones (2004) 'Uncovering 'Cultural Meaning': Problems and Solutions', *Behavior and Philosophy*, 32:2, 247–68; and C. Geertz (1973) *The Interpretation of Cultures: Selected Essays* (New York: Basic Books).
10. Q. Skinner, 'Meaning and Understand in the History of Ideas', 53.
11. G. Eley (1990) 'Is all the World a Text? From Social History to the History of Society two Ddecades Later', in G. M. Spiegel (ed.) (2005) *Practicing History: New Directions in Historical Writing after the Linguistic Turn* (London: Routledge), p. 38. See also E. Hobsbawm (Winter 1971) 'From Social History to the History of Society' in *Daedalus, Historical Studies Today*, 100:1, 20–45.
12. This is for a number of reasons, the most significant of which is that the nature of OE vocabulary makes comparison of it with modern English, in the methodology used throughout this chapter, somewhat problematic. For example, the OE term *bærbære* can be defined as 'barbarous', as is done in John R. Clark Hall's *A Concise Anglo-Saxon Dictionary*. However, it would be difficult to argue from this that it indicates a perception of a category of 'barbarous' persons, as is argued in section three, due to the nature and distribution of those OE texts which survive to the present day. The *Thesaurus of Old English*, a child project of *HTOED*, marks *bærbære* as a rare glossarial term, and a search of the Toronto *Old English Corpus* finds only one use of this term, in glosses to the Canterbury Psalter (Cambridge, Trinity College, MS. R.17.1), which is a trilingual psalter with many overwritings and erasures in its Anglo-Norman and OE glosses (see Gibson, Heslop and Pfaff 1992). Deciding from this single use whether an OE term is appropriate to use as the basis of a sense-family in this chapter is highly problematic, given the limited surviving OE corpus, and without the benefit of scholarship and investigation

taken by editors of the *OED* over the last century to mark obsolete or rare words and provide contextual evidence from a range of times. It is hoped that the completion of the comprehensive and authoritative Toronto *Dictionary of Old English*, alongside the *Thesaurus of Old English*, will help in this area. For now, this chapter restricts itself to the Middle English period onwards.

13. B. Harry; J. Moir (ed) ([1475]1889) *The Acts and Deidis of Schir William Wallace, Knicht of Ellerslie* (Edinburgh: Scottish Text Society).
14. *Parliamentary Debates: House of Commons*, 21 August 1860, vol. 160, c. 1642.
15. For more information about this concept in earlier Indo-European languages, see '19.55 Stranger' in C.D. Buck (ed) (1949) *A Dictionary of Selected Synonyms in the Principal Indo-European Languages* (Chicago: University of Chicago Press), p.1349–50.
16. G. Chaucer, L.D. Benson (eds) (1988) *The Riverside Chaucer*, p. 520 (*Troilus and Criseyde*, 3.529). Showing the close relation between these two words, although the Riverside uses *fremed*, there are five MSS which have 'wild(e) and tame' in the same place, and some editors (including Caxton) use the same. Chaucer earlier in *Troilus* has 'Lat be to me your fremde maner speche' (2.248), which mirrors sense-family 3.2 below.
17. *Parliamentary Debates: House of Commons,* Mr Richard Cherry (Attorney-General of Ireland), 20 March 1908 vol. 186 c988; Lord John Manners, 1 April 1870 vol. 200 cc1070–1; Mr Francis Channing, 5 June 1899 vol. 72 c302.
18. J. Miers (1826) *Travels in Chile and La Plata, Including Accounts Respecting the Geography, Geology, Statistics, Government, Finances, Agriculture, Manners and Customs, and the Mining Operations in Chile. Collected during a Residence of Several Years in These Countries*, Vol. I (London: Baldwin, Cradock, and Joy), p. 39.
19. C. Darwin (1839) *Journal and Remarks: The Voyage of the Beagle* (London), chapter 5.
20. W. Lithgow ([1632]1906) *The Totall Discourse of the Rare Adventures, Painefull Peregrinations of long Nineteene Yeares Travayles from Scotland to the most Famous Kingdomes in Europe, Asia and Affrica ['The Rare Adventures of William Lithgow']* (Glasgow: Glasgow University Press), p. 261.
21. On the subject of the onomatopoeia of barbar, Liddell and Scott's A *Greek-English Lexicon* points to the passage in Strabo's *Geography* (7 BCE - 23 CE) where, in the Harvard translation,

the word 'barbarian' was at first uttered onomatopoetically in reference to people who enunciated words only with difficulty and talked harshly and raucously…those they called barbarians in the special sense of the term, at first derisively, meaning that they pronounced words thickly or harshly; and then we misused the word as a general ethnic term, thus making a logical distinction between the Greeks and all other races (Strabo 14.2.28).

22. W. Bonde (1526) *Here begynneth a deuout treatyse in Englysshe, called the Pylgrimage of Perfection*, 1st edn, in 'barbarous, adj.'. *OED* online. March 2011. Oxford University Press (accessed: 17 May 2011). http://www.oed.com/view/Entry/15397 (accessed: 17 May 2011).
23. T. Starkey (1538) *Dialogue Pole & Lupset,* in 'barbarous, adj.'. *OED* online. March 2011. Oxford University Press. http://www.oed.com/view/Entry/15397 (accessed: 17 May 2011).

24. Sydney Smith to Francis Jeffrey (27 March 1814). Our italics. In 'barbarous, adj.'. *OED* online. March 2011. Oxford University Press (accessed: 17 May 2011). http://www.oed.com/view/Entry/15397 (accessed: 17 May 2011).

25. P. De Mornay (1587) *A Woorke Concerning the Trewnesse of the Christian Religion*, 1st edn, in 'barbarous, adj.'. *OED* online. March 2011. Oxford University Press. http://www.oed.com/view/Entry/15397 (accessed: 17 May 2011).

26. W. Shakespeare (1623) *Twelfth Night*, IV.1.

27. D. Livingstone (2004) *Travels and Researches in Southern Africa* (London: Kessinger), pp. 25–6.

28. 'Herriot Admits Pact Not Aimed at Debt to U.S.' *Washington Post*, 16 July 1932, p. 1. The quote has been variously and erroneously attributed to Wilde, Churchill, Georges Clemenceau, Bernard Shaw and others.

29. R. Holinshed (1570) *Scottish Chronicles*, in '† barbarious, adj.'. *OED* online. March 2011. Oxford University Press. http://www.oed.com/view/Entry/15387 (accessed: 17 May 2011).

30. O. Goldsmith (1762) *The Citizen of the World*, 1st book edn, 2 vols, in '† barbarious, adj.'. *OED* online. March 2011. Oxford University Press. http://www.oed.com/view/Entry/15387 (accessed: 17 May 2011).

31. J. Dryden (1700) *Fables Ancient and Modern*, 1st edn, in 'barbarian, n. and adj.' *OED* online. March 2011. Oxford University Press. http://www.oed.com/view/Entry/15380 (accessed: 17 May 2011).

32. A.F.M. Willich (1798) *Elements of the Critical Philosophy: Containing a Concise Account of Its Origin and Tendency; a View of All the Works Published by Its Founder*, in 'semi-barbarian, n.'. *OED* online. March 2011. Oxford University Press. http://www.oed.com/view/Entry/175600 (accessed 17 May 2011).

33. '† incivil, adj.'. *OED* online. June 2011. Oxford University Press. http://www.oed.com/view/Entry/93531 (accessed 17 May 2011).

34. J. Locke (1689) *Two Treatises of Government: In the Former, the False Principles and Foundation of Sir Robert Filmer, And His Followers, Are Detected and Overthrown. The Latter Is an Essay Concerning the True Original, Extent, and End of Civil-Government* (London).

35. J. Scott (September 2000) 'The Sovereignless State and Locke's Language of Obligation', *American Political Science Review*, 94:3, 547; and J. Waldron (Winter 1989) 'John Locke: Social Contract versus Political Anthropology', *The Review of Politics*, 51:1, 3–28.

36. Waldron, 'John Locke', 4–5.

37. Locke, *Two Treatises of Government*, Vol. II, p. 219.

38. A. Cowley (1647) *The Welcome (The Mistress)*.

39. 'uncivilised, adj.'. *OED* online. June 2011. Oxford University Press. http://www.oed.com/view/Entry/210392?redirectedFrom= uncivilised (accessed 17 May 2011).

40. A. Kipps (1840) *Narrative of the Voyages Round The World, Performed by Captain James Cook* (London: Richardson), p. 312.

41. H.T. Cheever (1855) *The Island World of the Pacific: Being A Travel Through the Sandwich or Hawiian Islands and Other Parts of Polynesia* (New York: Harper and Brothers), p. 359.

42. See, for example, H. Fischer and M. Mann (2004) *Colonialism as Civilizing Mission: Cultural Ideology in British India* (London: Anthem); and A. Twells (2009) *The Civilising Mission and the English Middle Class, 1792–1850: The 'Heathen' at Home and Overseas* (Basingstoke: Palgrave Macmillan).

43. R. Southey (1814) *Carmina Aulica*, vii. ii.
44. R. Burton (ed. I. Burton) (1893) *Personal Narrative of a Pilgrimage to Al-Madinah & Meccah* (London: Tylston & Edwards), p. 17.
45. United States Department of the Interior (1988) *Arctic National Wildlife Refuge: Final Comprehensive Conservation Plan, Environmental Impact Statement, Wilderness Review, and Wild River Plans*.
46. E. Hobsbawm (1990) *Nations and Nationalism Since 1780* (Cambridge: Cambridge University Press), p. 91.
47. L. Colley (1992, 2003) *Britons: Forging the Nation, 1707–1837* (London: Pimlico), p. 17.
48. Francis Herring (1602) *J. Oberndoerffer's Anatomyes of the True Physition and Counterfeit Mounte-Banke*.
49. 'mountainous, adj.'. *OED* online. March 2011. Oxford University Press. http://www.oed.com/view/Entry/122904 (accessed: 14 June 2011).
50. Ibid.
51. This term is originally from Italian, where it referred to outsiders living beyond the Alps. See also Blackwood's (October 1817–1905) *Edinburgh Magazine*, (Edinburgh: William Blackwood; London: T. Cadell and W. Davis), in 'tramontane, adj. and n.'. *OED* online. March 2011. Oxford University Press. http://www.oed.com/view/Entry/204513 (accessed: 14 June 2011).
52. Alfred Noyes (1908) *William Morris*, in 'jungle, n.'. *OED* online. March 2011. Oxford University Press. http://www.oed.com/view/Entry/102075 (accessed: 14 June 2011)
53. *Chambers's Journal of Popular Literature* (7th series vols. 1–21, 3 December 1910–28 November 1931), 'jungli, adj. and n.'. *OED* online. March 2011. Oxford University Press. http://www.oed.com/view/Entry/102079 (accessed: 14 June 2011).

Index

Index compiled by the editors

Printed and bound by CPI Group (UK) Ltd, Croydon, CR0 4YY